Energy, Environment, Ecology and Society

Energy, Environment, Ecology and Society

Dr. Pushpendra
• Ph.D. M.Tech., NET-UGC, NET-ASRB
Assistant Professor
Department of Applied Science and Humanities
AKG Engineering College
Ghaziabad (U.P.)

Er. Upendra Singh
B. Tech

(An ISO 9001:2008 Certified Company)
VAYU EDUCATION OF INDIA
2/25, Ansari Road, Darya Ganj, New Delhi-110 002

Energy, Environment Ecology and Society

ISBN: 978-93-80712-01-7

First Edition: 2011

Reprint : 2014

Price: ₹ 200/-

Printed & bounded in India

Published by:

(An ISO 9001:2008 Certified Company)

VAYU EDUCATION OF INDIA

2/25, Ansari Road, Darya Ganj, New Delhi-110 002

Ph.: 91-11-43526600, 41564445

Fax: 91-11-41564440

E-mail: vei@veiindia.com

Web: www.veiindia.com

Dedicated To
Swami Maharishi
Dayanand Saraswati

PREFACE

Energy, Environment, Ecology and Society as a scientific discipline. These are emerging area with tremendous potential. Increasing population has necessitated rapid industrialization and greater urbanization. This has caused great harms to each component of environment. Every citizen should be aware of the natural state of environment, its capacity to adjust and its consequential problems. Environmental Studies has been made a compulsory subject at undergraduate level in India.

Technological advancements have often led to environmental degradation. Rapid industrialization, expanding population and exploitation of scarce natural resources have led to environmental problems like global-warming, ozone depletion, acid rain, freshwater crisis, deforestation, and desertification. Perceiving the imminent threats to the life support systems, emphasis has now shifted to sustainable development. This cannot be achieved without the involvement of masses from all walks of life scientist, academicians, social scientists, students and policy makers. Making it mandatory to those so that they may be acquainted with environmental science ecology and ecosystem, is necessary. Under standing of various interaction with human activity, ways and means for their co-existence is also necessary.

The present book entitled *Energy, Environment, Ecology and Society* has been written specifically to graduates of engineering and technology and pharmacy students of colleges and institutions affiliated to U.P. Technical University, Lucknow. It aims to present all the scientific fundamentals in one easy-to-understand format for an undergraduate. All the topics of the syllabus are covered, comprehensive, lucid and organised manner. It also covers the basics required for the design, operation, analysis, and modeling of natural as well engineered environmental systems. It also emphasizes the connections among different specialty areas of Environmental Science - renewable and non-renewable resources, ecosystem, biodiversity and its significance, wastes water treatment, air quality engineering, solid and hazardous waste management and remediation, and socio-legal and moral issues involved in man-environment interaction are also discused in this book.

A Hon'ble Supreme Court of India passed an order in 1991 for the introduction of a common course on Environment in colleges and universities at undergraduate levels for all disciplines. But the order was not properly implemented. Displeased with non-compliance of this order, the Supreme Court again ordered in 2003 for the introduction of Environment. As a compulsory subject at higher secondary level in schools and undergraduate levels in colleges and even issued warning of legal action.

The introduction of the common course like environment, ecology etc. obviously brought confusion in the academic communities due to the lack of suitable textbooks lack of orientation about the subject among the teachers and students of various disciplines was also problem creating. The authors, with their long experience in environmental teaching and research, took up the challenge and brought out a standard textbook.

The book is written as per syllabus and the various units associated with it have been presented in a simple to suit the requirements of the course. Glossary of key terms is given at the end for easy understanding of the subject while exercises are intended to reinforce the knowledge of the students.

The book will be useful for the undergraduate students of arts, science commerce engineering medicine pharmacy management and low who have environment related subject in their course.

Industrial advancements have often led to environmental degradation. Rapid industrialization modern agricultural practices, population explosion and over exploitation of natural resources have led to environmental problems like global-warming, ozone depletion, acid rain, freshwater crisis, deforestation, and desertification. Perceiving the imminent threats to the life support systems, emphasis has now shifted to sustainable development. This obviously cannot be achieved without the involvement of masses from all walks of life scientist, academicians, social scientists, students and policy makers, making it mandatory for them to be acquainted with environmental science ecology and ecosystem study.

The book is written as per the coverage of various topics associated with the subject.

The authors also welcome constructive suggestions and comments from fellow teachers and beloved students.

psdhama@yahoo.co.in, Dr. Pushpendra

ACKNOWLEDGMENT

First of all, I am extremely thankful to God and my teachers for guiding, encouraging and for helping me during this work and facilitating my work to be carried out successfully.

I would like to express my sincere thanks to, Dr.T.N.R. Bishnoi, Dr. Krishan Kumar, Prof. C.K. Sharma, Prof. V.K. Garg, Prof. A.K. Sharma, Prof. C.P. Kaushik, Prof. Anubha Kaushik, Jitendra Pal, Prof. B.S. Katkar, Prof. B.K. Kuthiayala (Vice Chaceller-MLCu; Bhopal), Prof. SVS Rana (VC - BKU, Jhansi), Dr. D.S. Malik, Dr. P.K. Joshi, Prof. Dinesh Bhatt, Prof. R.P. Sharma, Prof. Santosh Satya providing me help in this work, avail the facility and all indispensable help to carry out this work smoothly.

My special thanks to my freiends colleages Mr. Kapil Kumar, Dr. Ashish Pathak, Dr. B.B. Verma, Mr. Vikash Rathi, Dr. Ruchira Goerl, Advocat Mr. Sharma, Dr. B.S. Chuhan, Prof. S.P. Pandey, Proof Ramesh Mishara, Mr. Kundan Mishara, Prof. Satendra Sharma, Prof. Sanjeev Goyal, Prof. J.P.Singh, Dr.Y.K. Agarwal, Dr. D.B. Ojha, Mr. Ajay Sharma, Prof. Avinash Gaur, Dr. Deepti Sharma Saba Firdosh and Ravinder Khaiwal for providing me the necessary though and assisting in organizing the field visits.

I place on record my sincere appreciation of Dr. Reshu Choudhary and for sparing their valuable time and helping me out of problems this work. Also my friends for their valuable suggestions and sharing some ideas about the subject making the book in a manner.

Finally yet importantly I express my gratitude to my parents, uncle, brother and sisters for their blessing and moral support.

psdhama@yahoo.co.in,

Dr. Pushpendra

ENERGY, ENVIRONMENT, ECOLOGY AND SOCIETY

According to Prescribed Syllabus
for
Rajiv Gandhi Proudyogiki Vishwavidyalya
Bhopal (M.P.)

SYLLABUS

ENERGY, ENVIRONMENTAL, ECOLOGY AND SOCIETY (BE -202)

Unit-1 Energy

Sources of energy, renawabe and nonrenewable, fossil fuels, coal, oil, gas, geothermal, hydrogen, solar, wind, hydal, nuclear sources.

Unit-2 Ecosystem

Segments of environment: atmosphere, hydrosphere, lithosphere, biosphere; cycles in the ecosystem-water, carbon, nitrogen, biodiversity: threats and conservation.

Unit-3 Air and Sound Pollution.

Air pollution: air pollutants classification, (primary and secondary pollutants) , adverse effects of pollutants, causes of air pollution chemical, photochemical, green house effect, ozone layer depletion, acid rain.

Sound pollution: causes controllind measures, measurement of sound pollution (deciblage), industrial and non industrial.

Unit-4 Water Pollution

Water pollution- meaning and definition of water pollution, pollutants in water, adverse effects of water pollution; treatment of effluent- domestic and industrial waste water.

Soil pollution: soil profiles, pollutants in soil, their adverse effects, controlling measures.

Unit-5 Society and Ethics

Society and ethics- impacts of waste on society, solid waste managemet (nuvclear, thermal, plastic, medicalagricultural, domestic and e-waste); ethics and moral values, ethical situations, objectives of ethics and its study; Prelimnary studies regarding environmental protection acts, environmental impact assessment.

CONTENTS

Unit-I

Chapter 1

General View of Energy Regarding the Demand and Supply

1.1 ENERGY SYSTEM

Energy is used up and lost as heat as it moves through ecosystems. More over, new energy is continually added to the earth in the form of solar radiation. Actualy earth is an open system in case of energy. On the other hand, Nutrients and other materials, are continually recirculated within ecosystems, with the flow of energy and there are no new inputs or losses from the planet. In terms of materials, earth is a closed system. Energy and materials are essential for ecosystem structure, function, and composition. For example, every one know number of calories (a measure of energy) in gram of certain carbon compounds or materials such as fats or carbohydrates contain.

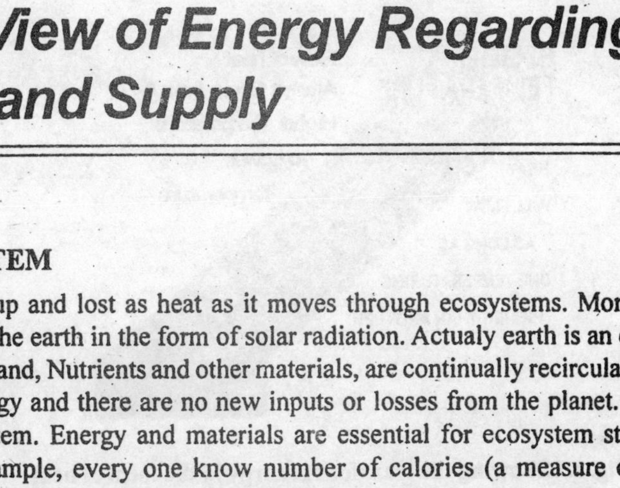

Fig. 1.1: Showing the usage of basic concept of heat flow useful for energy system

1.1.2 Flow of Heat

During the biological, the process energy (heat or heat flow) is constantly flowing into and out of all objects, including living objects. Heat flow occur from a higher temperature to a lower temperature. The bigger the difference in temperature between two objects, the faster the heat flows. If temperatures are the same,. there is no change in energy due to zero heat flow. Radiation and Conduction are the methods of heat transfer. Convection is a Special type of conduction. Heat has the units of energy and heat flow has the units of power. **Energy** is flowing into and out of body of living beings and everything else. Energy from the food you eat as a card carrying member of the *Food Chain*, though energy does get into animals in that way too.

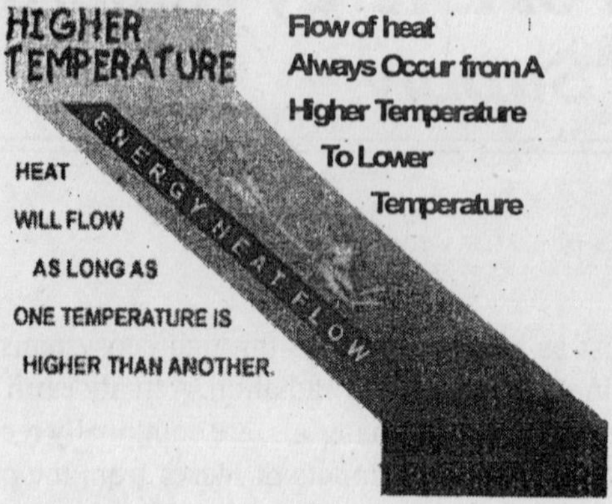

Fig. 1.2 Showing the transfer of energy in the form of heat

Energy flows into living beings body from the surrounding air, from surrounding objects, and from the sun. Energy also flows out of body into the surrounding air, into the surrounding objects, and even into outer space. This type of energy transfer from one place to another place is driven by differences in temperature and is called heat flow. It is a big deal—one of the major driving forces of nature. Heat flow from the sun to this planet (earth) is the force that makes weather, the mother of all earthly driving forces. Heat flow from the sun to this planet. Plants and algae and some types of bacteria is the energizer of photosynthesis the provide of food for almost all living beings. The way that each animal is made and behaves and where they can live, has a lot to do with heat flow. Due to heat flow, cold-blooded reptiles and insects only come out in the summer. There are a lot reptiles and insects in equatorial climates and arctic climates.

Warm-blooded mammals and birds with their high metabolisms and hotter bodies can live and move in some cold places. However, they have good dry fur or feathers, or a good layer of blubber, and plenty of high energy food to keep that body heat coming.

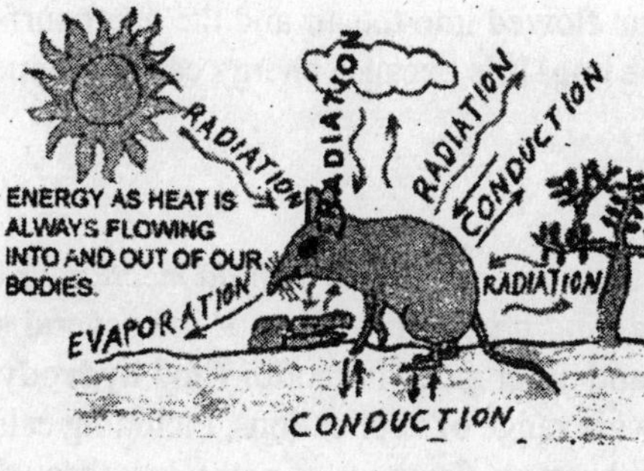

Fig. 1.3: Showing the flow of heat with the living beings and their surrounding

Human beings put on a jacket during winter, or wear shorts on a hot day, for adjusting heat flow. It helps the body to keep its temperature very close to 38°C (98.6°F). It's a never ending struggle. Energy as heat is always flowing out of, and into, your body. It's dangerous to be too hot and dangerous to be too cold. Just like Goldilocks' porridge, our body temperature has to be "just right". Animals and human engineers use all kinds of clever ways to transfer heat. Elephant ears act like giant radiators to transfer heat out of their bodies. Car radiators are used to transfer heat out of the car engine. There are countless fascinating examples. Now we will explore some fascinating examples of how animals and human made machines use the same basic principles of heat flow, along with some clever techniques, to keep their operating temperatures "just right".

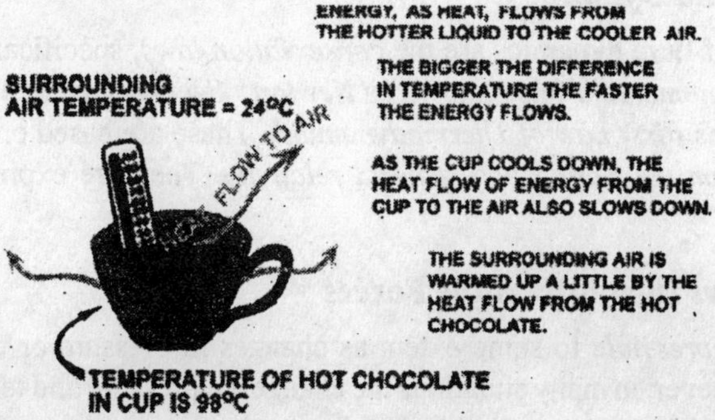

Fig. 1.4: Showing the exchange flow of heat form non livings things to surrounding

Let's consider a cup of hot chocolate in the light of our new found wisdom. The cup will only cool down if the air surrounding the cup is cooler than the hot chocolate. It flows by conduction into the air around the cup. It also travels by radiation into the cooler surfaces around the cup, like walls and cupboards.

The air in the room heated up. It is not noticed because the large room can easily absorb that amount of added heat energy without much change in temperature. However, with the help of thermometer it could be measure upto very small fractions of a degree. In addition, if you put hundreds of cups of hot chocolate in the kitchen it might get pretty hot. According to the *First Law of*

Thermodynamics, the energy that flowed into the air and the other surfaces in the room exactly equals the energy that flowed out of the cup. It is because energy can't disappear. The total amount of energy never changes.

1.2 FLUID FLOW

In *physics*, **fluid dynamics** is a sub-discipline of *fluid mechanics* that deals with **fluid flow**—the *natural science* of *fluids* (*liquids* and *gases*) in motion. It has several sub disciplines itself, including *aerodynamics* (the study of air and other gases in motion) and **hydrodynamics** (the study of liquids in motion). Fluid dynamics has a wide range of applications, including calculating *forces* and *moments* on *aircraft*. It helps in determining the *mass flow rate* of *petroleum* through pipelines, predicting *weather* patterns, understanding *nebulae* in *interstellar* space and modeling fission weapon detonation. Some of its principles are even used in *traffic engineering*, if traffic is considered as a continuous fluid.

Fluid dynamics offers a systematic structure that underlies these practical disciplines. It embraces empirical and semi-empirical laws derived from *flow measurement* and used to solve practical problems. The solution to a fluid dynamics problem typically involves calculating various properties of the fluid, such as *velocity*, *pressure*, *density*, and *temperature*, as functions of space and time. Historically, *hydrodynamics* meant something different than today. Before the twentieth century, hydrodynamics was synonymous with fluid dynamics. It still reflected in names of some fluid dynamics topics, like *magneto hydrodynamics* and *hydrodynamic stability*—both also applicable in, as well as being applied to, gases.

1.2.1 Equation of Fluid Dynamic

The foundations of fluid dynamics are the *conservation laws*, specifically, *conservation of mass*, *conservation of linear momentum* (also known as *Newton's Second Law of Motion*), and *conservation of energy* (also known as *First Law of Thermodynamics*). These are based on *classical mechanics* and are modified in *quantum mechanics* and *general relativity*. They are expressed using the *Reynolds Transport Theorem*.

1.2.2 Compressible *vs* Incompressible Forces

All fluids are *compressible* to some extent as changes in pressure or temperature will result in changes in density. However, in many situations the changes in pressure and temperature are sufficiently small that the changes in density are negligible. In this case the flow can be modeled as an *incompressible flow*. Otherwise, the more general *compressible flow* equations must be used.

Mathematically, incompressibility is expressed by saying that the density of a fluid parcel does not change as it moves in the flow field, *i.e.*,

$$\frac{D\rho}{Dt}$$

Where D/Dt is the *substantial derivative*, which is the sum of local and *convective derivatives*. This additional constraint simplifies the governing equations, especially in the case when the fluid has a uniform density.

1.2.3 Viscous *vs* In viscid

Viscous problems are those in which fluid friction has significant effects on the fluid motion. The *Reynolds number*, which is a ratio between inertial and viscous forces, can be used to evaluate whether viscous or in viscid. *Stokes flow* is flow at very low Reynolds numbers, *Re* j=1, such that inertial forces can be neglected compared to viscous forces. On the contrary, high Reynolds numbers indicate that the inertial forces are more significant than the viscous (friction) forces. Therefore, we may assume the flow to be an *inviscid flow*, an approximation in which we neglect *viscosity* completely, compared to inertial terms.

1.2.4 Steady vs Unsteady Flow

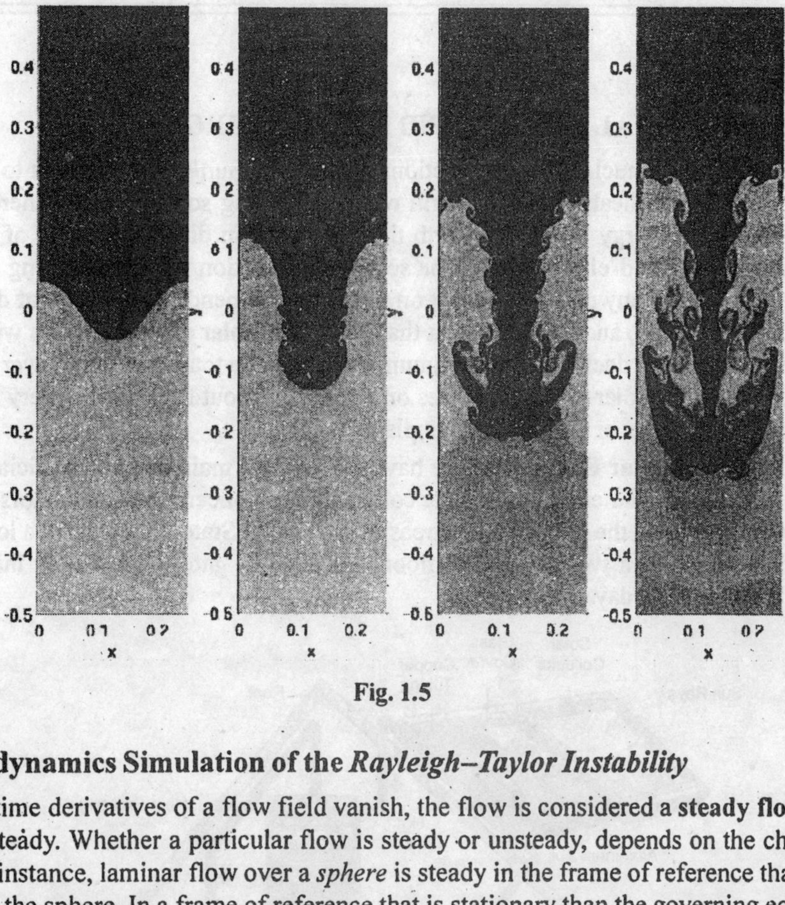

Fig. 1.5

1.2.5 Hydrodynamics Simulation of the *Rayleigh–Taylor Instability*

If all the time derivatives of a flow field vanish, the flow is considered a **steady flow**. Otherwise, it is called unsteady. Whether a particular flow is steady or unsteady, depends on the chosen *frame of reference*. For instance, laminar flow over a *sphere* is steady in the frame of reference that is stationary with respect to the sphere. In a frame of reference that is stationary than the governing equations of the same problem without taking advantage of the steadiness of the flow field. Although strictly unsteady flows, time-periodic problems can often be solved by the same techniques as steady flows. For this reason, they can be considered to be somewhere between steady and unsteady.

Chapter 2

Sources of Energy

2.1 NON-CONVENTIONAL ENERGY AND SOLAR ENERGY

Radiation produced by nuclear fusion reactions deep in the Sun's core reaches to this planet so Sun provides almost all the heat and light, Earth receives coming solar radiation therefore sustains every living being. Solar energy travels to, Earth through space in discrete packets of energy called *photons*. The atmosphere and clouds absorb or scatter the fraction of the incoming sunlight. The amount of light that reaches any particular point on the ground depends on the time of day, the day of the year, the amount of cloud, and the latitude at that point. The solar intensity varies with the time of day, peaking at solar noon and declining to a minimum at sunset. The total radiation power (1.4 kilowatts per square meter, called the solar constant) varies only slightly, about 0.2 percent every 30 years. Any substantial change would alter or end life on this planet (Earth).

Direct Collection of Solar Energy: People have devised two main types of artificial collectors to directly capture and utilize solar energy: flat plate collectors and concentrating collectors. Both require large surface areas exposed to the Sun. Even in areas of the United States that receive a lot of sunshine, a collector surface as big as a two-car garage floor is needed to gather the energy that one person typically uses during a single day.

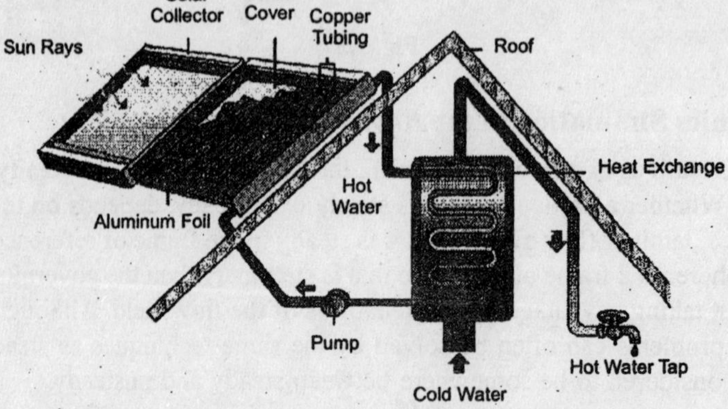

Fig. 2.1: Showing the mechanism and process for the collection of solar energy

Solar Heating

Flat plate collectors utilize the sun's energy to warm a carrier fluid, which in turn provides usable heat to a household. The carrier fluid (may also be water) flows through copper tubing in the solar collector. During the process it absorbs some of the sun's energy. Next, the carrier fluid moves to the heat exchange, where the carrier fluid warms water that is used by the household. Finally, a pump moves the carrier fluid back to the solar collector to repeat the cycle.

Fig. 2.2: Solar Home

in this solar home in Corrales, New Mexico, a flat plate solar collector (*lower right*) provides energy to heat water pumped by the windmill. The water is stored in large drums on the side of the home.

2.2 WIND ENERGY

Energy contained in the force of the winds blowing across the earth's surface. When harnessed, Wind energy can be converted into mechanical energy for performing work such as pumping water, grinding grain, and milling. By connecting a spinning rotor (an assembly of blades attached to a hub) to an electric generator, modern wind turbines convert wind energy, into electrical energy. Wind is created when warmed air over sun-heated land rises, leaving a vacuum in the space it once occupied. Cooler surrounding air then rushes in to fill the vacuum. This movement of rushing air results as wind.

Windmills have since been used to mill grain, pump water, saw timber, and provide other forms of mechanical energy. Wind is a clean and renewable source of energy. Modern wind turbines are being installed in countries such as Germany, Denmark, India, China, and the United States to supplement more traditional sources of electric power, such as burning coal. Design improvements such as more efficient rotor blades combined with an increase in the numbers of wind turbines installed, have helped to increase the world's wind energy generating capacity about150 percent since 1990.

The Modern Wind Turbine: During the 1930s, interest in powering electric lighting and appliances on homes across the Great Plains led to the development of small, battery-charging wind turbines. These are called wind chargers. They were early forerunners of the small two or three-bladed wind turbines used today to provide electricity for remote residences, and to provide electricity to villages in developing countries. The oil crisis of the 1970s spurred efforts into developing wind energy as an alternative source of electrical power. Many countries launched programs to develop modern wind turbines. Denmark was successful in developing modern wind turbines. Countries such as the United States have adopted this technology to develop wind energy resources. The modern wind turbine is the result of design and material advances made during the 1980s and 1990s, It have enabled wind turbines to become increasingly efficient. Modern wind turbines the same size as the traditional European windmill can generate 250 to 300 kilowatts of power—a nearly tenfold increase in efficiency.

Fig. 2.3

The intermittent nature of wind energy does not affect consumers when wind turbines are tied to an electrical network or power grid. Many wind turbines in North America, Europe, and parts of Asia are connected to large electricity networks. The effect of windless days can be offset by production from other power-generating sources, such as coal-fired plants and hydroelectric plants if they are connected to the power grid. Such systems help to provide reliable power supplies to consumers. People located in remote sites those depends on electricity from wind turbines often use batteries or a backup generator to provide auxiliary power during periods without sufficient wind.

Operationally, modern wind turbines are as reliable as conventional power plants. Most commercial wind turbines are offline (down for maintenance or repair) less than 3 percent of the time. Wind turbines are also known for their longevity. Many turbines have been generating electricity since the early 1980s. Many American farm windmills have been in continuous use for generations, while some traditional European windmills have been working for almost 300 years.

2.3 GEOTHERMAL ENERGY

Energy contained intense heat that continually flows outward from deep of Earth. This heat originates primarily in the core. Some heat is generated in the crust, the planet's outer layer, by the decay of radioactive elements that are in all rocks. The crust, which is about 5 to 75 km (about 3 to 47 mi) thick, insulates the surface from the hot interior, which at the core may reach temperatures from 4000° to 7000°C (7200° to 12,600°F). Where the heat is concentrated near the surface, it can be used as a source of energy.

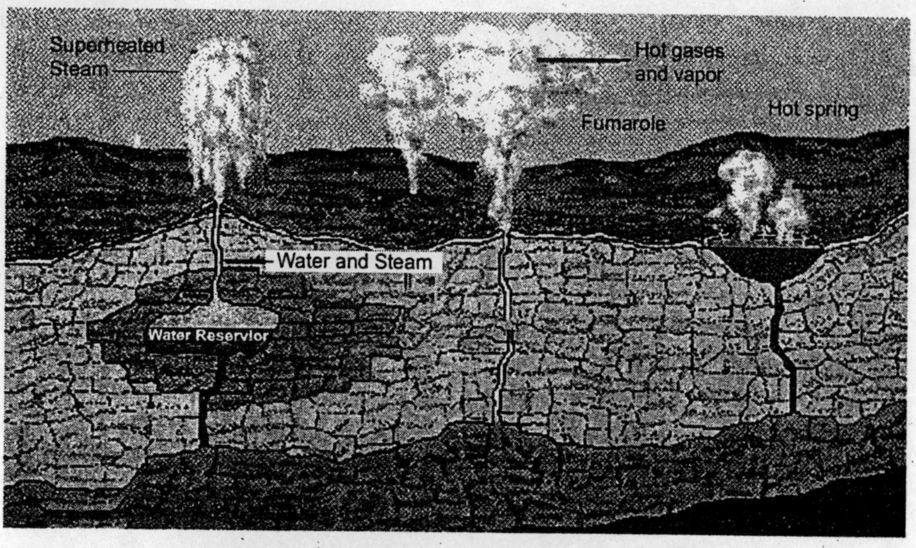

Fig. 2.4: Showing the formation of natural geysers

Geysers are caused when underground chambers of water are heated to the boiling point by volcanic rock. When heat causes the water to boil, pressure forces a superheated column of steam and water to the surface. Because most geothermal reservoirs are capped by overlying rock, the heated water cannot escape, remaining underground instead. If a geothermal reservoir is sufficiently close to the surface, the heated water can be piped to the surface and used to produce energy.

Geothermal Reservoirs

In certain areas, water seeping down through cracks and fissures in the crust. If it meets to the hot rock and is heated to high temperatures. Some of this heated water circulates back to the surface and appears as hot springs and geysers. However, the rising hot water may remain underground in areas of permeable hot rock, forming geothermal reservoirs. Geothermal reservoirs, which may reach temperatures of more than 350°C (700°F). It can provide a powerful source of energy. Geothermal reservoirs within about 5 km (about 3 mile) of Earth's surface can be utilized by drilling a well. The hot water or steam from wells can be used to turn turbine generators to produce electricity. A power plant that uses this natural source of hot water or steam is called a geothermal power plant. At the beginning of the 21st century, there were some 380 geothermal power plants in 22 countries around the world with a combined installed capacity of about 8,000 megawatts.

Geothermal energy provided 1.6 percent of the world's total electricity, serving the electricity needs of about 60 million people, mostly in developing countries. About 2.5 percent of the electricity produced in the United States came from geothermal power plants. The electricity produced from geothermal power in the United States represented about 37 percent of the world's electricity from geothermal power. The United States, the Philippines, Italy, Mexico, Indonesia, Japan, New Zealand, and Iceland are the largest producers of geothermal energy. There are three types of geothermal power plants: flash steam plants, dry steam plants, and binary plants.

Fig. 2.5: Showing Geothermal Energy Plant for electricity generation

Geothermal energy plants generate electricity and heat by harnessing the heat energy contained within the earth. The earth transfers its energy to deep-lying circulating water. The plants access this energy with wells and pumps. Geothermal energy is attractive because it creates almost no environmental pollution. However, the number of sites where geothermal energy can be economically extracted is limited.

2.4 BIOMASS ENERGY

Biofuel, any solid, liquid, or gaseous fuel produced from organic (comming form living beings) matter. Biofuel is produced either directly from plants or indirectly from industrial, commercial, domestic, or agricultural wastes. There are several methods for the development of biofuels: the burning of dry organic wastes (such as household refuse, industrial and agricultural wastes, straw, wood, and peat); the fermentation of wet wastes (such as animal dung) in the absence of oxygen to produce biogas (containing up to 60 percent methane), or the fermentation of sugarcane or corn to produce alcohol and esters; and energy forestry (producing fast-growing wood for fuel).

Though the first plants appeared on land only about half a billion years ago. Today green plant account for by far the largest proportion of the earth's biomass. From macroscopic to microscopic species of duckweed, the plant kingdom is an extraordinarily diverse and long-lived group that makes the life of animals, fungi, and other organisms possible.

Fig. 2.6: Tree Cutting for various uses

A logger fells a tree using a chain saw. Once the tree is down, the log will be mechanically dragged or lifted to a landing in the forest. Further it will be cut into shorter lengths to be trucked to a sawmill. Many countries that have well-developed forest industries process almost all tree parts into wood products, creating little waste.

Its members provide oxygen, shelter, and the foundation of the food web, determining the traits of the organisms that depend on them in a huge variety of habitats. Their beauty, fragrance, and amazing traits fascinate and bring intellectual and aesthetic pleasure to many humans.

Unlike conventional power plants, which are owned by large private or public companies, Denmark's wind turbines are often owned by the farmers on whose land they stand, or by farmers' cooperatives. The revenue produced by the wind a turbine typically flows directly into the local community and to the manufacturers and service firms that maintain them. Denmark also draws on a form of renewable energy known as biomass (biological materials derived from plants). Small, locally based power plants burn straw and other agricultural waste to produce electricity as well as hot water for local heating.

2.5 OCEAN ENERGY

The oceans also collect solar energy so act as a store solar energy. A significant fraction of the Sun's radiation reflects or scatters from the water's surface. The remaining fraction enters the water and rapidly diminishes with depth as the energy is absorbed and converted to heat or chemical energy. This absorption creates differences in temperature between layers of water in the ocean called temperature gradients. In some locations, these differences approach 20°C (36°F) over a depth of a few hundred meters. These large masses of water existing at different temperatures create a potential for generating power. Energy flows from the high-temperature water to the low-temperature water (Thermodynamics). The flow can be harnessed, to turn a turbine to produce electricity. Such systems, called ocean thermal energy conversion (OTEC) systems, require enormous heat exchangers and other hardware in the ocean to produce electricity in the megawatt range.

Tidal Energy: The energy of tides has been harnessed to produce electricity. In 1966, a tidal power plant with a capacity of 240,000 kW went into operation on the Rance River, an estuary of the English Channel in northwestern France. The incoming tide of the river flows through a dam, driving turbines, and tnen is trapped behind the dam. When the tide ebbs, the trapped water is released and flows back through the dam, again driving the turbines. Such tidal power plants are most efficient if the difference between high and low tides is great, as in the Rance estuary, where the difference is 8.5 m (28 ft). The highest tides in the world occur in the Bay of Fundy in Canada. In Bay of fundy the difference between high and low tide is about 18 m (about 60 ft). The erection of a tidal power plant across Passamaquoddy Bay, an arm of the Bay of Fundy, has long been contemplated.

Ocean Thermal Energy Conversion (OTEC)

Fig. 2.7: Showing Tidal pool for harnessing tidal energy

The fluctuation of the tide allows for a unique environment along shorelines. The current continually circulates and replenishes a rich supply of nutrients along beaches. Organisms living there must be adapted to both buffeting waves and frequent shifts from open air to complete submersion. Marine organisms adapt to the constantly changing surroundings in a variety of ways. Starfish use suction-cup feet, barnacles fix permanently to large objects like rocks and boats, and seaweed anchors firmly to the ocean floor. When the tide goes out, pockets of water remain trapped in rocks, depressions in the sand, and natural basins called tidal pools (one shown here during low title).

The oceans also collect and store solar energy. A significant fraction of the Sun's radiation reflects or scatters from the water's surface. The remaining fraction enters the water and rapidly diminishes with depth as the energy is absorbed and converted to heat or chemical energy.

This absorption creates differences in temperature between layers of water in the ocean called temperature gradients. In some locations, these differences approach 20°C (36°F) over a depth of a few hundred meters. These large masses of water existing at different temperatures create a potential for generating power. Energy flows from the high-temperature water to the low-temperature water.

2.6.1 Ocean Thermal Energy Conversion (OTEC)

Ocean thermal energy conversion (*OTEC* or *OTE*) uses the *temperature* difference that exists between deep and shallow waters to run a *heat engine*. As in any heat engine, the greatest efficiency and power is produced with the largest *temperature* difference. This temperature difference generally increases with decreasing latitude i.e., near the *equator*, in the *tropics*. The main technical challenge of OTEC was to generate significant amounts of power from this very small temperature ratio. Changes in efficiency of heat exchange in modern designs allow performance approaching the theoretical maximum efficiency. The *oceans* are continually heated by the *sun,* they cover nearly 70% of the *Earth*'s surface. The temperature difference contains a vast amount of *solar energy*, which can potentially be harnessed. If this extraction could be made cost effective on a large scale, it could provide a source of *renewable energy* required to deal with *energy shortages* and other energy problems. The total energy available is one or two *orders of magnitude* higher than other ocean energy options such as *wave power*. But the small magnitude of the temperature difference makes energy extraction comparatively difficult due to low *thermal efficiency*. Earlier OTEC systems had an overall efficiency of only 1 to 3% (the theoretical maximum efficiency lies between 6 and 7%). Current designs under review will operate closer to the theoretical maximum efficiency. An OTEC plant operates at a low overall efficiency, it can be configured to operate continuously as a *Base load* power generation system. Any thorough *cost-benefit analysis* should include these factors to provide an accurate assessment of performance, efficiency, operational, construction costs, and *returns on investment*. The concept of a heat engine is very common in *thermodynamics engineering*. A heat engine is a thermodynamic device placed between a high temperature reservoir and a low temperature reservoir. As heat flows from one to the other, the engine converts some of the heat energy to *work* energy. This principle is used in *steam turbines* and *internal combustion engines*, while *refrigerators* reverse the direction of flow of both the heat and work energy.

Fig. 2.8: The only heat cycle suitable for OTEC, is the *Rankine cycle* using a low-pressure turbine. Although Systems may be either closed-cycle or open-cycle. View of a land based OTEC facility

There have been many periodic attempts to develop and refine OTEC technology starting in the 1800s. In 1881, *Jacques Arsene d'Arsonval*, a *French physicist*, proposed tapping the thermal energy of the ocean. It was d'Arsonval's student, *Georges Claude* who actually built the first OTEC plant, in *Cuba* in 1930. The system generated 22 kW of *electricity* with a low-*pressure turbine*. In 1931, *Nikola Tesla* released "On Future Motive Power" which covered an ocean thermal energy conversion system. In 1935, Claude constructed another plant, this time aboard a 10,000-ton cargo vessel moored off the coast of *Brazil*. Weather and waves destroyed both plants before they could become net power generators.

Working Principles: Some experts believe that it could become cost-competitive with conventional power technologies. OTEC could produce gigawatts of electrical power, and in conjunction with *electrolysis*, could produce enough hydrogen to completely replace all projected global fossil fuel.

- Land based plant
- Shelf based plant
- Floating plant

Depending on the cycle used they may be classified as

- Closed cycle
- Open cycle
- Hybrid cycle

Cold seawater is an integral part of each of the three types of OTEC systems: closed-cycle, open-cycle, and hybrid. To operate, the cold seawater must be brought to the surface. This can be accomplished through direct pumping. A second method is to desalinate the seawater near the sea floor; this lowers its density, which will cause it to "float" up through a pipe to the surface.

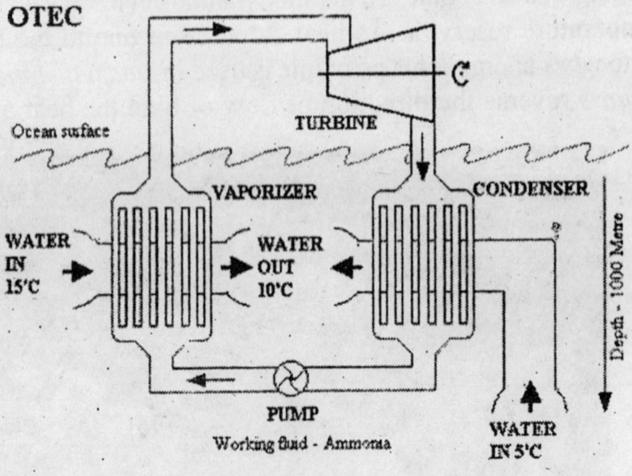

Fig. 2.9: Showing the energy production process of a Closed Cycle OTEC Plant

Closed-cycle: Closed-cycle systems use fluid with a low boiling point, such as *ammonia*, to rotate a *turbine* for electricity Generation. Warm surface *seawater* is pumped through a *heat exchanger* where the low-boiling-point fluid is vapourized. The expanding vapor turns the turbo-generator. Then, cold, deep seawater—pumped through a second heat exchanger—condenses the vapor back into a liquid, which is then recycled through the system.

Open-cycle: Open-cycle OTEC uses the tropical oceans' warm surface water to make electricity. When warm *seawater* is placed in a low-pressure container, it boils. The expanding *steam* drives a low-pressure turbine attached to an *electrical generator*. The steam, which has left its *salt* and contaminants behind in the low-pressure container, is pure *fresh water*. It is condensed back into a liquid by exposure to cold temperatures from deep-ocean water. This method has the advantage of producing *desalinized* fresh water, suitable for *drinking water* or *irrigation*.

Hybrid Cycle: A hybrid cycle combines the features of both the closed-cycle and open-cycle systems. In a hybrid OTEC system, warm seawater enters a vacuum chamber where it is flash-evaporated into steam, similar to the open-cycle evaporation process. The steam vapourizes the *ammonia* working fluid of a closed-cycle loop on the other side of an *ammonia* vaporizer. The vapourized fluid then drives a turbine to produce electricity. The steam condenses within the heat exchanger and provides *desalinated water*. The electricity produced by the system can be delivered to a utility grid or used to manufacture *methanol*, *hydrogen*, *refined metals*, ammonia, and similar products.

2.6.2 Applications

Chilled-soil agriculture: OTEC technology also supports *chilled-soil agriculture*. When cold seawater flows through underground pipes, it chills the surrounding soil. The temperature difference between plant roots in the cool soil and plant leaves in the warm air allows many plants that evolved in *temperate climates* to be grown in the *subtropics*.

Aquaculture: *Aquaculture* is the most well-known byproduct of OTEC. It is widely considered one of the most important ways to reduce the financial and energy costs of pumping large volumes of water from the deep ocean. Deep ocean water contains high concentrations of essential nutrients that are depleted in surface waters due to biological consumption.

Hydrogen production: *Hydrogen* can be produced *via electrolysis* using electricity generated by the OTEC process. The steam generated can be used as a relatively pure medium for electrolysis with electrolyte compounds added to improve the overall efficiency. OTEC technology can be scaled to generate large quantities of hydrogen. OTEC installations on islands, platforms, barges and ships have the potential for large scale, global hydrogen generation with supply to major ports *via hydrogen tanker* ships.

Mineral extraction: Another undeveloped opportunity is the potential to mine ocean water for its 57 elements contained in salts and other forms. In the past, most economic analyses concluded that mining the ocean for trace elements dissolved in solution would be unprofitable, in part because much energy is required to pump the large volume of water needed. With OTEC plants supplying the pumped water, the remaining problem is the cost of the extraction process.

Cost and economics: For OTEC to be viable as a power source in terms of global utilization, the technology must have equal tax and subsidy treatment as competing energy sources. As OTEC systems have not yet been widely deployed, estimates of their costs are uncertain. One study estimates power generation costs as low as US $0.07 per kilowatt-hour, compared with $0.05–$0.07 for subsidized wind systems.

Beneficial factors that should be taken into account include OTEC's status as a renewable resource (with no combustion or waste products or limited fuel supply), the amount of area in which it is available. The geopolitical effects of dependence and reliance on petroleum, the development of alternate forms of ocean power such as wave energy, tidal energy and *methane hydrates*, and the possibility of combining it with *solar energy*, *aquaculture*, refrigeration and air conditioning, hydrogen production or filtration for trace minerals to obtain multiple uses from a single pump system.

Classification: OTEC systems can be classified as two types based on the thermodynamic cycle

(1) Closed cycle and

(2) Open cycle.

Open/Claude cycle: In this scheme, warm surface water at around 27°C is admitted into an evaporator in which the pressure is maintained at a value slightly below the *saturation pressure*.

Water entering the evaporator is therefore vaporized.

$H_1 = H_f$

Where H_f is *enthalpy* of liquid water at the inlet temperature, T_1.

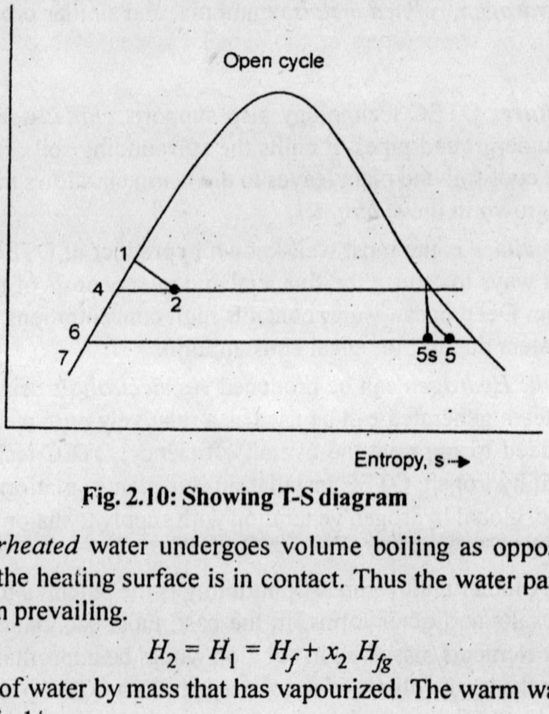

Fig. 2.10: Showing T-S diagram

This temporarily *superheated* water undergoes volume boiling as opposed to pool boiling in conventional boilers where the heating surface is in contact. Thus the water partially flashes to steam with a two-phase equilibrium prevailing.

$$H_2 = H_1 = H_f + x_2 H_{fg}$$

Here, x_2 is the fraction of water by mass that has vapourized. The warm water mass flow rate per unit *turbine* mass flow rate is $1/x_2$.

The low pressure in the evaporator is maintained by a vacuum pump that also removes the dissolved non-condensable gases from the evaporator. The evaporator now contains a mixture of water and steam of very low "*quality*". The steam is separated from the water as saturated vapour. The remaining water is saturated and is discharged back to the ocean in the open cycle. It expands in a special low pressure turbine.

$$H_3 = H_g$$

Here, H_g corresponds to T_2. For an ideal *isentropic* (*reversible adiabatic*) turbine,

$$S_{5,3} = S_3 = S_f + x_{5,3}\, S_{fg}$$

The above equation corresponds to the temperature at the exhaust of the turbine, T_5. $x_{5,s}$ is the mass fraction of vapor at state 5.

The enthalpy at T_5 is,

$$H_{3,s} = H_f + x_{5,s}\, H_{fg}$$

This enthalpy is lower. The adiabatic reversible turbine work = $H_3 - H_{5,s}$.

Actual turbine work $W_T = (H_3 - H_{5,s}) \times$ *polytropic efficiency*

$$H_5 = H_3 - \text{actual work}$$

The condenser temperature and pressure are lower. Since the turbine exhaust will be discharged back into the ocean anyway, a direct contact condenser is used.

$H_6 \approx H_f$ at T_5. T_7 is the temperature of the exhaust mixed with cold sea water, as the vapour content now is negligible,

$$H_7 \approx H_f \text{ at } T_7$$

The cold water flow rate *per* unit turbine mass flow rate,

$$m_c = \frac{H_5 - H_6}{H_6 - H_7}$$

Turbine mass flow rate, $M_T = \dfrac{\text{turbine work required}}{W_T}$

Warm water mass flow rate, $\dot{M}_w = \dot{M}_{Tmw}$

Cold water mass flow rate $\dot{M}_c = \dot{M}_{Tmc}$

Closed/Anderson cycle: The high-pressure, high-temperature gas then is expanded in the turbine to yield turbine work, W_T. The working fluid is slightly superheated at the turbine exit and the turbine typically has an efficiency of 90% based on reversible, adiabatic expansion. From the turbine exit, the working fluid enters the condenser where it rejects heat, $-Q_C$, to the cold sea water. The condensate is then compressed to the highest pressure in the cycle, requiring condensate pump work, W_C. The major additional parasitic energy requirements in the OTEC plant are the cold water pump work, W_{CT}, and the warm water pump work, W_{HT}. Denoting all other parasitic energy requirements by W_A, the net work from the OTEC plant, W_{NP} is

$$W_{NP} = W_T + W_C + W_{CT} + W_{HT} + W_A$$

The thermodynamic cycle undergone by the working fluid can be analyzed without detailed consideration of the parasitic energy requirements. From the first law of thermodynamics, the energy balance for the working fluid as the system is

$$W_N = Q_H + Q_C$$

where $W_N = W_T + W_C$ is the net work for the thermodynamic cycle. For the special idealized case in which there is no working fluid pressure drop in the heat exchangers,

$$Q_H = \int_H T_H ds$$

and

$$Q_C = \int_C T_H ds$$

so that the net thermodynamic cycle work becomes

$$W_N = \int_H T_H ds + \int_C T_H ds$$

Subcooled liquid enters the evaporator. Due to the heat exchange with warm sea water, evaporation takes place and usually superheated vapor leaves the evaporator. This vapor drives the turbine and two phase mixture enters the condenser heat exchangers should increase to endure high pressure especially on the evaporator side.

Technical difficulties: Degradation of heat exchanger performance by dissolved gases:

A very important technical issue pertaining to the Claude cycle is the performance of direct contact heat exchangers operating at typical OTEC boundary conditions. As the warm sea water raises in the intake pipes, the pressure decreases to the point where gas begins to evolve. If a significant amount of gas comes out of the solution, designing a gas trap before the direct contact heat exchangers may be justified.

Degradation of heat exchanger performance by microbial fouling: Because raw seawater must be passed through, the heat exchanger care must be taken to maintain good thermal conductivity. *Biofouling* layers as thin as 25 to 50μ^m can degrade heat exchanger performance by as much as 50%. The apparent discrepancy between the level of fouling and the heat transfer impairment is the result of a thin layer of water trapped by the microbial growth on the surface of the heat exchanger.

Improper sealing: The evaporator, turbine, and condenser operate in partial vacuum ranging from 3% to 1% atmospheric pressure. This poses a number of practical concerns. First, the system must be carefully sealed to prevent in-leakage of atmospheric air that can severely degrade or shut down operation. Second, the specific volume of low-pressure steam is very large compared to that of the pressurized working fluid used in the case of a closed cycle OTEC. This means components must have large flow areas to ensure steam velocities do not attain excessively high values.

Fig. 2.11

2.7 COOKING FUELS

Scientists are keen on developing strategies and policies for creating universal access to clean cooking fuels and electricity. We have been considering the requirements to increased supply of LPG for cooking in the rural and semi-urban areas of India. There are other important alternatives to traditional cooking fuels in the form of modernised biomass-fuels; however, the use of LPG has been considered as a short/medium term option, *i.e.*, a transition fuel (or a complement) to bio-based fuels. The LPG study has necessitated estimates of the possible increase in demand and an appropriate supply network. Attempts have been made to address the problems regarding increased LPG use in rural and semi-urban areas.

2.7.1 Biogas

Biogas typically refers to a *gas* produced during the biological breakdown of *organic matter* in the absence of *oxygen*. Biogas originates from biogenic material and is a type of *biofuel*. One type of biogas is produced by *anaerobic digestion* or *fermentation* of biodegradable materials such as ***biomass***, ***manure***, ***sewage***, ***municipal waste***, ***green waste*** and *energy crops*. This type of biogas comprises primarily ***methane*** and *carbon dioxide*. The other principal type of biogas is *wood gas* that is created by ***gasification*** of wood or other biomass. This type of biogas is comprised primarily of ***nitrogen***, ***hydrogen***, and ***carbon monoxide***, with trace amounts of *methane*.

The gases methane, hydrogen and carbon monoxide can be combusted or oxidized with oxygen. Biogas can be used as a low-cost fuel in any country for any heating purpose, such as cooking. It can also be used in modern *waste management* facilities where it can be used to run any type of *heat engine*, to generate either mechanical or electrical power. Biogas can be compressed, much like *natural gas*, and used to power *motor vehicles*. Biogas is a *renewable fuel*, so it qualifies for renewable *energy subsidies* in some parts of the world.

2.7.2 Producer Gas

Producer Gas is a generic term referring to the following gases.

Wood gas: produced in a *gasifier* to power cars with ordinary internal combustion engines.

Town gas: manufactured gas, originally produced from coal, for sale to consumers and municipalities.

Syngas: used as a fuel source or as an intermediate for the production of other chemicals.

Modern 'natural gas' used in homes is far less toxic, and has an onion-like scent added to it for identifying leaks.

A mixture of carbon monoxide and nitrogen made by passing air over very hot carbon. Usually some steam is added to the air and the mixture contains hydrogen. The gas is used as a fuel in some industrial processes.

2.7.3 Biomass Conversion Technology

Bioenergy is an important topic to include in a foresight analysis of the world agricultural markets. In the recent Agricultural Outlook report from OECD—FAO, it is concluded that one of the main drivers for agricultural market development in the period 2007-2016 is the growing use of cereals, sugar, oilseeds and vegetable oils to satisfy the needs of a rapidly increasing biofuel industry. It focuses on emerging technologies in relation to bioenergy, specifically biofuels for the transportation sector, and the role of bioenergy in sustainable energy production and uses.

The Problem

Present world population increases dramatically and even with low future growth rate, the world population size will at the earliest get to a plateau around year 2040 with a population size of nearly 8 billion. The world society is increasing its energy consumption dramatically. This demand is mainly based on fossil fuel availability. Today, about 80% of the total primary energy supply consists of fossil fuel. According to a reference, the largest increase in energy supply until 2030 will be in the fossil fuels coal and gas. However, as concluded in the Agricultural Outlook from OECD-FAO, these predictions may be misleading and biomass may increase more rapidly.

The transport sector is increasing dramatically and consumes at present about 25% of the world energy supply.

Fig. 2.12

2.7.4 Direct Fired or Conventional Steam Boiler

Most of the woody biomass-to-energy plants use direct-fired system or conventional steam boiler, whereby biomass feedstock is directly burned to produce steam leading to generation of electricity. In a direct-fired system, biomass is fed from the bottom of the boiler and air is supplied at the base. Hot combustion gases are passed through a heat exchanger in which water is boiled to create steam.

Biomass is dried, sized into smaller pieces and then pelletized or briquetted before firing. Pelletization is a process of reducing the bulk volume of biomass feedstock by mechanical means to improve handling and combustion characteristics of biomass. Wood pellets are normally produced from dry industrial wood waste, as *e.g.*, shavings, sawdust and sander dust. Pelletization results in:

1. Concentration of energy in the biomass feedstock
2. Easy handling, reduced transportation cost and hassle-free storage
3. Low-moisture fuel with good burning characteristics
4. Well-defined, good quality fuel for commercial and domestic use

2.7.5 Biomass Gasification

Gasification processes convert biomass into combustible gases. In practice, conversion efficiencies ranging from 60% to 90% are achieved. Gasification processes can be direct as using air or oxygen to generate heat through exothermic reactions. Although it may be indirect transferring heat to the reactor from the outside. The gas can be burned to produce industrial or residential heat. It may also be use to run engines for mechanical or electrical power, or to make synthetic fuels.

Biomass gasifiers are of two kinds – updraft and downdraft. In an updraft unit, biomass is fed in the top of the reactor and air is injected into the bottom of the fuel bed. The efficiency of updraft gasifiers ranges from 80 to 90 per cent because of efficient counter-current heat exchange between the rising gases and descending solids. However, the tars produced by updraft gasifiers imply that the gas must be cooled before it can be used in internal combustion engines. Thus, in practical operation, updraft units are used for direct heat applications while downdraft ones are employed for operating internal combustion engines.

Large scale applications of gasifiers include comprehensive versions of the small scale updraft and downdraft technologies, and fluidized bed technologies. The superior heat and mass transfer of fluidized beds leads to relatively uniform temperatures throughout the bed, better fuel moisture utilization, and faster rate of reaction, resulting in higher throughput capabilities.

Chapter 3

Renewable and Nonrenewable Energy Sources

3.1 FORMS OF ENERGY

3.1.1 Thermal Energy

This energy is used for Cooking Heating, Drying, Distillation, Electricity Power generation, Cooling, Refrigeration etc purposes.

Some gadgets and devices of thermal energy: Solar cooker, Flat plate solar cookers, Concentrating collectors, Solar hot water systems (Domestic and Industrial), Solar pond, Solar hot air systems, Solar Dryers, Solar timber kilns, solar stills, Solar photovoltaic systems, Solar pond, Concentrating collectors, Power Tower, Air conditioning, Solar collectors, coupled to absorption, Refrigeration systems are the examples of the devices related the thermal energy.

3.1.2 Chemical Energ

This energy is being used for purposes: Cooking Mechanicals Applications, Pumping, Power generation, Transportation etc. purposes.

Some of the gadgets and other devices: Biogas plant, Gasifier, Burner, Gasifier engine pump sets, Stirling engine pump sets, Producer gas/ Biogas based engine generator sets, turbine generators.

3.1.3 Potential/Kinetic energy

This energy is being used for: Power generation.

3.1.4 Kinetic energy

This energy is used for: Sailing ships, Pumping water/Irrigation, Grinding Grains, Power generation.

Some of the gadgets and other devices: Sails, Windmills, Wind turbines.

Half a kilo of dry plant tissue can produce as much as 1890 k Cal of heat which is equivalent to the heat available from a quarter of kilogram of coal. Geothermal manifestations are wide spread in India in the form of 340 hot spring sites.

3.2 ENERGY RESOURCES

Energy is the key input for domestic needs. It is also essential for industrial and economic development. It is a pre-requisite for sustaining industrial growth. With industrialization, the need of energy has continuously grown. The application areas of energy are mentioned below.

Main application area of energy demand:

1. In power plant
2. In transport sector
3. In space technology
4. In military uses
5. In industrial sector
6. For domestic purpose

3.2.1 Classification of Energy on the Basis of Availability

(a) Primary energy resources: These are directly obtained from the various components of environment. Their examples are

1. Fossil fuels such as coal etc.
2. Nuclear fuel such as uranium etc.
3. Hydro energy
4. Solar energy
5. Geothermal energy
6. Wind energy
7. Ocean energy
8. Biomass energy
9. Hydrogen energy

(b) Secondary energy resources: They do not exist in nature; they are derived from primary energy resources. The examples are:

1. Petrol
2. Compressed natural gas
3. Electrical energy based on coal etc.
4. Plutonium etc. which are derived from uranium

3.2.2 Classification of Energy on the Basis of Being Older and Newer in Use

(a) Conventional energy resources: The examples are:

(*i*) Fossil fuel
(*ii*) Nuclear energy
(*iii*) Hydro energy

(b) Non conventional energy resources: The examples are:

(i) Solar energy

(ii) Wind energy
(iii) Geothermal energy
(iv) Hydrogen energy
(v) Biomass energy

3.2.3 Classification of Energy on The Basis of Type of Their Uses:

(a) Commercial fuel: Their examples are:
(*i*) Coal
(*ii*) Petrol
(*iii*) Diesel
(*iv*) CNG
(*v*) LPG
(*vi*) Electricity

(b) Non commercial fuels: Their examples are:
(i) Cow dung
(ii) Agricultural waste
(iii) Fuel wood

3.3 HARNESSING OF RENEWAL ENERGY RESOURCES

To bridge the gap between the supply and the demand, some of the efforts are required to ensure availability of power to meet the countries ever increasing demand some offers are as:

(*i*) Exploitation of renewal source of energy like biogas, solar energy, wind energy etc. specially to meet the demand of the rural areas

(*ii*) Energy conservation

(*iii*) Accelerated exploitation of convectional energy sources like natural gas, solar energy, wind energy etc.

Renewal energy source: They are the energy resources that are found free in nature and have no fear of getting over with the period of time examples are solar energy, wind energy, tidal energy etc.

Solar energy: The energy obtains from the sun is called solar energy. The solar energy is utilized by converting it into two forms:

1. Thermal conversion: This occurs by the direct heating.
2. Photo conversions: This is the indirect conversion.

3.3.1 Application of Solar Energy

Solar water heater: It is used to rise the temperature of a liquid such as water. It is used in hotel hospital houses.

Solar cooker: It is used to prepare food by the use of solar energy. It uses few basic elements like box, mirror etc., which are available with various capacities?

Solar drying: The food products are kept dry by keeping them into a cabinet called dryer.

Solar furnace: A high temperature can be achieved by concentrating the solar energy, which is the basic principle of furnace. The temperature is very high from outside atmosphere.

Solar evaporator: It is used to produce salt from costal areas.

Solar greenhouse: A green house is a chamber covered by glass or plastic. It acts as the solar radiation collector.

Solar refrigeration and air conditioning: The solar energy is also utilized to preserve medicine and other useful materials by refrigeration and air conditioning.

3.3.2 Solar Energy's Advantages and Disadvantages

Advantages:

(*i*) They are pollution free.

(*ii*) They do not require serious attention. In solar cooker food is neither over flown nor burnt if they are exposed for a long time. The taste of the food remains natural and the nutrition value remains in it.

(*iii*) Noiseless product

(*iv*) Cheap

(*v*) Low maintenance cost

(*vi*) Occupy less space

(*vii*) No harmful gas involve

(*viii*) No harmful waste

Disadvantages:

(*i*) Fail to work at night, in cloudy days

(*ii*) All system is useless in rainy season

(*iii*) Unable to cook all type of food items

(*iv*) Take more time then other system

Non-conventional energy is *energy* generated from *natural resources* such as *sunlight, wind, rain, tides*, and *geothermal heat*, which are *renewable* (naturally replenished). In 2006, about 18% of global final energy consumption came from renewable, with 13% coming from traditional *biomass*, which is mainly used for *heating*, and 3% from *hydroelectricity. New renewables* (small hydro, modern biomass, wind, solar, geothermal, and biofuels) accounted for another 2.4% and are growing very rapidly. The share of renewables in *electricity generation* is around 18%, with 15% of global electricity coming from hydroelectricity and 3.4% from new renewables.

Wind power is growing at the rate of 30% annually, with a worldwide installed capacity of 157,900 megawatts (MW). It is widely used in Europe, Asia, and the United States. The annual manufacturing output of the photovoltaics industry reached 6,900 MW in 2008, and photovoltaic (PV) power stations are popular in Germany and Spain. Solar-thermal power stations operate in the USA and Spain. The world's largest geothermal power installation is The Geysers in California, with a rated capacity of 750 MW. Brazil has one of the largest renewable energy programs in the world, involving production of ethanol fuel from sugar cane. Ethanol now provides 18% of the country's automotive fuel. Ethanol is also widely available in the USA.

Renewable technologies are also suited to small off-grid applications, sometimes in rural and remote areas, where energy is often crucial in human development. Kenya has the world's highest household solar ownership rate with roughly 30,000 small (20–100 watt) solar power systems sold per year.

Some renewable energy technologies are criticized for being intermittent or unsightly, yet the renewable energy market continues to grow. Climate change concerns, coupled with high oil prices, peak oil, and increasing government support, are driving increasing renewable energy legislation, incentives and commercialization.

3.4 MAIN SOURCES OF RENEWABLE ENERGY

Renewable energy flows involve natural phenomena such as sunlight, wind, tides and geothermal heat, as the International Energy Agency explains:

Renewable energy is derived from natural processes that are replenished constantly. In its various forms, it derives directly from the sun, or from heat generated deep within the earth. It also includes electricity and heat generated from solar, wind, ocean, hydropower, biomass, geothermal resources, and biofuels and hydrogen derived from renewable resources. Each of these sources has unique characteristics which influence how and where they are used.

3.4.1 Wind Power

Airflows can be used to run wind turbines. Modern wind turbines range from around 600 kW to 5 MW of rated power. Although turbines with rated output of 1.5–3 MW have become the most common for commercial use. The power output of a turbine is a function of the cube of the wind speed, so as wind speed increases, power output increases dramatically. Areas where winds are stronger and more constant, such as offshore and high altitude sites are preferred locations for wind farms. Typical capacity factors are 20–40%, with values at the upper end of the range in particularly favourable sites.

Globally, the long-term technical potential of wind energy is believed to be five times total current global energy production, or 40 times current electricity demand. This could require large amounts of land to be used for wind turbines, particularly in areas of higher wind resources. Offshore resources experience mean wind speeds of ~90% greater than that of land. Therefore offshore resources could contribute substantially more energy. This number could also increase with higher altitude ground-based or airborne wind turbines. Wind power is renewable and produces no greenhouse gases during operation.

3.4.2 Hydropower

Energy in water can be harnessed and used. Since water is about 800 times denser than air, even a slow flowing stream of water, can yield considerable amounts of energy. There are many forms of water energy. The Hoover Dam when completed in 1936 was both the world's largest electric-power generating station and the world's largest concrete structure.

Fig. 3.1: Showing the potential of hydropower

Hydroelectric energy is a term usually reserved for large-scale hydroelectric dams. Examples are the Grand Coulee Dam in Washington State and the Akosombo Dam in Ghana. Micro hydro systems are hydroelectric power installations that typically produce up to 100 kW of power. They are often used in water rich areas as a remote-area power supply (RAPS). There are many of these installations around the world, including several delivering around 50 kW in the Solomon Islands. Damless hydro systems derive kinetic energy from rivers and oceans without using a dam.

Ocean energy describes all the technologies to harness energy from the ocean and the sea. It includes marine current power, ocean thermal energy conversion, and tidal power.

Solar Energy

Solar energy is the energy derived from the sun through the form of solar radiation. Solar powered electrical generation relies on photovoltaics and heat engines. A partial list of other solar applications includes space heating and cooling through solar architecture, daylighting, solar hot water, solar cooking, and high temperature process heat for industrial purposes.

Solar technologies are broadly characterized as either passive solar or active solar depending on the way of capture, convert and distribution of solar energy. Active solar techniques include the use of photovoltaic panels and solar thermal collectors to harness the energy. Passive solar techniques include orienting a building to the Sun. It can be done by selecting materials with favorable thermal mass or light dispersing properties, and designing spaces that naturally circulate air.

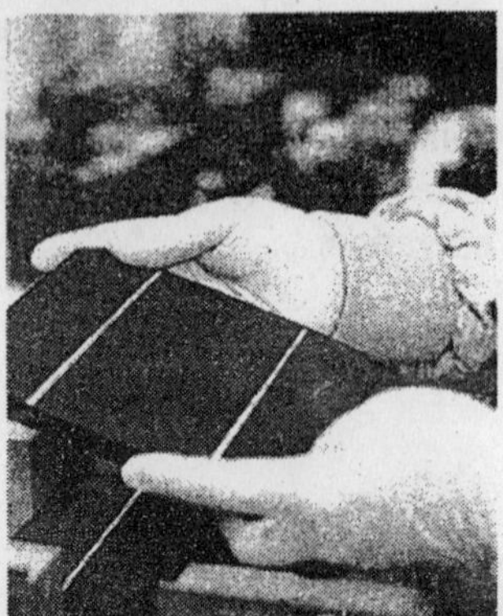

Fig. 3.2 Monocrystalline Solar Cell

3.4.3 Biofuel

Liquid biofuel is usually either bioalcohol such as bioethanol or oil such as biodiesel. Bioethanol is an alcohol made by fermenting the sugar components of plant materials and it is made mostly from sugar and starch crops. Cellulosic biomass, such as trees and grasses, are also used as feedstocks for ethanol production. Ethanol can be used as a fuel for vehicles in its pure form, usually it is used as a gasoline additive to increase octane and improve vehicle emissions. Bioethanol is widely used in the USA and in Brazil: Biodiesel is made from vegetable oils, animal fats or greases. Biodiesel can be used as a fuel for vehicles in its pure form. Usually it is used as a diesel additive to reduce levels of particulates, carbon monoxide, and hydrocarbons from diesel-powered vehicles. Biodiesel is produced from oils or fats using transesterification and is the most common biofuel in Europe. Biofuels provided 1.8% of the world's transport fuel in 2008.

3.4.4 Geothermal energy

Ultimately, this energy derives from heat in the Earth's core. Geothermal energy is obtained by tapping the heat of the earth itself. It is obtained both from kilometers deep into the Earth's crust in some places of the globe or from some meters in geothermal heat pump in all the places of the planet. It is expensive to build a power station but operating costs are low resulting in low energy costs for suitable sites.

Fig. 3.3 Krafla Geothermal Station in Northeast Iceland

Three types of power plants are used to generate power from geothermal energy: dry steam, flash, and binary. Dry steam plants take steam out of fractures in the ground and use it to directly drive a turbine that spins a generator. Flash plants take hot water, usually at temperatures over 200°C, out of the ground, and allows it to boil. As it rises to the surface then separates the steam phase in steam/water separators and then runs the steam through a turbine. In binary plants, the hot water flows through heat exchangers, boiling an organic fluid that spins the turbine. The condensed steam and remaining geothermal fluid from all three types of plants are injected back into the hot rock to pick up more heat.

The geothermal energy from the core of the Earth is closer to the surface in some areas than in others. Where hot underground steam or water can be tapped and brought to the surface. It may be used to generate electricity. Such geothermal power sources exist in certain geologically unstable parts of the world such as Chile, Iceland, New Zealand, United States, the Philippines and Italy. The two most prominent areas for this in the United States are in the Yellowstone basin and in northern California. Iceland produced 170 MW geothermal power through geothermal energy. Some 8000 MW of capacity is operational in total.

There is also the potential to generate geothermal energy from hot dry rocks. Holes at least 3 km deep are drilled into the earth. Some of these holes pump water into the earth, while other holes pump hot water out. The heat resource consists of hot underground radiogenic granite rocks, which heat up when there is enough sediment between the rock and the earths surface. Several companies in Australia are exploring this technology.

3.5 RENEWABLE ENERGY COMMERCIALIZATION

When comparing renewable energy sources with each other and with conventional power sources, three main factors must be considered:

(a) Capital costs (including, for nuclear energy, waste-disposal and decommissioning costs);

(b) Operating and maintenance costs;

(c) Fuel costs (for fossil-fuel and biomass sources—for wastes, these costs may actually be negative).

These costs are all brought together, using discounted cash flow. Inherently, renewables are on a decreasing cost curve, while non-renewables are on an increasing cost curve. In 2009, costs are comparable among wind, nuclear, coal, and natural gas, but for CSP—concentrating solar power—and PV (photovoltaics) are somewhat higher. There are additional costs for renewables in terms of increased grid interconnection to allow for variability of weather and load. These have been shown in the pan-European case to be quite low—overall, wind energy costs about the same as present-day power.

3.5.1 Growth of Renewables

From the end of 2004 to the end of 2008, solar photovoltaic (PV) capacity increased sixfold to more than 16 gigawatts (GW), wind power capacity increased 250 percent to 121 GW, and total power capacity from new renewables increased 75 percent to 280 GW. During the same period, solar heating capacity doubled to 145 gigawatts-thermal (GWth), while biodiesel production increased sixfold to 12 billion liters per year and ethanol production doubled to 67 billion liters per year.

Table: 3.1

Selected Renewable Energy Indicators

Selected global indicators	2006	2007	2008
Investment in new renewable capacity (annual)	63	104	120 billion USD
Existing renewables power capacity, including large-scale hydro	1,020	1,070	1,140 GWe
Existing renewables power capacity, excluding large hydro	207	240	280 GWe
Wind power capacity (existing)	74	94	121 GWe
Biomass heating			~250 GWth
Solar hot water/Space heating			145 GWth
Geothermal heating			~50 GWth
Ethanol production (annual)	39	50	67 billion liters
Countries with policy targets for renewable energy use		66	73

3.6 WIND POWER MARKET

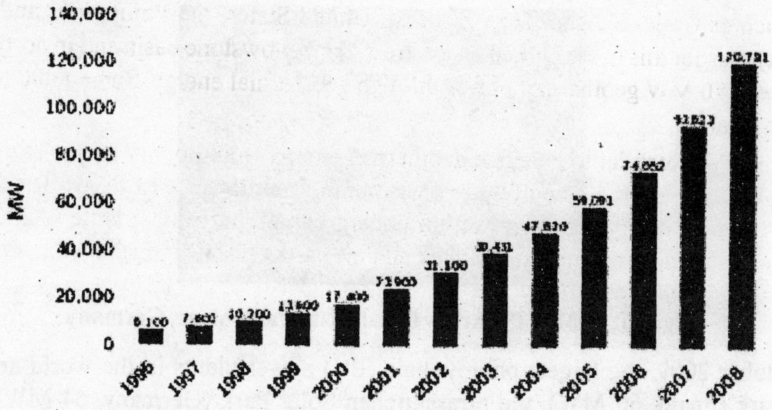

Fig. 3.4 Wind Power: Worldwide Installed Capacity 1996–2008

At the end of 2009, worldwide wind farm capacity was 157,900 MW, representing an increase of 31 percent and wind power supplied some 1.3% of global electricity consumption. Wind power accounts for approximately 19% of electricity use in Denmark, 9% in Spain and Portugal, and 6% in Germany and the Republic of Ireland. The United States is an important growth area and installed U.S. wind power capacity reached 25,170 MW at the end of 2008.The United Kingdom is the world's leading generator of offshore wind power, followed by Denmark.

3.7 NEW GENERATION OF SOLAR THERMAL PLANTS

Fig. 3.5: Solar Towers from left: PS10, PS20.

Large solar thermal power stations include the 354 MW Solar Energy Generating Systems power plant in the USA, Nevada Solar One (USA, 64 MW), Andasol 1 (Spain, 50 MW), Andasol 2 (Spain, 50 MW), PS20 solar power tower (Spain, 20 MW), and the PS10 solar power tower (Spain, 11 MW).

The solar thermal power industry is growing rapidly with 1.2 GW under construction as of April 2009. Spain is the epicenter of solar thermal power development with 22 projects for 1,037 MW under construction, all of which are projected to come online by the end of 2010. In the United States, 5,600 MW of solar thermal power projects have been announced. In developing countries, three World Bank projects for integrated solar thermal/combined-cycle gas-turbine power plants in Egypt, Mexico, and Morocco have been approved.

World's Largest Photovoltaic Power Plants

Fig. 3.6: 40 MW PV Array installed in Waldpolenz, Germany

As of October 2009, the largest photovoltaic (PV) power plants in the world are the Olmedilla Photovoltaic Park (Spain, 60 MW), the Strasskirchen Solar Park (Germany, 54 MW), the Lieberose Photovoltaic Park (Germany, 53 MW), the Puertollano Photovoltaic Park (Spain, 50 MW), the Moura photovoltaic power station (Portugal, 46 MW), and the Waldpolenz Solar Park (Germany, 40 MW). Many of these plants are integrated with agriculture and some use innovative tracking systems that follow the sun's daily path across the sky to generate more electricity. There are no fuel costs or emissions during operation of the power stations. Topaz Solar Farm is a proposed 550 MW solar photovoltaic power plant which is to be built northwest of California Valley in the USA at a cost of over $1 billion. High Plains Ranch is a proposed 250 MW solar photovoltaic power plant which is to be built on the Carrizo Plain, northwest of California Valley.

However, when it comes to renewable energy systems and PV, it is not just large systems that matter. Building-integrated photovoltaics or "onsite" PV systems have the advantage of being matched to end use energy needs in terms of scale. So the energy is supplied close to where it is needed.

3.8 USE OF ETHANOL FOR TRANSPORTATION

Fig. 3.7: E95 trial bus operating in São Paulo, Brazil

Since the 1970s, Brazil had an ethanol fuel program that has allowed the country to become the world's second largest producer of ethanol followed by United States and the world's largest exporter. Brazil's ethanol fuel program uses modern equipment and cheap sugar cane as feedstock, and the residual cane-waste (bagasse) is used to process heat and power. There are no longer light vehicles in Brazil running on pure gasoline. By the end of 2008 there were 35,000 filling stations throughout Brazil with at least one ethanol pump.

Most cars on the road today in the U.S. can run on blends of up to 10% ethanol. Motor vehicle manufacturers already produce vehicles designed to run on much higher ethanol blends. Ford, Daimler. Chrysler, and GM are among the automobile companies that sell "flexible-fuel" cars, trucks, and minivans that can use gasoline and ethanol blends. The blending ranging from pure gasoline up to 85% ethanol (E85). By mid-2006, there were approximately six million E85-compatible vehicles on U.S. roads. The challenge is to expand the market for biofuels beyond the farm states where they have been most popular to date. Flex-fuel vehicles are assisting in this transition because they allow drivers to choose different fuels based on price and availability.

3.9 HYDROELECTRICITY

The major advantage of hydroelectric systems is the elimination of the cost of fuel. Other advantages include longer life than fuel-fired generation, low operating costs, and the provision of facilities for water sports. Operation of pumped-storage plants improves the daily load factor of the generation system. Overall, hydroelectric power can be far less expensive than electricity generated from fossil, fuels or nuclear energy, and areas with abundant hydroelectric power attract industry. However, there are several disadvantages of hydroelectricity systems. These include: dislocation of people living where the reservoirs are planned, flooding of the reservoir, disruption of aquatic ecosystems and birdlife, adverse impacts on the river environment, potential risks of sabotage and terrorism, and in rare cases catastrophic failure of the dam wall.

Hydroelectric power is now more difficult to site in developed nations because most major sites within these nations are either already being exploited or may be unavailable for other reasons such as environmental considerations.

Large hydroelectric power is considered to be a renewable energy by a large number of sources. However, many groups have lobbied for it to be excluded from *renewable electricity standards*, any initiative to promote the use of renewable energies. Some organizations, including US federal agencies, will specifically refer to "non-hydro renewable energy". Many laws exist that specifically label "small hydro" as renewable or sustainable and large hydro as not. Furthermore, the line between what is small or large also differs by governing body.

3.10 WIND FARMS

A wind farm, has one of the lowest environmental impacts of all energy sources.

Wind power is one of the most environmentally friendly sources of renewable energy. Wind power occupies less land area per kilowatt-hour (kWh) of electricity generated than any other energy conversion system, apart from rooftop solar energy, and is compatible with grazing and crops.

It generates the energy used in its construction in just 3 months of operation, yet its operational lifetime is 20–25 years. Greenhouse gas emissions and air pollution produced by its construction are low and declining. There are no emissions or pollution produced by its operation.

Fig. 3.7

In substituting coal power, wind power produces a net decrease in greenhouse gas emissions and air pollution. Modern wind turbines are almost silent and rotate so slowly (in terms of revolutions per minute) that they are rarely a hazard to birds.

Studies of birds and offshore wind farms in Europe have found that there are very few bird collisions. Several offshore wind sites in Europe have been in areas heavily used by seabirds. Improvements in wind turbine design, including a much slower rate of rotation of the blades and a smooth tower base instead of perchable lattice towers, have helped reduce bird mortality at wind farms. However, older smaller wind turbines may be hazardous to flying birds.

Chapter 4

Fossil Fuels, Coal, Oil and Gas: Sources of Energy

4.1 NON-RENEWABLE ENERGY RESOURCES

All machines run on some form of energy — some of these such as the fossil fuels — cause harm to the environment.

4.1.1 Fossil Fuels

The Industrial Revolution in Europe in the 19th century fired man's search for alternative sources of fuel to meet energy needs of the mushrooming industries. With the realization that fossil fuels could meet this requirement, the energy needs of the world were fulfilled for the time being. Fossil fuels are called so because they have been derived from fossils. They were formed millions of years ago during the time of the dinosaurs. They are fossilized organic remains that over millions of years have been converted to oil, gas and coal. As their formation takes so long, these sources are also called non-renewable.

These fuels are made up of decomposed plant and animal matter. When plants, dinosaurs, and other ancient creatures died, they decomposed and buried, layer upon layer under the ground. Their decomposed remains gradually changed over the years. It took millions of years to form these layers into a hard, black rock-like substance called coal, a thick liquid called oil or petroleum, and natural gas means the three major forms of fossil fuels. Fossil fuels are usually found below ground. Coal is either mined or dug out while oil and natural gas are pumped out. Coal is widely distributed and is easier to locate in compression oil and gas.

Fossil fuels take millions of years to make, but burn and disappear with in seconds. Once they are used, they cannot be reused. People have irretrievably damaged the planet by extracting and burning these fuels. It is best not to waste fossil fuels as they are not renewable. We have to learn to conserve these sources of energy. Every year millions of tonnes of coal are consumed as energy. This has led to globai warming, (climate change) and the depletion of resources. At present, the worldwide burning of coal, oil, and natural gas releases billions of tonnes of carbon dioxide (measured as carbon) into the atmosphere every year.

Burning of any fossil fuel means addition of pollutants of some sort. Even if the fuel is low in sulphur, the atmosphere contains nitrogen, which combines with oxygen at the high burning temperatures found in boilers, jet, or car engines. This yields oxides of nitrogen, like sulphur dioxide they dissolves in rain to form nitric acid and process results into acid precipitation. Both gases are poisonous to humans. Mining and exploration for fossil fuels can cause disturbance to the surrounding ecosystem. The burning of fossil fuels emits oxides of sulphur and nitrogen into the atmosphere.

4.1.2 Coal

Coal is by far the most abundant fossil fuel on earth. It is essentially carbon and is mainly used as a combustion fuel. The large-scale use of coal began with the Industrial Revolution in the 19th century. As the number of industries increased, demand for more sources of energy grew. Coal is the product of plants, mainly trees that died hundreds of millions of years ago. Due to water logging in low-lying swampy areas or in slowly sinking lagoons, dead trees and plants, did not decompose as they normally would. The dead plant matter was covered with water and protected from the oxidizing effect of air. The action of certain bacteria released the oxygen and hydrogen, making the residue richer and richer in carbon. Thick layers of this carbon-rich substance, called peat, built up over thousands of years. As more material accumulated above the peat, the water was squeezed out leaving just carbon-rich plant remains. Pressure and temperature further compressed the material. This aided the process of producing coal as more gases were forced out and the proportion of carbon continued to increase. The carbon slowly metamorphosed into coal over millions of years. There are three main types of coal: lignite, bituminous, and anthracite. Lignite and bituminous have a lesser percentage of carbon therefore burn faster. They release a great deal of pollutants into the atmosphere. Anthracite has about 98% carbons and therefore burns slowly and releases much less smoke. Coal of all types contains sulphur to some degree. Sulphur is the worst of the pollutants and causes damage to human health and to vegetation. Though petroleum gained importance over the 20th century and continues to do so but coal remains essential for the industrial sector. It is the principal heat source for electricity generation in most countries and is used directly in such heavy industries as iron and steel making.

Until recently, most coal came from underground mines. But now there are a large number of opencast mines. Underground coal mines are notorious killers due to roof falls and explosions. Accidents have resulted in the deaths of hundreds of miners. Almost 80% of today's coal comes from surface strip mines (opencast mines), which is much safer. Huge earth-moving equipment strips off the soils and rocks covering the buried coal seams. The land is backfilled and returned to normal after the coal has been removed, thereby repairing the landscape. Many companies do not refill the excavated area and leave it damaged. Most countries have now enforced backfilling by law.

Coal Mining in India

India has about seven per cent of the world's proven coal reserves. Coal supplies more than 50% of the country's total energy requirements. By current estimates, the reserves are enough to meet India's needs for at least another 100 years. Coal mining in India dates back to the 18th century. The regulation of its use in the industrial sector was conceived in 1923. In 1972–73, the Indian government nationalized the coal industry, primarily to develop the sector, since it was considered to be of strategic importance for rapid industrial development. India's coal demand is expected to increase several fold within the next 5 years due to the completion of ongoing coal-based power projects, metallurgical and other industries.

Coal is the dominant source of fuel in the industrial sector, with a share of nearly 72.5% in the total energy consumption. The industrial sector is the largest consumer of electricity, with a share of 41% of the total consumption. The transport sector is the largest consumer of petroleum products. it accounts for nearly 50% of the total consumption. The small amount of coal presently consumed adds atmospheric pollutants, some of which precipitate into the ground and water.

4.1.3 Oil and Gas

Almost all oil and natural gas are found deep underground in tiny holes in rocks. Millions of years ago a sea covered much of what is now dry land. In prehistoric times, tiny plants and animals lived in the sea. When these creatures died, they sank to the bottom of the sea, and got buried in layers of mud and sand. As the ages passed, this organic material sank deeper and deeper. The earth's crust changed its shape, put intense pressure and heat on what were once only plants and tiny animals.

Heat from the earth's interior and the weight of the overlying rocks gradually changed the energy-containing substances in the accumulated plants into hydrocarbon liquids and gases. As millions of years passed, these deposits turned into chemicals that are now called 'hydrocarbons'. Hydrocarbons are simple molecules made up of carbon and hydrogen atoms joined together in chains or in rings. These molecules, being light and mobile, migrated upwards through the rocks but eventually became trapped beneath impermeable rock structures in the earth's crust. Much of the oil and gas production now comes from underneath the sea-bed. As the technology for extraction continues to advance, production becomes possible from deeper and deeper waters. But the supplies are limited. Every drop of oil burnt ads to the monumental environment problems already created by pumping gases like carbon dioxide into the atmosphere. Many scientists worry that this continual release of carbon dioxide is an important cause of global warming. Natural gas is usually found underground near an oil source. It is a mixture of light hydrocarbons including methane, ethane, propane, butane, and pentane. Other compounds found in natural gas include carbon dioxide, helium, hydrogen sulphide, and nitrogen. It is found around the world, but the largest reserves are in the former Soviet Union and the Middle East. This gas is lighter than air and is highly inflammable, made up mainly of a gas called methane. Methane is a simple chemical compound that is made up of carbon and hydrogen atoms. Natural gas usually has no odour and cannot be seen. Before it is sent to the pipelines and storage tanks, it is mixed with a chemical that gives it a strong odour, like rotten eggs. The odour makes it easy to detect a leak. Natural gas is the cleanest burning fossil fuel. When it is burned, it gives off less carbon dioxide than oil or coal, virtually no sulphur dioxide, and only small amounts of nitrous oxides. Natural gas is mostly composed of methane and other light hydrocarbons. The carbon and the hydrogen in methane combine with oxygen when natural gas is burned, giving off heat. Coal and oil contain proportionally more carbon than natural gas, therefore giving off more carbon dioxide per unit of energy produced. Natural gas gives off 50% of the carbon dioxide released by coal and 25% less carbon dioxide than oil. Carbon dioxide is the most important greenhouse gas contributing to global warming. To find oil and natural gas, companies drill through the earth to the deposits deep below the surface. The oil and natural gas are then pumped from below the ground by oil rigs. Usually then they travel through pipelines. At oil refineries, crude oil is split into various types of products by heating the thick black oil. The products include gasoline, diesel fuel, aviation fuel, home heating oil, oil for ships, and oil to burn in power plants to make electricity. Oil is used for transportation—cars, airplanes, trucks, buses, and motorcycles. Oil is stored in large tanks until it is sent to various places to be used. Oil is also made into many different products—fertilizers for farms, clothes, toothbrush, plastic bottle, and plastic pen. There are thousands of other products that come from oil. Almost all plastic comes originally from oil. Oil is transported in huge pipelines and tanker ships to places where it is made into other products. The origin of the oil industry in India can be traced back to the last part of the 19th century when petroleum was discovered in Digboi in north-east India. Thereafter large numbers of oil fields have been discovered. This has led to the setting up of refineries to process the oil and gas for use in various sectors.

4.1.4 LPG — Liquefied Petroleum Gas

LPG is the abbreviation or short form for liquefied petroleum gas. Like all fossil fuels, it is a non-renewable source of energy. It is extracted from crude oil and natural gas. The main composition of LPG is hydrocarbons containing three or four carbon atoms. The normal components of LPG thus, are propane (C_3H_8) and butane (C_4H_{10}). Small concentrations of other hydrocarbons may also be present. Depending on the source of the LPG and how it has been produced, components other than hydrocarbons may also be present. LPG is a gas at atmospheric pressure and normal ambient temperatures, but it can be liquefied when moderate pressure is applied or the temperature is reduced. It can be easily condensed, packaged, stored and utilized. This makes it an ideal energy source for a wide range of applications. Normally, the gas is stored in liquid form under pressure in a steel container, cylinder or tank. The pressure inside the container will depend on the type of LPG (commercial butane or commercial propane) and the outside temperature.

At the time of start using LPG, some of the pressure in the container is released. Some of the liquid LPG then boils to produce vapour. Heat is needed to convert the liquid to vapour which is known as the latent heat of vaporization. As the liquid boils, it draws the heat energy from its surroundings. This explains why containers feel cold to touch and why, if there is a heavy off-take, water may appear on the container. At the time of stop using LPG, the pressure will return to the equilibrium value for the surrounding temperature. The pressure of the LPG in the container varies with the surrounding temperature. It is also much higher than is needed by the appliances that use it. It needs to be controlled to ensure a steady supply at constant pressure. This is done by a regulator, which limits the pressure to suit the appliance that is being fuelled. It is a colourless and odourless gas to which foul-smelling gas ethyl mercaptan is added so that leak can be easily detected.

LPG is highly inflammable and must therefore be stored away from sources of ignition and in a well-ventilated area, so that any leak can disperse safely. Another reason for care is that LPG vapour is heavier than air, so any leakage will sink to the ground and accumulate in low lying areas and may be difficult to disperse. LPG expands rapidly when its temperature rises. So whenever a container is filled, sufficient space is left to allow for such expansion. LPG will cause natural rubber and some plastics to deteriorate. This is why only hoses and other equipment specifically designed for LPG should be used. Although, LPG is non-toxic, its abuse (like that of solvents) is highly dangerous. LPG should always be kept away from children whenever possible. Liquid petroleum gases were discovered in 1912 when Dr. Walter Snelling, an American scientist, realized that these gases could be changed into liquids and stored under moderate pressure. From 1912 and 1920, LPG uses were developed. The first LPG cook stove was made in 1912, and the first LPG—fueled car was developed in 1913. The LPG industry began sometime shortly before World War I. At that time, a problem in the natural gas distribution process popped up. Gradually facilities were built to cool and compress natural gas, and to separate the gases that could be turned into liquids (including propane and butane). LPG was sold commercially by 1920.

Chapter 5

Geothermal, Hydrogen and Solar Energy Sources

5.1 SOLAR ENERGY

Solar energy intermittence and its varying radiation intensity are the key factors affecting solar energy efficiency. For example, radiation intensity of solar energy in the same place varies with season, climate, weather day and night. In general, it is difficult to match the energy demand of some users with variety of solar energy. Therefore, solar energy storage is one of the critical problems of present solar energy application research. Ways of storing solar energy can be roughly classified into three types.

5.1.1 Sensible Heat Storage

In middle and low temperature solar energy systems, water and stones are the best and cheapest storing energy medium. The heat energy collected by solar energy collectors increases the temperature of the medium, so the heat energy is stored in the medium. When needed, the heat energy is desorbed for use. The density of sensible heat storing energy is low, and the period of it is short.

5.1.2 Latent Heat Storage

The latent heat storage from phase transformation is characterized by high energy storing density and long storage period. Nevertheless, the medium is easily cooled. Once this happens, crystallization of the medium is made difficult.

For this type of storage, the storing energy medium is required to have the features of big energy absortivity, small variety of volume, little corrosion and good repeatability. Presently, sulphate, nitrate and hydrate carbonates are usually used as the medium.

5.1.3 Chemical Reaction Energy Storage

In this type, the endothermic reaction of chemical material is used to store heat energy. When the inverse process takes place, the heat can be released. Some inorganic oxides are usually used as the medium.

The merits of this type are high capacity for storing heat and long storage period. Nevertheless, the high temperature required by endothermic reactions, results in high equipment costs.

5.2 STORING SOLAR ENERGY BY ZEOLITE METHOD

Zeolite is a aluminosilicate mineral of alkali (alkaline earth metal) it contains crystal water. Its general chemical formula is

$$A_mX_pO_{2p} + nH_2O$$

Where A represents Ca, Na, K, Ba, and Sr; X represents Al and Si. Zeolites consist of three dimensional networks of AlO_4 and SiO_4 tetrahedra linked by sharing of all oxygen atoms. The aluminosilicate frameworks of zeolites are remarkably open and contain channels, and interconnected voids partially filled with cation and water molecules. The intracrystalline voids make up from 20 to 50% of the total crystal volume of most zeolites. When zeolites are heated, water molecules in the intracrystalline voids are partially or wholly desorbed. After being desorb, the water molecules can be adsorbed in the air or water again, and crystal lattice construction of zeolite are not damaged.

Zeolites have extremely nonlinear adsorption isotherms to water. The feature of adsorbing and desorbing water makes zeolites a new type of material for storing solar energy and to be showed off. When zeolites are heated, water molecules in it escape, and heat energy is stored in it. In the meantime; when water molecules are adsorbed again, the heat energy in zeolites is released. These two process can be shown by chemical equation as follow:

$$A_mX_pO_{2p} + nh_2O = A_mX_pO_{2p} + nH_2O \text{ (endothermic)}$$
$$A_mX_pO_{2p} + nh_2O = A_mX_pO_{2p} + nH_2O \text{ (endothermic)}$$

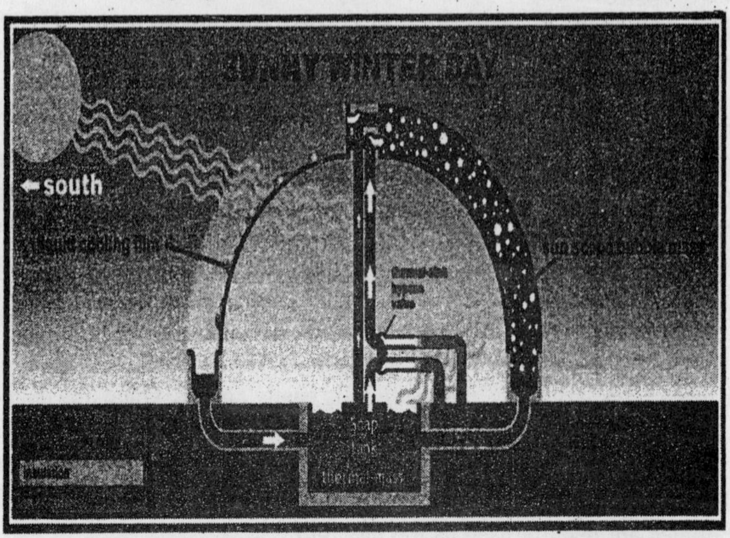

Fig. 5.1: Showing the storage process fo Solar Energy

Apparatus for collecting solar energy comprises one or more solar energy collectors attached to a frame that floats on a pool of water and means for orienting the frame relative to the azimuthal direction of the sum. The solar energy collectors are preferably horizontal elongate parabolic reflectors. They may also float on the pool of water and which can be rotated about their longitudinal axes to orient them relative to the elevation of the sun. Solar rays reflected by such reflectors are absorbed by elongate absorption devices placed at the focal points of the parabolic reflectors. The absorption devices are preferably of a novel design that provides for removal of the energy of the absorbed rays by means of a working fluid that passes through the device. The parabolic reflectors preferably have body portions composed of a novel constructional material that comprises a plurality of hollow glass bodies that are connected together.

5.2.1 Solar Energy Collection And Storage System

A solar energy collection and storage system comprising of a three dimensional enclosure having at least one glass wall facing the sun for admitting sunlight. A solar collector having a position behind said at least one glass wall contained within said enclosure for collecting radiant energy, a first pump contained within said enclosure, a storage tank contained within said enclosure. First pipes connecting said solar collector, said first pump and said storage tank contained within said enclosure creating a first closed loop system for a first liquid to flow within, a vacuum pump connected to said enclosure providing said enclosure with a vacuum. Second pipes and a heat exchanger contained within said storage tank connected to said second pipes. Said second pipes and a second pump connecting said heat exchanger to a heat. Energy device that is external to said three dimensional enclosure creating a second closed loop wherein heat stored in said storage tank and collected from said collector is transferred to said heat energy device via second pipes and second pump by a second liquid.

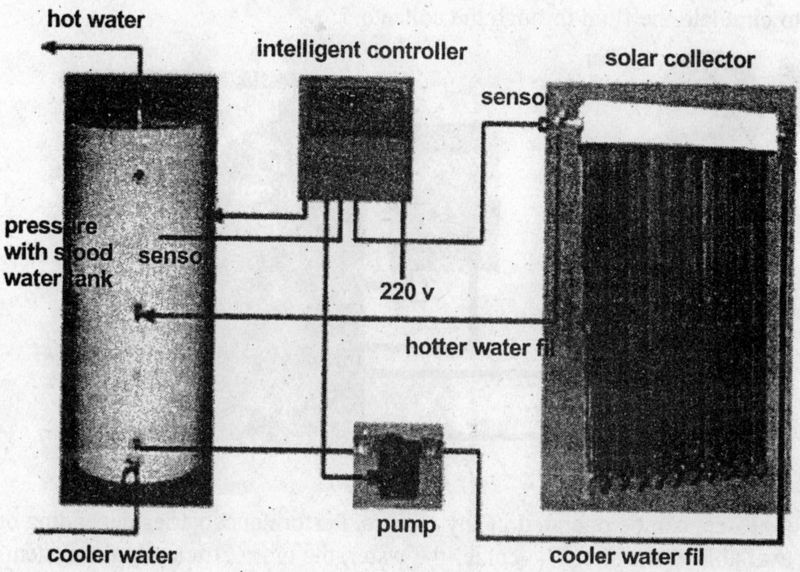

Fig. 5.2: Complete Solar System

A solar energy collection and storage system as claimed in claim 1 wherein said first liquid used in said first closed loop has a boiling point that is higher than an amount of heat collected by said collector.

A solar energy collection and storage system as claimed in claim 2, wherein said first liquid is oil. A solar energy collection and storage system as claimed in claim 3, wherein said heat energy device is configured to activate when a temperature in said storage tank reaches a predetermined threshold temperature. A solar energy collection and storage system as claimed in claim 2, wherein said second liquid used in said second closed loop has a boiling point that is lower than an amount of heat collected by said collector. A solar energy collection and storage system as claimed in claim 5, wherein said heat energy device is configured to activate when a temperature in said storage tank reaches a predetermined threshold temperature. A solar energy collection and storage system as claimed in claim 2, wherein said heat energy device is configured to activate when a temperature in storage tank reaches a predetermined threshold temperature.

5.3 SOLAR WATER HEATER

Solar water heaters are cost competitive in many applications when you account for the total energy costs over the life of the system. Although the initial cost of solar water heaters is higher than that of conventional water heaters, the fuel (sunshine) is free. Plus, they are environmentally friendly. To take advantage of these heaters, you must have an un shaded, south-facing location (a roof, for example) on your property. These systems use the Sun to heat either water or a heat-transfer fluid, such as a water-glycol antifreeze mixture, in collectors generally mounted on a roof. The heated water is then stored in a tank similar to a conventional gas or electric water tank. Some systems use an electric pump to circulate the fluid through the collectors.

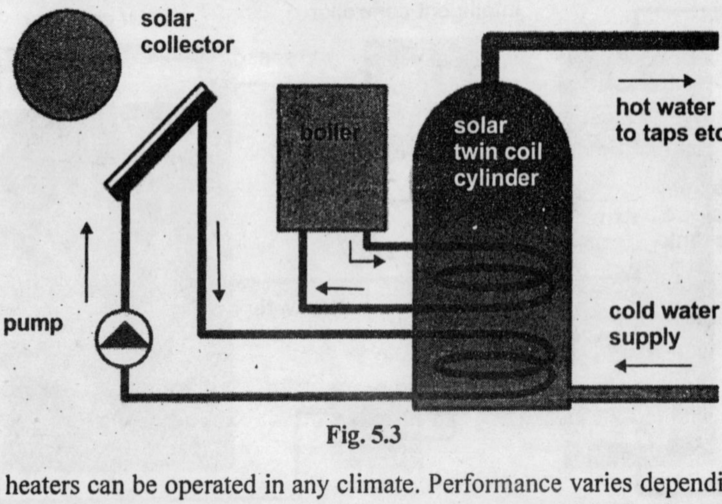

Fig. 5.3

Solar water heaters can be operated in any climate. Performance varies depending on how much solar energy is available at the site. The colder the water, the more efficiently the system operates. In almost all climates, conventional backup system in required In fact, many building codes require you to have a conventional water heater as the backup.

Before investing in any solar energy system, it is more cost effective to invest in making your home more energy efficient. Taking steps to use less hot water and to lower the temperature of the hot water.

First steps are installing low-flow showerheads or flow restrictors in shower heads and faucets, insulating current water heater, and insulating any hot water pipes that pass through unheated areas also a useful thing .

5.3.1 Solar Water Heater Basics

Solar water heaters are made up of collectors, storage tanks, and, depending on the system, electric pumps. There are three types of collectors: flat plate, evacuated-tube and concentrating collectors. A flat plate collector, the most common type, is an insulated, weather-proofed box containing a dark absorber plate under one or more transparent or translucent covers. Evacuated-tube collectors are made up of rows of parallel, transparent glass tubes. Each tube consists of a glass outer tube and an inner tube or absorber. It is covered with a selective coating that absorbs solar energy well but inhibits radioactive heat loss. The air is withdrawn ("evacuated") from the space between the tubes to form a vacuum, which eliminates conductive and convective heat loss.

Concentrating collectors for residential applications, are usually parabolic. It use mirrored surfaces to concentrate the sun's energy on an absorber tube (called a receiver) containing a heat-transfer fluid. Most commercially available solar water heaters require a well-insulated storage tank. Many systems use converted electric water heater tanks or plumb the solar storage tank in series with the conventional water heater.

5.3.2 Types of Solar Water Heater

Active System

Active systems use electric pumps, valves, and controllers to circulate water or other heat-transfer fluids through the collectors. They are usually more expensive than passive systems but they are more efficient. Active systems are usually easier to retrofit than passive systems because their storage tanks do not need to be installed above or close to the collectors. As they use electricity, they will not function in a power outage. Active systems range in price from about $2,000 to $4,000 installed.

Open Loop Active System

Open-loop active systems use pumps to circulate household water through the collectors. This design is efficient with lowers operating costs but is not appropriate if your water is hard or acidic because scale with corrosion quickly disable the system. These open-loop systems are popular in nonfreezing climates such as Hawaii. They should never be installed in climates that experience freezing temperatures for sustained periods. They can installed in mild but occasionally freezing climates but requires freeze protection.

Close Loop Active System

Such systems pump heat-transfer fluids (usually a glycol-water antifreeze mixture) through collectors. Heat exchangers transfer the heat from the fluid to the household water stored in the tanks. Double-walled heat exchangers prevent contamination of household water. Some codes require double walls when the heat-transfer fluid is anything other than household water. Closed-loop glycol systems are popular in areas subject to extended freezing temperatures because they offer good freeze protection. However, glycol antifreeze systems are a bit more expensive to buy and install, the glycol must be checked each year and changed every 3 to 7 years. Although it also depends on glycol quality and system temperatures.

Pump in Active System

The pumps in solar water heaters have low power requirements. Some companies now include direct current (DC) pumps powered by small solar-electric (photovoltaic or PV) panels. PV panels convert sunlight into DC electricity. Such systems cost nothing to operate and continue to function during power outages.

Passive System

Passive systems move household water or a heat-transfer fluid through the system without pumps. Passive systems have no electric components to break. This makes them generally more reliable, easier to maintain, and possibly longer lasting than active systems. Passive systems can be less expensive than active systems, but they can also be less efficient. Installed costs for passive systems range from about $1,000 to $3,000, depending on whether it is a simple batch heater or a sophisticated thermo siphon system.

Batch Heater

Batch heaters are also known as "bread box" or integral collector storage systems. They are simple passive systems consisting of one or more storage tanks placed in an insulated box that has a glazed side facing the sun. Batch heaters are inexpensive and have few components—in other words, less maintenance and fewer failures. A batch heater is mounted on the ground or on the roof if the roof structure is strong enough to support it. Some batch heaters use "selective" surfaces on the tank(s). These surfaces absorb sun well but inhibit radiative loss.

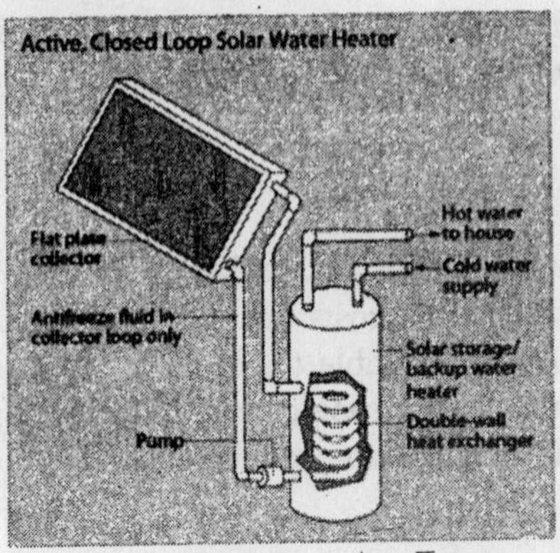

Fig. 5.4

Thermo Siphon System

A thermo siphon system relies on warm water rising, a phenomenon known as natural convection, to circulate water through the collectors and to the tank. In this type of installation, the tank must be above the collector. As water in the collector heats, it becomes lighter and rises naturally into the tank above. Meanwhile, cooler water in the tank flows down pipes to the bottom of the collector, resulting circulation throughout the system. The storage tank is attached to the top of the collector so that thermo siphoning can occur. These systems are reliable and relatively inexpensive but require careful planning in new construction because the water tanks are heavy. They can be freeze-proofed by circulating an antifreeze solution through a heat exchanger in a closed loop to heat the household water.

5.4 BENEFIT OF SOLAR WATER SYSTEM

There are many benefits of a solar water heater and number one is economics. Solar water heater economics compare quite favorably with those of electric water heaters. Although economics aren't quite so attractive when compared with those of gas water heaters. Heating water with the sun also means long-term benefits, such as being cushioned from future fuel shortages and price increases, and environmental benefits.

Solar Energy System: Solar Radiation Data

Solar energy, radiant light and heat from the sun, has been harnessed by humans since ancient times using a range of ever-evolving technologies. Solar radiation, along with secondary solar-powered resources such as wind and wave power, hydroelectricity and biomass, account for most of the available renewable energy on earth. Only a minuscule fraction of the available solar energy is used. Solar powered electrical generation relies on heat engines and photovoltaics. Solar energy's uses are limited only by human ingenuity. A list of solar applications includes space heating and cooling through solar architecture, potable water via distillation and disinfection, day lighting, solar hot water and solar cooking. To harvest the solar energy, the most common way is to use solar panels.

Solar technologies are broadly characterized as either passive solar or active solar depending on the way they capture, convert and distribute solar energy. Active solar techniques include the use of photovoltaic panels and solar thermal collectors to harness the energy. Passive solar techniques include orienting a building to the Sun, selecting materials with favorable thermal mass or light dispersing properties, and designing spaces that naturally circulate air.

5.4.1 Energy From The Sun

Solar Radiation

About half of the incoming solar energy reaches the Earth's surface. The Earth receives 174 pet watts (PW) of incoming solar radiation at the upper atmosphere. Approximately 30% is reflected back to space while the rest is absorbed by clouds, oceans and various bodies of earth surface. The spectrum of radiation at the Earth's surface is mostly spread across the visible and near-infrared ranges with a small part in the near-ultraviolet.

Earth's surface, oceans and atmosphere absorb solar radiation, and this raises their temperature. Warm air containing water vapours from the oceans rises, causing atmospheric circulation or convection. The air reaches a high altitude, where the temperature is low, water vapour condenses into clouds. It results into rain on the Earth surface by completing the water cycle. The latent heat of water condensation amplifies convection, producing atmospheric phenomena such as wind, cyclones and anti-cyclones. Sunlight absorbed by the oceans and land masses keeps the surface at an average temperature of 15°C. Green plants convert solar energy into chemical energy, by photosynthesis, which produces food, wood and the biomass.

The total solar energy absorbed by Earth's atmosphere, oceans and land masses is approximately 3,850,000 exajoules (EJ) per year. It is more energy in one hour than the world used in one year. Photosynthesis captures approximately 3,000 EJ per year in biomass. The amount of solar energy reaching the surface of the planet is so vast that in one year it is about twice as much as will ever be obtained from all of the Earth's non-renewable resources of coal, oil, natural gas, and mined uranium combined.

Solar energy can be harnessed in different levels around the world. It Depend on a geographical location the closer to the equator the more potential solar energy is available. The solar, wind or biomass would be sufficient to supply all of our energy needs. However, the increased use of biomass has had a negative effect on global warming and dramatically increased food prices by diverting forests and crops into biofuel production.

5.5 APPLICATIONS OF SOLAR TECHNOLOGY

Average insulation showing land area (small black dots) required to replace the world primary energy supply with solar electricity. 18 TW is 568 Exajoule (EJ) per year. Insulation for most people is from 150 to 300 W/m² or 3.5 to 7.0 kWh/m²/day.

Solar energy refers primarily to the use of solar radiation for practical ends. However, all renewable energies, other than geothermal and tidal, derive their energy from the sun.

Solar technologies are broadly characterized as either passive or active depending on the way they capture, convert and distribute sunlight. Active solar techniques use photovoltaic panels, pumps, and fans to convert sunlight into useful outputs. Passive solar techniques include selecting materials with favorable thermal properties, designing spaces that naturally circulate air, and referencing the position of a building to the Sun. Active solar technologies increase the supply of energy and are considered supply side technologies, while passive solar technologies reduce the need for alternate resources and are generally considered demand side technologies.

5.5.1 Architecture and Urban Planning

Passive solar building design and Urban heat island:

University of Technology in Germany won the 2007 Solar Decathlon in Washington, this passive house designed specifically for the humid and hot subtropical climate.

Fig. 5.5

Sunlight has influenced building design since the beginning of architectural history. Advanced solar architecture and urban planning methods were first employed by the Greeks. They oriented their buildings toward the south to provide light and warmth. The common features of passive solar architecture are orientation relative to the Sun, compact proportion (a low surface area to volume ratio), selective shading (overhangs) and thermal mass. It such features are tailored to the local climate and environment, they can produce well-lit spaces that produce a comfortable temperature range. Socrates' Megaton House is a classic example of passive solar design. The most recent approaches to solar design use computer modeling tying together solar lighting, heating and ventilation systems in an integrated solar design package. Active solar equipment such as pumps, fans and switchable windows can complement passive design and improve system performance.

Urban heat islands (UHI) are metropolitan areas with higher temperatures than that of the surrounding environment. The higher temperatures are a result of increased absorption of the Solar light by urban materials such as asphalt and concrete, which have lower albedos and higher heat capacities in comparison to the natural environment. A straightforward method of counteracting the UHI effect is to paint buildings, roads white, and plant trees. Using these methods, a hypothetical "cool communities" program in Los Angeles has projected that urban temperatures could be reduced by approximately 3°C at an estimated cost of US $1 billion, giving estimated total annual benefits of US $530 million from reduced air-conditioning costs and healthcare savings.

5.5.2 Agriculture and Horticulture

Greenhouses like these in the Westland municipality of the Netherlands grow vegetables, fruits and flowers. Agriculture and horticulture seek to optimize the capture of solar energy in order to optimize the productivity of plants. Techniques such as timed planting cycles, tailored row orientation, staggered heights between rows and the mixing of plant varieties can improve crop yields. While sunlight is generally considered a plentiful resource, the exceptions highlight the importance of solar energy to agriculture. During the short growing seasons of the Little Ice Age, French and English farmers employed fruit walls to maximize the collection of solar energy.

Fig. 5.6

These walls acted as thermal masses and accelerated ripening by keeping plants warm. Early fruit walls were built perpendicular to the ground and facing south, but over time, sloping walls were developed to make better use of sunlight. In 1699, Nicolas Fatio de Duillier even suggested using a tracking mechanism which could pivot to follow the Sun. Applications of solar energy in agriculture aside from growing crops include pumping water, drying crops, brooding chicks and drying chicken manure. More recently, the technology has been embraced by vinters, who use the energy generated by solar panels to power grape presses.

Greenhouses convert solar light to heat, enabling year-round production and the growth (in enclosed environments) of specialty crops and other plants not naturally suited to the local climate. Primitive greenhouses were first used during Roman times to produce cucumbers year-round for the Roman emperor Tiberius. The first modern greenhouses were built in Europe in the 16th century to keep exotic plants brought back from explorations abroad. Greenhouses remain an important part of horticulture today, and plastic transparent materials have been used to similar effect in polytunnels and row covers.

5.5.3 Solar lighting

Day lighting features such as this oculus at the top of the Pantheon, in Rome, Italy have been in use since antiquity.

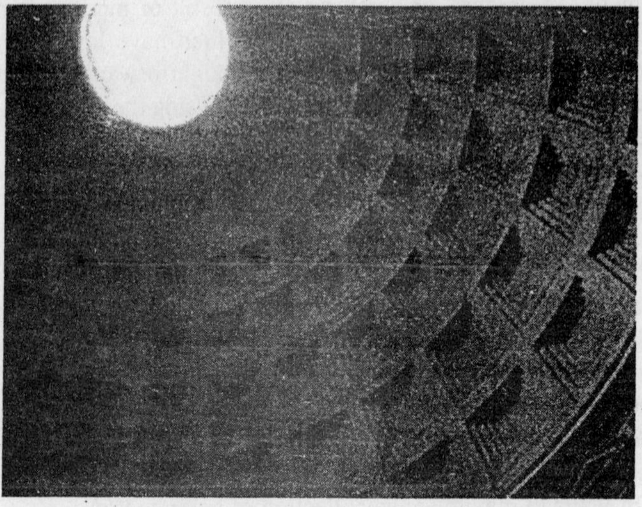

Fig. 5.7

The history of lighting is dominated by the use of natural light. The Romans recognized a right to light as early as the 6th century and English law echoed these judgments with the Prescription Act of 1832. In the 20th century, artificial lighting became the main source of interior illumination but daylighting techniques and hybrid solar lighting solutions are ways to reduce energy consumption.

Day lighting systems collect and distribute sunlight to provide interior iilumination. This passive technology directly offsets energy use by replacing artificial lighting, and indirectly offsets non-solar energy use by reducing the need for air-conditioning.

Although difficult to quantify, the use of natural lighting also offers physiological and psychological benefits compared to artificial lighting.

Day lighting design implies careful selection of window types, sizes and orientation; exterior shading devices may be considered as well. Individual features include saw tooth roofs, clerestory windows, light shelves, skylights and light tubes. They may be incorporated into existing structures, but are most effective when integrated into a solar design package that accounts for factors such as glare, heat flux and time-of-use. When day lighting features are properly implemented, they can reduce lighting-related energy requirements by 25%.

Hybrid solar lighting is an active solar method of providing interior illumination. HSL systems collect sunlight using focusing mirrors that track the Sun and use optical fibers to transmit it inside the building to supplement conventional lighting. In single-story applications, these systems are able to transmit 50% of the direct sunlight received.

Solar lights that charge during the day and light up at dusk are a common sight along walkways. Although daylight saving time is promoted as a way to use sunlight to save energy, recent research has been limited and reports contradictory results: several studies report savings, but just as many suggest no effect or even a net loss, particularly when gasoline consumption is taken into account. Electricity use is greatly affected by geography, climate and economics, making it hard to generalize from single studies.

5.6 SOLAR THERMAL

Solar Thermal Energy

Solar thermal technologies can be used for water heating, space heating, space cooling and process heat generation.

Water heating

Fig. 5.8: Solar hot water and solar comb system

Solar Water Heaters Facing the Sun to Maximize Gain

Solar hot water systems use sunlight to heat water. In low geographical latitudes (below 40 degrees) from 60 to 70% of the domestic hot water, use with temperatures up to 60°C can be provided by solar heating systems. The most common types of solar water heaters are evacuated tube collectors (44%) and glazed flat plate collectors (34%) generally used for domestic hot water; and unglazed plastic collectors (21%) used mainly to heat swimming pools.

As of 2007, the total installed capacity of solar hot water systems is approximately 154 GW. China is the world leader in their deployment with 70 GW installed as of 2006 and a long term goal of 210 GW by 2020. Israel and Cyprus are the per capita leaders in the use of solar hot water systems with over 90% of homes using them. In the United States, Canada and Australia heating swimming pools is the dominant application of solar hot water with an installed capacity of 18 GW as of 2005.

Process Heat

Solar pond, Salt evaporation pond, and Solar furnace STEP parabolic dishes used for steam production and electrical generation. Solar concentrating technologies such as parabolic dish, trough and Schaeffer reflectors can provide process heat for commercial and industrial applications. The first commercial system was the Solar Total Energy Project (STEP) in Shenandoah, Georgia, USA where a field of 114 parabolic dishes provided 50% of the process heating, air conditioning and electrical requirements for a clothing factory. This grid-connected cogeneration system provided 400 kW of electricity plus thermal energy in the form of 401 kW steam and 468 kW chilled water, and had a one hour peak load thermal storage.

Evaporation ponds are shallow pools that concentrate dissolved solids through evaporation. The use of evaporation ponds to obtain salt from sea water is one of the oldest applications of solar energy. Modern uses include concentrating brine solutions used in leach mining and removing dissolved solids from waste streams.

Clothes lines, clotheshorses, and clothes racks dry clothes through evaporation by wind and sunlight without consuming electricity or gas. In some states of the United States legislation protects the "right to dry" clothes.

Unglazed transpired collectors (UTC) are perforated sun-facing walls used for preheating ventilation air. UTCs can raise the incoming air temperature up to 22°C and deliver outlet temperatures of 45–60°C. The short payback period of transpired collectors (3 to 12 years) makes them a more cost-effective alternative than glazed collection systems. As of 2003, over 80 systems with a combined collector area of 35,000 m² had been installed worldwide, including an 860 m² collector in Costa Rica used for drying coffee beans and a 1,300 m² collector in Coimbatore, India used for drying marigolds.

5.7 ELECTRICAL GENERATION

Solar Power

Sunlight can be converted into electricity using photovoltaic's (PV), concentrating solar power (CSP), and various experimental technologies. PV has mainly been used to power small and medium-sized applications, from the calculator powered by a single solar cell to off-grid homes powered by a photovoltaic array. For large-scale generation, CSP plants like SEGS have been the norm but recently multi-megawatt PV plants are becoming common. Completed in 2007, the 14 MW power station in Clark County, Nevada, United States and the 20 MW site in Beneixama, Spain are characteristic of the trend toward larger photovoltaic power stations in the United States and Europe.

As an intermittent power source, solar power requires a backup supply, which can partially be complemented with wind power. Local backup usually is done with batteries, while utilities normally use pumped-hydro storage. The Institute for Solar Energy Supply Technology of the University of Kassel in Germany pilot-tested a combined power plant linking solar, wind, biogas and hydro storage to provide load-following power around the clock, entirely from renewable sources.

Solar Vehicles

Australia hosts the World Solar Challenge where solar cars like the Nuna race through a 3,021 km (1,877 mi) course from Darwin to Adelaide. Development of a solar powered car has been an engineering goal since the 1980s. The World Solar Challenge is a biannual solar-powered car race, where teams from universities and enterprises compete over 3,021 kilometers (1,877 mi) across central Australia from Darwin to Adelaide. In 1987, when it was founded, the winner's average speed was 67 kilometers per hour (42 mph) and by 2007 the winner's average speed had improved to 90.87 kilometers per hour (56.46 mph). The North American Solar Challenge and the planned South African Solar Challenge are comparable competitions that reflect an international interest in the engineering and development of solar powered vehicles.

Fig. 5.9: Solar vehicle, electric boat, and solar balloon

Some vehicles use solar panels for auxiliary power, such as for air conditioning, to keep the interior cool, thus reducing fuel consumption. In 1975, the first practical solar boat was constructed in England. By 1995, passenger boats incorporating PV panels began appearing and are now used extensively. In 1996, Kenichi Horie made the first solar powered crossing of the Pacific Ocean, and the sun catamaran made the first solar powered crossing of the Atlantic Ocean in the winter of 2006–2007. There are plans to circumnavigate the globe in 2010.

Conventional Collector: A new type of flat plate solar collector was utilized for heating fuel oil. In a previous work, two identical flat plate collectors of the conventional fin tube configuration were investigated. One collector was filled with fuel oil, and the other was filled with water. It was found that the efficiency of the fuel oil collector was 25% less than that of the water collector.

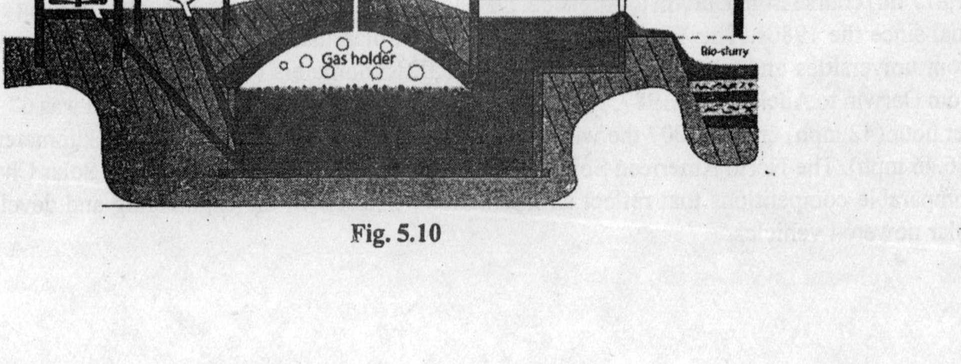

Fig. 5.10

In this work, two collectors were tested. One was the same conventional water collector, and the other was a trickle collector whose working fluid was fuel oil. It was found that the efficiency of the fuel oil collector was 15–19% less than that of the water collector. Comparing the results of this work with those of the previous one, it was found that the efficiency of the fuel oil-trickle collector is 4–9% larger than that of a conventional one filled with fuel oil. It is concluded that a considerable portion of the efficiency lost formerly due to changing the working fluid from water to fuel oil in the conventional collector was almost regained by changing the collector type to be a trickle one.

Fig. 5.11

Solar energy collectors are special kind of heat exchangers that transform solar radiation energy to internal energy of the transport medium. The major component of any solar system is the solar collector. This is a device which absorbs the incoming solar radiation, converts it into heat, and transfers this heat to a fluid (usually air, water, or oil) flowing through the collector. The solar energy thus collected is carried from the circulating fluid either directly to the hot water or space conditioning equipment or to a thermal energy storage tank from which can be drawn for use at night and/or cloudy days.

There are two types of solar collectors: non-concentrating or stationary and concentrating. A non-concentrating collector has the same area for intercepting and for absorbing solar radiation whereas a sun-tracking concentrating solar collector usually has concave reflecting surfaces to intercept and focus the sun's beam radiation to a smaller receiving area, thereby increasing the radiation flux. Solar energy collectors are also distinguished by their motion, *i.e.,* stationary, single axis tracking and two-axes tracking and the operating temperature.

The performance of a solar collector depends mainly on its optical and thermal efficiencies, determined according to various methods outlined in international standards. The collector optical efficiency depends on the properties of the materials (and their coating) used for the collector construction (absorptance transmittance, remittance), and the incident angle modifier, which applies to both stationary and concentrating collector. For the latter, the collector acceptance angle, which determines the tracking mechanism allowable error, is also required. The collector thermal performance depends on the collector instantaneous thermal efficiency and the collector time constant, which depends on the thermal capacity of the collector.

The performance of a solar system can be evaluated with various design methods, like the f-chart and the utilizability method, whereas a detailed analysis of the systems can be obtained by using a number of programs, like TRNSYS, WATSUN, Polysun, F-Chart and many others.

Lately artificial intelligence methods have been used for the design, simulation and prediction of long-term performance of solar collectors and systems. These include the use of artificial neural networks, genetic algorithms, expert systems, fuzzy systems and various hybrid systems which combine two or more the above technologies.

Solar collectors can be used in a large variety of applications. The main areas of applications include:

Solar water heating, which includes thermosyphon, integrated collector storage systems, air systems, direct circulation and indirect water heating systems.

Solar space heating systems, which includes both water and air systems.

Solar refrigeration, which includes both adsorption and absorption systems.

Industrial process heat systems, which include both low temperature (air and water based) applications and solar steam generation systems.

Solar desalination systems, which include both direct (solar stills) and indirect systems (conventional desalination equipment powered by solar collectors).

Solar thermal power generation systems, which include the parabolic trough systems, the power tower or central receiver systems and the parabolic dish systems (dish/Stirling engine).

Current research trend is focused on the development of new coating materials for solar collectors, which could increase absorptance and reduce remittance, thus increase the optical and thermal efficiency of the collector. This includes the use of innovative coatings and nanotechnology.

Solar Collectors: Different Types and Fields of Application

Solar collectors transform solar radiation into heat and transfer that heat to a medium (water, solar fluid, or air). Then solar heat can be used for heating water, to back up heating systems or for heating swimming pools.

5.8 THE USE OF SOLAR HEAT

The heart of a solar collector is the absorber, which is usually composed of several narrow metal strips. The carrier fluid for heat transfer flows through a heat-carrying pipe, which is connected to the absorber strip. In plate-type absorbers, two sheets are sandwiched together allowing the medium to flow between the two sheets. Absorbers are typically made of copper or aluminum.

Swimming pool absorbers, on the other hand, are usually made of plastic (mostly EPDM, but also of polypropylene and polyethylene), as the lower temperatures involved do not require greater heat capacity. Heating and storage are united in a *reservoir collector.* Arrays of reservoir collectors do not need circulating pumps or regulating mechanisms, as the drinking water is warmed and stored right in the collector.

Highly Efficient Absorber Surfaces

Absorbers are usually black, as dark surfaces demonstrate a particularly high degree of light absorption. The level of absorption indicates the amount of short-wave solar radiation being absorbed that means not being reflected. As the absorber warms up to a temperature higher than the ambient temperature, it gives off a great part of the accumulated solar energy in form of long-wave heat rays. The ratio of absorbed energy to emitted heat is indicated by the degree of emission.

In order to reduce energy loss through heat emission, the most efficient absorbers have a *selective surface coating.* This coating enables the conversion of a high proportion of the solar radiation into heat, simultaneously reducing the emission of heat.

The usual coatings provide a degree of absorption of over 90%. Solar paints that can be mechanically applied to the absorbers (with either brushes or sprays), are less or not at all selective, as they have a high level of emission. Galvanic ally applied selective coatings include black chrome, black nickel, and aluminum oxide with nickel. Relatively new is a titanium-nitride-oxide layer, which is applied via steam in a vacuum process. This type of coating stands out not only because of its quite low emission rates, but also because its production is emission-free and energy-efficient.

Flat-plate Collectors

A flat-plate collector consists of an absorber, a transparent cover, a frame, and insulation. Usually an iron-poor solar safety glass is used as a transparent cover, as it transmits a great amount of the short-wave light spectrum.

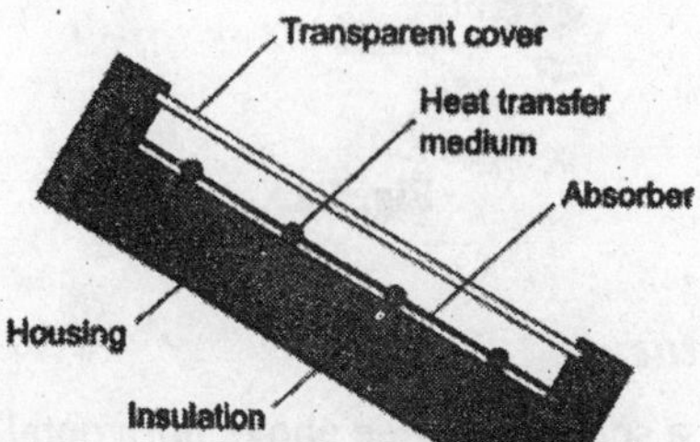

Fig. 5.12: Sketch of a flat-plate collector

Simultaneously, only very little of the heat emitted by the absorber escapes the cover (greenhouse effect).

In addition, the transparent cover prevents wind and breezes from carrying the collected heat away (convection). Together with the frame, the cover protects the absorber from adverse weather conditions. Typical frame materials include aluminum and galvanized steel; sometimes fiberglass-reinforced plastic is used.

The insulation on the back of the absorber and on the side walls lessens the heat loss through conduction. Insulation is usually of polyurethane foam or mineral wool, though sometimes mineral fiber insulating materials like glass wool, rock wool, glass fiber or fiberglass are used.

Flat collectors demonstrate a good price-performance ratio as well as a broad range of mounting possibilities (on the roof, in the roof itself or unattached).

In order to reduce heat loss within the frame by convection, the air can be pumped out of the collector tubes. Such collectors then can be called evacuated-tube collectors. They must be re-evacuated once every one to three years.

5.9 EVACUATED-TUBE COLLECTORS

In this type of vacuum collector, the absorber strip is located in an evacuated and pressure proof glass tube. The heat transfer fluid flows through the absorber directly in a U-tube or in countercurrent in a tube-in-tube system. Several single tubes, serially interconnected, or tubes connected to each other via manifold, make up the solar collector. A heat pipe collector incorporates a special fluid that begins to vaporize even at low temperatures. The steam rises in the individual heat pipes and warms up the carrier fluid in the main pipe by means of a heat exchanger. The condensed liquid then flows back into the base of the heat pipe.

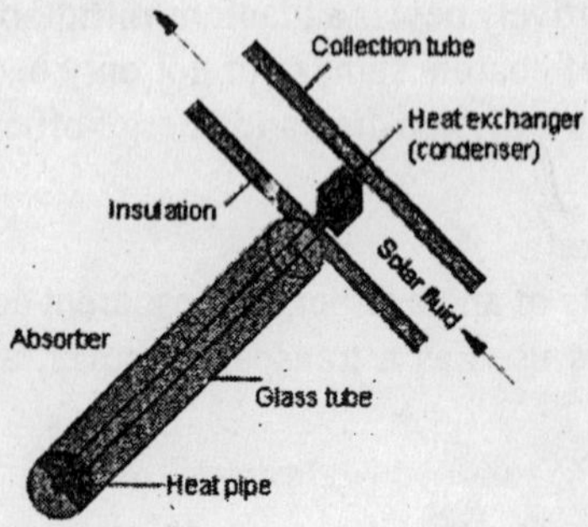

Fig. 5.13

Sketch of a Heat Pipe Collector

The pipes must be angled at a specific degree above horizontal so that the process of vaporizing and condensing functions. There are two types of collector connection to the solar circulation system. Either the heat exchanger extends directly into the manifold ("wet connection") or it is connected to the manifold by a heat-conducting material ("dry connection"). A "dry connection" allows exchanging individual tubes without emptying the entire system of its fluid. Evacuated tubes offer the advantage that they work efficiently with high absorber temperatures and with low radiation. Higher temperatures also may be obtained for applications such as hot water heating, steam production, and air conditioning.

Energy Solar Collector Provide

The efficiency of a solar collector is defined as the quotient of usable thermal energy versus received solar energy. Besides thermal loss there, always is optical loss as well. The conversion factor or optical efficiency h0 indicates the percentage of the solar rays penetrating the transparent cover of the collector (transmission) and the percentage being absorbed. It is the product of the rate of transmission of the cover and the absorption rate of the absorber.

5.10 EFFICIENCY GRAPH OF SOLAR COLLECTOR PERFORMANCE

The heat loss is indicated by the thermal loss factor or k-value. This is given in watt per m² collector surface and the particular temperature difference (in °C) between the absorber and its surroundings. The higher the temperature difference, the more heat is lost. Above a specific temperature difference, the amount of heat loss equals the energy yield of the collector, so that no energy at all is delivered to the solar circulation system. A good collector will have a high conversion factor and a low k-value.

Table: 5.1

Type of Collector	*Conversion Factor*	*Thermal Loss Factor in W/m² °C*	*Temperature Range in °C*
Absorber (uncovered)	0,82 to 0,97	10 to 30	up to 40
Flat-plate collector	0,66 to 0,83	2,9 to 5,3	20 to 80
Evacuated-plate collector	0,81 to 0,83	2,6 to 4,3	20 to 120
Evacuated-tube collector	0,62 to 0,84	0,7 to 2,0	50 to 120
Reservoir collector	about 0,55	about 2,4	20 to 70
Air collector	0,75 to 0,90	8 to 30	20 to 50

Solar water heater performance is often presented as a graph, or set of three performance variables. Values may be provided based on gross area, aperture area or absorber area. In Europe, aperture or absorber is often used, in the US, gross area is often used. It doesn't really matter which values is used, as long as you use the correct value. ie. Don't use absorber area when using performance values based on gross area. To adjust from one to the other, multiply by the size difference, *i.e.*, If absorber area = $0.6m^2$ & gross area = $1.1m^2$ then (1.1/0.6 = 1.83), so multiply the performance factors by 1.83 to convert from gross to absorber. The three performance variables for the Apricots solar collector as provided by the SPF testing laboratory in Switzerland (SPF report C632LPEN) are as follows (for metric calculations, based on absorber area):

Conversion Factor: 0 = 0.717

Loss Coefficient: $a_1 = 1.52\ W/(m^2K)$

Loss Coefficient: $a_2 = 0.0085\ W/(m^2K^2)$

As well as the three performance variables shown above, insulation level (G) in $Watts/m^2$, ambient temperatures (Ta) and average manifold temperature (Tm) must be known. These values give the value **x**, also sometimes presented as T*m, used in the formula below.

$$\eta\ (x) = \eta\ o—a1.\ (X) –a2.\ G.\ (X)^2\ [x=(Tm–Ta)/G]$$

(Other slightly different forms of this formula are used, but provide the same result)

How to use the formula

Based on the ambient temperature, average manifold temperature and insolation level, firstly calculate the value for X.

For example: At 2:40pm; ambient temperature of 25°C (77°F); average water temp [(Tinlet + Texit)/2] of 50°C (122°F); insolation level of $800Watts/m^2$ ($252Btu/ft^2$).

$$x = (50–25)/800 = 0.03125$$

Now enter all the values into the formula:

$$□(x) = 0.717 – (1.52*0.03125) – (0.0085*800*0.03125^2)$$

$$□(x) = 0.717 – 0.0475 – 0.0066 = 0.663$$

The solar conversion efficiency for that specific point in time and set of environmental conditions is 66.3%. That is: 66.3% of the energy provided by the sun is actually used to heat the water.

Based on the assumption that those three environmental factors (G Tm and Ta) are stable for a period of one hour, then 800 × 0.663 = 530.4 Watts of energy per m^2 of absorber area will be used to heat the water (168 Btu/ft^2). 530.4Watts is equivalent to 456 kcal, which could heat 100L of water by 4.56°C (20 Gallons by 10.9°F) Below is a graph showing the performance curves for the Apricots solar collector at three different insulation levels, from 0 to 80°C delta-t. In most cases the delta-t values will be in the range of 20–50°C, with higher values present for high temperature heating such a for absorption cooling applications, or during very cold weather. Except for when the delta-t is zero, conversion efficiency is dependent on solar isolation levels, with higher insulation yielding greater levels of solar conversion.

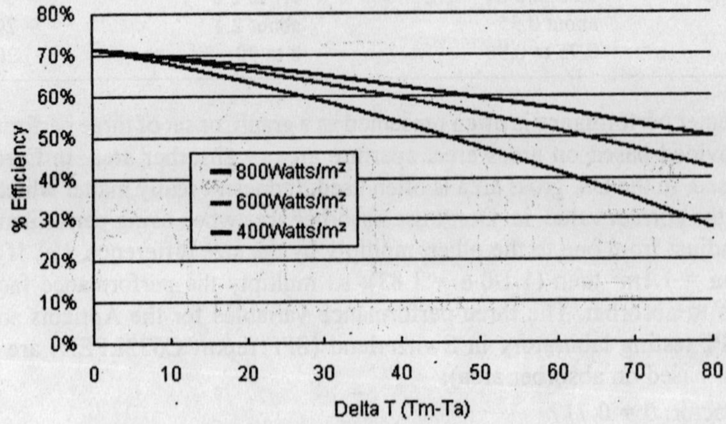

Fig. 5.14: Apricus Solar Collector Performance Curves

In reality, ambient temperature will fluctuate, and the manifold temperature will gradually increase as the water is heated. Furthermore, insulation levels may fluctuate with intermittent cloud cover. In order to more accurately calculate energy output per day/month/year a more complete set of environmental data must be considered and many (hourly) performance calculations throughout the day taken. Your local Apricots distributor can provide estimates of average monthly and annual performance, heat output and thus solar contribution for your location. One factor that is not considered in the straight performance calculations outlined above is the affect of transversal or longitudinal IAM values (Incidence Angle Modifier). Considering IAM is important as for Apricots solar collectors it accounts for as much as an additional 25% in total daily heat output values.

Suitability of Collector for Situation?

The desired temperature range of the material to be heated is the most important factor in choosing the correct type of collector. An uncovered absorber is certainly not suitable for producing process heat. The amount of radiation on that spot, exposure to storms, and the amount of space must all be carefully considered when planning a solar array.

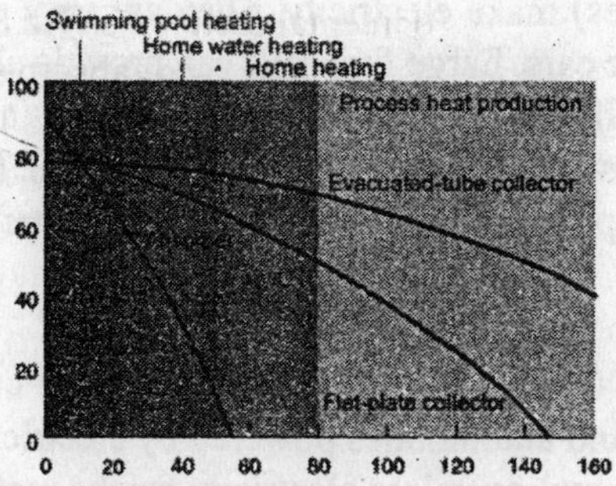

Fig. 5.15 Graph of efficiency and temperature ranges of various types of collectors (radiation; 1000 W/m²)

The specific costs of collectors are also important. Evacuated-tube collectors are substantially more expensive (at 511,.29–1278, 23 Euro /m² collector surface) than flat-plate collectors (153,34 to 613,55 Euro/m²) or even plastic absorbers (25,60 to 102,26 Euro/m²). However, a good collector does not guarantee a good solar system. Rather, all components should be of high quality and similar capacity and strength. On line, biomonitors used as a tool for toxicity reduction evaluation of in situ groundwater remediation techniques.

5.11 HYDROGEN AS ENERGY

Hydrogen is the simplest element known to man. Each atom of hydrogen has only one proton. It also the most plentiful gas in the universe. Stars are made primarily of hydrogen. The sun is a giant ball of hydrogen and helium gases in the sun core, hydrogen atoms combine to form helium atoms. This process-called fusion gives off radiant energy. This radiant energy sustains life on earth. It gives us light and makes plants grow. It makes the wind blow and rain fall. It is stored as chemical energy fossil fuels. Most of the energy we use today came from the sun's radiant energy.

Since hydrogen doesn't exit on earth as a gas, we must separate it from other elements. We can separate hydrogen atoms from water, biomass or natural gas molecules. The two most common methods for producing hydrogen are steam reforming and electrolysis (water splitting).scientists have even discovered that some algae and bacteria give off hydrogen. Stem reforming is currently the least expensive method of producing hydrogen and accounts for about 95 percent of the hydrogen produced in the United States. it is used in industries to separate hydrogen atoms from carbon atoms in methane (CH_4).because methane is a fossil fuels, the process of steam reforming results in greenhouse gas emissions that are linked with global warming.

Electrolysis is a process that splits hydrogen from water. It results in no emissions but it is currently a very expensive process new technologies are being developed all the time.

Uses of Hydrogen

The national aeronautics and space administration (NASA) is the primary user of hydrogen as an energy fuel; it has used hydrogen for years in the space program. Liquid hydrogen lifts the space shuttle into orbit. Hydrogen batteries called fuel cells power the shuttle electrical systems. The only by products is pure water, which the crew uses as drinking water.

Hydrogen fuel cells (batteries) make electricity. They are very efficient, but expensive to build. Small fuel cells can power electric cars. Large fuel cells can provide electricity in out of the way places with no power lines. Won't be built for a while. However, fuel cells are being used in some place as a source of emergency power to hospitals and to wilderness locations. Portable fuel cells are being sold to provide longer power for laptop computer, cell phones, and military application.

Hydrogen user in Vehicles

There are currently about 200 hyrogen-fueued vehicles in the united state–mostly in California. Most of these vehicles are buses and automobiles powered by electric motors. they store hydrogen gas or liquid on board and convert the hydrogen into electricity for the motor using a fuel cell only a few of these vehicles burn the hydrogen directly (producing almost no pollution).

The Future of Hydrogen

Hydrogen has great potential as an environmentally clean energy fuel and as a way to reduce reliance on imported energy sources. Before hydrogen can play a bigger energy role and becomes a widely used alternative to gasoline, many new facilities and make hydrogen, store it and move it, we will need economical fuel cells. In addition, consumers will need the technology and the education to safely use it.

Chapter 6

Wind, Hydal and Nuclear Sources of Energy

6.1 WIND ENERGY SYSTEM AND WIND ENERGY DATA

Distribution of wind speed (red) and energy (blue) for all of 2002 at the Lee Ranch facility in Colorado. The histogram shows measured data, while the curve is the Rayleigh model distribution for the same average wind speed. Energy is the Betz limit through a 100 m (328 ft) diameter circle facing directly into the wind. Total energy for the year through that circle was 15.4 gigawatt-hours (GW·h).

The Earth is unevenly heated by the sun, such that the poles receive less energy from the sun than the equator; along with this, dry land heats up (and cools down) more quickly than the seas do. The differential heating drives a global atmospheric convection system reaching from the Earth's surface to the stratosphere that acts as a virtual ceiling. Most of the energy stored in these wind movements can be found at high altitudes where continuous wind speeds of over 160 km/h (99 mph) occur. Eventually, the wind energy is converted through friction into diffuse heat throughout the Earth's surface and the atmosphere.

The total amount of economically extractable power available from the wind is considerably more than present human power use from all sources. An estimated 72 terawatt (TW) of wind power on the Earth potentially can be commercially viable, compared to about 15 TW average global power consumption from all sources in 2005. Not all the energy of the wind flowing past a given point can be recovered (see Betz' law).

6.1.1 Distribution of Wind Speed

The strength of wind varies, and an average value for a given location does not alone indicate the amount of energy a wind turbine could produce there. To assess the frequency of wind speeds at a particular location, a probability distribution function is often fit to the observed data. Different locations will have different wind speed distributions. The Weibull model closely mirrors the actual distribution of hourly wind speeds at many locations. The Weibull factor is often close to 2 and therefore a Rayleigh distribution can be used as a less accurate, but simpler model. Because so much power is generated by higher wind speed, much of the energy comes in short bursts.

The 2002 Lee Ranch sample is telling; half of the energy available arrived in just 15% of the operating time. The consequence is that wind energy from a particular turbine or wind farm does not have as consistent an output as fuel-fired power plants; utilities that use wind power provide power from starting existing generation for times when the wind is weak thus wind power is primarily a fuel saver rather than a capacity saver. Making wind power more consistent requires that various existing technologies and methods be extended, in particular the use of stronger inter-regional transmission lines to link widely distributed wind farms. Problems of variability are addressed by grid energy storage, batteries, pumped-storage hydroelectricity and energy demand management.

6.1.2 Electricity Generation

Typical components of a wind turbine (gearbox, rotor shaft and brake assembly) being lifted into position. In a wind farm, individual turbines are interconnected with a medium voltage (often 34.5 kV), power collection system and communications network. At a substation, this medium-voltage electrical current is increased in voltage with a transformer for connection to the high voltage electric power transmission system. The surplus power produced by domestic microgenerators can, in some jurisdictions, be fed into the network and sold to the utility company, producing a retail credit for the microgenerators' owners to offset their energy costs.

Fig. 6.1

Grid Management

Induction generators, often used for wind power, require reactive power for excitation so substations used in wind-power collection systems include substantial capacitor banks for power factor correction. Different types of wind turbine generators behave differently during transmission grid disturbances, so extensive modelling of the dynamic electromechanical characteristics of a new wind farm is required by transmission system operators to ensure predictable stable behaviour during system faults (see Low voltage ride through). In particular, induction generators cannot support the system voltage during faults, unlike steam or hydro turbine-driven synchronous generators. Doubly-fed machines—wind turbines with solid-state converters between the turbine generator and the collector system—generally have more desirable properties for grid interconnection. Transmission systems operators will supply a wind farm developer with a *grid code* to specify the requirements for interconnection to the transmission grid. This will include power factor, constancy of frequency and dynamic behaviour of the wind farm turbines during a system fault.

Capacity Factor

Since wind speed is not constant, a wind farm's annual energy production is never as much as the sum of the generator nameplate ratings multiplied by the total hours in a year. The ratio of actual productivity in a year to this theoretical maximum is called the capacity factor. Typical capacity factors are 20–40%, with values at the upper end of the range in particularly favourable sites. For example, a 1 MW turbine with a capacity factor of 35% will not produce 8,760 MW·h in a year (1 × 24 × 365), but only 1 × 0.35 × 24 × 365 = 3,066 MW·h, averaging to 0.35 MW. Online data is available for some locations and the capacity factor can be calculated from the yearly output.

Unlike fueled generating plants, the capacity factor is limited by the inherent properties of wind. Capacity factors of other types of power plant are based mostly on fuel cost, with a small amount of downtime for maintenance. Nuclear plants have low incremental fuel cost, and so are run at full output and achieve a 90% capacity factor. Plants with higher fuel cost are throttled back to follow load. Gas turbine plants using natural gas as fuel may be very expensive to operate and may be run only to meet peak power demand. A gas turbine plant may have an annual capacity factor of 5–25% due to relatively high energy production cost.

According to a 2007 Stanford University study published in the Journal of Applied Meteorology and Climatology, interconnecting ten or more wind farms can allow an average of 33% of the total energy produced to be used as reliable, baseload electric power, as long as minimum criteria are met for wind speed and turbine height. In a 2008 study released by the U.S. Department of Energy's Office of Energy Efficiency and Renewable Energy, the capacity factor achieved by the wind turbine fleet is shown to be increasing as the technology improves. The capacity factor achieved by new wind turbines in 2004 and 2005 reached 36%.

Penetration

Wind energy "penetration" refers to the fraction of energy produced by wind compared with the total available generation capacity. There is no generally accepted "maximum" level of wind penetration. The limit for a particular grid will depend on the existing generating plants, pricing mechanisms, capacity for storage or demand management, and other factors. An interconnected electricity grid will already include reserve generating and transmission capacity to allow for equipment failures; this reserve capacity can also serve to regulate for the varying power generation by wind plants. Studies have indicated that 20% of the total electrical energy consumption may be incorporated with minimal difficulty.

These studies have been for locations with geographically dispersed wind farms, some degree of dispatchable energy, or hydropower with storage capacity, demand management, and interconnection to a large grid area export of electricity when needed. Beyond this level, there are few technical limits, but the economic implications become more significant. Electrical utilities continue to study the effects of large (20% or more) scale penetration of wind generation on system stability and economics.

At present, a few grid systems have penetration of wind energy above 5%: Denmark (values over 19%), Spain and Portugal (values over 11%), Germany and the Republic of Ireland (values over 6%). For instance, in the morning hours of 8 November 2009, wind energy produced covered more than half the electricity demand in Spain, setting a new record, and without problems for the network.

The Danish grid is heavily interconnected to the European electrical grid, and it has solved grid management problems by exporting almost half of its wind power to Norway. The correlation between electricity export and wind power production is very strong:

Intermittency and Penetration Limits

Electricity generated from wind power can be highly variable at several different timescales: from hour to hour, daily, and seasonally. Annual variation also exists, but is not as significant. Related to variability is the short-term (hourly or daily) predictability of wind plant output. Like other electricity sources, wind energy must be "scheduled". Wind power forecasting methods are used, but predictability of wind plant output remains low for short-term operation.

Because instantaneous electrical generation and consumption must remain in balance to maintain grid stability, this variability can present substantial challenges to incorporating large amounts of wind power into a grid system. Intermittency and the non-dispatchable nature of wind energy production can raise costs for regulation, incremental operating reserve, and (at high penetration levels) could require an increase in the already existing energy demand management, load shedding, or storage solutions or system interconnection with HVDC cables. At low levels of wind penetration, fluctuations in load and allowance for failure of large generating units requires reserve capacity that can also regulate for variability of wind generation. Wind power can be replaced by other power stations during low wind periods. Transmission networks must already cope with outages of generation plant and daily changes in electrical demand. Systems with large wind capacity components may need more spinning reserve (plants operating at less than full load).

Pumped-storage hydroelectricity or other forms of grid energy storage can store energy developed by high-wind periods and release it when needed. Stored energy increases the economic value of wind energy since it can be shifted to displace higher cost generation during peak demand periods. The potential revenue from this arbitrage can offset the cost and losses of storage; the cost of storage may add 25% to the cost of any wind energy stored, but it is not envisaged that this would apply to a large proportion of wind energy generated. The 2 GW Dinorwig pumped storage plant in Wales evens out electrical demand peaks, and allows base-load suppliers to run their plant more efficiently. Although pumped storage power systems are only about 75% efficient, and have high installation costs, their low running costs and ability to reduce the required electrical base-load can save both fuel and total electrical generation costs.

In particular, geographic regions, peak wind speeds may not coincide with peak demand for electrical power. In the US states of California and Texas, for example, hot days in summer may have low wind speed and high electrical demand due to air conditioning. Some utilities subsidize the purchase of geothermal heat pumps by their customers, to reduce electricity demand during the summer months by making air conditioning up to 70% more efficient; widespread adoption of this technology would better match electricity demand to wind availability in areas with hot summers and low summer winds. Another option is to interconnect widely dispersed geographic areas with an HVDC "Super grid".

In the USA it is estimated that to upgrade the transmission system to take in planned or potential renewables would cost at least $60 billion Total annual US power consumption in 2006 was 4 thousand billion kW.h. Over an asset life of 40 years and low cost utility investment grade funding, the cost of

$60 billion investment would be about 5% p.a. (*i.e.*, $3 billion p.a.) Dividing by total power used gives an increased unit cost of around $3,000,000,000 × 100/4,000 × 1 = 0.075 cent/kW.h.

In the UK, demand for electricity is higher in winter than in summer, and so are wind speeds. Solar power tends to be complementary to wind. On daily to weekly timescales, high pressure areas tend to bring clear skies and low surface winds, whereas low pressure areas tend to be windier and cloudier. On seasonal timescales, solar energy typically peaks in summer, whereas in many areas wind energy is lower in summer and higher in winter.

Thus, the intermittencies of wind and solar power tend to cancel each other somewhat. A demonstration project at the Massachusetts Maritime Academy shows the effect. The Institute for Solar Energy Supply Technology of the University of Kassel pilot-tested a combined power plant linking solar, wind, biogas and hydrostorage to provide load-following power around the clock, entirely from renewable sources.

A report from Denmark noted that their wind power network was without power for 54 days during 2002. Wind power advocates argue that these periods of low wind can be dealt with by simply restarting existing power stations that have been held in readiness or interlinking with HVDC. Electrical grids with slow-responding thermal power plants and without ties to networks with hydroelectric generation may have to limit the use of wind power. Three reports on the wind variability in the UK issued in 2009, generally agree that variability of wind needs to be taken into account, but it does not make the grid unmanageable; and the additional costs, which are modest, can be quantified. A 2006 International Energy Agency forum presented costs for managing intermittency as a function of wind-energy's share of total capacity for several countries, as shown:

Table: 6.1

Increase in system operation costs, Euros per MW·h, for 10% and 20% wind share

	10%	20%
Germany	2.5	3.2
Denmark	0.4	0.8
Finland	0.3	1.5
Norway	0.1	0.3
Sweden	0.3	0.7

Capacity Credit and Fuel Saving

Many commentators concentrate on whether or not wind has any "capacity credit" without defining what they mean by this and its relevance. Wind does have a capacity credit, using a widely accepted and meaningful definition, equal to about 20% of its rated output (but this figure varies depending on actual circumstances). This means that reserve capacity on a system equal in MW to 20% of added wind could be retired when such wind is added without affecting system security or robustness. However, the precise value is irrelevant since the main value of wind (in the UK, worth 5 times the capacity credit value) is its fuel and CO_2 savings.

Fig: 6.2: "Wind farm and its impact on economic"

6.2 WILD FARM

A **wind farm** is a group of wind turbines in the same location used for production of electric power. Individual turbines are interconnected with a medium voltage (usually 34.5 kV) power collection system and communications network. At a substation, this medium-voltage electrical current is increased in voltage with a transformer for connection to the high voltage transmission system.

Spain, Denmark, and Germany are Europe's main wind energy producers. A large wind farm may consist of a few dozen to several hundred individual wind turbines, and cover an extended area of hundreds of square miles, but the land between the turbines may be used for agricultural or other purposes. A wind farm may be located off-shore to take advantage of strong winds blowing over the surface of an ocean or lake.

6.3 LOCATION PLANNING

A quantity called Wind Power Density (WPD) is used to select locations for wind energy development. The WPD is a calculation relating to the effective force of the wind at a particular location, frequently expressed in term of the elevation above ground level over a period of time. It takes into account velocity and mass. Color coded maps are prepared for a particular area describing, for example, "Mean Annual Power Density, at 50 Meters." The results of the above calculation are used in an index developed by the National Renewable Energy Lab and referred to as "NREL CLASS." The larger the WPD calculation the higher it is rated by class.

Access to the power grid must be taken into mind. The further from the power grid, there will be need for more transmission lines to span from the farm directly to the power grid or transformers will have to be built on the premises depending upon the types of turbines being used. Wind farm siting can be highly controversial, particularly when sites are picturesque or environmentally sensitive, such as having substantial bird life, or requiring roads to be built through pristine areas. These areas are generally non-residential due to the noise concerns and setback requirements.

6.4 WIND SPEED

Generally, wind generators are practical if windspeed is 10 mph (16 km/h or 4.5 m/s) or greater. An ideal location would have a near constant flow of non-turbulent wind throughout the year with a minimum likelihood of sudden powerful bursts of wind. An important factor of turbine siting is also access to local demand or transmission capacity.

Usually sites are preselected on basis of a wind atlas, and validated with wind measurements. Meteorological wind data alone is usually not sufficient for accurate siting of a large wind power project. Collection of site specific data for wind speed and direction is crucial to determining site potential. Local winds are often monitored for a year or more, and detailed wind maps constructed before wind generators are installed. To collect wind data a meteorological tower is installed with instruments at various heights along the tower.

All towers include anemometers to determine the wind speed and wind vanes to determine the direction. The towers generally vary in height from 30 to 60 meters. The towers primarily are guyed steel-pipe structures that are left to collect data for one to two years and then disassembled. Data is collected by a data logging device that stores and transmits data for analysis. Great attention must be paid to the exact positions of the turbines (a process known as *micro-siting*) because differences of 30 m can nearly double energy production.

For smaller installations where such data collection is too expensive or time consuming, the normal way of prospecting for wind-power sites is to directly look for trees or vegetation that are permanently "cast" or deformed by the prevailing winds. Another way is to use a wind-speed survey map or historical data from a nearby meteorological station, although these methods are less reliable.

6.5 ALTITUDE

The wind blows faster at higher altitudes because of the reduced influence of drag. The increase in velocity with altitude is most dramatic near the surface and is affected by topography, surface roughness, and upwind obstacles such as trees or buildings. Typically, the increase of wind speeds with increasing height follows a wind profile power law, which predicts that wind speed rises proportionally to the seventh root of altitude. Doubling the altitude of a turbine, then, increases the expected wind speeds by 10% and the expected power by 34%.

6.6 WIND PARK EFFECT

The "wind park effect" refers to the loss of output due to mutual interference between turbines. Wind farms have many turbines and each extracts some of the energy of the wind. Where land area is sufficient, turbines are spaced three to five rotor diameters apart perpendicular to the prevailing wind, and five to ten rotor diameters apart in the direction of the prevailing wind, to minimize efficiency loss. The loss can be as low as 2% of the combined *nameplate* rating of the turbines.

In a large wind park, due to "multifractal" effects between individual rotors, the behaviour deviates significantly from Kolmogorov's turbulence scaling for individual turbines.

6.7 ENVIRONMENTAL AND AESTHETIC IMPACT

Livestock Wind Turbine and Continue to Graze

Compared to the environmental effects of traditional energy sources, the environmental effects of wind power are relatively minor. Wind power consumes no fuel, and emits no air pollution, unlike fossil fuel power sources. The energy consumed to manufacture and transport the materials used to build a wind power plant is equal to the new energy produced by the plant within a few months of operation. Garrett Gross, a scientist from UMKC in Kansas City, Missouri states, "The impact made on the environment is very little when compared to what is gained." While a wind farm may cover a large area of land, many land uses such as agriculture are compatible.

Danger to birds and bats has been a concern in many locations. Some dismiss the number of birds killed by wind turbines as negligible when compared to the number that die as a result of other human activities, and especially the environmental impacts of using non-clean power sources. Others are in very strong disagreement with the placement of wind farms. New evidence suggests that the critically endangered California Condor is being killed at the Tehachapi Pass wind farm in Southern California. Bat species appear to be at risk during key movement periods. Almost nothing is known about current populations of these species and the impact on bat numbers because of mortality at windpower locations. Offshore wind sites 10 km or more from shore do not interact with bat populations but their placement is of great concern if there are nearby bird colonies.

Aesthetics have also been an issue in some areas. In the USA, the Massachusetts Cape Wind project was delayed for years mainly because of aesthetic concerns. In the UK, repeated opinion surveys have shown that more than 70% of people either like, or do not mind, the visual impact. According to a town councillor in Ardrossan, Scotland, the overwhelming majority of locals believe that the Ardrossan Wind Farm has enhanced the area, saying that the turbines are impressive looking and bring a calming effect to the town.

6.8 EFFECT ON POWER GRID

Utility-scale wind farms must have access to transmission lines to transport energy. The wind farm developer may be obligated to install extra equipment or control systems in the wind farm to meet the technical standards set by the operator of a transmission line. The company or person that develops the wind farm can sell the power on the grid through the transmission lines, moreover the company ultimately chooses whether to hold on to the rights or sell the farm or parts of it to big business.

TYPES

Onshore: Turbine installations in hilly or mountainous regions tend to be on ridgelines generally three kilometers or more inland from the nearest shoreline.

Nearshore: Turbine installations are on land within three kilometers of a shoreline or on water within ten kilometers of land.

Offshore: Wind development zone are generally considered to be beaten kilometer or more from land. Offshore wind turbines are less obtrusive than turbines on land, as their apparent size and noise is mitigated by distance.

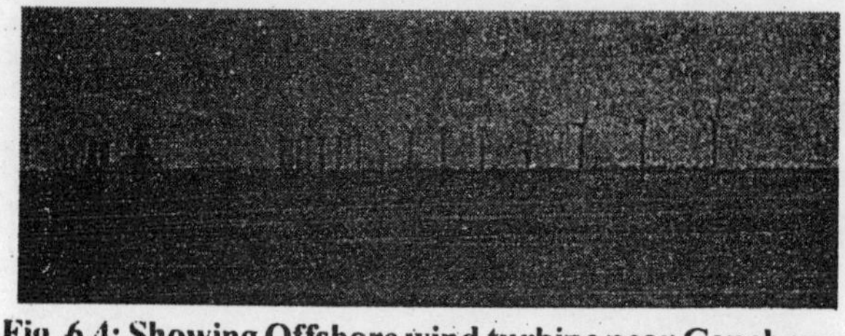

Fig. 6.4: Showing Offshore wind turbine near Copehngen

6.9 FIXED BOTTOM, FOUNDATION BASED TOWER TECHNOLOGIES

Offshore installation monopile wind turbines are generally more expensive than onshore installations but this depends on the attributes of the site. Offshore fixed-bottom towers are generally taller than onshore towers (the submerged height is included). Offshore foundations may be more expensive to build. Power transmission done from offshore turbines is through undersea cable. Offshore saltwater environments also raise maintenance costs by corroding the towers.

Repairs and maintenance are usually more costly than on onshore turbines, motivating operators to reduce the number of wind turbines for a given total power by installing the largest available units. Offshore saltwater wind turbines are outfitted with extensive corrosion protection measures including coatings and cathodic protection, which may not be required in fresh water locations.

6.10 DEEP WATER, FLOATING TURBINE TECHNOLOGIES

In 2009, the first deep-water, large-capacity, floating wind turbine is being built by Statoil Hydro. The 2.3 MW turbines can be anchored in water 120–700 m deep. It will be tested off the coast of Norway for two years. The 120-meter-tall tower was towed 10 km offshore into the Amoy Fjord, in 220-meter-deep water, off of Stavanger, Norway on 2009 for a two year test run. Through 2003, existing offshore wind turbine technology deployments had been limited to water depths of 30-meters utilizing *fixed-bottom technology* which necessarily limits deployments to the near-coastal sea surface.

Worldwide deep-water wind resources are extremely abundant in deep-water areas with depths up to 600 meters, which are thought to best facilitate transmission of the generated electric power to shore communities. The U.S. deep-water wind resource is second only to China. Although limited early conceptual work on deep-water floating turbine technologies was done in 1972, it was not until the mid 1990's. After the onshore, foundation-tower, commercial wind industry was well established, that design of deep-water technologies. It was taken up again by the mainstream research community.

New deep-water, floating-turbine technologies are only recently beginning to be deployed. The first large-capacity floating wind turbine is the Hywind, a 2.3 MW turbine in 220-meter deep water in the North Sea, 10 km southwest of Karmøy, Norway.

6.11 WIND FARM IN INDIA

At the end of September 2007, India had 7660 MW of wind generating capacity and is the fourth largest market in the world. Indian Wind Energy Association has estimated that with the current level of technology, the 'on-shore' potential for utilization of wind energy for electricity generation is of the order of 65,000 MW. There are about a dozen wind pumps of various designs providing water for agriculture, afforestation, and domestic purposes, all scattered over the country. The wind farms are predominantly present in the states of Tamil Nadu, Maharashtra, Karnataka and Gujarat. Other states like Andhra Pradesh, Rajasthan, Kerala and Madhya Pradesh have a very good potential.

Fig. 6.5: A wind farm in Aralvaimozhy, Tamil Nadu, India

6.12 WIND ENERGY

Wind-generated power is a variable resource the amount of electricity produced at any given point in time by a given plant depends on wind speeds, air density, and turbine characteristics (among other factors). If wind speed is too low (less than about 2.5 m/s) then the wind turbines will not be able to make electricity, and if it is too high (more than about 25 m/s) the turbines will have to be shut down to avoid damage. The output from a single turbine can vary, greatly and rapidly as local wind speeds vary. As more turbines are connected over larger and larger areas the average power output becomes less variable.

Intermittence: A single wind turbine is highly intermittent. Theoretical arguments often claim that a large wind farm spread over a geographically diverse area will as a whole rarely stop producing power altogether, however this is in contradiction to the observed variability in total power output of wind turbines installed in Ireland and Denmark.

Capacity Factor: Wind power typically has a capacity factor of 20–40%.

Dispatchability: Wind power is "highly non-dispatchable"

Capacity Credit: At low levels of penetration, the capacity credit of wind is about the same as the capacity factor. As the concentration of wind power on the grid rises, the capacity credit percentage drops.

Variability: Site dependent. Sea breezes are much it is more constant than land breezes.

Reliability: A wind farm is highly reliable although highly intermittent. The output at any given time will only vary gradually due to falling wind speeds or storms (the latter necessitating shut downs). A typical wind farm is unlikely to have to shut down in less than half an hour at the extreme, whereas an equivalent sized power station can fail totally instantaneously and without warning. The total shut down of a wind farm is highly predictable via weather forecasting.

According to a study of wind in the United States, ten or more widely-separated wind farms connected through the grid could be relied. As reliable, baseload power, as long as minimum criteria are met for wind speed and turbine height. As wind power is generated by large numbers of small generators, individual failures do not have large impacts on power grids. This feature of wind has been referred to as resiliency.

Wind power is affected by air temperature because colder air is more dense and therefore more effective at producing wind power. Therefore, wind power is affected seasonally (more output in winter than summer) and by daily temperature variations. During the 2006 California heat storm output from wind power in California significantly decreased to an average of 4% of capacity for 7 days. A similar result was seen during the 2003 European heat wave, when the output of wind power in France, Germany, and Spain fell below 10%.

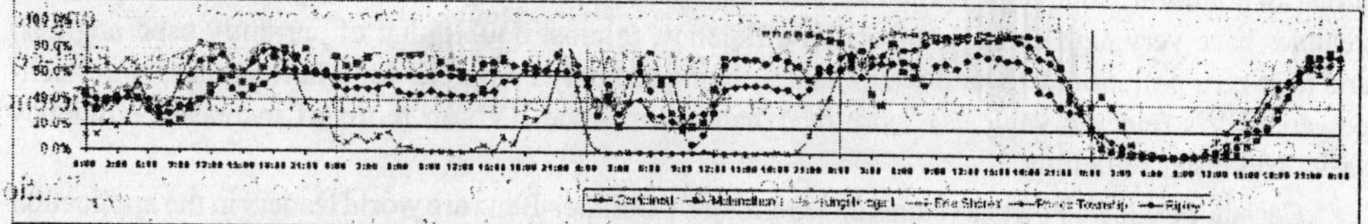

Fig. 6.6: Showing 5 days of hourly output of five wind farms in Ontario

6.13 NON-RENEWABLE ENERGY SOURCE

Non renewable energy have accumulated in nature over a long span of time and can not be quickly replenished if exhausted? After crude oil is removed from the ground, it is sent to a refinery by pipeline ship or barge. In a refinery different parts of the crude oil are separated into useable petroleum crude oil. It is measured in barrels (abbreviated "bbls"). One barrel of crude oil when refined produces about 20 gallons of finished motor gasoline and 7 gallons of diesel as well as other petroleum products. Most of the petroleum products are used propane to heat their homes.

Dr. Homi Bhabha is considered the father of nuclear power development in India.

Atomic and nuclear power Can be used to make electricity. But first the energy must be released. It can be released from atoms in two ways: nuclear fusion and nuclear fission. In nuclear fusion, energy is released when atoms are combined or fused together to form a large atom. This is the same method by this sun produces energy. In nuclear fission, atoms are split apart to from smaller atoms releasing energy. Nuclear power plants use nuclear fission to produce electricity. The first controlled fission of an atom was carried out in Germany in 1938.

6.14 NUCLEAR FUEL –URANIUM

The fuel most widely used by nuclear plants for nuclear fission is uranium. Uranium is nonrenewable, thought it is to common metal found in rocks all over the world. Nuclear plants use a certain kind of uranium is quite common. It is about 100times more common than silver, U-235 is relatively rare. Once uranium is mined the U-235must be extracted and processed before it can be used as a fuel.

During nuclear fission, a small particle called a neutron hits the uranium atom and splits it. This process releasing a great amount of energy as heat and radiation. Moreover more neutrons are also released. These neutrons go on to bombard other uranium atoms and the process repeats itself over and over again, this phenomenon is called a chain reaction.

6.15 FUEL CELLS

Fuel cells are electrochemical devices that convert the chemical energy of a fuel directly very efficiently. They convert the chemical energy into electricity (DC) and heat, thus they are for far away from combustion. The most suitable fuel for such cells is hydrogen or a mixture of compounds containing hydrogen. A fuel cell consists of an electrolyte sandwiched between two electrodes. Oxygen passes over one electrode and hydrogen over the other. They react electrochemically to generate electricity, water, and heat. fuel cells have been used in space flights and combined supplies of heat and power, Their use in electric vehicles are the best option available to dramatically reduce urban air pollution. Compared to vehicles powered by the internal combustion engine, fuel-cell powered vehicles have very high energy conversion efficiency, (almost double that of currently used engines) and near-zero pollution. CO_2 and water vapour being the only emissions for whole process. Fuel-cell-powered EV's (electric vehicles) score over battery operated EV's in terms of increased efficiency easier and faster refuelling.

Canada's Ballad's Power Systems and Germany's Dailmer-Benz are world leaders in the application of fuel cell technology for meeting transportation needs. In India, diesel buses are a major means of transport and these emit significant quantities of SPM and SO_x (Oxider of suphur). Thus, fuel-cell powered buses could be introduced with relative ease and yet make a positive impact on urban air quality. Such buses are already in operation in Vancouver in Canada and in Illinois and California in the USA. Though rapid progress has been made, high initial cost is still the biggest hurdle in the widespread commercialization of fuel cells.

6.15.1 Fuel Cells for Power Generation

India has a large gap between the demand and supply of power. Conventional large-scale power plants use non-renewable fuels with significant adverse environmental impacts. Fuel cell systems are excellent alternates for small-scale decentralized power generation. Fuel cells can supply combined heat and power to commercial buildings, hospitals, airports and military installation at remote locations. Fuel cells have efficiency levels up to 55% as compared to 35% of conventional power plants. The emissions are very less in comparision to enginers as only CO_2 and water vapors being the only emissions. Fuel cell systems are modular (i.e. additional capacity can be added whenever required with relative ease) and can be set up wherever power is required.

Hydel Energy Energy from Water Sources

The energy in the flowing water can be used to produce electricity. Waves result due to the interaction of the wind with the surface of the sea. It represent a transfer of energy from the wind to the sea. Energy can be extracted from these tides by creating a reservoir or basin behind a barrage and then passing tidal waters through turbines in the barrage to generate electricity.

Mini or Micro Hydro power

Hydro power is one of the best, cheapest, and cleanest sources of energy. Although, with big dams, there are many environmental and social problems. Such problems also have been seen in the case of the Tehri and the Narmada Projects. However small dams are, free from these problems. This is fact that one of the earliest known renewable energy sources in the country is hydro power. For the last few hundred years, people living in the hills of the Himalayas have been using water mills, or chakki, to grind wheat. The 130 kW small hydropower plant in Darjeeling set up in 1897, was the first in India. Besides being free from the problem of pollution. Such plants are also free from issues and controversies that are associated with the bigger projects. They are not affecting the lives of thousands of people living along the banks of the rivers, destruction of large areas under forest, and seismological threats. New environmental laws affected by the danger of global warming have made energy from small hydropower plants more relevant. These small hydropower plants can serve the energy needs of remote rural areas independently. The real challenge in a remote area lies in successful marketing of the energy. Local industries should be encouraged to use this electricity for sustainable development. It is a technology with enormous potential, which could exploit the water resources to supply energy to remote rural areas. It also eliminates most of the negative environmental impacts associated with large hydro power projects.

Energy From the Sea, Thermal, Tidal and Wave Energy

Large amounts of solar energy are stored in the oceans and seas. On an average, the 60 million square kilometers of the tropical seas absorb solar radiation. It is equivalent to the heat content of 245 billion barrels of oil. Scientists feel that if this energy can be trapped a large source of energy will be available to the tropical and other countries. The process of harnessing this energy is called OTEC (Ocean Thermal Energy Conversion). It uses the temperature differences between the surface of the ocean and the depths of about 1000m to operate a heat engine, which produces electric power. Energy is also obtained from waves and tides. The first wave energy project with a capacity of 150 MW has been set up at Vizhinjam near Trivanthpuram. A major tidal wave power project costing of ₹ 5000 crores is proposed to be set up in the Hanthal Creek in the Gulf of Kutch in Gujarat. In some countries such as Japan small scale power generators run by energy from waves used as power sources.

Geothermal Energy

All the organisms exists between two great sources of energy, the hot rocks beneath the surface of the earth and the sun in the sky. Our ancestors were aware about the value of geothermal energy. They bathed and cooked in hot springs. Today it has been recognized that this resource has potential for much broader application. The core of the earth is very hot and it is possible to make use of this geothermal energy (in Greek it means heat from the earth). These are areas with volcanoes, hot springs, geysers, and methane even under the water in the oceans and seas. In some countries, such as in the USA water is pumped from underground hot water deposits and used to heat people's houses. The utilization of geothermal energy for the production of electricity dates back to the early part of the twentieth century. For 50 years the generation of electricity from geothermal energy was confined to Italy and interest in this technology was slow to spread elsewhere. In 1943, the use of geothermal hot water was pioneered in Iceland.

In India, Northwestern Himalayas and the western coast are considered as geothermal areas. The Geological Survey of India has already identified more than 350 hot spring sites, which can be explored as areas to tap geothermal energy. Satellites like the IRS-1 have played an important role, through infrared photographs of the ground, in locating geothermal areas. The Puga valley in the Ladakh region has the most promising geothermal field. An experimental 1-kW generator is already in operation in this area. It is being used mainly for poultry farming, mushroom cultivation, and pashmina-wool processing.

Co-generation

Co-generation is the concept of producing two forms of energy from one fuel. One of the forms of energy must always be heat and the other may be electricity or mechanical energy. In a conventional power plant, fuel is burnt in a boiler to generate high-pressure steam. This steam is used to drive a turbine, which in turn drives an alternator through a steam turbine to produce electric power. The exhaust steam is generally condensed to water that goes back to the boiler. As the low-pressure steam has a large quantum of heat that is lost in the process of condensing. The efficiency of conventional power plants is only around 35%. In a cogeneration plant, very high efficiency levels, in the range of 75%–90% can be reached. This is so, because the low-pressure exhaust steam coming out of the turbine is not condensed, but used for heating purposes in factories or houses. Since co-generation can meet both power and heat needs.

It has other advantages as well in the form of significant cost savings for the plant and reduction in emissions of pollutants due to reduced fuel consumption. Even at conservative estimates, the potential of power generation from co-generation in India is more than 20,000 MW. Since India is the largest producer of sugar in the world, bagasse-based cogeneration is being promoted. The potential for cogeneration thus lies in facilities with joint requirement of heat and electricity. Primarily sugar and rice mills, distilleries, petrochemical sector and industries such as fertilizers, steel, chemical, cement, pulp and paper, and aluminum are the industries with the potential of co-generation energy.

Nuclear Power Plants and Electricity

Most power plants burn fuel to produce electricity, but not nuclear power plant. Electric generation may use the heat given off during fission as fuel. Fission takes place insides the reactor of a nuclear power plant. At the center of the reactor is the core, which contains the uranium fuel. The uranium fuel is formed into ceramic pellets. These are about the size of our fingertip, but each one produces the same amount of energy as 150 gallons of oil. These energy-rich pellets are stacked end to end. A bundle of fuel rods is called a fuel assembly. Fission generate heats in a reactor just as coal generates heat in a boiler. The heat is use to boil water into steam. The steam turns to the turbine blades. As they turn, they drive generator that make electricity. After ward the steam converts into water and water can be used again and again.

Type of Reactors

As there are different approaches to design and building. Scientists have developed different types of nuclear power plants. Tow types are used boiling water reactors (BWRs) and pressurized water reactors (PWRs). India has 10 nuclear reactors at 5 nuclear powers stations that produce 20% of India's electricity.

In the BWR the water heated by the reactor core turns directly into steam in the reactor vessel and is it used to power the turbine-generator. In a PWR the water passing thought the reactor core is kept under pressure so that it does not turn in to steam.

Steam to drive the turbine is generated in a separate piece of equipment called a steam generator. A steam generator is a giant cylinder with thousands of tube in it though the hot radioactive water can flow outside the tubes in the steam generator. Clean water boils and eventually turns to steam. The clean waters may come from several sources like ocans, lakes or river. The radioactive water flows back to the reactor core, where it is reheated only to flow back to the steam generator.

Nuclear reactors are machines that contain and control chain reactions while releasing heat at a controlled rate. In electric power plants, the rectors supply the heat to turn water into steam, which drives-generators. The electricity travels through high voltage transmission lines and low voltage distribution lines to home, schools, hospitals, factories, office buildings, rail system and other users.

Nuclear Power and the Environment

Compared to electricity generated by burning fossil fuels, nuclear energy is clean. Nuclear power plants produce no pollution or carbon dioxide. Although but a small amount of emissions results from processing the uranium that is use in nuclear reactors.

Like all industrial processes, nuclear power generation also has by-product wastes. There are like spend (used) fuels other radioactive waste and heat-spent fuels. Radioactive wastes are the principal environment concern for nuclear power. Most nuclear waste is low-level radioactive waste. It consists of ordinary tolls, protective clothing, wiping clothes and disposable item. These have been contaminated with small amounts of radioactive dust or particles. These materials are subject to special regulation that governs their disposal so they will not encounter the outside environment.

On the other hand, the spent fuel assemblies are highly radioactive must these be stored in specially designed pools resembling large swimming pools (water cools the fuel and acts as shield) or in specially designed dry storage containers. An increasing number of reactor operators now store their older and less spent fuel in dry storage facilities using special outdoor concrete or steel containers with air cooling.

Uses of Energy

A lot of energy is used in our homes, in businesses in industry and for traveling. The industrial sector uses about on third of the total energy. The residential and commercial sector combined use more than this *i.e.*, 40% of total energy. Theses two sectos use more energy in coporation to all type of building such as houses, offices stores restaurants and palace of worship. Energy used for transportation accounts for more than Quarter of all energy.

London Smog (Chemical Smog)

This type of smog is thought to be caused by sulphur dioxide. It is formed by combination of smoke, dust, fog and SO_2. Chemical smog is usually formed around some industrial and power plants. It is generally bad in early morning hours and become worse after sunrise, due to sunlight included oxidation of SO_2 to SO_3 followed by reaction with humidity. Sulphuric acid is formed in this type of smog, which is very harmful. It creat harms specially to people suffering form bronchial diseases such as asthma or emphysema.

On Thursday, December 4, 1952, a high temperature air mass moved over Southern England. It creates a temperature inversion phenomenon and caused white fog to settle over London. As the particulate and sulphur dioxide levels rose. Due to the extensive use of coal-fired heating and power production system, the fog began to blacken. The high pressure area stalled and the pollutant build-up worsened further, since there were no air currents to disperse the smog. By Friday morning, visibility was zero. According to an Eye-witness such was the state that white collar became almost black within 20 minutes.

The smog so formed was intensely irritation to the human respiratory system. As a result most of the people soon developed red eyes, hurning throats and nagging coughs. Soon reports of smog related deaths began to come in the elderly. The poople with chronic respiratory problems became the first casualty; followed by young and healthy persons. More than 4,000 people died before the fog disappearances on December 9, 1952.

Los Angles Smog (Photochemical Smog)

Photo chemical smog is associated with adverse meteorological conditions (inversion conditions). Such type of situations occurs if air movement is restricted in summers in highly motorized areas. The first noticed incidence of photochemical smog was is los Angles USA, in the mid 1940's. Thus it is sometimes referred as los angles smog.

Photo-chemical smog is oxidizing smog having a high concentrating of oxidants. Photochemical smog is a mixture of reactants and products. These results due to the interaction between volatile organic compounds VOCs and oxidants (such as NO_x, O_3, CO etc). The primary pollutants in photochemical smog are nitric oxide and hydrocarbons. These primary pollutants convert rapidly in to the secondary pollutants like ozone, nitrates PAN (peroxyacetylnitrate) oxidized hydrocarbons and photochemical aerosols. In presence these chemicals eye and lung irritation occur. They damage the crops lead to the cracking of rubber damage of plants organs etc.

In India Bombay and Calcutta are located in ideal conditions for the formation of photochemical smog, but it may be masked by smoke and SO_2. In a vastly oversimplified from the production of photochemical smog can be represented by the following equation. However, in actual practice, there are many complex reactions which take place in the formation of photochemical smog. However, in actual practice, many complex reactions take place in the formation of photochemical smog.

NUCLEAR ENERGY

The growth of nuclear power combined with the shift from carbon-heavy fuels such as coal and oil to carbon-light fuels like gas. Nuclear energy may contribute to the gradual de-carbonization' of the world energy system. Nuclear energy has tremendous potential but any leakage from the reactor may cause devastating nuclear pollution. Disposal of nuclear waste is also a big problem.

Nuclear Power in India is still not very well developed. There are seven nuclear power stations operating in India. These are located at Tarapur (Maharashta); Rana Pratap Sagar near Kota (Rajasthan), Kalpakkan (Tamil Naidu) and Norora (U.P.). After the signing of 123 civil Nuclear Agreement between Indian government and US govt, the way for the growth of nuclear power generation in India has become open. Many new nuclear power plant projects are under process with other expert countries.

Nuclear energy is the energy that is hidden inside each atom. The ancient Greeks believed that the smallest part of nature is an atom. However, they did not know 2000 years ago that atoms are made up of further smaller particles. They were not aware about the nucleus of protons and neutrons, surrounded by electrons, which swirl around the nucleus much like the earth revolves around the sun. One of the laws of the universe is that matter and energy can neither be created nor destroyed. However, they can be changed various in forms. Matter can be changed into energy. Albert Einstein's famous mathematical formula $E = mc^2$ explains this. The equation says: E [energy] equals m [mass] times c^2 [c stands for the speed or velocity of light]. This means that mass multiplied by the square of the velocity of light. Scientists used Einstein's equation as the key to unlock atomic energy and to create atomic bombs.

An atom's nucleus can be split apart. This is known as fission. During this process, a tremendous amount of energy in the form of both heat and light is released by the initiation of a chain reaction it. this energy, slowly released, can be harnessed to generate electricity. If is released all at once. It results in a tremendous explosion as in an atomic bomb. Nuclear energy can also be harnessed by fusion. A fusion reaction occurs when two hydrogen atoms combine to produce one helium atom. This reaction takes place at all times in the sun.

Uranium is the main element required to run a nuclear reactor. Uranium is mined from many places around the world. It is processed to get enriched uranium, *i.e.,* the radioactive isotope into tiny pellets. These pellets are loaded into long rods that are put into the power plant's reactor. Inside the reactor of an atomic power plant, uranium atoms are split apart in controlled chain reaction. Other fissile material includes plutonium and thorium.

In a chain reaction, particles released by the splitting of the atom strike other uranium atoms and split them. The particles released by this further split other atoms in a chain process. In nuclear power plants, control rods are used to keep the splitting regulated. These are called moderators. The chain reaction gives off heat energy. This heat energy is used to boil heavy water in the core of the reactor. Therefore, instead of burning a fuel, nuclear power plants use the energy released by the chain reaction to change the energy of atoms into heat energy.

The heavy water from the nuclear core is sent to another section of the power plant. In section heavy water heats another set of pipes filled with water to make steam. The steam in this second set of pipes rotates a turbine to generate electricity.

In atomic bombs, almost pure pieces of uranium-235 or plutonium, of a precise mass and shape, must be brought together and held together with great force. These conditions are not present in a nuclear reactor. The reaction also creates radioactive material. This material could harm organisms if released, so it is kept in a solid form. A strong concrete dome is built around the reactor to prevent this material from escaping in case of an accident.

Chernobyl, Three Mile Island, and other nuclear accidents have increased the fear of harnessing nuclear energy. Another issue with international and local implications is the storage and disposal of radioactive wastes both for nuclear reactors making electricity and the production of military weapons. Earlier disposal practices, such as dumping of nuclear waste at sea, have been completely stopped by formal treaty. This has been implemented due to environmental concerns and by cessation of furtive scuttling of nuclear submarines. Regimes for transport and temporary storage of civil and defense nuclear wastes now function, although sites and designs for permanent disposal have yet to be accepted. People are concerned about both low and high level radioactive wastes. With the rise of nuclear electrification, the volume of spent fuel and other wastes has risen substantially. In some countries such as the US, the volume of high-level waste from commercial power plants has now reached hundreds of millions of tonnes.

Experiences with nuclear programmes differ and the future of nuclear power remains uncertain because of public reaction. Nevertheless, in the past few years the capacity of operating nuclear plants has increased more than twenty fold. There are more than 400 nuclear power plants providing about 7% of the world's primary energy and about 25% of the electric power in industrialized nations.

Chapter 7

Food Chains

7.1 THE TRANSFORMATION OF ENERGY

The transformations of energy in an ecosystem begin first with the input of energy comming from the sun. Energy from the sun is captured by the process of photosynthesis. Carbon dioxide is combined with hydrogen (derived from the splitting of water molecules) to produce carbohydrates (CHO). Energy is stored in the high energy, bonds of adenosine triphosphate, ATP.

The ecologist have prooven virtually all energy available to organisms originates in plants. As it is the first step in the production of energy for living things, it is called ***primary production***. ***Herbivores*** obtain their energy by consuming plants or plant products, ***carnivores*** eat herbivores, and ***detritivores*** consume the droppings and carcasses of all organisms.

Portrays is a simple food chain, in which energy comming from sun, is captured by plant photosynthesis. It flows from lower ***trophic level*** to higer trophic level via the ***food chain***. A trophic level is composed of organisms that make a living in the same way. As either they are ***primary producers*** (plants), ***primary consumers*** (herbivores) or ***secondary consumers*** (carnivores). Dead tissue and waste products are produced at all levels. Scavengers, detritivores, and decomposers collectively account for the use of all such "waste". Consumers of carcasses and fallen leaves may be other animals, such as crows and beetles, ultimately these are the microbes that finish the job of decomposition. The amount of primary production varies a great deal from place to place, due to differences in the amount of solar radiation and the availability of nutrients and water.

Energy transfer through the food chain is inefficient. This means that less energy is available at the herbivore level than at the primary producer level, less yet at the carnivore level, and so on. The result is a pyramid of energy, with important implications for understanding the quantity of life that can be supported.

Usually when we think of food chains we visualize green plants, herbivores, and so on. These are referred to as ***grazer food chains***, because living plants are directly consumed. In many circumstances, the principal energy input is not green plants but dead organic matter. These are called ***detritus food chains***. Examples include the forest floor or a woodland stream in a forested area, a salt marsh, and most obviously, the ocean floor in very deep areas where all sunlight is extinguished 1000's of meters above.

Talking about food chains, in reality the organization of biological systems is much more complicated : it can be represented by a simple "chain". There are many food links and chains in an ecosystem, and we refer to all of these linkages as a **food web**. Food webs can be very complicated, where it appears that ***"everything is connected to everything else"*** and it is important to understand what the most important linkages are in any particular food web.

7.2 BIOGEOCHEMISTRY

We study the linkages in a food web these are most important. One obvious way is to study the flow of energy or the cycling of elements. For example, the cycling of elements is controlled in part by organisms, which store or transform elements, and in part by the chemistry and geology of the natural world. The terms Biogeochemistry is defined as the study of how living systems influence, and is controlled by, the geology and chemistry of the earth. Thus biogeochemistry encompasses many aspects of the abiotic and biotic world.

There are several main **principles and tools** that biogeochemists use to study earth systems. Most of the major environmental problems can be analyzed using biogeochemical principles and tools. These problems include global warming, acid rain, environmental pollution, and increasing greenhouse gases. The principles and tools that we use can be broken down into three major components: **element ratios, mass balance, and element cycling.**

1. Element Ratios

In biological systems, we refer to important elements as ***"conservative"***. These elements are often nutrients. "conservative", mean that an organism can change only slightly the amount of these elements in their tissues if they are to remain in good health. It is easiest to think of these conservative elements in relation to other important elements in the organism. For example, in healthy algae the elements C, N, P, and Fe have the following ratio, called the ***Redfield ratio*** after the oceanographer who discovered it:

$$C : N : P : Fe = 106 : 16 : 1 : 0.01$$

Once we know these ratios, we can compare them to the ratios that we measure in a sample of algae to determine if the algae are lacking in one of these limiting nutrients.

2. Mass Balance

Another important tool that biogeochemists use is a simple mass balance equation to describe the state of a system. The system could be a snake, a tree, a lake, or the entire globe. Using a mass balance approach we can determine whether the system is changing and how fast it is changing. The equation is:

$$\text{NET CHANGE} = \text{INPUT} + \text{OUTPUT} + \text{INTERNAL CHANGE}$$

In this equation the net change in the system from one time to another is determined. It may be performed by knowing what the inputs are, what the outputs are, and what the internal change in the system was. The example is of the acidification of a lake, considering the inputs and outputs and internal change of acid in the lake.

3. Element Cycling

Element cycling describes where and how fast elements move in a system. There are two general classes of systems as mentioned earlier: closed and open systems. A closed system refers to a system where the inputs and outputs are negligible compared to the internal changes. Examples of such systems would include a bottle, or our entire globe. There are two ways we can describe the cycling of materials within this closed system, either by looking at the rate of movement or at the pathways of movement.

Rate = number of cycles/time* as rate increases, productivity increases

Pathways is important because of different reactions that may occur

In an open system, there are inputs and outputs as well as the internal cycling. Thus we can describe the rates of movement and the pathways, just as the closed system, but we can also define a new concept called the residence time. The residence time indicates how long on average an element remains within the system before leaving the system.

Rate

Pathways

Residence time, Rt

Rt = total amount of matter/output rate of matter

7.3 CONTROLS ON ECOSYSTEM FUNCTION

Now that we have learned something about how ecosystems are put together and how materials and energy flow through ecosystems we can better address the question of "what controls ecosystem function"? There are two dominant theories of the control of ecosystems. The first, called bottom-up control, states that it is the nutrient supply to the primary producers that ultimately controls ecosystems function. If the nutrient supply is increased, the resulting increase in production of autotrophs is propagated through the food web. More over all of the other trophic levels will respond to the increased availability of food energy and materials.

The second theory, called top-down control, states that predation and grazing by higher trophic levels on lower trophic levels ultimately controls ecosystem function. For example, if you have an increase in predators, that increase will result in fewer grazers, and that decrease in grazers will result in turn in more producers that are primary because fewer of them are being eaten by the grazers. Thus, the control of population numbers and overall productivity "cascades" from the top levels of the food chain down to the bottom trophic levels.

Often the case when there is a clear dichotomy to choose from, the answer regarding the correct theory lies somewhere in the middle. There is evidence from many ecosystem studies that both controls are operating to some degree, but that neither control is complete. For example, the "top-down" effect is often very strong at trophic levels near to the top predators, but the control weakens as you move further down the food chain. Similarly, the "bottom-up" effect of adding nutrients usually stimulates primary production, but the stimulation of secondary production further up the food chain is less strong or is absent.

Thus, we find that both of these controls are operating in any system at any time. We must understand the relative importance of each control in order to help us to predict how an ecosystem will behave or change under different circumstances, such as in the face of a changing climate.

7.4 Summary

Ecosystems are made up of abiotic (non-living, environmental) and biotic components. These basic components are important to nearly all types of ecosystems. Ecosystem ecology looks at energy transformations and biogeochemical cycling within ecosystems. Energy is continually input into an ecosystem in the form of light energy some of the energy is lost during each transfer to a higher tropic level. Nutrients, on the other hand, are recycled within an ecosystem, and their supply normally limits biological activity. So, "energy flows, elements cycle".

Energy is moved through an ecosystem *via* a food web, which is made up of interlocked food chains. Energy is first captured by photosynthesis (primary production). The amount of primary production determines the amount of energy available to higher trophic levels. The study of chemical elements cycle through an ecosystem is termed biogeochemistry. A biogeochemical cycle can be expressed as a set of stores (pools) and transfers, and can be studied using the concepts of "stoichiometry", "mass balance", and "residence time". Ecosystem function is controlled mainly by two processes, "top-down" and "bottom-up" controls. A biome is a major vegetation type extending over a large area. Biome distributions are determined largely by temperature and precipitation patterns on the Earth's surface

7.5 Ecosystem Energy Flow and Models

This model represents the flow of energy through the different components of an ecosystem. It is a classic compartmental model, conforming to conventional System Dynamics notation, and could be represented in any of the standard System Dynamics visual modelling packages. The model has five compartments, representing the energy content in each of five ecosystem compartments:

The primary food chain, consisting of

(a) Plants

(b) Herbivores

(c) Carnivores

The detritus chain, consisting of

(d) Detritus

(e) Detritivores

The flows show the processes that move energy from one compartment to the next. The overlapping circles represent clouds, signifying a System Dynamics. The thin arrows represent influences, and indicate which compartments are deemed to influence each flow: i.e the flow rate is dependent on the value in the compartment.

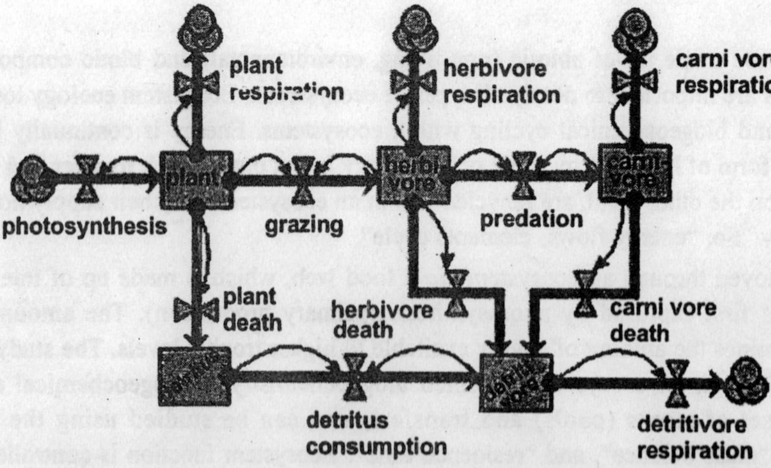

Fig. 7.1: Showing flow of Matter Energy

Photosynthesis explains process regarding comming energy from the sun is captured by green plants and used to make food. Most of this energy is used to carry on the plant's life activities. The rest of the energy is passed on as food to the next level of the food chain.

The figure above shows energy flow in a simple food chain. At each level of the food chain, about 90% of the energy is lost in the form of heat. The total energy passed from one level to the next is only about one-tenth of the energy received from the previous organism. Therefore, towards upward the food chain, there is less energy available. Animals located at the top of the food chain need a lot more food to meet their energy needs.

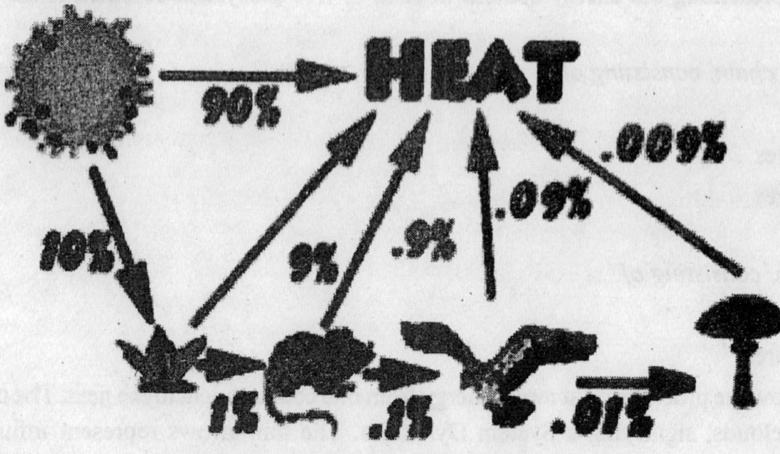

Fig. 7.2: Showing the 10% low of Energy

7.6 Food Chain

A food chain consists of a series of organisms in which the first organism is eaten by a second and the second is eaten by third and so on. During this process, nutrients and energy in the eaten organism are transferred to the organism that eats it. Most of the food comes from simple food chains derived from human-controlled agricultural ecosystems. For example, the beef comes from a cow that ate corn. The corn received its energy from the sun.

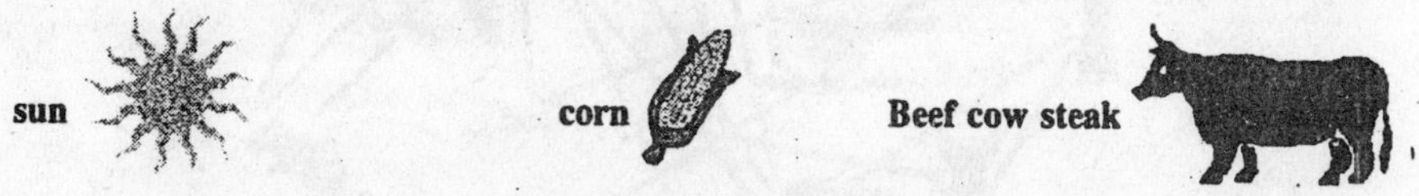

Fig. 7.3 Human Controlled Food Chain

However, in natural ecosystems, a hawk may eat a snake that may have received its energy from a mouse, a frog, or a rabbit. If it ate a mouse, that mouse may have consumed seeds from any number of plants. None of these food chains is exactly alike, which makes studying energy transfer complex.

Fig. 7.4 Natural Food Chain Representing

Food Webs

Organisms are classified based upon the number of energy transfers through a food web. Photoautotrophic production of organic matter represents the first energy transfer in ecosystems and is classified as primary production. Consumption of a plant by a herbivore is the second energy transfer, thus herbivores occupy the second trophic level. It is also known as secondary production. Consumer organisms that are one, two, or three transfers from photoautotrophs are classified as primary, secondary, and tertiary consumers. Moving through a food web, energy is lost during each transfer as heat, as per the second law of thermodynamics. Consequently, the total number of energy transfers rarely exceeds four or five. With energy loss during each transfer, little energy is available to support organisms at the highest levels of a food web.

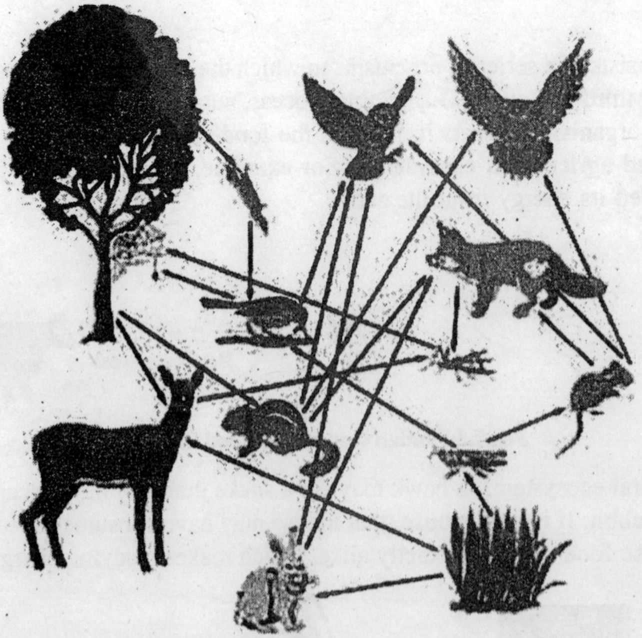

Fig. 7.5

Energy Pyramids Show:

- That the amount of available energy decreases down towards the top of the food chain.
- It takes a large number of producers to support a small number of primary consumers.
- It takes a large number of primary consumers to support a small number of secondary consumers.

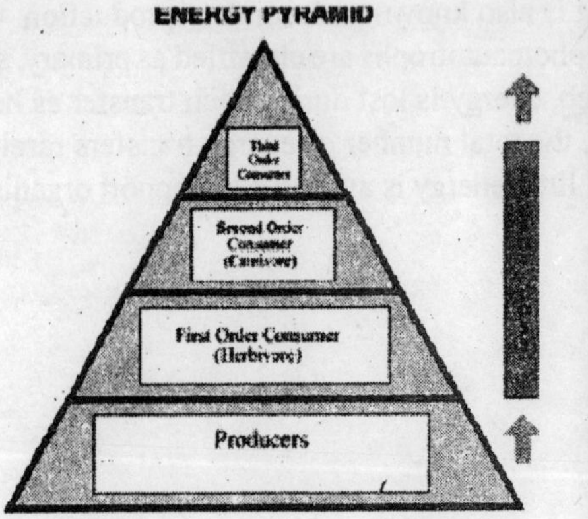

Fig. 7.6

Fig. 7.7

Showing the pyramides of energy

REVIEW QUESTIONS

SHORT ANSWER

1. Give the Name the major natural energy resources.
2. Give examples of (a) renewable and (b) non renewable energy resources;
3. What is the significance of forest resources?
4. State the function of decomposers in an ecosystem.
5. What is biomagnification?
6. What is ecosystem?
7. What is a Biome?
8. What is Green belt?
9. What is Biofertilizer?

SHORT NOTES, WRITE NOTES ON THE FOLLOWING:

1. Nitrogen cycle
2. Carbon cycle
3. Phosphate cycle
4. Sulphur cycle
5. Hydrologic cycle
6. Biogas
7. Hydroelectricity
8. Ozone layer depletion
9. Geothermal energy
10. Hydrogen fuel

DIFFERENTIATE BETWEEN THE

1. Renewable and Nonrenewable energy sources
2. Food chain and food web
3. Environment and Ecology
4. Nuclear Energy and Atombomb

LONG ANSWER

1. What are the sources of water? Name also the sources of freshwater. Express their quantities in term of percentage of water resources.
2. The important energy. Mention their impartance also.
3. Give an account of environmental factors for the balanced ecosystem. How can imbancing of the ecosystem it be prevented?

4. What arc major minerals for nuclear energy.
5. How do you classify energy sources? Name some energy sources
6. Name conventional non confrontational sources of energy compare their effects on environment.
7. What are the products of combustion of coal? Discuss their damaging effect on environment?
8. Solar energy is the energy for future in I ad in." Elucidate.
9. Comment on: "Wood is a major renewable energy resource - it offers multiple benefits to man, but it is vanislung fast."

Put a tick mark (against the correct answer/answers iii the boxes given). This feedback exercise will help the student to test their understanding of the subject matter and will sustain their interest in environmental science.

1. Environment means
   a. A beautiful landscape
   b. Industrial production the atmosphere
   c. Sum total of conditions that affect the life and development of all organisms on earth
2. environmental studies involve studies of
   a. Evolution of life
   b. All aspects of human enviroinment the atmosphere
   c. Nitrogen cycle
   d. the agriculture
3. The killer Bhopal Disaster was
   a. Methyl isocynate carboy
   b. Accidental fire in the factorythe atmosphere
4. The quality of environment has steadily suffered due to
   a. Man-made activities
   b. Air, water, soil and food pollution
   c. Public awareness
   d. the atmosphere
5. Environmental degradation has been due to
   a. Poverty of the developing countries
   b. Poor quality of life
   c. The atmosphere
   d. Over-consumption of earth's resources by the developed countries
6. The earth was born
   a. 6.0 billion years ago 10,000 years ago
   b. 9.5 billion years ago
   c. 4.5 billion years ago
   d. the atmosphere

7. The first living form (blue-green algae) appeared on earth
   a. 3.5 billion years ago
   b. 6.0 billion years ago
   c. 5.0 billion years ago
   d. the atmosphere
8. Soil has an important role as it
   a. gives us space for building houses
   b. produces food for us and animals
   c. provides highways for traffic
   d. the atmosphere
9. Soil, suitable for agriculture, consists of
   a. micro-organisms only 5 %
   b. organic and 95 % inorganic matter
   c. rock powder and water
   d. the atmosphere
10. Biosphere means
    a. the earth's crust only
    b. all living species in the earth's crust, air and water
    c. micro-organisms only
    d. the atmosphere
11. The earth swings back and forth between hot and cold periods
    a. with the rise and fall of carbon dioxide concentration
    b. with increased deforestation
    c. with change in ocean currents
    d. the atmosphere
12. Our supply and reserves of freshwater
    a. from hydrological cycle
    b. from carbon cycle
    c. from snowf
    d. all the atmosphere

Unit-II

Chapater 8

Environment and its Segments

8.1 INTRODUCTION TO ENVIRONMENT

Environment is defined as the surroundings in which the organism lives. The environment may be the physical environment, the chemical environment or the biological environment. The environment has three components abiotic, biotic and energy. The abiotic environment includes the air (atmosphere), water (hydrosphere) and land (lithosphere). The biotic components of environment includes the plants, animals and the microbes.

Fig. 8.1 Showing the environment with various energy and non living things

Organisms are dependent on the environment to fulfil their needs. Man is also constantly interacting with the environment in order to fulfil his needs. These needs include the basic needs of, food mate and shelter in addition to the social needs like entertainment, medicines, etc. The things that man requires for his survival and comfort are called the resources. The environment is a reservoir of resources. Maintaining the resources of the environment and their careful use is called conservation. The conservation of environment also involves the conservation of the natural resources.

A healthy environment is an absolute necessity for the well-being of all organisms. All our needs, are being met by the environment. However, man having reached the pinnacle of evolution is trying to bring about changes in the environment to suit his convenience. Unfortunately, this convenience is temporary. In the long run, man is losing out on a healthy environment.

8.2 Components of Environment

Atmosphere: The **atmosphere of Earth** is a mixture of gases surrounding the planet Earth. Atmosphere is retained by Earth's gravity. The atmosphere protects life on Earth by absorbing ultraviolet solar radiation, warming the surface through heat retention (greenhouse effect), and reducing temperature extremes between day and night. Dry air contains about 78% nitrogen, 21% oxygen, 0.93% argon, 0.038% carbon dioxide, with very small amounts of other gases. Air also contains a variable amount of water vapor, on average around 1% by volume.

The atmosphere has a mass of about five quintillion (5×10^{18}) kg, three quarters of which is within about 11 km (6.8 mi; 36,000 ft) of the surface. The atmosphere becomes lets dense with increasing altitude, with no definite boundary between the atmosphere and outer space. An altitude of 120 km (75 mi) is where atmospheric effects become noticeable during atmospheric reentry of spacecraft. The Kármán line, at 100 km (62 mi), also is often regarded as the boundary between atmosphere and outer space.

STRUCTURE OF THE ATMOSPHERE

Earth's atmosphere can be divided into five main layers. These layers are mainly determined by whether temperature increases or decrease with altitude. From highest to lowest, these layers are:

Exosphere: The outermost layer of Earth's atmosphere extends towards upward. The particles in this zone are so far apart that they can travel hundreds of km without colliding with one another. Since the particles rarely collide, the atmosphere no longer behaves like a fluid. These free-moving particles follow ballistic trajectories and may migrate into and out of the magnetosphere. The exosphere is mainly composed of hydrogen and helium.

Thermosphere: Temperature increases with height in the thermosphere. It extends from the mesopause up to the thermopause. The temperature of this layer can raise to 1,500°C (2,730°F), though the gas molecules are so far apart that temperature in the usual sense is not well defined. The International Space Station orbits have been established in this layer, between 320 and 380 km (200 and 240 mi). The top of the thermosphere is the bottom of the exosphere, called the exobase. Its height varies with solar activity and ranges from about 350–800 km (220–500 mi; 1,100,000–2,600,000 ft).

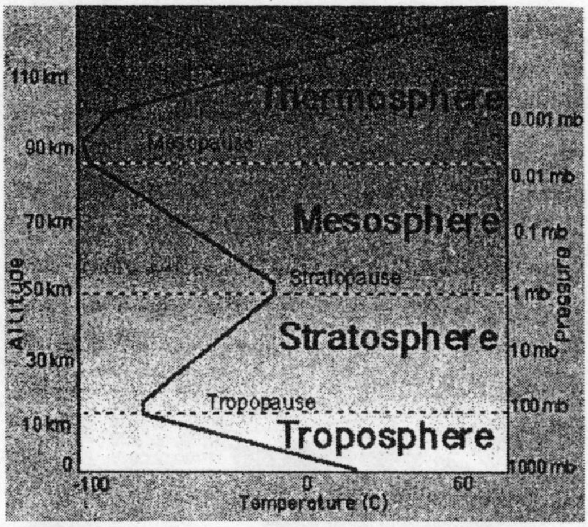

Fig. 8.2

Mesosphere: The mesosphere extends from the stratopause to 80–85 km (50–53 mi; 260,000–280,000 ft). It is the zoen where most meteors burn up comming from space. Temperature decreases with height in the mesosphere. The mesopause boundry is the layer with the minimum temperature that marks the top of the mesosphere, is the coldest place on Earth and has an average temperature around-100°C (–148.0°F; 173.1 K).

Stratosphere: The stratosphere extends from tropopause to about 51 km 32 mi; 170,000 ft. Temperature increases with height, which restricts turbulence and mixing. The stratopause, which is the boundary between the stratosphere and mesosphere, typically is at the hight of 50 to 55 km (31 to 34 mi; 160,000 to 180,000 ft). The pressure here is 1/1000th sea level.

Troposphere: The troposphere begins at the surface and extends up to 7 km (23,000 ft) at the poles and 17 km (56,000 ft) at the equator, with variation due to weather. The troposphere is mostly heated by transfer of energy from the surface, so on average the lowest part of the troposphere is warmest and temperature decreases with altitude. It promotes vertical mixing hence the origin of its name in the Greek word is, *trope*, meaning turn or overturn. The troposphere contains roughly 80% of the mass of the atmosphere. The tropopause is the boundary between the troposphere and stratosphere.

8.2.2 Hydrosphere

A **hydrosphere** (from Greek - *hydor*, "water" and *sphaira*, "sphere") in physical geography describes the combined mass of water found beneath and over the surface of the planet. The total mass of the Earth's hydrosphere is about 1.4×10^{18} tonnes, which is about 0.023% of the Earth's total mass. About 20×10^{12} tonnes of this is in the Earth's atmosphere (the volume of one tonne of water is approximately 1 cubic metre). Approximately 71% of the Earth's surface means an area of about 361 million square kilometres (139.5 million square miles), is covered by ocean.

One more Hydrosphere

A thick hydrosphere is thought to exist around the Jovian moon Europa. Outer layer of this hydrosphere is almost entirely ice, but current models predict that the cause of tidal flexing of the moon in its orbit around Jupiter. The volume of Europa's hydrosphere is, 2.3 times that of Earth. It has been suggested may also possess sub-surface oceans. However, the ice **covering is expected to be thicker on Jupiter's.**

8.2.3 Lithosphere

The **lithosphere** Originates from the Greek litheem for "rocky" and ["sphaira"] for "sphere") is the rigid meons outermost shell of a rocky planet. It comprises the crust and the portion of the upper mantle that behaves elastically on time scales of thousands of years or greater.

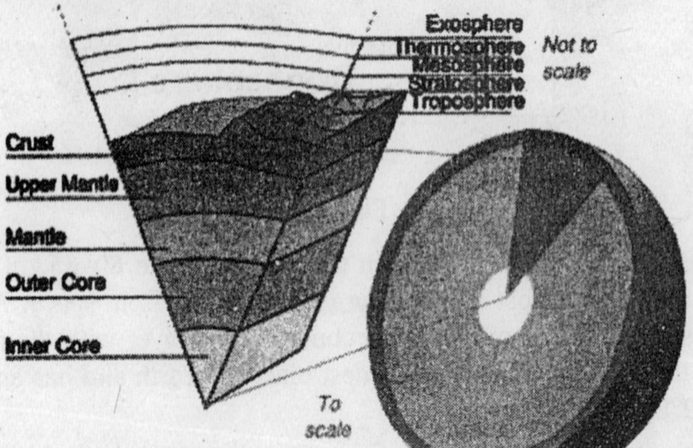

Fig. 8.3: Showing various zones Earth cut away from core to Exosphere

The lithosphere includes the crust and the uppermost mantle, which constitute the hard and rigid outer layer of the Earth. The lithosphere is underlain by the asthenosphere, the weaker, hotter, and deeper part of the upper mantle. The boundary between the lithosphere and the underlying asthenosphere is defined by a difference in response to stress. The lithosphere remains rigid for very long periods of geologic time in which it deforms elastically and through brittle failure. The asthenosphere deforms viscously and accommodates strain through plastic deformation. The lithosphere is broken into tectonic plates.

The concept of the lithosphere as Earth's strong outer layer was developed by Barrell, who wrote a series of papers introducing the concept. The concept was based on the presence of significant gravity anomalies over continental crust. He inferred that there must exist a strong upper layer (which he called the lithosphere) above a weaker layer which could flow (which he called the asthenosphere). These ideas were expanded by Daly (1940), and have been broadly accepted by geologists and geophysicists. Although these ideas about lithosphere and asthenosphere were developed long before plate tectonic theory was articulated in the 1960s. The concepts that strong lithosphere exists and that this rests on weak asthenosphere are essential to that theory. The lithosphere provides a conductive lid atop the convecting mantle; as such, it affects heat transport through the Earth.

There are two types of lithosphere:

- Oceanic lithosphere, which is associated with Oceanic crust and exists in the ocean basins
- Continental lithosphere, which is associated with Continental crust.

8.4 SOME INCIDENCE IN ENVIRONMENT AND IT'S COMPONENTS

8.4.1 Global Warming

The addition of certain pollutants like the carbon dioxide gases increases the temperature of the earth. These gases remain close to the surface of earth, forming an insulating layer. The surface becomes hot due to the solar radiations. This radiation is normally reflected back into the space. However, due to the presence of the insulating layer the heat remains within the earth's atmosphere and increases its temperature. This phenomenon is called global warming. the reduction in the forest cover also contributes to the heating of earth.

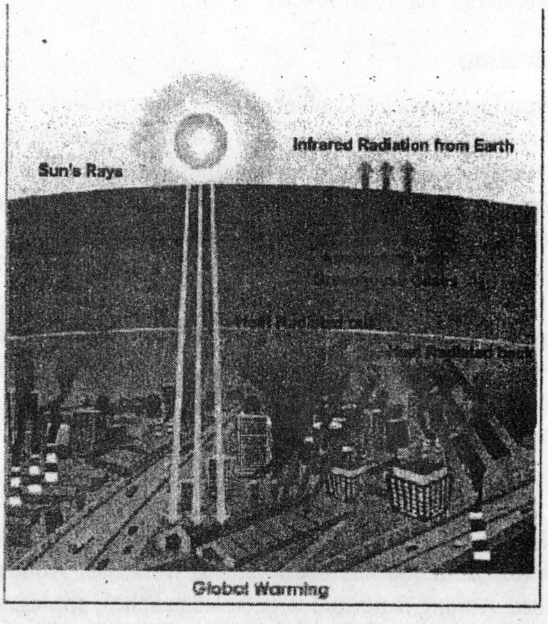

Fig. 8.4: Showing the mechanism of Global Warming

Global warming results in the melting of polar ice caps. This inturn results in the rise in the level of ocean waters. It is also called as the inhanced greenhouse effect. Greenhouses are the covered areas where the temperature is artificially kept higher than the surrounding cold environment for the growth of plats.

8.4.2 OZONE DEPLETION

Ozone (O_3) is a molecule formed by three atoms of oxygen while oxygen (O_2), is essential for all aerobic forms of life. Ozone is a deadly poison. It is an allotrop of oxygen however, at the higher levels of the atmosphere, ozone performs an essential function. It shields the surface of the earth from ultraviolet (UV) radiation FROM the Sun. UV radiation causes skin cancer, damage to eyes, and affect immune system also. It can also affect global rainfall and may cause ecological disturbances.

$$O_2 \underrightarrow{UV} O + O$$

$$O + O_2 \rightarrow \underset{\text{ozone}}{O_3}$$

Ozone at the higher levels of the atmosphere is a product of UV radiation acting on oxygen (O_2) molecule. The higher energy UV radiations split apart some molecular oxygen (O_2) into free oxygen O) atoms. These atoms at combine with the molecular oxygen to form ozone as shown in the equations.

The decline of ozone content in the atmosphere began in the 1980s. This decrease has been linked to synthetic chemicals LIKE chlorofluorocarbons (CFCs) which are used AS refrigerants and in fire extinguishers. in 1987, the United Nations Environment Programme (UNEP) succeeded in forging an agreement to freeze CFC production AT 1986 levels.

8.4.3 Biological Magnification

Extensive usage of several pesticides and other chemicals to protect our crops from diseases and pests has resulted their entry into food chains the entry of these harmful chemicals into bodies. of organisms creat several problems through the food chain these chemicals are washed down either into soil or into the water bodies. From the soil, these are absorbed by the plants along with water and minerals, and from the water bodies these are taken up by aquatic plants and animals. This is one of the ways in which they enter the food chain. As these chemicals are not degradable, they get accumulated progressively at each trophic level. As human beings occupy the top level in food chain, the maximum concentration of these chemicals gets accumulated in bodies. This phenomenon is known as **biological magnification**. This is the reason as food grains such as wheat and rice, vegetables and fruits, and even meat, contain varying amounts of pesticide residues. They cannot always be removed by washing or other means.

8.4.4 Problems in Food Chain

Persisten Organic Pollutants [POP] or Pesticidess enter desenter our food chain through various methods. DDT, a very harmful pesticide has been banned from use. Almost all ready made foods contain two or more pesticides. Among fruits and vegetables peaches, apples, spinach and lettuce have the highest amount of pesticide content. Onions have the least followed by papaya. Dieldrin and DDE are the most commonly used pesticides. DDE is a break down product of DDT. Dieldrin is an organochlorine pesticide. Use of organically grown food items is one way of reducing pesticide intake.

8.4.5 Wastes

Accumulation of wastes due to its improper disposal is a major problem in our country. Population in India has been growing at a rapid rate. With this increase, there has also been an increase in the amount of wastes being produced especially in the cities. Every person, on an average generates about 400 to 500 grams of wastes per day. At this rate, in a city of about 10 lakh people around 500 tonnes of wastes is being produced every day.

8.5 PROTECTING THE ENVIRONMENT

Protecting the natural environment is paramount especially when travelling. Check out how you can conserve local eco-systems: Always try and use local energy and water as efficiently as possible in line with local practices. You may come from a city blessed with heavy annual rainfall, but the odds are the village youre staying in.

Fig. 8.5

- Dont leave taps running or use water intensive practices such as hand washing only a few or single items of clothing at a time in countries where water is sparse.
- Check that any soaps or detergents you use are biodegradable, always washing dishes and utensils away from streams and lakes.
- Never litter. Find a bin or recycle it. Find out how to recycle waste most efficiently from your hotel or hostel. Try not to bring any superfluous containers or packaging that you do not intend to take back home.
- Never put rubbish bags down beside a garbage bag or pile of rubbish sacks as wild animals are more likely to tear them open and disperse the rubbish, bottles and cans can seriously injure animals and plastic bags suffocate animals when consumed.
- Travellers should be aware that not all countries employ the same levels of animal welfare protection. so be discerning when visiting zoos and marine parks abroad.
- Animals are not to amuse us, so do not support this trend by visiting circus, festivals and carnivals where performing animals are used.
- In natural areas, be aware that your movements are affecting your surroundings. Move cautiously, do not take any natural keepsakes and always stay to marked footpaths.

8.5.1 Rainwater Harvesting

Rain water harvesting (RWH) is the accumulating and storing, of rainwater. Rainwater harvesting has been used to provide drinking water, water for livestock, water for irrigation and to refill aquifers in a process called ground water recharge. Rainwater collected from the roofs of houses, local institutions, and from specially prepared areas of ground, can make an important contribution to water con servation. In some cases, rainwater may be the only available, or economical, water source. Rainwater systems are simple to construct from inexpensive local materials, and are potentially successful in most habitable locations.

Fig. 8.6: Rainwater harvesting a single can contribute

Roof rainwater can be of good quality and may not require treatment before consumption. However, some rooftop materials may produce rainwater that is harmful to human health. Household rainfall catchments systems are appropriate in areas with an average rainfall greater than 200 mm per year, and no other accessible water sources. There are a number of types of systems to harvest rainwater ranging from simple to complex industrial systems. Generally, rainwater is harvested either from the ground or from a roof. The rate at which water can be collected from either system is dependent on the plan area of the system, its efficiency, and the intensity of rainfall.

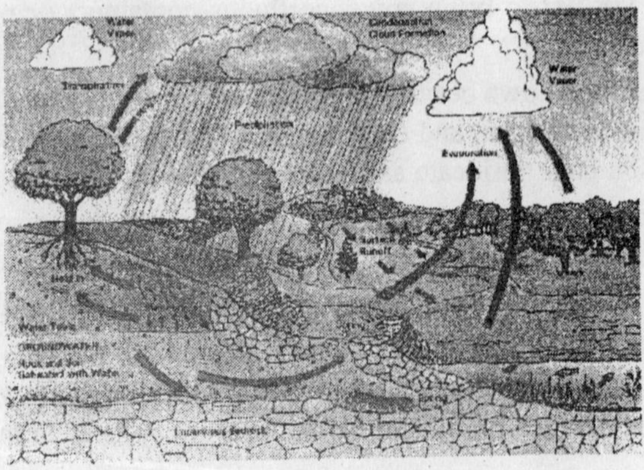

Fig. 8.7: Showing the hydrological cycle

8.5.2 Ground Catchments Systems

Ground catchments systems channel water from a prepared catchment area into storage. Generally, they are only considered in areas where rainwater is very scarce and other sources of water are not available. They are more suited to small communities than individual families. If properly designed, ground catchments can collect large quantities of rainwater.

8.5.3 Roof Catchments Systems

Roof catchments systems channel rainwater that falls onto a roof into storage via a system of gutters and pipes. The first flush of rainwater after a dry season should be allowed to run to waste as it will be contaminated with dust, bird droppings etc. Roof gutters should have sufficient incline to avoid standing water. They must be strong enough, and large enough to carry peak flows. Storage tanks must be covered to prevent mosquito breeding and to reduce evaporation losses, contamination and algal growth. Rainwater harvesting systems require regular maintenance and cleaning to keep the system hygienic and in good working order.

CATCHMENT SURFACE

Fig. 8.8: Showing Ground cat chment

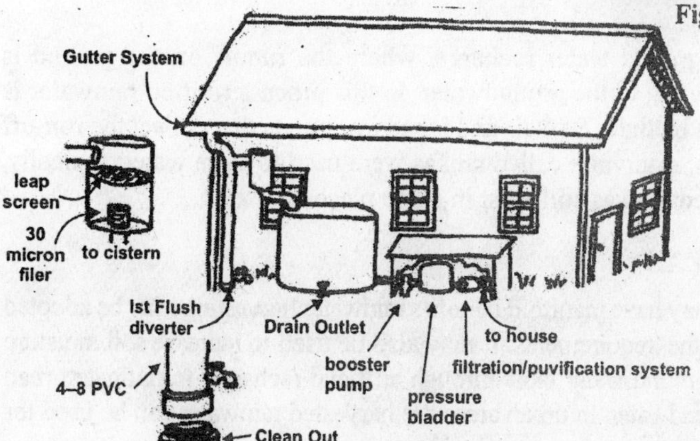

Fig. 8.9: Showing the Roof Cat chment system

8.5.4 Subsurface Dyke

A subsurface dyke is built in an aquifer to obstruct the natural flow of groundwater, thereby raising the groundwater level with increasing the amount of water stored in the aquifer. The subsurface dyke at Krishi Vigyan Kendra, Kannur under Kerala Agricultural University with the support of ICAR, has become an effective method for ground water conservation by means of rain water harvesting technologies. The sub-surface dyke has demonstrated that it is a feasible method for conserving and exploiting the groundwater resources specially in caseds Kerala state. The dyke is now the largest rainwater harvesting system in that region.

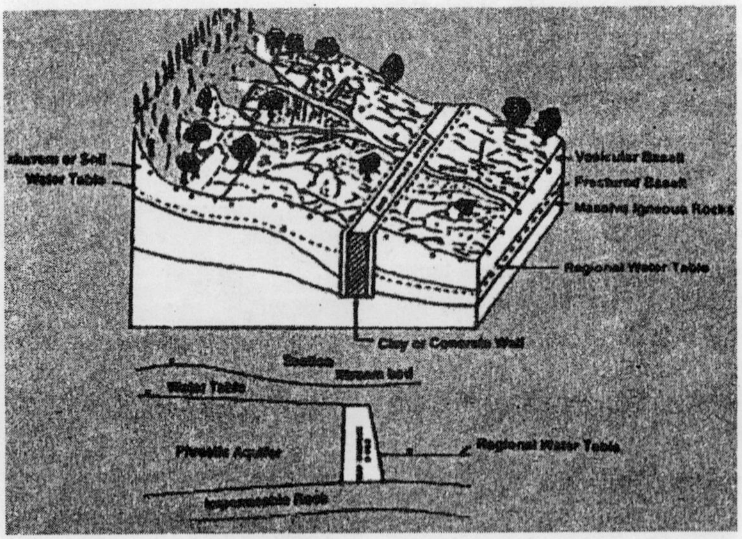

Fig. 8.10: Subsurface Dyke

8.5.5 Ground water Recharge

Rain water may also be used for ground water recharge, where the runoff on the ground is collected and allowed to be absorbed, adding to the groundwater. In this process rooftop rainwater is collected and stored in sump. In India this includes Bawdis and johads, or ponds that collect the run-off from small streams in wide area. In India, reservoirs called tankas were used to store water; typically, they were shallow with mud walls. Ancient tankas still exist in some places.

8.6 ADVANTAGES IN URBAN AREAS

Rainwater harvesting in urban areas may have manifold benefits rainwater harvesting may be adopted in cities to provide supplemental water for the requirements. It may also be used to increase soil moisture levels for urban greenery, to increase the ground water table through artificial recharge, to mitigate urban flooding and to improve the quality of groundwater. In urban areas the harvested rainwater can be used for flushing, toilets washing laundry.

Indeed, in hard water areas it is superior to mains water for this. It can also be used for showering or bathing. It may require treatment prior to use for drinking purposes. In New Zealand, many houses away from the larger towns and cities routinely rely on rainwater collected from roofs as the only source of water for all household activities. This is almost inevitably the case for many holiday homes.

Fig. 8.11: Mechanism of ground water

Quality of Rain Water

As rainwater may be contaminated, it is often not considered suitable for drinking without treatment. However, there are many examples of rainwater being used for all purposes including drinking. Rainwater harvested from roofs can contain animal and bird faeces, mosses and lichens and dust. It may also contain particulates from urban pollution, pesticides, and inorganic ions from the sea (Ca, Mg, Na, K, Cl, SO_4), and dissolved gases (CO_2, NO_x, SO_x). High levels of pesticide have been found in rainwater in with the highest concentrations in the first rain the concentration of these and other contaminants are reduced significantly by diverting the initial flow of water to waste as described above. The water may need to be analyzed properly, and used in a way appropriate to its safety for example, harvested rainwater is boiled in parabolic solar cookers before being used for drinking is many areas. In Brazil alum and chlorine is added to disinfect water before consumption. So-called "appropriate technology" methods, such as solar water disinfection, provide low-cost disinfection options for treatment of stored rainwater for drinking.

8.7 SIZE OF THE SYSTEM

It is important that the system is sized to meet the water demand throughout the dry season. The size of the storage tank should be big enough to meet the daily water requirement throughout the dry season. In addition, the size of the catchments area or roof should be large enough to fill the tank.

8.7.1 Use of the Technology Around the World

Currently in China and various other countries, rooftop rainwater harvesting is being practiced for providing, water for livestock, water for small irrigation and a way to replenish ground water levels. Gansu province inh China and semi-arid north east Brazil have the largest rooftop rainwater harvesting projects ongoing. In Rajasthan, India rainwater harvesting has traditionally been practiced by the people of the Thar Desert. In Bermuda, the law requires all new construction to include rainwater harvesting adequate for the residents.

The U.S. Virgin Islands have a similar law.

In the Indus Valley Civilization, Elephanta Caves and Kanheri Caves in Mumbai rainwater harvesting alone has been used to supply in their water requirements.

In the United Kingdom, water butts are oft-found in domestic gardens to collect rainwater that is then used to water the garden. In the Ayerwaddy Delta of Myanmar, the groundwater is saline and communities rely on mud lined rainwater ponds to meet their drinking water needs throughout the dry season. Some of these ponds are centuries old and are treated with great reverence and respect.

Until 2009 in Colorado, water rights laws restricted rainwater harvesting; a property owner who captured rainwater was deemed to be stealing it from those who have rights to take water from the watershed.

8.8 ENVIRONMENTAL MANAGEMENT SYSTEM

Environmental Management System (EMS) refers to the management of an organization's environmental programs in a comprehensive, systematic, planned and documented manner. It includes the organizational structure, planning and resources for developing, implementing and maintaining policy for environmental protection.

Serves as a tool to improve environmental performance. Provides a systematic way of managing an organization's environmental affairs.

EMS is the aspect of the organization's overall management structure that addresses immediate and long-term impacts of its products, services and processes on the environment gives order and consistency for organizations to address environmental concerns through the allocation of resources, assignment of responsibility and ongoing evaluation of practices.

8.9 FOCUSES ON CONTINUAL IMPROVEMENT OF THE SYSTEM

8.9.1 The EMS Model

An EMS follows a Plan-Do-Check-Act Cycle, or PDCA. It shows the process of first developing an environmental policy, planning the EMS, and then implementing it. The process also includes checking the system and acting on it. The model is continuous because an EMS is a process of continual improvement in which an organization is constantly reviewing and revising the system. This model can be used by a wide range of organizations from manufacturing facilities to service industries including government agencies.

Policy Statement is a statement of the organization's commitment to the environment. Identification of Significant Environmental Impacts on environmental attributes of products, activities, services, and their effects on the environment. It includes.

1. Development of Objectives and Targets environmental goals for the organization
2. Implementation plans to meet objectives and targets
3. Training instruction to ensure employees are aware and capable of fulfilling their environmental responsibilities

8.11.2 Management Review

Existing environmental management activities be integrated into the EMS.

An EMS is flexible and does not require organizations to necessarily "retool" their existing activities. An EMS establishes a management framework by which an organization's impacts on the environment can be systematically identified and reduced. For example, many organizations, including counties and municipalities, have active and effective pollution prevention activities underway. These could be incorporated into the overall EMS.

EMS can be used to assist with maintaining compliance. As an example, the Massachusetts DEP has opted to assist with the use of EMS in compliance cases. The EPA also produces Guidance on the Use of EMS in Enforcement.

ISO, ISO 14000, and ISO 14001.

ISO stands for the International Organization for Standardization, located in Geneva, Switzerland. ISO is a non-governmental organization established in 1947. The organization mainly functions to develop voluntary technical standards that aim at making the development, manufacture and supply of goods and services more efficient, safe and clean.

ISO 14000 refers to a family of voluntary standards and guidance documents to help organizations environmental issues in the family the standards for Environmental Management Systems, environmental and EMS auditing, environmental labeling, performance evaluation and life-cycle assessment are included.

In September 1996, the International Organization for Standardization published the first edition of ISO 14001, the Environmental Management Systems standard. This is an international voluntary standard describing specific requirements for an EMS. ISO 14001 is a specification standard to which an organization may receive certification or registration. ISO 14001 is considered the foundation document of the entire series. A second edition of ISO 14001 was published in 2004, updating the standard.

The U.S. body that provides input into the standard's development is the U.S. TAG (Technical Advisory Group) to TC 207 (Technical Committee). This same body has established a formal process to respond to questions that may arise regarding clarification of the ISO 14001. Responses will reflect the interpretation of the Standard as intended during the drafting of the Standard and may be found in the "Clarification of Intent of ISO 14001.

8.9.3 Standards Developed

All the ISO standards are developed through a voluntary, consensus-based approach. ISO has different member countries across the globe. Each member country develops its position on the standards and these positions are then negotiated with other member countries. Draft versions of the standards are sent out for formal written comment and each country casts its official vote on the drafts at the appropriate stage of the process. Within each country, various types of organizations can and do participate in the process. These organizations include industry, government (federal and state), and other interested parties, like various non-government organizations. For example, EPA and states participated in the development of the ISO 14001 standard and are now evaluating its usefulness through a variety of pilot projects.

The 17 requirements of the ISO 14001:2004 standard.

Environmental Policy: Develop a statement of the organization's commitment to the environment.

Environmental Aspects and Impacts: Identify environmental attributes of products, activities and services and their effects on the environment.

Legal and Other Requirements: Identify and ensure access to relevant laws and regulations.

Objectives and Targets and Environmental Management Program: Set environmental goals for the organization and plan actions to achieve objectives and targets.

Structure and Responsibility: Establish roles and responsibilities within the organization.

Training, Awareness and Competence: Ensure that employees are aware and capable of their environmental responsibilities.

Communication: Develop processes for internal and external communication on environmental management issues.

EMS Documentation: Maintain information about the EMS and related documents.

Document Control: Ensure effective management of procedures and other documents.

Operational Control: Identify, plan and manage the organization's operations and activities in line with the policy, objectives and targets, and significant aspects

Emergency Preparedness and Response: Develop procedures for preventing and responding to potential emergencies.

Monitoring and Measuring: Monitor key activities and track performance including periodic compliance evaluation.

Evaluation of Compliance: Develop procedure to periodically evaluate compliance with legal and other requirements.

Nonconformance and Corrective and Preventive Action: Identify and correct problems and prevent recurrences.

Records: Keep adequate records of EMS performance.

EMS Audit: Periodically verify that the EMS is effective and achieving objectives and targets.

Management Review: Review the EMS.

8.9.4 Legislation and Standards

The Environmental Liability Directive [ELD] 2004/35/EC is one of the most important instruments that your business will need to comply EMS. It came into force across Europe during 2009 and for example it became law on the 1st March 2009 converting the various national Pollution Prevention Guidelines (PPGs) such as the UK PPG11, PPG18 and PPG21 into requirements. Failure to comply can result in fines and more significantly reformation reinstatement costs which can run into many millions of Euro or Dollars. In this Directive there is a requirement to mitigate the effects of events such as spills and firewater. The Directive makes it clear that it is the site owner's responsibility to contain spills and firewater on site using some form of containment apparatus such as sealing the drains.

Within the European Union (EU) legislation was introduced to encourage businesses to voluntarily adopt ISO 14000. Regulation (EC) No 761/2001 of the European Parliament and of the Council of 19 March 2001, allowed voluntary participation by organizations in a Community eco-management and audit scheme Eco-Management and Audit Scheme (EMAS).

The implementation of a robust EMS, which may incorporate ISO 14001, should lead to improve environmental performance, including better and more consistent legal compliance. The ISO 14000 standards reflect different aspects of environmental management. The following list outlines the broad coverage of each:

Environmental Management Systems: 14001-2004, 14002, 14004

Environmental Auditing: 19011

Environmental Labeling: 14020, 14021, 14022, 14023, 14024, 14025

Life Cycle Assessment: 14040, 14041, 14042, 14043

Chapter 9

Atmosphere, Constituents and Structure

9.1 SUSTAINABILITY

Sustainability is the capacity to endure. In ecology, the word sustainability describes about the biological systems diverse being them and productive over time. For humans it is the potential for long-term maintenance of wellbeing, which in turn depends on the wellbeing of the natural world and the responsible use of natural resources. Achieving sustainability will enable the Earth to continue supporting human life sustainability has become a wide-ranging term that can be applied to almost every facet of life on Earth. Long-lived and healthy wetlands and forests are examples of sustainable biological systems. Invisible chemical cycles redistribute water, oxygen, nitrogen and carbon through the world's living and non-living systems, wet lands and forests have sustained life for millions of years. As the earth's human population has increased, natural ecosystems have declined and changes in the balance of natural cycles. It creats a negative impact on both humans and other living systems..

According to the Earth Policy Institute, there is abundant scientific evidence that humanity is living unsustainably. Human use of natural resources to within sustainable limits will require a major collective effort. Methods of living more sustainably can take many forms from reorganizing living conditions (*e.g.*, ecovillages, eco-municipalities and sustainable cities), reappraising economic sectors (perm culture, green building, sustainable agriculture), or work practices (sustainable architecture), using science to develop new technologies (green technologies, renewable energy), to adjustments in individual lifestyles that conserve natural resources.

9.2 DEFINITION AND MEANING OF SUSTAINBILITY

A representation of sustainability showing how both economy and society are constrained by environmental limits. Definitions of sustainability often refer to the "three pillars" of social, environmental and economic sustainability. The word sustainability is derived from the Latin *sustainer* (*tenere*, to hold; *sus*, up). Dictionaries provide more than ten meanings for *sustain*, the main ones being to "maintain", "support", or "endure". Since the 1980s *sustainability* has been used more in the sense of human sustainability on plane.. Earth and this has resulted in the most widely quoted definition of sustainability and sustainable development. As per the Brundtland Commission of the United Nations on March 20, 1987: "sustainable development is development that meets the needs of the present without compromising the ability of future generations to meet their own needs." At the 2005 World Summit it was noted that this requires the reconciliation of environmental, social and economic demands. This view has been expressed as an illustration using three overlapping ellipses indicating that the three pillars of sustainability are not mutually exclusive and can be mutually reinforcing.

For many environmentalists the idea of sustainable development is an oxymoron as development seems to entail environmental degradation. Ecological economist Herman Daly has asked, "what use is a sawmill without a forest?" From this perspective, the economy is a subsystem of human society, which is itself a subsystem of the biosphere and a gain in one sector is a loss from another. This can be illustrated as three concentric circles.

A universally-accepted definition of sustainability is elusive because it is expected to achieve many things. It needs to be factual and scientific, a clear statement of a specific "destination". The simple definition "sustainability is improving the quality of human life while living within the carrying capacity of supporting eco-systems", though vague, conveys the idea of sustainability having quantifiable limits. However, sustainability is also a call to action, a task in progress or "journey" and therefore a political process, so some definitions set out common goals and values. The Earth Charter speaks of "a sustainable global society founded on respect for nature, universal human rights, economic justice, and a culture of peace."

To add complication the word *sustainability* is applied not only to human sustainability on Earth, but to many situations and contexts over many scales of space and time, from small local ones to the global balance of production and consumption. It can also refer to a future intention: "sustainable agriculture" is not necessarily a current situation but a goal for the future, a prediction. For all these reasons sustainability is perceived, at one extreme, as nothing more than a feel-good buzzword with little meaning or substance but, at the other, as an important but unfocused concept like "liberty" or "justice". It has also been described as a "dialogue of values that defies consensual definition".

Sustainability, science and environmental science form the basis for much of the philosophical and analytic framework of sustainability. Quantitative data is collected through sustainability measurement and this data is then used in governance for sustainability.

9.3 SCALE AND CONTEXT

Sustainability is studied and managed over many scales (levels or frames of reference) of time and space and in many contexts of environmental, social and economic organization. The focus ranges from the total carrying capacity (sustainability) of planet Earth to the sustainability of economic sectors, ecosystems, countries, municipalities, neighborhoods, home gardens, individual lives, individual goods, services, lifestyles, and so on. In short, it can entail the full compass of biological and human activity or any part of it. As Daniel Bodkin author and environmentalist, has stated: "We see a landscape that is always in flux, changing over many scales of time and space."

9.4 CONSUMPTION POPULATION, TECHNOLOGY, RESOURCES

The overall driver of human impact on Earth systems is the consumption of biophysical resources. Human consumption can be divided into three key components: population numbers, levels of consumption (affluence), and impact per unit of resource use impact per unit of resource use depends on the technology used. It has been expressed through an equation:

$$I = P \times A \times T$$

Where: I = Environmental impact, P = Population, A = Affluence, T = Technology

Historically, humanity has responded to a demand for more resources by trying to increase supply. As supplies inevitably become depleted sustainable practices are encouraged through demand management for all goods and services by promoting reduced consumption, using renewable resources where possible, and encouraging practices that minimize resource intensity while maximizing resource productivity. Careful resource management can be applied at many scales, from economic sectors like agriculture, manufacturing and industry, to work organizations, the consumption patterns of households and individuals are directly related to the resource demands of individual goods and services.

9.5 ENVIRONMENTAL DIMENSION

Atmosphere: In March 2009 at a meeting of the Copenhagen Climate Council 2,500 climate experts from 80 countries issued a keynote statement that there is now "no excuse" for failing to act on global warming. It is also stated that without strong carbon reduction targets "abrupt or irreversible" shifts in climate may occur that "will be very difficult for contemporary societies to cope with". Management of the global atmosphere now involves assessment of all aspects of the carbon cycle to identify opportunities to address human-induced climate change and this has become a major focus of scientific research because of the potential catastrophic effects on biodiversity and human communities.

9.6 OCEANS

A selection of the world's saltwater fish: Ocean circulation patterns have a strong influence on climate and weather and, in turn, the food supply of both humans and other organisms. Scientists have warned of the possibility, under the influence of climate change, of a sudden alteration in circulation patterns of ocean currents that could drastically alter the climate in some regions of the globe. Major human environmental impacts occur in the more habitable regions of the ocean fringes – the estuaries, coastline and bays. Ten per cent of the world's population – about 600 million people – lives in low-lying areas vulnerable to sea level rise.

Water covers 71% of the Earth's surface. Of this, 97.5% is the salty water of the oceans and only 2.5% freshwater, most of which is locked up in the Antarctic ice sheet. The remaining freshwater is found in lakes, rivers, wetlands, the soil, aquifers and atmosphere. All life depends on the solar-powered global water cycle, the evaporation from oceans and land to form water vapor that later condenses from clouds as rain, which then becomes the renewable part of the freshwater supply. Awareness of the global importance of preserving water for ecosystem services has only recently emerged as, during the 20th century, more than half the world's wetlands have been lost along with their valuable environmental services. Biodiversity-rich freshwater ecosystems are currently declining faster than marine or land ecosystems making them the world's most vulnerable habitats.

9.7 LAND

Loss of biodiversity stems largely from the habitat loss and fragmentation produced by the human appropriation of land for development, forestry and agriculture as natural capital is progressively converted to man-made capital. Land use change is fundamental to the operations of the biosphere because alterations in the relative proportions of land dedicated to urbanization, agriculture, forest, woodland, grassland and pasture have a marked effect on the global water, carbon and nitrogen biogeochemical cycles and this can impact negatively on both natural and human systems.[At the local human scale, major sustainability benefits accrue from the pursuit of green cities and sustainable parks and gardens.

9.8 FORESTS

Since the Neolithic Revolution, about 47% of the world's forests have been lost to human use. Present-day forests occupy about a quarter of the world's ice-free land with about half of these occurring in the tropics[In temperate and boreal regions forest area is gradually increasing (with the exception of Siberia), but deforestation in the tropics is of major concern.

Beech Forest – Grib Pskov, Denmark

Forests moderate the local climate and the global water cycle through their light reflectance (albedo) and evapo transpiration. They also conserve biodiversity, protect water quality, preserve soil and soil quality, provide fuel and pharmaceuticals, and purify the air. These free ecosystem services have no market value and so forest conservation has little appeal when compared with the economic benefits of logging and clearance which, through soil degradation and organic decomposition returns carbon dioxide to the atmosphere

Cultivated land

Main article—Sustainable agriculture: A rice paddy, Rice, wheat, corn and potatoes make up more than half the world's food supply feeding more than six billion human bodies takes a heavy toll on the Earth's resources. This begins with the appropriation of about 38% of the Earth's land surface and about 20% of its net primary productivity.[91] Added to this are the resource-hungry activities of industrial agribusiness – everything from the crop need for irrigation water, synthetic fertilizers and pesticides to the resource costs of food packaging, transport (now a major part of global trade) and retail. Food is essential to life. However, the list of environmental costs of food production is a long one: top soil depletion, erosion and conversion to desert from constant tillage of annual crops;

Overgrazing; salinization; sodification; waterlogging;

High levels of fossil fuel use;

Reliance on inorganic fertilisers and synthetic organic pesticides;

Reductions in genetic diversity by the mass use of monocultures;

Water resource depletion;

Pollution of water bodies by run-off and groundwater contamination.

Chapter 10

Hydrosphere, Lithosphere and Biosphere

Environment may be defined as the sum total of all situations and influences which affects the development and life of organisms of all kinds. Every living organism has its own environment. Environment may be categorised into various categories as under:

10.1 ENVIRONMENTAL SEGMENTS

- Atmosphere
- Lithosphere
- Hydrosphere
- Biosphere

10.1.1 Atmosphere

Atmosphere comprises of a mixture of gases and it extends up to about 500 km above the surface of the earth. The atmosphere surrounding the earth acts as a gaseous blanket by protecting the earth from dangerous cosmic radiations from outer space and helps in sustaining life on earth. The atmosphere screens the dangerous U.V. radiation from the sun (<300 nm) and transmits only the radiations in the range 300 nm to 2500 nm. The atmosphere plays a vital role in maintaining the heat balance on the earth by absorbing the infra red radiations received from sun and remitted by the earth as long wave radiation.

10.1.2 Lithosphere

The outer mantle of the solid earth, consisting of minerals occurring in the earth's crust and soil. The soil is a complex mixture of minerals, organic matter, air and water.

10.1.3 Hydrosphere

It includes all types of water resources – oceans, seas, rivers, lakes, streams reservoirs, and glaciers, polar ice caps and ground water. Only 1% of total available water is meant for human consumption.

10.1.4 Biosphere

The region of earth where life exists and includes a global girdle extending from about 10,000 m below sea-level to 6000 above sea-level. Thus the biosphere covers the entire realm of living organisms and their interactions with the other segments of the environment. Biosphere: - The biosphere is composed of all living organism. Plants, animals, and one-celled organism, are all parts of the biosphere. Most of the planet's life is found from three meters below the ground to thirty meters above it and in the top 200 meters of the oceans and seas. Within the biosphere, living things form ecological communities based on the physical surroundings of an area. These communities are referred to as biomes *e.g.*, Desert, grasslands, and tropical rainforests.

10.2 HYDROSPHERE AND CHEMISTRY OF WATER

10.2.1 About the Water

Water is a very important substance, as it makes up the larger part of an organism's body. Inside the body of a human being, there is a skeleton, which makes your body solid and makes sure you can stand up without falling apart. Water is also a kind of skeleton. It consists of tiny particles, the atoms, just like every other substance on earth. One of these atoms is called hydrogen and the other is called oxygen. As you probably know, the air that we breathe also contains oxygen. One particle of water is called a molecule. When lots of water molecules melt together we can see the water and drink it or use it, for instance to flush a toilet.

A water molecule built up: A water molecule consists of three atoms; an oxygen atom and two hydrogen atoms, which are bond together like little magnets. The atoms consist of matter that has a nucleus in the centre. The difference between atoms is expressed by atomic numbers. The atomic number of an atom depends on the number of protons in the nucleus of the atom. Protons are small positively charged particles. Hydrogen has one proton in the nucleus and oxygen has eight. There are also uncharged particles in the nucleus, called neutrons.

Next to protons and neutrons, atoms also consist of negatively charged electrons, which can be found in the electron cloud around the nucleus. The number of electrons in an atom equals the number of protons in the nucleus. The attraction between the protons and electrons is what keeps an atom together.

10.2.2 A Water Molecule Weight

The weight of a molecule is determined by the atomic masses of the atoms that it is built of. The atomic mass of an atom is determined by the addition of the number of protons and neutrons in the nucleus, because the electrons hardly weight anything. When the atomic masses of the separate atoms are known, one simply has to add them up to find the total atomic mass of a molecule, expressed in grams per mol. A mol is an express ion of the molar weight of a molecule, derived from the weight of a hydrogen molecule, which is 1 mol. Hydrogen has a relative atomic mass of 1 g/ mol and oxygen has a relative atomic mass of 16 g/mol. Water consists of one oxygen atom and two hydrogen atoms. This means that the mass of a water molecule is 1 g + 1 g + 16 g = 18 g/mol.

The mol air weight of separate atoms can be found in the periodic table of Mendeleev.

States (phases), of water: Water exists in three states: solid, liquid and gaseous. At a normal temperature of about 25°C it is liquid, but below 0°C it will freeze and turn to ice. Water can be found in the gaseous state above 100°C, this is called the boiling point of water, at which water starts to evaporate. The water turns to gas and is then odorless and colorless. How fast water evaporates depends on the temperature; if the temperature is high, water will evaporate sooner.

Water changes phase: The changes from a liquid to a solid or to a gas are called phase changes. When a substance such as water changes phase, its physical appearance changes, but not its chemical properties. This is because the chemical structure remains the same, but the molecules of which it consists will float a little further apart. In the solid state the water molecules are fairly close together, but in the liquid state they are a bit further apart. The water becomes liquid as a result of parting molecules. As water changes from liquid to gas the molecules will part even further, that is why we cannot detect it.

Ice float on water: When substances freeze, usually the molecules come closer together. Water has an abnormality there: it freezes below 0°C, but when temperatures go below 4°C, water starts to expand again and as a result, the density becomes lower. Density of a substance means the weight in kilograms of a cubic meter of a substance. When two substances are mixed but do not dissolve in one another, the substance with the lowest density floats on the other substance. In this case, that substance is ice, due to the decreased density of water.

Water-soluble substances are : Polarity determines if a substance is water-soluble. A polar substance is a substance that has two kinds of 'poles', as in a magnet. When another substance is also poll air the poles of the substances attract each other and as a result the substances mix. A substance then dissolves in water. Substances that contain no 'poles' are called poll air substances. Oil for instance is a poll air substance, as oil does not dissolve in water. In fact, it floats on water, just like ice, due to its lesser density.

10.2.3 Hard Water

When water is referred to as 'hard' this simply means, that it contains more minerals than ordinary water. These are especially the minerals calcium and magnesium. The degree of hardness of the water exceeds, when more calcium and magnesium dissolve. Magnesium and calcium are positively charged ions. Because of their presence, other positively charged substances will dissolve less easy in hard water than in water that does not contain calcium and magnesium. This is the cause of the fact that soap doesn't really dissolve in hard water.

10.2.4 Physical and Chemical Properties

Physical properties of a substance are properties that have everything to do with the substance's appearance. Chemical properties are properties that are often used in chemistry, to address the state of a substance. Physical and chemical properties can tell us something about the behaviour of a substance in certain circumstances. There are several different physical and chemical properties, which are often used alternately. We can name the following:

- **Density.** The density of water means the weight of a certain amount of water. It is usually expressed in kilograms per cubic meter. (Physical)
- **Thermal properties.** This refers to what happens to water when it is heated; at which temperature it becomes gaseous and that sort of thing. (Physical)
- **Conductivity.** This means the amount of electricity that water can conduct. It is expressed in a chemical magnitude. (Physical)
- **Light absorption.** This is the amount of light a certain amount of water can absorb over time. (chemical)
- **Viscosity.** This means the syrupiness of water and it determines the mobility of water. When the temperature rises, the viscosity degrades; this means that water will be more mobile at higher temperatures. (physical)
- **The pH.** The pH has its own scale, running up from 1 to 14. The pH shows whether a substance is acid (pH 1–6), neutral (pH 7) or basic (pH 8–14). The number of hydrogen atoms in the substance determines the pH. The more hydrogen atoms a substance contains, the lower the pH will be. A substance that contains many hydrogen atoms is acid. We can measure the pH by dipping a special coloring paper in the substance, the colors shows which pH the substance has. (Chemical)
- **Alkalinity.** This is the capacity of water to neutralize an acid or a base, so that the pH of the water will not change.

10.2.5 Chemistry of Hard and Soft Water

Hard water is any water containing an appreciable quantity of dissolved minerals. Soft water is treated water in which the only action (positively charged ion) is sodium. The minerals in water give it a characteristic taste. Some natural mineral waters are highly sought for their flavor and the health benefits they may confer. Soft water, on the other hand, may taste salty and may not be suitable for drinking. Extremely hard water may shorten the life of plumbing and lessen the effectiveness of certain cleaning agents. If hard water is heated, the carbonates precipitate out of solution, forming scale in pipes and tea kettles.

In addition to narrowing and potentially clogging the pipes, scale prevents efficient heat transfer, so a water heater with scale will have to use a lot of energy to give you hot water. Soap is less effective in hard water because its reacts to form the calcium or magnesium salt of the organic acid of the soap. These salts are insoluble and form grayish soap scum, but no cleansing lather. Detergents, on the other hand, lather in both hard and soft water. Calcium and magnesium salts of the detergent's organic acids form, but these salts are soluble in water. Hard water can be softened (have its minerals removed) by treating it with lime or by passing it over an ion exchange resin. The ion exchange resins are complex sodium salts. Water flows over the resin surface, dissolving the sodium. The calcium, magnesium, and other cations precipitate onto the resin surface. Sodium goes into the water, but the other cations stay with the resin. Very hard water will end up tasting saltier than water that had fewer dissolved minerals.

Most of the ions have been removed in soft water, but sodium and various anions (negatively charged ions) remain. Water can be deionized by using a resin that replaces cations with hydrogen and anions with hydroxide. With this type of resin, the cations stick to the resin and the hydrogen and hydroxide that are released combine to form pure water.

10.3 WATER CYCLE

The movement of water around, over, and through the Earth is called the **water cycle**. The **water cycle** technically known as the **hydrologic cycle** or **hydrological cycle** is the continuous circulation of water within the Earth's hydrosphere, and is driven by solar radiation. This includes the atmosphere, land, surface water and groundwater. As water moves through the cycle, it changes state between liquid, solid, and gas phases. Water moves from compartment to compartment, such as from river to ocean, by the physical processes of evaporation, precipitation, infiltration, runoff, and subsurface flow.

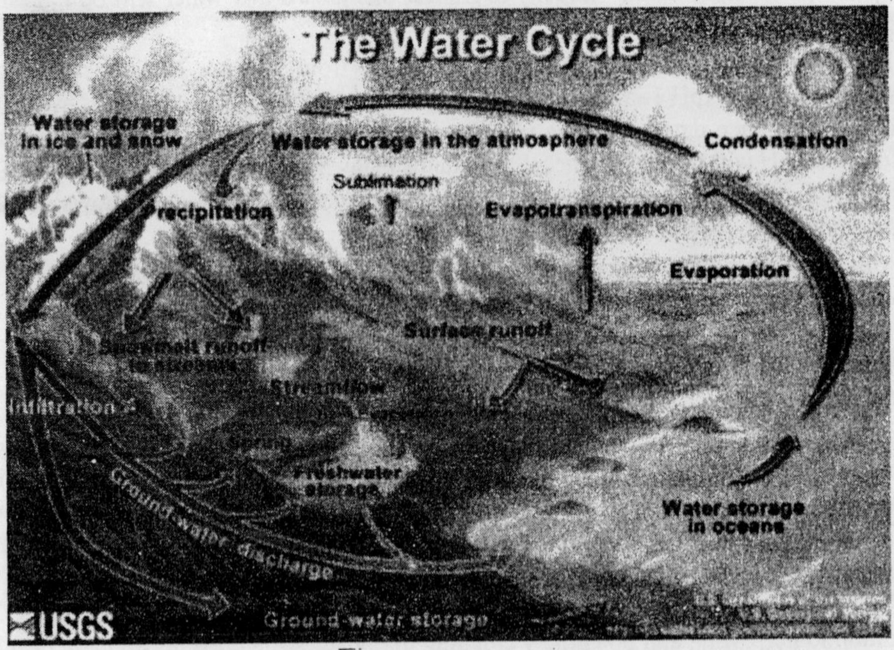

Fig. 10.1: From Wikipedia, the free encyclopedia

The water cycle is the continuous movement of water over, above, and beneath the Earth's surface. It is powered by solar energy, as it is a cycle, there is neither beginning nor end. As water moves around in the hydrosphere, it changes state among liquid, vapour, and ice. The time taken for water to move from one place to another varies from seconds to thousands of years, and the amount of water stored in different parts of the hydrosphere ranges up to 1.37 billion km³, which is contained in the oceans. Despite continual movement within the hydrosphere, the total amount of water at any one time remains essentially constant. Movement of water takes place by a variety of physical and biophysical processes. The two processes responsible for moving the greatest quantities of water are precipitation and evaporation, transporting 505,000 km³ of water each year. The flow of water along rivers transports an intermediate amount of water, and sublimation of ice directly to vapour transports relatively very little. The different processes are as follows.

Precipitation is condensed water vapor that falls to the Earth's surface. Most precipitation occurs as rain, but also includes snow, hail, fog drip, graupel, and sleet. Approximately 505,000 km³ of water fall as precipitation each year, 398,000 km³ of it over the oceans.

Canopy interception is the precipitation that is intercepted by plant foliage and eventually evaporates back to the atmosphere rather than falling to the ground.

Snowmelt refers to the runoff produced by melting snow.

Runoff includes the variety of ways by which water moves acrıss the land. This includes both surface runoff and channel runoff. As it flows, the water may infiltrate into the ground, evaporate into the air, become stored in lakes or reservoirs, or be extracted for agricultural or other human uses.

Infiltration is the flow of water from the ground surface into the ground. Once infiltrated, the water becomes soil moisture or groundwater.

Subsurface Flow is the flow of water underground, in the vadose zone and aquifers. Subsurface water may return to the surface (*eg.*, as a spring or by being pumped) or eventually seep into the oceans. Water returns to the land surface at lower elevation than where it infiltrated, under the force of gravity or gravity induced pressures. Groundwater tends to move slowly, and is replenished slowly, so it can remain in aquifers for thousands of years.

Evaporation is the transformation of water from liquid to gas phases as it moves from the ground or bodies of water into the overlying atmosphere. The source of energy for evaporation is primarily solar radiation. Evaporation often implicitly includes **transpiration** from plants, though together they are specifically referred to as **evapotranspiration**. Approximately 90% of atmospheric water comes from evaporation, while the remaining 10% is from transpiration. Total annual evapotranspiration amounts to approximately 505,000 km³ of water, 434,000 km³ of which evaporates from the oceans.

Sublimation is the state change directly from solid water (snow or ice) to water vapor.

Advection is the movement of water in solid, liquid, or vapour states through the atmosphere. Without advection, water that evaporated over the oceans could not precipitate over land.

Condensation is the transformation of water vapour to liquid water droplets in the air, producing clouds and fog.

10.3.2 Reservoirs

In the context of the water cycle, a reservoir represents the water contained in different steps within the cycle. The largest reservoir is the collection of oceans, accounting for 97% of the Earth's water. The next largest quantity (2%) is stored in solid form in the ice caps and glaciers. The water contained within all living organisms represents the smallest reservoir.

Table: 10.1
Volume of water stored in the water cycle's reservoirs

Reservoir	*Volume of water(10^6 km^3)*	*Percent of total*
Oceans	1370	97.25
Ice caps & glaciers	29	2.05
Groundwater	9.5	0.68
Lakes	0.125	0.01
Soil moisture	0.065	0.005
Atmosphere	0.013	0.001
Streams & rivers	0.0017	0.0001
Biosphere	0.0006	0.00004

The volumes of water in the fresh water reservoirs, particularly those that are available for human use, are important water resources.

10.4 BIOSPHERE

Life, as far as is known, exist only on earth. The reason for this is that the various physical conditions to sustain life occur only on the earth. Even on the earth, the conditions favorable for life exist in certain areas only. Further, all kinds of environment are not suitable for all forms of life. For instance, the land organisms cannot live in water and vice versa. All the living organisms and all the parts of the earth and its atmosphere inhabited by them together with the various physicochemical factors prevailing in these together with their abiotic environment form a biosphere. In short, all the ecosystem of the world constitutes a biosphere. The biosphere is also called the ecosphere. The concept of biosphere was introduced by an Australian geologist, Edward Seuss, in 1875. It was placed on a firm footing by a Russian mineralogist Vernadsky in 1926.

10.4.1 Extent of Biosphere

Life is confined to a thin shell, about 24 km thick, on the earth's surface. It occurs in the ocean down to about 9,000 m, below the surface of land for about 300 m., and in the air to about 15,000 m life is more abundant at the interfaces are too low ; concentration of CO_2 and O_2 is too little and cosmic radiation is too high. At great depths, light becomes a limiting factor for life. Life exists virtually everywhere in the biosphere, even in hot springs and Polar Regions. However, there is no life in the extremely dry regions, frozen mountains peaks and poles, live volcanoes and toxic sea basin. Life is not uniformly distributed in the biosphere. Some parts have more life, or produce more biomass, than others produce. Maximum life occurs in the tropics rain forests and coral reefs, and is searce in the tundra, snow-clad mountains, deserts, and hot springs.

10.4.2 Biosphere, an Open as Well as a Closed System

A closed system is one that receives no input from outside nor turns out any products. An open system is that which gets input from outside and sends out certain products.

Chapter 11

Various Cycles in the Ecosystem—water, Carbon and Nitrogen

11.1 THE TERM ECOSYSTEM

Introduction

The term ecosystem refers to the combined physical and biological components of an environment. An ecosystem is generally an area within the natural environment in which physical (abiotic) factors of the environment, such as rocks and soil, function together along with interdependent (biotic) organisms, such as plants and animals, within the same habitat. Ecosystems can be permanent or temporary. Ecosystems usually form a number of food webs. The term ecosystem was coined in 1930 by Roy Clapham to mean the combined physical and biological components of an environment. British ecologist Arthur Tansley later refined the term, describing it as "The whole system, including not only the organism-complex, but also the whole complex of physical factors forming what we call the environment".

Examples of Ecosystems

Aquatic ecosystem
Coral reef
Desert
Forest
Lentic
Lotic
Marine ecosystem
Prairie
Savanna
Taiga
Tundra

Urban ecosystem

Biomes etc.

Fig. 11.1

Biomes are a classification of globally similar areas, including ecosystems, such as ecological communities of plants and animals, soil organisms and climatic conditions. Biomes are in part defined based on factors such as plant structures (such as trees, shrubs, and grasses), leaf types (such as broadleaf and needleleaf), plant spacing (forest, woodland, savanna), and climate. Unlike ecozones, biomes are not defined by genetic, taxonomic, or historical similarities. Biomes are often identified with particular patterns of ecological succession and climax vegetation.

11.2 A FUNDAMENTAL CLASSIFICATION OF BIOMES IS

Terrestrial (land) biomes

Freshwater biomes

Marine biomes

Types of Ecosystems: *Ecosystems may be categorized in different manners. Following are some examples of diverse ecosystems:*

Riverine Ecosystem

River ecosystem

Stream ecosystem

Spring ecosystem

Lacustrine Ecosystem:

Pond ecosystem
Lake Ecosystem

Marine ecosystem:

Coastal water ecosystem
Estuary ecosystem
Lagoon ecosystem
Coral reef ecosystem
Soft-bottom continental shelf ecosystem
Upwelling continental shelf ecosystem
Open ocean ecosystem
Polar ocean ecosystem (the Artic and Antarctic oceans)
Boundary ecosystem (where one body of water meets another (estuaries and lagoons); where a body of water meets land (wetlands); where one land area meets another land type)
Soil ecosystem
Polar ecosystem (in Polar Regions, such as polar barrens and tundra)
Mountain ecosystem
Agroecosystem (farms, livestock production systems)
Forest ecosystem
Grassland ecosystem
Urban ecosystem (cities, suburbs)

11.3 Key Features of Ecosystems

The accumulated body of empirical evidence concerning natural, disturbed and managed ecosystems identifies key features of ecosystem structure and function that can be distilled into the following points. Change is neither continuous and gradual nor consistently chaotic. Rather it is episodic, with periods of slow accumulation of natural capital such as biomass or nutrients, punctuated by sudden releases and reorganization of that capital as the result of internal or external natural processes or of human-imposed catastrophes. Rare events, such as hurricanes, or the arrival of invading species, can unpredictably shape structure at critical times or at locations of increased vulnerability. Critical processes function at radically different rates and span several orders of magnitude, but these rates cluster around a few dominant frequencies.

Spatial attributes are neither uniform nor scale invariant over all scales. Rather, productivity and textures are patchy and discontinuous at all scales from the leaf, to the landscape, to the planet. There are several different ranges of scales each with different attributes of patchiness and texture (Holling 1992) and each controlled by a specific set of abiotic and biotic processes. Therefore scaling up from small to large cannot be a process of simple aggregation: non-linear processes organize the shift from one range of scales to another.

Ecosystems do not have a single equilibrium with homeostatic controls to remain near it. Rather, multiple equilibria define functionally different states, and normal movement between states maintains structure and diversity. On the one hand, destabilizing forces are important in maintaining diversity, resilience and opportunity. On the other hand, stabilizing forces are important in maintaining productivity and biogeochemical cycles. Policies and management that apply fixed rules for achieving constant yields (*e.g.,* fixed carrying capacity of cattle or wildlife, or fixed sustainable yield of fish or wood), independent of scale, lead to systems that increasingly lose resilience *i.e.,* to ones that suddenly break down in the face of disturbances that previously could be absorbed. Ecosystems are moving targets, with multiple futures that are uncertain and unpredictable.

11.4 PROCESSES OF ECOSYSTEMS

This figure with the plants, zebra, lion, and so forth illustrates the two main ideas about how ecosystems function: ***ecosystems have energy flows*** and ***ecosystems cycle materials***. These two processes are linked, but they are not quite the same.

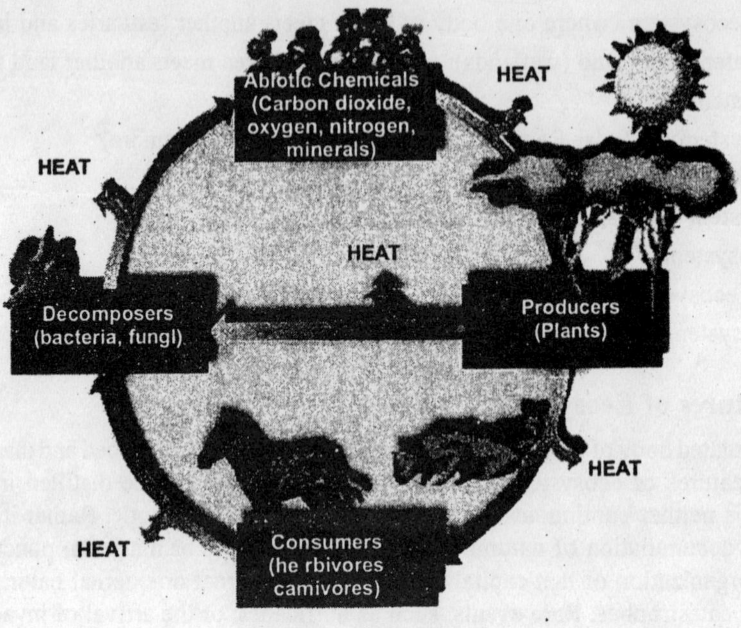

Fig. 11.2: Showing the flows and material way cycles

Energy enters the biological system as light energy, or photons, is transformed into chemical energy in organic molecules by cellular processes including photosynthesis and respiration, and ultimately is converted to heat energy. This energy is dissipated, meaning it is lost to the system as heat; once it is lost it cannot be recycled. Without the continued input of solar energy, biological systems would quickly shut down. Thus the earth is an *open system* with respect to energy.

Elements such as carbon, nitrogen, or phosphorus enter living organisms in a variety of ways. Plants obtain elements from the surrounding atmosphere, water, or soils. During decomposition these materials are not destroyed or lost, so the earth is a ***closed system*** with respect to elements although it becomes exception if a meteorite entering the system. The elements are cycled endlessly between their biotic and abiotic states within ecosystems. Those elements whose supply tends to limit biological activity are called ***nutrients.***

11.4.1 Transformation of Energy

The transformations of energy in an ecosystem begin first with the input of energy from the sun. Energy from the sun is captured by the process of photosynthesis. Carbon dioxide is combined with hydrogen (derived from the splitting of water molecules) to produce carbohydrates (CHO). Energy is stored in the high energy, bonds of adenosine triphosphate, or ATP

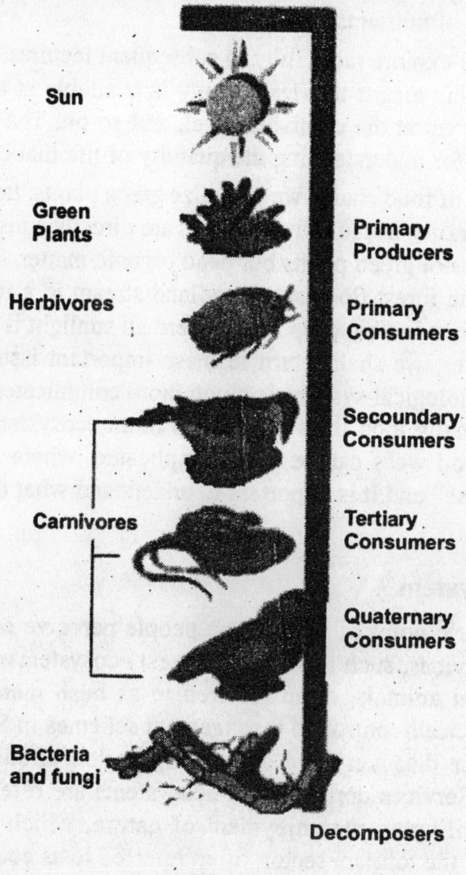

Fig. 11.3

The prophet Isaah said "all flesh is grass", earning him the title of first ecologist, because virtually all energy available to organisms originates in plants. Because it is the first step in the production of energy for living things, it is called **primary production** (click here for a primer on photosynthesis). **Herbivores** obtain their energy by consuming plants or plant products, **carnivores** eat herbivores, and **detritivores** consume dead organisms.

Portrays a simple food chain, in which energy from the sun, captured by plant photosynthesis, flows from **trophic level** to trophic level via the **food chain.** A trophic level is composed of organisms that make a living in the same way that is they are all **primary producers** (plants), **primary consumers** (herbivores) or **secondary consumers** (carnivores). Dead tissue and waste products are produced at all levels. Scavengers, detritivores, and decomposers collectively account for the use of all such "waste" — consumers of carcasses and fallen leaves may be other animals, such as crows and beetles, but ultimately it is the microbes that finish the job of decomposition. Not surprisingly, the amount of primary production varies a great deal from place to place, due to differences in the amount of solar radiation and the availability of nutrients and water.

For reasons that we will explore more fully in subsequent lectures, **energy transfer through the food chain is inefficient.** This means that less energy is available at the herbivore level than at the primary producer level, less yet at the carnivore level, and so on. The result is a pyramid of energy, with important implications for understanding the quantity of life that can be supported.

Usually when we think of food chains we visualize green plants, herbivores, and so on. These are referred to as **grazer food chains,** because living plants are directly consumed. In many circumstances, the principal energy input is not green plants but dead organic matter. These are called **detritus food chains.** Examples include the forest floor or a woodland stream in a forested area, a salt marsh, and most obviously, the ocean floor in very deep areas where all sunlight is extinguished 1000's of meters above. In subsequent lectures, we shall return to these important issues concerning energy flow in reality the organization of biological systems is much more complicated than can be represented by a simple "chain". There are many food links and chains in an ecosystem, and we refer to all of these linkages as a **food web.** Food webs can be very complicated, where it appears that **"everything is connected to everything else"** and it is important to understand what the most important linkages are in any particular food web.

11.4.2 Function of Ecosystem

From an anthropocentric point of view, some people perceive ecosystems as production units that produce goods and services, such as wood by forest ecosystems and grass for cattle by natural grasslands. Meat from wild animals, often referred to as bush meat in Africa, has proven to be extremely successful under well-controlled management schemes in South Africa and Kenya. Much less successful has been the discovery and commercialization of substances of wild organism for pharmaceutical purposes. Services derived from ecosystems are referred to as ecosystem services. They may include: (1) facilitating the enjoyment of nature, which may generate many forms of income and employment in the tourism sector, often referred to as eco-tourisms, (2) water retention, thus facilitating a more evenly distributed release of water, (3) soil protection, open-air laboratory for scientific resea ch, etc.

A greater degree of species or biological diversity — popularly referred to as Biodiversity — of an ecosystem may contribute to greater resilience of an ecosystem, because there are more species present at a location to respond to change and thus "absorb" or reduce its effects. This reduces the effect before the ecosystem's structure is fundamentally changed to a different state. This is not universally the case and there is no proven relationship between the species diversity of an ecosystem and its ability to provide goods and services on a sustainable level: Humid tropical forests produce very few goods and direct services and are extremely vulnerable to change, while many temperate forests readily grow back to their previous state of development within a lifetime after felling or a forest fire. Some grassland have been sustainably exploited for thousands of years as Mongolia, Africa, European peat and mooreland communities.

11.4.3 Flow of CO_2 in an Ecosystem

The Sun's energy, stored by plants (primary producers) during photosynthesis, passes through the food chain to other organisms to ultimately power all living processes. Since the industrial revolution the concentrated energy of the Sun stored in fossilized plants as fossil fuels has been a major driver of technology which, in turn, has been the source of both economic and political power. In 2007 climate scientists of the IPCC concluded that there was at least a 90% probability that atmospheric increase in CO_2 was human-induced, mostly as a result of fossil fuel emissions but, to a lesser extent from changes in land use. Stabilizing the world's climate will require high income countries to reduce their emissions by 60–90% over 2006 levels by 2050 which should hold CO_2 levels at 450–650 ppm from current levels of about 380 ppm. Above this level and temperatures could rise by more than 2°C (36°F) to produce "catastrophic" climate change.

11.5 BIOGEOCHEMICAL CYCLES

The cycling of chemical elements required by life between the living and nonliving parts of the environment. Some examples of these chemical elements are H_2O, P, S, N_2, O_2 and C. These elements cycle in either a gas cycle or a sedimentary cycle; some cycle as both a gas and sediment. In a gas cycle elements move through the atmosphere. Main reservoirs are the atmosphere and the ocean. In a sedimentary cycle elements move from land to water to sediment. Main reservoirs are the soil and sedimentary rocks.

Table: 11.1

Gas Cycles	*Sedimentary Cycles*
Carbon	Phosphorus
Nitrogen	Sulfur
Oxygen	

11.5.1 Life and Biogeochemical Cycles

Life on earth is inextricably linked to climate through a variety of interacting cycles and feedback loops. In recent years there has been a growing awareness of the extent to which human activities, such as deforestation and fossil fuel burning, have directly or indirectly modified the biogeochemical and physical processes involved in determining the earth's climate. These changes in atmospheric processes can disturb a variety of the ecosystem services that humanity depends upon. In addition to helping to maintain relative climate stability and a self-cleansing, oxidizing environment, these services include protection from most of the sun's harmful ultraviolet rays, mediation of runoff and evapotranspiration (which affects the quantity and quality of fresh water supplies and helps control floods and droughts), and regulation of nutrient cycling among others.

Before further discussion of these services, it is important to review briefly how life and climate interact. The transport and transformation of substances in the environment, through life, air, sea, land, and ice, are known collectively as biogeochemical cycles. These global cycles include the circulation of certain elements, oi nutrients, upon which life and the earth's climate depend. One way that climate influences life is by regulating the flow of substances through these biogeochemical cycles, in part through atmospheric circulation.

It is critical for the survival and health of human beings and ecological systems and is part of the climatic state. When water vapor condenses to form clouds, more of the sun's rays are reflected back into the atmosphere, usually cooling the climate. Conversely, water vapor is also an important greenhouse gas in the atmosphere, trapping heat in the infrared part of the spectrum in the lower atmosphere. The water or hydrologic cycle intersect with most of the other element cycles, including the cycles of carbon, nitrogen, sulfur, and phosphorus, as well as the sedimentary cycle. The processes involving each one of these elements may be strongly coupled with that of other elements, and ultimately, with important regional and global scale climatic or ecological processes. Managing and finding solutions to many of the important environmental problems facing humanity begins with understanding and integrating biogeochemical cycles and the scales at which they operate.

Examples of these links include world climate and the potential threat of global climate change; agricultural productivity and its strong reliance on climatic factors including temperature and precipitation, and on the availability of nutrients; the cleansing of toxics in soils and streams through precipitation and runoff; acid precipitation and the perturbation of ecosystem processes. The depletion of stratospheric ozone and its potential threat to human health and the food chain; and the often destructive interaction with natural cycles of other manmade compounds such as pesticides and synthetic hormones.

11.6 THE HYDROLOGIC AND SEDIMENTARY CYCLES

While the total amount of water found on earth may seem huge, the amount of precipitating freshwater available to people is a tiny fraction of this total. Earth's renewable supply of water is continually distilled and distributed through the hydrological cycle. It falls from the sky as precipitation, collects in lakes, rivers and oceans or seeps into the ground, and eventually evaporates or transpires, accumulating as water vapor in clouds, ready to begin the sun powered cycle again. Water is transferred to the air from the leaves of plants primarily from a process called transpiration. This, combined with evaporation from bodies of water and the soil, is known as evapotranspiration.

Evaporation of ocean water is about six times as large globally as evapotranspiration on land, although in the centers of continents evapotranspiration may be the main local source of water vapor. Changes in the global climate may cause changes in the hydrologic cycle. Increases in temperature and evaporation are expected to cause increases in precipitation, which may further affect runoff and soil moisture, and eventually influence vegetation patterns and world agriculture.

The sedimentary cycle is tied to the hydrological cycle through precipitation. Water carries materials from the land to the oceans, where they can be deposited as sediments. On a shorter time-scale, the sedimentary cycle includes the processes of physical or chemical erosion, nutrient transport, and sediment formation for which water flows are mostly responsible. On a geologically longer time-scale, the processes of sedimentation, chemical transformation, uplift, sea floor spreading, and continental drift operate. The hydrological and sedimentary cycles are intertwined with the distribution of the amounts and flows of six important elements - hydrogen, carbon, oxygen, nitrogen, phosphorus, and sulfur. These elements, or macronutrients, combine in various ways to make up more than 95% of all living things. Appropriate quantities of them in proper balance and in the right places are required to sustain life. Although great stocks of all of these nutrients exist in the earth's crust in different (but not always accessible) forms, at any one time the natural supply of these vital elements is limited. Therefore, they must be recycled for life to regenerate continuously.

11.7 THE NITROGEN CYCLE

Nitrogen exists in a variety of forms in natural systems and its compounds are involved in numerous biological and abiotic processes. Nitrogen, in its gaseous form of N_2, makes up almost 80 percent of the atmosphere. This constitutes the major storage pool in the complex cycle of nitrogen through ecosystems. Some of this gas is converted in the soils and waters to ammonia (NH_3), ammonium (NH^{4+}), or many other nitrogen compounds.

The process is known as nitrogen fixation, and, in the absence of industrial fertilizers, is the primary source of nitrogen to all living things. Biological nitrogen fixation is mediated by special nitrogen-fixing bacteria and algae. On the land, these bacteria often live on nodules on the roots of legumes where they use energy from plants to do their work. In freshwater and, possibly, in marine systems, cyanobacteria fix nitrogen. Once nitrogen has been fixed in the soil or aquatic system, it can follow two different pathways. It can be oxidized for energy in a process called nitrification or assimilated by an organism into its biomass in a process called ammonia assimilation.

Plants incorporate the appropriate forms of fixed nitrogen into their tissues through their root systems. The plants then use it to manufacture amino acids and convert it into proteins. Nitrogen, fixed as proteins in the bodies of living organisms, eventually returns via the nitrogen cycle to its original form of nitrogen gas in the air. The process of denitrification starts when plants containing the fixed nitrogen either are eaten or die. Fixed nitrogen products in dead plants, animal bodies, and animal excreta encounter denitrifying bacteria that undo the work done by the nitrogen-fixing bacteria. Generally, N_2 is the end-product of denitrification, but nitrous oxide (N_2O) is also produced in smaller quantities it is up to about ten percent.

The disruption of the nitrogen cycle by human activity plays an important role in a wide-range of environmental problems ranging from the production of tropospheric smog to the perturbation of stratospheric ozone and the contamination of groundwater. Nitrous oxide, for example, is a greenhouse gas like carbon dioxide and water vapor that can trap heat near the earth's surface. It also destroys stratospheric ozone. Eventually nitrous oxide in the stratosphere is broken down by ultraviolet light into nitrogen dioxide (NO_2) and nitric oxide (NO), which can catalytically reduce ozone. Nitrogen oxides are chemically transformed back to either N_2 or to nitrate or nitrite compounds, which may later get used by plants after they are washed by the rain back to the earth's surface. Nitrate rain is acidic and can cause ecological problems as well as serve as a fertilizer to vegetation.

11.8 THE SULFUR CYCLE

Another example of a major biogeochemical cycle of significance to climate and life is the sulfur cycle. Living things require certain safe, low levels of this nutrient. The sulfur cycle can be thought of as beginning with the gas sulfur dioxide (SO_2) or the particles of sulfate (SO_4^{-2}) compounds in the air. These compounds either fall out or are rained out of the atmosphere. Plants take up some forms of these compounds and incorporate them into their tissues. Then, as with nitrogen, these organic sulfur compounds are returned to the land or water after the plants die or are consumed by animals. Bacteria are important here as well since they can transform the organic sulfur to hydrogen sulfide gas (H_2S). In the oceans, certain phytoplankton can produce a chemical that transforms to SO_2 that resides in the atmosphere. These gases can re-enter the atmosphere, water, and soil, and continue the cycle.

In its reduced oxidation state, the nutrient sulfur plays an important part in the structure and function of proteins. In its fully oxidized state, sulfur exists as sulfate and is the major cause of acidity in both natural and polluted rainwater. This link to acidity makes sulfur important to geochemical, atmospheric, and biological processes such as the natural weathering of rocks, acid precipitation, and rates of denitrification. Sulfur is also one of the main elemental cycles most heavily perturbed by human activity. Estimates suggest that emissions of sulfur to the atmosphere from human activity are at least equal or probably larger in magnitude than those from natural processes. Like nitrogen, sulfur can exist in many forms: as gases or sulfuric acid particles. Sulfuric acid particles contribute to the polluting smog that engulfs some industrial centers and cities where many sulfur containing fuels are burned. Such particles floating in air also known as sulfate aerosols can cause respiratory diseases or cool the climate by reflecting some extra sunlight to space.

The lifetime of most sulfur compounds in the air is relatively short (*e.g.,* days). Superimposed on these fast cycles of sulfur are the extremely slow sedimentary-cycle processes or erosion, sedimentation, and uplift of rocks containing sulfur. In addition, sulfur compounds from volcanoes are intermittently injected into the atmosphere, and a continual stream of these compounds is produced from industrial activities.

These compounds mix with water vapor and form sulfuric acid smog. In addition to contributing to acid rain, the sulfuric acid droplets of smog form a haze layer that reflects solar radiation and can cause a cooling of the earth's surface. While many questions remain concerning specifics, the sulfur cycle in general, and acid rain and smog issues in particular are becoming major physical, biological, and social problems.

Fig. 11.4

11.9 THE CARBON CYCLE

Carbon, the key element of all life on earth, has a complicated biogeochemical cycle of great importance to global climate change. The carbon cycle includes four main reservoirs of stored carbon: as CO_2 in the atmosphere; as organic compounds in living or recently dead organisms; as dissolved carbon dioxide in the oceans and other bodies of water; and as calcium carbonate in limestone and in buried organic matter (in the form of natural gas, peat, coal, and petroleum).

Ultimately, the cycling of carbon through each of these reservoirs is tightly tied to living organisms. Plants continuously extract carbon from the atmosphere and use it to form carbohydrates and sugars to build up their tissues through the process of photosynthesis. Animals consume plants and use these organic compounds in their metabolism. When plants and animals die, CO_2 is formed again as the organic compounds combine with oxygen during decay. Not all of the compounds are oxidized, however, and a small fraction is transported and redeposited as sediment and trapped where it can form deposits of coal and petroleum. Carbon dioxide from the atmosphere also dissolves in oceans and other bodies of water.

Fig. 11.5

Aquatic plants use it for photosynthesis and many aquatic animals use it to make shells of calcium carbonate ($CaCO_3$). The shells of dead organisms (*e.g.*, phytoplankton or coral reefs) accumulate on the sea floor and can form limestone that is part of the sedimentary cycle. The relevant time-scales for these different processes vary over many orders of magnitude, from millions of years for the rock cycle and plate tectonics to days and even seconds for processes like photosynthesis and air-sea exchange.

CO_2 is a trace gas in the earth's atmosphere that has a substantial effect on earth's heat balance by absorbing infrared radiation. This gas, like water vapor (H_2O), CH_4, and N_2O, has a strong greenhouse effect. Life can alter the global concentration of CO_2 over very short time periods. During the growing season, CO_2 decreases in the atmosphere of the temperate latitudes due to the increasing sunlight and temperatures, which help plants to increase their rate of carbon uptake and growth. During the winter dormant period, more CO_2 enters the atmosphere than is removed by plants, and the concentration rises because plant respiration and the decay of dying plants and animals occur faster than photosynthesis. The land mass in the northern hemisphere is greater than in the southern hemisphere, thus the global concentration of CO_2 tracks the seasonality of terrestrial vegetation in the northern hemisphere.

Chapter 12

Biodiversity

12.1 BIOLOGICAL DIVERSITY

Biodiversity (Gk, bios = life ; diversity = forms) or biological diversity can be defined as the vast array of species of micro-organisms, algae, fungi, plants and animal occurring on the earth either in the terrestrial or aquatic habitats and the ecological complexes. Biodiversity differ from place to place. It is so because environmental condition of the area as well as the range of tolerance of the species determines whether or not a particular species can occur in that area. Results in the formation of polymorphs (individuals indifferently forms of a same species) in the sympatric (spatially contiguous) populations races in the allopathic (distantly placed) population and sub species in the geographically isolated populations thus genetic diversity provides the raw materials for adaptation changing environment and for the evolution of new life forms (speciation).

Speciation plays a key role in maintaining the diversity at both the species level and community level. As the environment becomes diversified, Genetic diversity within the species greatly increases. In addition, total genetic diversity of the community will also be in erase if there are many species.

12.1.1 Levels of Biodiversity

Biodiversity on earth exists in three levels of organization genetic diversity, species diversity and community and ecosystem diversity.

Genetic Diversity

Every living organisms store vast amount of genetic information. For instance, a bacteriophage has approximately 100 genes, mycoplasma 45–700 genes, Escherichia coli 4000 genes, Drosophila melanogaster 13000 genes, Oryza sativa 32000–50000 genes and Homo sapiens 35000–45000 genes. Genetic diversity is related to the variations of genes within species. The variations may be in different variants of same genes (alleles), in entire genes or in chromosomal structures. On account of genetic differences, all the individuals of the same species become different from one another in the details of body structure giving rise to multitude of intraspecific categories such as sub- species, varieties, races, strains, morphotypes, ecotypes etc.

All of these show variations of organism to the other. For example, there are various varities of mangoes, wheat, rice etc. similarly, there are various races of human beings such as Mangoloid, Negrito, Protoaustraloid etc. These differences are apparent in large-sized species of plants and animals but are too minute to be evident in small-sized species. Such morphological variations become distinctive at the level of species. Environment also plays an important role in imparting diversity of living organisms. Genetic changes due to mutations in the frequency of genes result in altered genotypes. Natural selection favours the several of those genotypes, which are suited to the prevailing environment.

Species Diversity

It is related to the variety in the number and richness of the species within a region and is measured at the level of 'species'. For example, big cats e.g. tiger (Panthera tigris), lion (Panthera leo) and snow leopard (Panthera unica) belong to the same genus panthera but they all differ at the species level. Similarly, taking example of plants, brinzal (Solanum melanogena), potato (Solanum tuberous) and tomato (Solanum lycopersicon) belong to the same genus solanum but them all too different at the species level. These species have attended the unique biological status of reproductive isolation.

Species richness refers to the numbers of species per unit area. As the areas of site increases, the number of species also increases due to more availability of natural resources however number of individuals of different specie as may very resulting in differences in evenness or equitability species diversity. let us take three sample areas in first sample areas there are three species of birds two species are represented by one bird each and the third species is represented by four birds. in the second sample area some three species exist but each species is represented by two birds each. This sample area depicts greater evenness and there fore this sample area will be considered more diverse than the first sample area in the third sample are there are percent two individuals each of an insect birds and a mammal as this area comprises taxonomically unrelated species it is the most diverse sample area. Thus, variations in the number of species, kinds of species as well as the number of individuals per species lead to greater diversity.

12.1.2 Community and Ecosystem Diversity

It is related to the different types of ecosystem/s e.g terrestrial and aquatic ecosystems. Fresh water ecosystems include lentic (*e.g.*, ponds, lake), lotic (*e.g.*, streams, rivers) and wetlands (*e.g.*, marshes, swamps, bogs) whereas marine ecosystems include open ocean, upwelling regions, and coastal ecosystems (*e.g.*, estuaries, coral reefs, mangroves etc.). Ecosystem diversity explains the diverse number of niches, tropic levels and various ecological processes that sustain energy flow, food webs and recycling of nutrients. Within particular geographical area, there may be variable number of ecosystems/habitats. The number of ecosystems present in a region is also a measure of biodiversity.

12.1.3 Alpha Diversity (within Community Diversity)

It refers to the diversity of organisms i.e. number of species in the given community or habitats. Species diversity and species evenness; the two indices are used in combination to represent alpha diversity.

12.1.4 Distribution of Species in a Community

In a community, species distribution is highly uneven. Five major factors determine the number of species in a particular community:

1. Historical factor *i.e.*, the time available for the colonization.
2. Number of potential colonizers *i.e.*, size of the species pool from which colonization occur.
3. The distance of the community from the source of colonizers.
4. Size of biotype that influence its structural biodiversity, and
5. There are a direct correlation between the number of species and the diversity of available resources. It is the number of available resources, the quality range in each resources, and the diversity resources in each quality category that influences the number of abundance of species in a community.

Species diversity of a community is analyzed easily on the basis of diversity indices1 which are rates vs. time mathematical expressions of species numbers (or importance) relationship.

Following three diversity indicates are commonly used:

d_1= S–1/log N

d_2= S/N

d_3 = S/1000 individuals

Where, S = Number of species

N = Number of individuals

It may be noted that 'e' and 'H' behave inversely to the index of dominance given above, and their high values indicated a poor concentration of dominance. Higher diversity means food chains and more cases of site-specific interactions such as mutualism, proto cooperation, parasitism etc. The result is greater possibility for negative feed back control, which reduces oscillations thereby increasing stability. Therefore, diversity is directly related to the stability of the community.

12.1.5 Beta Diversity

It refers to the rate of replacement of species along a gradient of habitats or communities within a given geographical region. It reveals differences in species composition of communities along altitudinal gradient, moisture gradient or any other environment gradient. If there is more heterogeneity in the habitats in a region or more dissimilarity between communities, then there will be more beta diversity.

12.1.6 Gamma diversity

It refers to the diversity of the habitats in the whole geographical region.

12.2 BIOGEOGRAPHICAL CLASSIFICATION OF INDIA

India is Asia's second largest nation and world's seventh largest country. As far as geographical location of the country is concerned, India is located between 8' 4' and 8' 4' north latitude and 68'7' and 97'25' east longitude. It measures 3,214 km from north to south and 2,993 km from east to west with a total land area of 3,287,263 sq. km. In the north-west, India borders Pakistan; in the north-east, China, Tibet, Nepal; and in the east Burma. Indian southern peninsula extends into the tropical waters of the Indian Ocean bounded by Bay of Bengal on the south-east and Arabian Sea on the south-west. On the north, north-east and north-west lay the Himalayan ranges.

The country is rich in biodiversity due to diversified climatic conditions that vary from the humid tropicall Western Ghats and the hot deserts of Rajasthan to diversity north-east regions of the country, from the cold desert of Ladakh and the icy mountains of Himalayas to the warm coats of peninsular India, the central fertile plains, providing innumerous microhabitats. The country has large number of species of microorganisms, plants and animals already known anc described.

The important feature of India's biodiversity is that the countıy has 10 biogeographically regions namely, Trans Himalaya, Himalaya, Desert, Semi-arid, Western Ghats, Deccan Peninsula, Gangetic Plain, Coasts, North-East and Islands. The various biogeographically regions and total area in square kilometers is shown below:

Sr.No Biogeography zone Total area (Sq. km)

1. Trans-Himalaya 1,86,200
2. Himalaya 3,47,200
3. Desert 2,25,000
4. Semi-desert 5,08,000
5. Western Ghats 14,21,000
7. Gangetic Plan3, 59,400
8. Coasts 13,000
9. North East1, 71,400
10. Islands (Andaman, Nikobar, Lakshadweep) 8,507

12.2.1 Trans-Himalayan Zone

It covers an area of 1, 86,200 sq. km in the cold, arid regions of Ladakh and Lahul Spiti. This zone has sparse alpine vegetation. The fauna of this zone includes wild sheep and goat, yak, Tibetan ass, gazelle antelope, snow leopard, Tibetan wolf, pika, marmot, migratory black-necked crane.

12.2.2 Himalaya

This zone extends from north-west region to Kashmir to the east up to NEFA comprising four biotic provinces north-west, west, central and east Himalayas. It extends up to 3, 47,200 sq. km. This zone has three zones of vegetation namely, sub-montane (tropical and subtropical) extending from plain-foothills upto 6000 ft. altitude: temperate or montane extending in this zone is more than the trans-Himalayan zone. It includes samber, goral, musk deer, serow, wild bear, snow leopard, brown bear, pheasanta etc. Sikkim stag, once prevalent, is now extinct.

12.2.3 Desert Zone

This zone includes Kutch, Thar and Ladakh provinces consisting of parts of Gujarat, Rajasthan, Haryana, Delhi and Jammu and Kashmir. It covers around 2, 25,000 sq. km area. (Area of Ladakh provides is not includes). The north-west desert region of Kutch and Thar has very hot and dry summer climate, while winters are cold. Rainfall is less than 700 mm. this region has mostly xerophytes (*e.g.,* Acacia nelotica, Prosopia specifera, Tecomella species etc.). the fauna of this region includes great Indian bustard, wild ass, desert fox, desert cat, sand grouse etc. the ladakh region, in the other hand, is the cold desert region having sparse vegetation.

12.2.4 Semi-Desert Zone

It extends up to 5,08,000 sq-km covering Madhya Pradesh, Chattisgarh, parts of Orissa and Gujarat. This zone has thorny, mixed deciduous and Sal type forest vegetation depending upon the rainfall. Endemic fauna includes lion of Gir.

12.2.5 Western Ghats

This zone extends 1,59,000 sq-km from Gujarat in the north to the cape Comorian in the south comprising the Malabar Coast and western Ghat mountains. This region has heavy rainfall. The vegetation of Western Ghats includes tropical moist evergreen forests, Sub-tropical or temperate evergreen forests, mixed deciduous forests and the mangrove forests. This region has very large number of endemic fauna and flora. Travacore tortoise and crane turtle are the threatened reptiles.

12.2.6 Deccan Peninsula

It covers 14,24,000 sq-km area comprising Deccan Plateau (South), Central Plateau, Eastern Plateau, Chhota Nagpur Plateau and Central Highlands. This region lies in the rain-shadow zone of the Western Ghats and thus has limited rainfall of about 100 mm. the forests of this zone have Boswellia serrata, Hardwickia pinnata, Tectona grandis etc. the fauna of this region comprises gair sambar, sloth bear, tiger, leopard, wild boar, barasingha, chowsinga, chital, wild buffalo, wild elephants etc.

12.2.7 Gangetic Plains

This zone extends up to the Himalaya foothills in the north covering 3,59,400 sq-km area. This zone is the most fertile belt comprising of Uttar Pradesh, Bihar and West Bengal States. The vegetation of the region is primarily of tropical moist and dry deciduous forests type. Different regions have characteristic vegetation. For instance, near the foothills of the Himalayas in the north-western Uttar Pradesh, Dalbergia sissoo and Acacia nelotica are most common trees; in the south-western Uttar Pradesh, Capparis aphylla, Acacia nelotica and Saccharum munja are dominant species ; Butea monosperma, Acacia catechu, Azadirachta indica, Ficus religiosa etc. are most common tn eastern Uttar Pradesh ; Gangetic delta region has dominant halophytic vegetation. The fauna includes blackbuck, barashinga, gazelle, elephants, rhinoceros, crocodile, turtle etc.

12.2.8 Coasts

The coastline of India has mangrove vegetation typical of estuarine tracts *e.g.*, at Ratna Giri (Maharashtra) and Pichavaram near Chennai, Fauna of the region includes dugong, inshore dolphin, marine and estuarine turtles, estuarine and salt water crocodile etc.

12.2.9 North-East zone

This zone is among the richest region of the country as far as flora is concerned. It has grasslands and dense tropical evergreen forests having Mesua ferrea, Dipterocarpus macrocarpus, Shorea robusta, Sterculia alata etc. important trees. This region receives the heaviest rainfall. The fauna of the region comprises elephants, rhinoceros, buffalo, swamp deer, pygmy hog etc.

12.2.10 Islands

The islands of Andaman and Nokibar in the Bay of Bengal and Lakshadweep islands in the Arabian Sea have wide variety of coastal vegetation e.g. mangroves, beech forests, and evergreen forests of tall trees. The area is rich in higher plants species and avian fauna. Of these, large number of species is endemic.

12.3 INDIA AS A MEGA DIVERSITY NATION

India has attained a unique distinction as it has been assigned the status of mega diversity nation along with 11 other countries namely, Australia, Brazil, China, kolumbia, Equador, Indonesia, Madagascar, Malaysia, Mexico, Peru and Zaire. It has valuable gene pools, which built the foundations of modern agriculture, horticulture, silviculture, pisciculture, poultry, piggery, dairy etc. Some salient-features of India's biodiversity, which render it as a mega diversity nation, are mentioned below:

The country has diversified climatic conditions that vary from the humid tropics Western Ghats and hot deserts of Rajasthan to diversified north-east region of the country, from the cold deserts of Ladakh and the icy mountains of Himalayas to the warni deccan Peninsula India, and the central fertile plains, providing innumerous microhabitats.

The country has 10 biogeographically region namely, trans Himalaya, Himalaya, Desert, Semi-arid, Western Ghats, Deccan Peninsula, Gangtic Plains, Coasts, North-East and Islands. Sub-tropical or temperature evergreen forests, mixed deciduous forests and the mangrove forests. This region has very large number of endemic fauna and flora. Travacore tortoise and crane turtle are the threatened reptiles.

India represents only 2.4% of the total land area of the world. However, in terms of biodiversity, its percent contribution is 10.53% of the known global biodiversity. Table 4.2 reveals recorded number of animal and plants species belonging to different taxonomic groups in India and the world as well as India's percent contribution to the world's biodiversity.

India has 95 national parks, 498 wild life sanctuaries, 13 biosphere, 6 wetlands and 5 world heritage sights. The country has also 29 tiger reserves.

1. Assam Kaziranga National park
2. Assam Manas Wildlife Sanctuary
3. Rajasthan Keoladeo Ghana National Park
4. Utter Pradesh Nanda Devi National Park
5. West Bengal Sunderban National Park

The country is rich in endemic flora and fauna. The richest regions are the Himalayas, Western Ghats, Indian Islands and North-Eastern Hills of India. Each biogeographically region has several habitats, biotic communities and ecosystem. Of the total flowering plants known and described from Indian region, nearly 33% are endemic to our country. Similarly, of the known vertebrate animal species from this country, 53% fresh water fishes, 60% amphibians, 36% reptiles and 10% mammals are endemic to our country. Still, there are region in India such as deep oceans. Biological diversity remains poorly explored.

In the revised classification, as per updated list of 25 hotspots of the world two hotspots figure in India sthe western ghats and indo Burma region covering North-east part of India. India is one of the 12 centers of 'origin' of cultivated plants'. As far as agro biodiversity is concerned, it is the origin place of 167 cultivated plants species and 320 species of their wild relatives. India is recognized as centre of origin of 30,000—50,000 varieties of rice, pigeon-pea, sugarcane, turmeric, ginger, mango etc. it ranks seventh in terms of contribution of world's agriculture. India has 26 recognized centers that have nearly a third of all the endemic flowering plants (angiosperms) identified and described till data.

The country has also very marine biodiversity. India's vast coastline, with exclusive economic zone of 202 million sq-kms, supports the most productive ecosystems such as coral reefs, mangroves, lagoons and estuaries. There are 342 species of corals belonging to 76 genera reported so far from India. In addition, about 42 species of mangrove plants have been reported.

12.4 BIODIVERSITY AT THE GLOBAL, NATIONAL AND LOCAL LEVELS

Although references of identification, classification and naming of organisms are available in Upanishads and Vedas, the credit of modern concept of classification and nomenclature goes to Carolus Linnaeus (1707–1778). It has been predicated that total number of species of organisms occupying the planet earth is around 30 million only. Nearly 61% of the known and described species are insects belonging to Phylum Arthropods. In the country, there are only 9700 species of birds and 4650 species of mammals known to us. Similarly, as per **Global Diversity information Facility and the Species** known and described. Our knowledge about viruses, bacteria, protests and Archaea is fragmentary. The available records revel that only 1,550 species of viruses, 4, 000 species of bacteria and 40, 000 species of protozoa are known. There are many more species that still not been described?

Country like India has great habitat diversity and therefore rich in species diversity. Large number of different taxonomic group have been described from India of the total 45,364 number of species of bacteria, algae, fungi, lichens, bryophytes and higher plants known from India, 17,500 species belong to Angiosperms and only 64 and 1,100 species of gymnosperms and pteridophytes respectively. Similarly, 89,315 species of animal's species are known a described from India.

12.5 GRADIENTS OF BIODIVERSITY

As one moves from the poles towards the equator (change in latitude), one finds progressive increase in biodiversity means the biodiversity is minimum at the poles. The temperate regions, with serve climate and short growing period for plants, reveal higher biodiversity than the Polar Regions. The biodiversity becomes the highest in the tropical rain forests. Following reasons have been mentioned for rich biodiversity in the tropics:

1. Rate of specification is more in the tropics. It is so because——
   (i) In the tropics, geographical isolation is enhanced as the environment is unseasoned and the populations of organisms restrict themselves to particular home range. These populations, unlike temperate population, do not feel the need to shift to other favorable habitats. The species specific characteristics, therefore, evolve more rapidly in the isolated population of the tropics.
   (ii) A longer growing seasons in the tropics allows many more generations in the year, allowing more opportunity for selection, for adaptation of courtship and mating which lead to reproductive isolation between species.

(iii) Rate of extinction of species is low. This is so because the environment that prevails in the tropics is nearly constant.

2. There is reduced competition among the species in the tropics. This is due to reasons mentioned below:
   (i) Greater resource availability in the tropics or use of fewer resources by each species.
   (ii) Limitation of population size by predation. This allows additional species to coexist on the resources left by the prey species.
3. The tropics environment is older, allowing more time for the evolution of much larger number of fauna and flora.

Surveys indicated that mean number of vascular species per 0.1 ha sample area in the tropics rain forests range from 118–236 as compared to only 21–48 species in the forests of temperate regions. Such a correlation between diversity and latitude has been depicted for ant species as well as for a wide variety of taxonomic group such as butterflies, months, birds and mammals. Biodiversity also changes with the change in attitude. It increases as one move from higher to lower altitudes. Decrease in temperature and greater seasonal variability are the two major factors responsible for lower diversity at higher altitudes. Worth mentioning is that a 1,000 m increase in altitudes results in nearly 6.5°C decrease in temperature.

12.6 VALUES OF BIODIVERSITY

Values of biodiversity can be mesure at three levels as Consumptive, productive and medicinal values

1. Source of food and improve varieties. However, 85% of the world's food production comes from the cultivating less than 20 plant species. Three carbohydrate-rich crops namely, wheat, corn (maize) and rice alone yield nearly two-third of the food production. To meet the food demands of increasing human population, man not only exploring new verities of plants but also animal food. Biodiversity is also used as a source for **breeding to improve the verities.** To improve the desired traits, commercial & domesticated species are crossbred with their wild relatives. In this way, disease resistant and high yielding verities of crops like wheat, rice, maize, sugarcane and fruits have been developed. For example, cross breeding of wild rich species (oryza nivara) has helped in developing new vareihes which are resistant to main rice diseases. Similarly, potato has been made resistant to late blight disease, potato mosaic virus and five races of cyst nematodes etc. through cross breeding experiments.

Also, hybrid animal verities have been produced to increase the production of milk, meat, eggs etc. This indicates the need for protecting biodiversity for breeding programmers in agriculture, horticulture, floriculture, animal husbandry, apiculture, sericulture, lac culture, piggery, poultry and fishery. Variety plants such as sunflower, coconut, soybean, cotton seed, groundnut, sesames, mustard, rap seed, oil palm are the sources of oils. A number of new species *e.g.*, jojoba seeds, wild gourd, bitter colocynth and many other are under investigation as potential sources of oils. Similarly, a number of animal species are also utilized to obtain fats and oils *e.g.*, fish oil etc.

12.7 IMPORTANT EXAMPLE

A specific case is cited to emphasize the need for conservation of wild life. A few years back, oil palm is the high-yielding rice verities were attacked by a new rice pest named brown plant hopper

(*Nilaparvata lunges*). In a worldwide search, only a few old rice verities from Kerala were found to have resistance to this pest. The resistant gene these verities has been introduced into the modern rice variety.

1. ***Life of a Crop variety:*** Change is the law of nature and it affects everything pests and pathogens evolve new strains, soils vary climates change. The consumer demands also change with time. Average life for a crop variety is only 5 to 15 years. Therefore, new varieties must be constantly produced to meet the changing requirements, and hence wild varieties must continue to persist for serving as gene banks to provide genes for producing new high-yielding, disease-resistant varieties. Sugarcane (*Saccharum offcinarum*) has been made resistant to red rot by introducing into it the gene for resistant form kahi (*Saccharum spontaneous*).
2. ***Fibers:*** A variety of plant species such as cotton, flax, hemp, jute, sun hemp, Agaves, Abaca (*Manila hemp*) etc. are the major sources of fibers. More and more variety of plants is being explored for obtaining superior fibers.
3. ***Plant:*** Species provide a variety of useful products such as gums, resins, tannins, paper, tea, coffee, dry-fruit etc. Similarly, animal species provide fur, skin, leather, honey, lac, silk, pearls, ivory, horns, articles etc. for trade.
4. **Drugs and Medicines:** Large number of substances with therapeutic properties is obtained from variety of plant species. For example, quinine is obtained from the bark of plant *Cinchona ledgeriana* to combat malaria; taxol from the bark of yew trees (*Taxus brevifolia, Taxus baccate*) for treating cancer; alkaloids such as vicristine and vinblastine from Rosy periwinkle plant (*Vinca rosea*)

12.8 BIODIVERSITY AND ITS CONSERVATION

It is pressured that life on this planet originated around 3.6 billion years ago. This mega event marked a major step of transformation of the inorganic to the organic realm. Subsequently, the original life forms underwent progressive changes from simple to complex forms in the course of ages and resulted in great variety of microorganisms, algae, fungi plants and animals in the conditions. These have inhabited and flourished in different habitats draped by characteristics physical conditions. Large and diverse communities of biota have, thus, occupied distinct climatic zones forming ecosystems. The concept of biodiversity first appeared in 1980. It is in fact, the shortened form of two words—'biological' and 'diversity'.

12.9 PHYSICAL CONDITIONS

The physical condition of a cropland depends upon geographic location (latitude and altitude), climatic factors and edaphic conditions. The likely influences of the physical condition are offset by selecting a crop suitable for the area, by growing it in appropriate season and by artificial irrigation and use of fertilizers and manures.

12.10 COMPOSITION

The composition of a biotic community in a cropland varies. The dominant plants species is the crop grown (monoculture). Some weeds invariable grow in every field. The animal populations of a cropland are of earthworms, nematode, rodents, insect pollinators and pests, some birds, and domestic animals. Decomposers are also present. The cropland biotic community is richest when crop is growing in it.

12.11 VULNERABILITY

Agro ecosystem is simple and efficient. However, due to lack of diversity of natural ecosystem, they are more vulnerable to sudden climatic changes. Drought, pests and disease may destroy the entire crop. It will not happen if there are more than one dominant plants populations in a field.

12.12 CHARACTERISTICS OF AGRO ECOSYSTEM

The agro ecosystem has many common features:

1. They are created by man and so termed as anthropogenic or artificial.
2. They are maintained and regulated by man means out put and input.
3. They lack the capacity of self-regulation.
4. They are aerated, irrigated and fed with manure and synthetic fertilizers. The use of the latter is responsible for water population.
5. They are protected against pathogens and pests by the use of pesticides. The latter are toxic to the organisms of higher tropic levels animals and humans. They fenced against the attacks of cattle and other animals.
6. They lack circulation of natural soil nutrients, hence needs for artificial manuring.
7. They lack stability because they are mostly monocultures and do not have diversity.
8. They are prone to destruction by drought, floods, pests, and diseases. Such destructions have caused famines in the past.
9. Crops grown in agro ecosystem are genetically improved so have higher yields.
10. Machinery is used in sowing, spraying and reaping the crops.
11. No biomass is left in the fields because of reaping.
12. Stubbles are burnt to add ash to the fields. However, it loads to the air pollution and is cape Nitrogen.

In short, the agro ecosystem are created, regulated, fed, protected and improved by humans, hence lack diversity, stability, circulation of nutrients, and self-regulation.

12.13 AGRO BIODIVERSITY

India ranks 7th in world. It is one of the 12 centers of origin of cultivated plant. There are enormous varieties of agro-products (grains, fruits and vegetable) produced in India. It is estimated that about 30000 to 50000 varieties of wheat, rice, pulse, sugarcane, potatoes, potato, ginger, turmeric, banana, pigeon pea, berries etc.

There are 167 crop species and their wild relatives. Glimpses of India's mega diversity can be understood by the following points.

As in India there are ten biographic regions and 12 biosphere reserves. The areas like.

Great Nicobar, Gulf of Mannar, Kanchanjanga, Mahas and Nanda Devi are the areas with rich biodiversity.

India as a mega diversity nation is has a very rich heritage of biodiversity at all three levels viz Genes species and ecosystems.Its richness may be assessed from the fact that it represents almost all the biogeographical regions of the world.

Salient Features: Ranking: it ranks 12th amongst the list of mega diversity nation of the world. Ranking in other respects are:

In plant diversity

In mammals diversity

In endemic vertebrae diversity

Agriculture and animal husbandary

Land: Its land area is about 2.4% of the total land area of the world.

Biodiversity share: Its biodiversity contribution is about 8.22% of the total global diversity.

Other contributions are:

Faunal contribution is about 7.31%

Floral contribution is about .88%

Plants Diversity: Plants diversity is high in bryophyte angio-sperms, family orchidacae etc.

There are six Ranigar Wet Lands:

Chikka Lake

Harika Lake

Keoladeo National park

Loktak Lake

Conservation of natural resources

Natural resource conservation

The conservation of natural resources is the fundamental problem. Unless we solve that problem, it will avail us little to solve all others.

—Theodore Roosevelt

Efforts to conserve and protect *global* biodiversity are a recent phenomenon. Prior to the global conservation era, there was the coming of the age of conservation. Some historians have linked this with the 1916 National Parks Act, which included the 'use without impairment' clause, sought by John Muir. This eventually resulted in the removal of a proposal to build a dam in Dinosaur National Monument in 1951.

Natural resource conservation, however, has a history that extends prior to the age of conservation. Resource ethics grew out of necessity through direct relations with nature. Regulation or communal restraint became necessary to prevent selfish motives from taking more than could be locally sustained, therefore compromising the long-term supply for the rest of the community. This social dilemma with respect to natural resource management is often called the "Tragedy of the Commons." From this principal, conservation biologists can trace communal resource based ethics throughout cultures as a solution to communal resource conflict. For example, the Alaskan Tlingit peoples and the Haida of the

Pacific Northwest had resource boundaries, rules, and restrictions among clans with respect to the fishing of Sockeye Salmon. These rules were guided by clan elders who knew life-long details of each river and stream they managed.

There are numerous examples in history where cultures have followed rules, rituals, and organized practice with respect to communal natural resource management. Conservation ethics are also found in early religious and philosophical writings. There are examples in the Tao, Shinto, Hindu, Islamic and Buddhist traditions. In Greek philosophy, Plato lamented about pasture land degradation: "What is left now is, so to say, the skeleton of a body wasted by disease; the rich, soft soil has been carried off and only the bare framework of the district left." In the bible, through Moses, God commanded to let the land rest from cultivation every seventh year. Before the 18th century, however, much of European culture considered it a pagan view to admire nature. Wilderness was denigrated while agricultural development was praised. However, as early as AD 680 a wildlife sanctuary was founded on the Farne Islands by St. Cuthbert in response to his religious beliefs.

12.14 CONSERVATION BIOLOGY

Conservation biology is the scientific study of the nature and status of Earth's biodiversity with the aim of protecting species, their habitats, and ecosystems from excessive rates of extinction. It is an interdisciplinary subject drawing on sciences, economics, and the practice of natural resource management. The term *conservation biology* was introduced as the title of a conference held at the University of California in La Jolla, California in 1978 organized by biologists Bruce Wilcox and Michael Soulé. The meeting was prompted by the concern among scientists over tropical deforestation, disappearing species, eroding genetic diversity within species.

The conference and proceedings that resulted. sought to bridge a gap existing at the time between theory in ecology and population biology on the one hand and conservation policy and practice on the other. Conservation biology and the concept of biological diversity (biodiversity) emerged together, helping crystallize the modern era of conservation science and policy.

The rapid decline of established biological systems around the world means that conservation biology is often referred to as a "Discipline with a deadline". Conservation biology is tied closely to ecology in researching the dispersal, migration, demographics, effective population size, inbreeding depression, and minimum population viability of rare or endangered species. Conservation biology is concerned with phenomena that affect the maintenance, loss, and restoration of biodiversity and the science of sustaining evolutionary processes that engender genetic, population, species, and ecosystem diversity. The concern stems from estimates suggesting that up to 50% of all species on the planet will disappear within the next 50 years, which has contributed to poverty, starvation, and will reset the course of evolution on this planet

12.15 CONTEXT AND TRENDS

Conservation biologists study trends and process from the paleontological past to the ecological present as they gain an understanding of the context related to species extinction. It is generally accepted that there have been five major global mass extinctions that register in Earth's history. These include: the Ordovician (440 mya), Devonian (370 mya), Permian–Triassic (245 mya), Triassic–Jurassic (200 mya), and Cretaceous (65 mya) extinction spasms. Within the last 10,000 years, human influence over the Earth's ecosystems has been so extensive that scientists have difficulty estimating the number of species lost; that is to say the rates of deforestation, reef destruction, wetland draining and other human acts are proceeding much faster than human assessment of species. The latest *Living Planet Report* by the World Wide Fund for Nature estimates that we have exceeded the bio-regenerative capacity of the planet, requiring 1.5 Earths to support the demands placed on our natural resources.

12.16 STATUS OF OCEANS AND REEFS

Global assessments of coral reefs of the world continue to report drastic and rapid rates of decline. By 2000, 27% of the world's coral reef ecosystems had effectively collapsed. The largest period of decline occurred in a dramatic "bleaching" event in 1998, where approximately 16% of all the coral reefs in the world disappeared in less than a year. *Coral bleaching* is caused by a mixture of environmental stresses, including increases in ocean temperatures and acidity, causing both the release of symbiotic algae and death of corals. Decline and extinction risk in coral reef biodiversity has risen dramatically in the past ten years. The loss of coral reefs, which are predicted to go extinct in the next century, will have huge economic impacts, threatens the balance of global biodiversity, and endangers food security for hundreds of millions of people. Conservation biology plays an important role in international agreements covering the world's oceans.

The oceans are threatened by acidification due to an increase in CO_2 levels. This is a most serious threat to societies relying heavily upon oceanic natural resources. A concern is that the majority of all marine species will not be able to evolve or acclimate in response to the changes in the ocean chemistry.

12.17 CONCEPTS AND FOUNDATIONS MEASURING EXTINCTION RATES

The five major extinction spasms measured by extinction levels in marine animal genera through time. Extinction rates are measured in a variety of ways. Conservation biologists measure and apply statistical measures of fossil records, rates of habitat loss, and a multitude of other variables such as loss of biodiversity as a function of the rate of habitat loss and site occupancy to obtain such estimates. The Theory of Island Biogeography is possibly the most significant contribution toward the scientific understanding of both the process and how to measure the rate of species extinction.

The current background extinction rate is estimated to be one species every few years. The measure of ongoing species loss is made more complex by the fact that most of the Earth's species have not been described or evaluated. Estimates vary greatly on how many species actually exist (estimated range: 3,600,000–111,700,000) to how many have received a species binomial (estimated range: 1.5–8 million). Less than 1% of all species that have been described have been studied beyond simply noting its existence.[51] From these figures, the IUCN reports that 23% of vertebrates, 5% of invertebrates and 70% of plants that have been evaluated are designated as endangered or conservation planning is threatened.

12.18 SYSTEMATIC CONSERVATION PLANNING

Systematic conservation planning is an effective way to seek and identify efficient and effective types of reserve design to capture or sustain the highest priority biodiversity values and to work with communities in support of local ecosystems. Margules and Pressey identify six interlinked stages in the systematic planning approach:

Compile data on the biodiversity of the planning region

Identify conservation goals for the planning region

Review existing conservation areas

Select additional conservation areas

Implement conservation actions

Maintain the required values of conservation areas

Conservation biologists regularly prepare detailed conservation plans for grant proposals or to effectively coordinate their plan of action and to identify best management practices. Systematic strategies generally employ the services of Geographic Information Systems to assist in the decision making process.

12.19 PRESERVATION

A preservationist differs from a conservation biologist through the principal of non-interference. Preservationists advocate for giving areas of nature and species a protected existence that halts interference from the humans.[4] In this regard, conservationists differ from preservationists in the social dimension, as conservation biology engages society and seeks equitable solutions for both society and ecosystems.

12.20 ETHICS AND VALUES

Conservation biologists are interdisciplinary researchers that practice ethics in the biological and social sciences. Chan states that conservationists must advocate for biodiversity and can do so in a scientifically ethical manner by not promoting simultaneous advocacy against other competing values. A conservationist researches biodiversity and reasons through a Resource Conservation Ethic, which identify what measures will deliver "the greatest good for the greatest number of people for the longest time." Some conservation biologists argue that nature has an intrinsic value that is independent of anthropocentric usefulness or utilitarianism. Intrinsic value advocates that a gene, or species, be valued because they have a utility for the ecosystems they sustain. Aldo Leopold was a classical thinker and writer on such conservation ethics whose philosophy, ethics and writings are still valued and revisited by modern conservation biologists. His writing is oftentimes required reading for those in the profession.

12.21 CONSERVATION PRIORITIES

A pie chart image showing the relative biomass representation in a rain forest through a summary of children's perceptions from drawings and artwork (left), through a scientific estimate of actual biomass (middle), and by a measure of biodiversity (right). Notice that the biomass of social insects (middle) far outweighs the number of species (right).

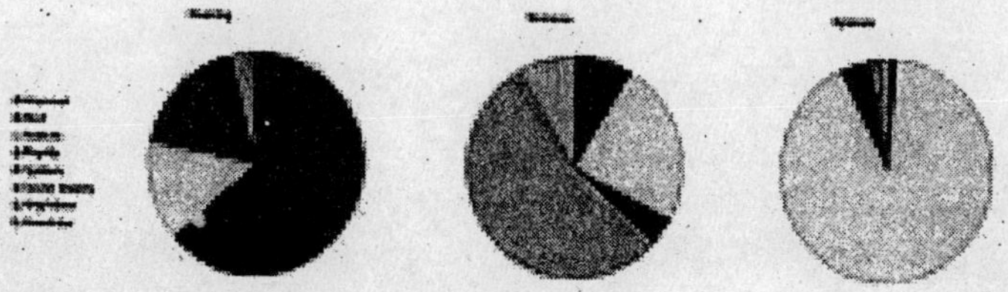

Fig. 12.1

While most in the community of conservation science "stress the importance" of sustaining biodiversity, there is debate on how to prioritize genes, species, or ecosystems, which are all components of biodiversity. While the predominant approach to date has been to focus efforts on endangered species by conserving *biodiversity hotspots*, some scientists and conservation organizations, such as the Nature Conservancy, argue that it is more cost effective, logical, and socially relevant to invest in *biodiversity coldspots*. The costs of discovering, naming, and mapping out the distribution every species, they argue, is an ill advised conservation venture. They reason it is better to understand the significance of the ecological roles of species.

Biodiversity hotspots and coldspots are a way of recognizing that the spatial concentration of genes, species, and ecosystems is not uniformly distributed on the Earth's surface. For example, 44% of all species of vascular plants and 35% of all species in four vertebrate groups are confined to 25 hotspots comprising only 1.4% of the land surface of the Earth."

Those arguing in favor of setting priorities for coldspots point out that there are other measures to consider beyond biodiversity. They point out that emphasizing hotspots downplays the importance of the social and ecological connections to vast areas of the Earth's ecosystems where biomass, not biodiversity, reigns supreme. It is estimated that 36% of the Earth's surface, encompassing 38.9% of the world's vertebrates, lacks the endemic species to qualify as biodiversity hotspot. Moreover, measures show that maximizing protections for biodiversity does not capture ecosystem services any better than targeting randomly chosen regions. Population level biodiversity (*i.e.*, cold spots) are disappearing at a rate that is ten times that at the species level. The level of importance in addressing biomass versus endemism as a concern for conservation biology is highlighted in literature measuring the level of threat to global ecosystem carbon stocks that do not necessarily reside in areas of endemism. A hotspot priority approachwould not invest so heavily in places such as steppes, the Serengeti, the Arctic, or taiga. These areas contribute a great abundance of population (not species) level biodiversity and ecosystem services, including cultural value and planetary nutrient cycling.

12.22 ECONOMIC VALUES AND NATURAL CAPITAL

Conservation biologists have started to collaborate with leading global economists to determine how to measure the wealth and services of nature and to make these values apparent in global market transactions. This system of accounting is called *natural capital* and would, for example, register the value of an ecosystem before it is cleared to make way for development. The WWF publishes its *Living Planet Report* and provides a global index of biodiversity by monitoring approximately 5,000 populations in 1,686 species of vertebrate (mammals, birds, fish, reptiles, and amphibians) and report on the trends in much the same way that the stock market is tracked. This method of measuring the global economic benefit of nature has been endorsed by the G8 + 5 leaders and the European Commission. Nature sustains many ecosystem services that benefit humanity.

Fig. 12.2

Many of the earths ecosystem services are public goods without a market and therefore no price or value. When the *stock market* registers a financial crisis, traders on Wall Street are not in the business of trading stocks for much of the planet's living natural capital stored in ecosystems. There is no natural stock market with investment portfolios into sea horses, amphibians, insects, and other creatures that provide a sustainable supply of ecosystem services that are valuable to society. The ecological footprint of society has exceeded the bio-regenerative capacity limits of the planet's ecosystems by about 30 percent, which is the same percentage of vertebrate populations that have registered decline from 1970 through 2005.

12.23 20th century conservation Roosevelt and Muir on Glacier Point in Yosemite National Park

In the 20th century, actions in the United Kingdom, United States, and Canada emphasized the protection of habitat areas pursuant to visions of such people as John Muir, Theodore Roosevelt, and Aldo Leopold. While the Canadian nor the United Kingdom governments did not pioneer the creation of National Parks as the United States did in the late 19th century, many far-sighted civil servants were dedicated to wildlife conservation and of notable mention. Some of these historical figures include Charles Gordon Hewitt and James Harkin. The term *conservation* came into use in the late 19th century and referred to the management, mainly for economic reasons, of such natural resources as timber, fish, game, topsoil, pastureland, and minerals. In addition, it referred to the preservation of forests (forestry), wildlife (wildlife refuge), parkland, wilderness, and watersheds. Western Europe was the source of much 19th century progress for conservation biology, particularly the British Empire with the Sea Birds Preservation Act 1869.

However, the United States made contributions to this field starting with thinking of Thoreau and taking form with the Forest Act of 1891, John Muir's founding of the Sierra Club in 1892, the founding of the New York Zoological Society in 1895 and establishment of a series of national forests and preserves by Theodore Roosevelt from 1901 to 1909. Not until the mid 20th century did efforts arise to target individual species for conservation, notably efforts in big cat conservation in South America led by the New York Zoological Society.

In the early 20th century the New York Zoological Society was instrumental in developing concepts of establishing preserves for particular species and conducting the necessary conservation studies to determine the suitability of locations that are most appropriate as conservation priorities; the work of Henry Fairfield Osborn Jr., Carl E. Akeley, Archie Carr and Archie Carr III is notable in this era. Akeley for example, having led expeditions to the Virunga Mountains and observed the mountain gorilla in the wild, became convinced that the species and the area were conservation priorities. He was instrumental in persuading Albert I of Belgium to act in defense of the mountain gorilla and establish Albert National Park (since renamed Virunga National Park) in what is now Democratic Republic of Congo.

By the 1970s, led primarily by work in the United States under the Endangered Species Act along with the Species at Risk Act (SARA) of Canada, Biodiversity Action Plans developed in Australia, Sweden, the United Kingdom, hundreds of species specific protection plans ensued. Notably the United Nations acted to conserve sites of outstanding cultural or natural importance to the common heritage of mankind. The programme was adopted by the General Conference of UNESCO in 1972. As of 2006, 830 sites are listed: 644 cultural, 162 natural. The first country to pursue aggressive biological conservation through national legislation was the United States, which passed back to back legislation in the Endangered Species Act (1966) and National Environmental Policy Act (1970), which together injected major funding and protection measures to large scale habitat protection and threatened species research. Other conservation developments, however, have taken hold throughout the world. India, for example, passed the Wildlife Protection Act of 1972.

In 1980, a significant development was the emergence of the urban conservation movement. A local organization was established in Birmingham, UK, a development followed in rapid succession in cities across the UK, then overseas. Although perceived as a grassroots movement, its early development was driven by academic research into urban wildlife. Initially perceived as radical, the movement's view of conservation being inextricably linked with other human activity has now become mainstream in conservation thought. Considerable research effort is now directed at urban conservation biology. The Society for Conservation Biology originated in 1985.

By 1992 most of the countries of the world had become committed to the principles of conservation of biological diversity with the Convention on Biological Diversity; subsequently many countries began programmes of Biodiversity Action Plans to identify and conserve threatened species within their borders, as well as protect associated habitats. The late 1990s saw increasing professionalism in the sector, with the maturing of organisations such as the Institute of Ecology and Environmental Management and the Society for the Environment.

Since 2000, the concept of landscape scale conservation has risen to prominence, with less emphasis being given to single-species or even single-habitat focused actions. Instead, an ecosystem approach is advocated by most mainstream conservationist, although concerns have been expressed by those working to protect some high-profile species. Ecology has clarified the workings of the biosphere; *i.e.*, the complex interrelationships among humans, other species, and the physical environment. The burgeoning human population and associated agriculture, industry, and the ensuing pollution, have demonstrated how easily ecological relationships can be disrupted.

REVIEW QUESTIONS-2

SHORT ANSWER

1. Write a short note on "Arsenic contamination of ground- water."
2. What are primary air pollutants?
3. How would you control carbon monoxide?
4. What is acid rain? Flow does it damage environment?
5. What is biodiversity?
6. What is a cyclone?
7. What is acid rain?
8. What are the units of extinction of biodiversity measurement?
9. How is infant mortality related to life expectancy?
10. What are greenhouse gases?
11. How does global warming affect the world climate and food production?
12. Population stabilization and sustainable c evelop men t
13. Human development index and India's rank in the world context.
14. Explain greenhouse effect.

SHORT NOTES, WRITE NOTES ON THE FOLLOWING:

1. Nitrogen cycle
2. Carbon cycle
3. Human Rights
4. Biodiversity Conservation
5. Hydro/sphere
6. Lithos sphere
7. Carrying capacity of the earth

DIFFERENTIATE BETWEEN THE

1. National park and sanctuary
2. In-situ and ex-situ conservation
3. Species and genetic biodiversity
4. Endangered and extinct species

LONG ANSWER

1. What is population explosion? How does it affect the economy of India?
2. What is meant by doubling time? Explain with reference to world population and Indian population.

3. Give a flow-sheet diagram of municipal waste water treatment (primary and secondary).
4. List water quality parameters for drinking water (USPH Standard) and give their permissible limits.
5. What are the causes of water pollution? Name the organic and inorganic water pollutants.

OBJECTIVE TYPE QUESTION

1. The source of atmospheric oxygen is
   (a) the nitrogen cycle
   (b) photosynthesis by green plants
   (c) exchange of oxygen in environmental segments
   (d) the atmosphere
2. The major reservoir of carbon dioxide is
   (a) the ocean beds
   (b) the atmosphere
   (c) plants and animals
   (d) the atmosphere
3. Forests are important
   (a) for life-support systems
   (b) renewable resources
   (c) the atmosphere
   (d) for animals only
4. India has been losing
   (a) very little forests each year
   (b) 1.3 million hectares of forests each year
   (c) the atmosphere
   (d) 100 million hectares of forests each year
5. The main causes for deforestation are
   (a) the atmosphere
   (b) increasing human and livestock population
   (c) timber business
   (d) tribal people
6. The aim of social forestry is to meet the demand for
   (a) firewood and fodder among rural people
   (b) furniture for urban people
   (c) removing pressure on natural forests
   (d) the atmosphere

7. Biodiversity involves
   (a) forests only
   (b) various living natural resources (plants, animals, micro-organisms)
   (c) human beings
   (d) the atmosphere
8. Extinction of species is
   (a) part of natural extinction
   (b) natural extinction accelerated by man-made extinction
   (c) due to natural disasters
   (d) the atmosphere
9. The P-Triangle is composed of
   (a) biodiversity
   (b) population, poverty and pollution
   (c) poverty, flood and drought
   (d) pressure, point and pollution
10. Indian population doubled
    (a) between 1901 and 1930
    (b) between 1950 and 1981
    (c) between 1941 and 1961
    (d) between 1951-1971
11. The countries with 1-billion population are
    (a) China and India
    (b) USA and Canada
    (c) France and Ger
    (d) the atmosphere
12. Population explosion occurs when
    (a) population increases at a slow rate
    (b) population size exceeds the carrying capacity

Answers

1. (c) 2. (a) 3. (a) 4. (b) 5. (b) 6. (c) 7. (b) 8. (b) 9. (b) 10. (b)
11. (a) 12. (b)

Unit-III

Chapter 13

Air Pollution: An Overview

13.1 INTRODUCTION

Pollution affects both, the living as well as the non-living components of the environment. It brings about drastic changes in the physical environment causing community wide problems by polluting the air, water and land; adversely affecting the health of humans and animals, and damaging plants and property. Main types of pollution are:

Air pollution
Water pollution
Marine pollution
Soil pollution
Noise pollution
Thermal pollution
Radioactive pollution.

Air Pollution

Air pollution may be defined as any chane in atmospheric composition or condition presence certain substances are present in such concentrations that they can produce undesirable effects on man and his environment.

13.2 CAUSES OF AIR POLLUTION

There are two main causes or sources of air-pollution:

A. Natural

B. Man-made or Anthropogenic

Classification of Air Pollutants: The air-pollutants are classified in two different ways

A. According to origin

B. According to state of matter

A. According to Origin

According to their origin the air pollutants may be classified as

- Primary pollutants
- Secondary pollutants
- Air Pollutants
- Contents
- Introduction
- Air Pollution
- Cause of Air Pollution
- Classification of Air Pollutant
- According to Origin
- Primary Pollutants
- Secondary Pollutants

13.2.1 Primary Pollutants

Those pollutants that are emitted directly from the sources and are found in the atmosphere in the form in which they were emitted are called primary pollutants. Examples of primary pollutants are Sulphur oxides, Nitrogen oxides, hydrocarbons, ash, smoke, dust, fumes, mist, sprays, radioactive compounds etc.

13.2.2 Secondary Pollutants

Those pollutants that are formed in the atmosphere by chemical interactions between primary pollutants and atmospheric constituents are called secondary pollutants. These are usually formed by a photochemical reaction or by hydrolysis or oxidation reactions in the atmosphere. Examples of secondary pollutants are Ozone, Sulphur trioxide, peroxyacytyl nitrate (PAN), aldehydes, ketones etc.

Classification of pollutants on the basis of State of Matter According to this property the air pollutants can be classified into two main categories:

Gaseous air pollutants

Particulate air pollutants

13.2.3 Gaseous matter as Air Pollutants

These are pollutants occurring in the gaseous state at normal temperature and pressure. Common gaseous pollutants are carbon dioxide, nitrogen oxides, Sulphur oxides, hydrocarbons and photochemical oxidants.

13.2.4 Particulate matter as Air Pollutants

All atmospheric substances that are not gases but may be suspended droplets, solid particles or mixtures of the two are generally referred to as particulates. Particulate pollutants are categorized according to size, mode of formation (source) or physical state.

a. Aerosols
b. Dust
c. Smoke
d. Fumes
e. Mist
f. Fog
g. Flyash
h. Soot
i. Natural Particulates

Effects of Air Pollution

Effects on human health

Effects on animals

Effects on plants

Effects on materials

Effect on climate

Effect on aesthetic beauty

Control of Air Pollution

The following methods are most effective for dealing with the control of air pollution:

Source correction method

Pollution control equipment

Diffusion of pollutant in air

Vegetation

Zoning

13.3 CHEMISTRY OF ATMOSPHERIC POLLUTANTS

A variety of air pollutants have known or suspected harmful effects on human health and the environment. In most areas of Europe, these pollutants are principally the products of combustion from space heating, power generation or from motor vehicle traffic. Pollutants from these sources may not only prove a problem in the immediate vicinity of these sources but can travel long distances, chemically reacting in the atmosphere to produce secondary pollutants such as acid rain or ozone.

13.3.1 Evolutionary Trends in Pollution Problems

In both developed and rapidly industrialising countries, the major historic air pollution problem has typically been high levels of smoke and SO_2 arising from the combustion of sulphur-containing fossil fuels such as coal for domestic and industrial purposes. Smogs resulting from the combined effects of black smoke, sulphate/acid aerosol and fog have been seen throughout Northern European cities for centuries, and still occur in many parts of the developing world. In economically developed countries, however, this problem has diminished over recent decades because of changing fuel-use patterns; the increasing use of cleaner fuels such as natural gas, and the implementation of effective smoke and emission control policies. These long-term changes in air pollution climate are also seen, often occurring very rapidly, in many developing countries. In both developed and developing countries, the major threat to clean air is now posed by traffic emissions. Petrol- and diesel-engined motor vehicles emit a wide variety of pollutants, principally carbon monoxide (CO), oxides of nitrogen (NO_x), volatile organic compounds (VOCs) and particulates, which have an increasing impact on urban air quality.

In addition, photochemical reactions resulting from the action of sunlight on NO2 and VOCs from vehicles leads to the formation of ozone, a secondary long-range pollutant, which impacts in rural areas often far from the original emission site. Acid rain is another long-range pollutant influenced by vehicle NOx emissions. In all except worst-case situations, industrial and domestic pollutant sources, together with their impact on air quality, tend to be steady-state or improving over time. However, traffic pollution problems are worsening world-wide. The problem may be particularly acute in developing countries with dramatically increasing vehicle fleets, infrastructural limitations, poor engine/emission control technologies and limited provision for maintenance or vehicle regulation.

Principal pollutants produced by industrial, domestic and traffic sources are mentioned below:

Sulphur Dioxide (SO_2).

Particulate Matter

Carbon Monoxide (CO)

Nitrogen Dioxide(NO_2)

Ozone (O_3)

Hydrocarbons

Benzene

1,3-Butadiene

TOMPs (Toxic Organic Micropollutants)

Lead (Pb) and Heavy Metals

Acid Deposition

Sulphur Dioxide

Sulphur dioxide is a corrosive acid gas that combines with water vapour in the atmosphere to produce acid rain. Wet and dry deposition has been implicated in the damage and destruction of vegetation and in the degradation of soils, building materials and watercourses. SO_2 in ambient air is also associated with asthma and chronic bronchitis. The principal source of this gas is power stations burning fossil fuels, which contain sulphur. Major SO_2 problems now only tend to occur in cities in which coal is still widely used for domestic heating, in industry and in power stations. As some power stations are now located away from urban areas, SO_2 emissions may affect air quality in both rural and urban areas. Since the decline in domestic coal burning in cities and in power stations overall, SO_2 emissions have diminished steadily and, in most European countries, they are no longer considered to pose a significant threat to health. Particular concern in the past was the combination of SO_2 and black smoke and particulate matter; current EC Directive Limit Values for SO_2 are defined in terms of accompanying black smoke levels, although these are likely to change.

13.4 PARTICLES (PM_{10})

Airborne particulate matter varies widely in its physical and chemical composition, source and particle size. PM_{10} particles (the fraction of particulates in air of very small size (<10 μm)) are of major current concern, as they are small enough to penetrate deep into the lungs and so potentially pose significant health risks. Larger particles meanwhile, are not readily inhaled, and are removed relatively efficiently from the air by sedimentation. Particles are often classed as either primary (those emitted directly into the atmosphere) or secondary (those formed or modified in the atmosphere from condensation and growth).

A major source of fine primary particles are combustion processes, in particular diesel combustion, where transport of hot exhaust vapour into a cooler tailpipe or stack can lead to spontaneous nucleation of "carbon" particles before emission. Secondary particles are typically formed when low volatility products are generated in the atmosphere, for example the oxidation of sulphur dioxide to sulphuric acid. The atmospheric lifetime of particulate matter is strongly related to particle size, but may be as long as 10 days for particles of about 1mm in diameter.

The principal source of airbourne PM_{10} matter in European cities is road traffic emissions, particularly from diesel vehicles. As well as creating dirt, odour and visibility problems, PM_{10} particles are associated with health effects including increased risk of heart and lung disease. In addition, they may carry surface-absorbed carcinogenic compounds into the lungs. Concern about the potential health impacts of PM_{10} has increased very rapidly over recent years. Increasingly, attention has been turning towards monitoring of the smaller particle fraction $PM_{2.5}$ capable of penetrating deepest into the lungs, or to even smaller size fractions or total particle numbers.

13.4.1 Carbon Monoxide

Carbon monoxide (CO) is a toxic gas that is emitted into the atmosphere because of combustion processes, and is formed by the oxidation of hydrocarbons and other organic compounds. In European urban areas, CO is produced almost entirely (90%) from road traffic emissions. CO at levels found in ambient air may reduce the oxygen-carrying capacity of the blood. It survives in the atmosphere for a period of approximately 1 month but is eventually oxidised to carbon dioxide (CO_2).

13.4.2 Nitrogen Dioxide (NO_2)

Nitrogen oxides are formed during high temperature combustion processes from the oxidation of nitrogen in the air or fuel. The principal source of nitrogen oxides — nitric oxide (NO) and nitrogen dioxide (NO_2), collectively known as NO_x - is road traffic, which is responsible for approximately half the emissions in Europe. NO and NO_2 concentrations are therefore greatest in urban areas where traffic is heaviest. Other important sources are power stations, heating plants and industrial processes.

Nitrogen oxides are released into the atmosphere mainly in the form of NO, which is then readily oxidised to NO_2 by reaction with ozone. Elevated levels of NO_x occur in urban environments under stable meteorological conditions, when the airmass is unable to disperse.

Nitrogen dioxide has a variety of environmental and health impacts. It is a respiratory irritant, may exacerbate asthma and possibly increase susceptibility to infections. In the presence of sunlight, it reacts with hydrocarbons to produce photochemical pollutants such as ozone. In addition, nitrogen oxides have a lifetime of approximately 1 day with respect to conversion to nitric acid. This nitric acid is in turn removed from the atmosphere by direct deposition to the ground, or transfer to aqueous droplets (e.g. cloud or rainwater), thereby contributing to acid deposition.

13.4.3 OZONE (O_3)

Ground-level ozone (O_3), unlike other primary pollutants mentioned above, is not emitted directly into the atmosphere, but is a secondary pollutant produced by reaction between nitrogen dioxide (NO_2), hydrocarbons and sunlight. Ozone can irritate the eyes and air passages causing breathing difficulties and may increase susceptibility to infection. It is a highly reactive chemical, capable of attacking surfaces, fabrics and rubber materials. Ozone is also toxic to some crops, vegetation and trees.

Whereas nitrogen dioxide (NO_2) participates in the formation of ozone, nitrogen oxide (NO) destroys ozone to form oxygen (O_2) and nitrogen dioxide (NO_2). For this reason, ozone levels are not as high in urban areas (where high levels of NO are emitted from vehicles) as in rural areas. As the nitrogen oxides and hydrocarbons are transported out of urban areas, the ozone-destroying NO is oxidised to NO_2, which participates in ozone formation.

Sunlight provides the energy to initiate ozone formation; near-ultra-violet radiation dissociates stable molecules to form reactive species known as free radicals. In the presence of nitrogen oxides, these free radicals catalyse the oxidation of hydrocarbons to carbon dioxide and water vapour. Partially oxidised organic species such as aldehydes, ketones and carbon monoxide are intermediate products, with ozone being generated as a by-product.

Since ozone itself is photodissociated (split up by sunlight) to form free radicals, it promotes the oxidation chemistry, and so catalyses its own formation (ie. it is an autocatalyst). Consequently, high levels of ozone are generally observed during hot, still sunny, summertime weather in locations where the airmass has previously collected emissions of hydrocarbons and nitrogen oxides (e.g. urban areas with traffic). Because of the time required for chemical processing, ozone formation tends to be downwind of pollution centres. The resulting ozone pollution or "summertime smog"may persist for several days and be transported over long distances.

13.4.4 HYDROCARBONS

There are two main groups of hydrocarbons of concern: volatile organic compounds (VOCs) and polycyclic aromatic hydrocarbons PAHs VOCs are released in vehicle exhaust gases either as unburned fuels or as combustion products, and are emitted by the evaporation of solvents and motor fuels. Benzene and 1,3-butadiene are of particular concern as they are known carcinogens. Other VOCs are important because of the role they play in the photochemical formation of ozone in the atmosphere. Benzene is an aromatic VOC, which is a minor constituent of petrol (about 2% by volume). The main sources of benzene in the atmosphere in Europe are the distribution and combustion of petrol. Combustion by petrol vehicles is the single biggest source (70% of total emissions) whilst the refining, distribution and evaporation of petrol from vehicles accounts for approximately a further 10% of total emissions. Benzene is emitted in vehicle exhaust not only as unburnt fuel but also as a product of the decomposition of other aromatic compounds. Benzene is a known human carcinogen.

1, 3-butadiene, like benzene, is a VOC emitted into the atmosphere principally from fuel combustion of petrol and diesel vehicles. Unlike benzene, however, it is not a constituent of the fuel but is produced by the combustion of olefins. 1, 3-butadiene is also an important chemical in certain industrial processes, particularly the manufacture of synthetic rubber. It is handled in bulk at a small number of industrial locations. Other than in the vicinity of such locations, the dominant source of 1, 3-butadiene in the atmosphere is the motor vehicle. 1, 3 Butadiene is also a known, potent human carcinogen.

13.4.5 Toxic Organic Micropollutants

TOMPs (Toxic Organic Micropollutants) are produced by the incomplete combustion of fuels. They comprise a complex range of chemicals some of which, although they are emitted in very small quantities, are highly toxic or carcinogenic. Compounds in this category include:

- PAHs (PolyAromatic Hydrocarbons)
- PCBs (PolyChlorinated Biphenyls)
- Dioxins
- Furans

13.4.6 Lead and Heavy Metals

Particulate metals in air result from activities such as fossil fuel combustion (including vehicles), metal processing industries and waste incineration. There are currently no EC standards for metals other than lead, although several are under development. Lead is a cumulative poison to the Central Nervous System, particularly detrimental to the mental development of children.

Lead is the most widely used non-ferrous metal and has a large number of industrial applications. Its single largest industrial use world-wide is in the manufacture of batteries (60–70% of total consumption of some 4 million tonnes) and it is used in paints, glazes, alloys, radiation shielding, tank lining and piping. As tetraethyl lead, it has been used for many years as an additive in petrol; most airborne emissions of lead in Europe therefore originate from petrol-engined motor vehicles. With the increasing use of unleaded petrol, however, emissions and concentrations in air have declined steadily in recent years.

13.4.7 ACID DEPOSITION

Acidification of water bodies and soils, and the consequent impact on agriculture, forestry and fisheries are the result of the re-deposition of acidifying compounds resulting principally from the oxidation of primary SO_2 and NO_2 emissions from fossil fuel combustion. Deposition may be by either wet or dry processes, and acid deposition studies often need to examine both of these acidification routes.

13.4.8 BIOLOGICAL MAGNIFICATION

Toxins and pollutants that cannot be degraded or completely excreted from living things are found in much higher concentrations in the tissues of top consumers than in their environment. This is the result of "biological magnification". For Example if A consumer eats 10 pounds of food and burns 80 to 90% of it for metabolism. Stable toxins are not burned but are stored in the consumer's tissues, accumulating by a factor of 10 or more over the concentration in the food. This magnification occurs at every step in the food chain and thus an environmental level of the toxin that is harmless can accumulate to health-threatening levels in top consumers, including humans.

A famous example of a toxin that was biologically magnified to the point of poisoning top consumers (birds of prey) was the insecticide DDT. This case is discussed on page 744 of your text. Another example is mercury. Mercury is released into the air from burning coal in power plants and from burning of refuse. It falls into the oceans from these human sources as well as from other natural sources. Ocean waters may have a concentration of mercury that is extremely low but it is magnified up to 100,000 times in the tissues of top consumers, such as swordfish and shark.

Mercury levels in swordfish and shark sold at fish markets can be above 1 part per million (ppm), which is the safe level of mercury in food established by the Food and Drug Administration. The FDA discourages consumption of shark and swordfish because of the mercury they contain. Canned tuna can have mercury levels up to 0.3 ppm. This is high enough that Consumers Union (publisher of Consumer Reports) recommends that pregnant women and young children, who are more susceptible to mercury poisoning than adults are, eat no more than one tuna sandwich a week. Low level mercury poisoning damages nerve cells and causes memory loss and loss of muscle coordination. These symptoms appear when blood levels of mercury exceed about 15 parts per billion.

Chapter 14

Classification of Air Pollutants (Primary and Secondary Pollutants)

14.1 POLLUTANTS

Any substance present in the environment in harmful concentration, which adversely alters the environment by damaging the growth rate of a species and by interfering with the food chains, affects the health, comfort and property etc. is considered as a pollutant.

Types of pollutants, on the basis of their natural disposal

Degradable pollutant

Non degradable pollutant

Degradable pollutants are those that can be decomposed, consumed, or reduced to acceptable levels by natural or artificial means. However, pollutants such as human sewage, animal, and crop wastes can be decompose only if the system is not overloaded. Certain chemicals decompose slowly, and can persist at harmful levels for decades like detergents and pesticides.

Non degradable pollutants include many radioactive materials, heavy metals and some plastics, which cannot be degraded by natural or artificial means. They must be controlled or prevented from reaching the environment.

14.2 ON THE BASIS OF ORIGIN

14.2.1 Primary Pollutant:

Which are emitted directly from the source *eg.,* Ash, fumes, dust, NO_2, SO_2 etc.

14.2.2 Secondary Pollutant

Which derived from primary pollutant after the photochemical reaction in the atmosphere.Eg., SO_3, NO_3, PAN etc.?

14.2.3 Quantitative pollutant

These are those substances normally occurring in the environment, who acquire the status of a pollutant when their concentration increased due to the unmindful activity of man.

14.2.4 Qualitative pollutant

These are those substances, which do not normally occur in nature but are added by man, for example, insecticides.

Environmental pollutants:

Deposited matter–Smoke, tar, dust, grit etc.

Gases–oxides of nitrogen, sulphur, CO, Halogens (chlorine, bromine, iodine)

Acids droplets–Sulphuric acid, nitric acid etc.

Fluorides

Metals–Mercury, lead, iron, zinc, nickel, tin, cadmium, chromium etc.

Agrochemicals–Biocides (pesticides, herbicides, fungicides, nematicides, bacteriacides, weedicides etc) and fertilizers.

Complex organic substances–Benzene, ether, acetic acid, benzpyrenes etc.

Photochemical oxidants–Photochemical smog, ozone, peroxyacetyl nitrate(PAN), NO_2, aldehydes, ethylene etc.

Solid wastes

Radioactive wastes

Noise

Table: 14.1 Types of pollution and pollutanty

Type of pollution	*Pollutant*
Air pollution suspended particulate matter	Sulphur dioxide, oxides of nitrogen etc.
Water pollution	Microorganisms, fluoride, cyanide, sulphate etc.
Soil pollution	Heavy materials like arsenic.
Food pollution	Pesticide, microorganisms, lead, cadmium etc.
Noise pollution	Industrial activity, traffic, and loudspeakers.

Sources of Pollution

There are two main sources of pollution:

Natural sources

Man made or anthroprogenic sources

Natural sources of pollution:

Volcanic eruptions

Forest fires

Dust storms

Bacteria. spores, cysts and pollens

Decay of organic matter in marshy places release methane.

Man made sources of pollution:

Industrialization

Invention of automobiles

Over population

Deforestation

Nuclear explosions

Over exploitation of resources

Construction of buildings, roads and dams

Explosives use in wars

Use of fertilizers and pesticides

14.3 QUARRING AND MINING

14.3.1 Pollutant

Any substance present in higher concentration which adversely alters the environment by reducing the growth rate of species and by interfering with the growth rate of species an by interfering with the food chain effects the health , comfort and property etc. is considered as a pollutant CO_2, SO_2, NO_2.

Classification of Pollutants:

These pollutants are classified on three bases:

On the basis of their natural disposal:

Bio degradable: They are naturally degraded by the action of natural source

Domestic organic waste

Domestic sewage

Non degradable: They are not degraded by the action of Natural Source

Chemicals

Pesticides

14.4 ON THE BASIS OF ORIGIN

14.4.1 Primary pollutants

Which are directly added or emitted into the atmosphere?

14.4.2 Secondary pollutants

Which are derived from primary pollutant after the photo chemical reaction in the atmosphere.

$SO_2 + H_2O \rightarrow H_2SO_4$ (acid rain)

HNO_3

HCl

On the basis of the existence in nature:

Quantitative (increase in quantity) NO_2, SO_2, N

Qualitative (included by us) Pesticides, DDT, fungicides

14.5 NATURAL SOURCES OF POLLUTION

Smoke and traces of gases produced from forest fires. Gases released from volcanic eruptions.

Volcanic ash and Dust from dust storms.

Marsh gas such as methane (CH_4) released from the decay of organic matter.

Bacterias, cysts, pollens, spores etc.

14.6 ANTHROPOGENIC OR MAN MADE SOURCES

Smoke and dust particles from industries, thermal power plants, automobile exhausts, marine exhausts, aircraft exhausts, Nuclear explosion, Explosives, fertilizers, pesticides etc.

Solid wastes due to over urbanization and over population.

Deforestation and destruction of Natural habitat

Construction of roads, buildings etc.

Medical waste and garbage

Micro particles of automobiles types

Cosmic rays which are fast moving highly energetic radiation.

Volcanoes

The terrestrial radiations from nuclides

Natural disasters

Pollen grains

Bacterial decomposition

Forest fire

Gases like NO_2, NO, SO_2, CO, CO_2, and Halogens.

Fluorides

Deposited matter

Acid droplets

Agro chemicals

Solid wastes

Radioactive wastes

Complex organic wastes/ substances

Photochemical oxidants

Metals like mercury, lead

Atomic reactors and nuclear fuel

Chapter 15

Causes of Air Pollution and Adverse Effects of Pollutants

15.1 ENVIRONMENTAL POLLUTION

Illustration in physical, chemical and biological properties of air, water and soil, which is harmful to human beings, plants, property, is known as Environmental Pollution.

In other words, Environment mean surrounding and pollution means to make anything dirty or to change the purity, which can be overall termed as presence of anything in our surroundings that can change the physical, chemical or biological property of air water and soil, are known as Environmental Pollution.

15.2 VARIOUS TYPES OF ENVIRONMENTAL POLLUTION

There are several types of pollutions

- Air pollution
- Water pollution
- Soil pollution
- Marine pollution
- Thermal pollution
- Noise pollution
- Industrial pollution
- Solid waste pollution

15.2.1 Air Pollution

The term "air pollution "means the substances that on local and regional scales harm animals, plants and people.

Causes of air pollution:

Carbon compounds

Sulphur compounds

Nitrogen compounds

Ozone

Fluorides

Hydro carbons

Metals

Photochemical products

Particulate waste

Biological particulate pollutants

Toxicants other than heavy metals

Effects of Air pollution on human health:

Irritation of eye, nose and throat

Irritation of respiratory system

Lead particles from automobile cause in lead poisoning, which results in conversion, coma and even death.

Radioactive fallout has somatic and genetic effects on future.

Mercury from combustion of fossil fuels and plants results in nerve, brain and kidney damage.

Plants

Ozone causes necrosis and damages the leaves

NO_2 causes premature leaf fall and suppressed growth of plants resulting in reduced yields of crop plants.

SO_2 bleaches the leaf surface and causes chlorosis (*i.e.*, loss of chlorophyll and yellowing of the leaf), especially in leafy vegetables.

PAN (peroxy acyl nitrate) damages leafy vegetables causing their premature fall, discoloration and curling of sepals.

Animals

When animals feed on the particulate coated plants, they get affected with Arsenic poisoning. Head poisoning results in bronchitis and lack of appetite in pet animals.

Properties

Chemical attack

Abrasion

Corrosion

Deposition and removal of materials.

15.3 THE MAPS

The MAPS instrument measures the distribution of carbon monoxide in the Earth's lower atmosphere (3 to 10 kilometers above the surface), from latitude 57 degrees North to latitude 57 degrees South. The MAPS measurements provide scientists with the only near-global database of atmospheric carbon monoxide levels. These unique measurements help scientists understand how well the atmosphere can cleanse itself of pollutants such as carbon monoxide. In addition, the MAPS measurements help scientists better understand both how far pollutants are transported from their source areas and the size of the sources.

15.3.1 Carbon Monoxide

Carbon monoxide (CO) is a colorless and odorless gas produced by the burning of fossil fuels, such as gasoline, and by the burning of forests and grasslands.

World-wide increases in human technological and agricultural activity are causing increasing amounts of carbon monoxide to be released into the air. Once in the atmosphere, carbon monoxide can be transported over long distances, eventually converting to carbon dioxide by reaction with a chemical called the hydroxyl radical (chemical symbol: OH). The OH radical is a key participant in the destruction and removal of greenhouse gases such as methane. Methane itself is important in the chemical cycle of stratospheric ozone.

As the amount of carbon monoxide in the atmosphere increases, its reactions with the OH radical may increase accordingly. This may leave less OH available to break down and remove greenhouse gases. Therefore, increases in carbon monoxide levels may cause subsequent decreases in OH levels, which can have long-term consequences on stratospheric ozone and the levels of various greenhouse gases, potentially influencing the Earth's climate. At present, the size of the various global carbon monoxide sources and their seasonal cycles are not well known.

15.3.2 Previous MAPS missions

The MAPS instrument has flown aboard the Space Shuttle four times: in November 1981 (STS-2), as the first science payload on the Space Shuttle, in October 1984 (STS-41G), and in April 1994 (STS-59) and October 1994 (STS-68). The November 1981 mission provided surprising results in that the greatest concentrations of carbon monoxide in the lower atmosphere were found over the Earth's tropical regions rather than over the industrialized Northern Hemisphere, as had been expected. The 1981 mission also showed that carbon monoxide concentrations vary greatly from region to region. The October 1984 mission (Fig. 1) confirmed the November 1981 finding that the burning of forests in South America and grasslands in Africa are significant sources of global tropospheric carbon monoxide during the Southern Hemisphere dry season.

Results from the April 1994 (STS-59) MAPS mission show low carbon monoxide mixing ratios in the Southern Hemisphere (very clean air), with a gradual increase in carbon monoxide levels in the Northern Hemisphere. In October 1994, the data revealed that the latitudinal gradient was reversed from the situation observed in April. The highest levels of carbon monoxide were measured over central Brazil, southern Africa, and over Indonesia where extensive fires and smoke plumes were reported by the astronaut crew.

15.3.3 Correlative Measurements

The space-based data from the MAPS instrument were correlated with a global network of intercalibrated ground- and aircraft-based measurements. To ensure the accuracy of the ground and aircraft measurements, every instrument was calibrated using the same four gas cylinders. This ensured that all the instruments had the same calibration standard (that they were "intercalibrated") and allowed for the intercomparison of carbon monoxide data measured by dozens of different instruments around the world.

The more than two dozen ground sites during the April and October 1994 missions included locations in the United States, South Africa, Russia, Germany, Bermuda, Ireland, Hong Kong, Australia and New Zealand. The aircraft underflights of the 1994 MAPS missions included the NASA DC-8, and aircraft from INPE, Brazil; CSIRO, Australia; the University of Maryland; and NOAA, Boulder.

15.3.4 The MAPS instrument

The MAPS shuttle flight hardware consists of an optical box, an electronics box, a tape recorder, and an infrared camera, all mounted to a single baseplate. This assembly is mounted to a Multi-Purpose Experiment Support Structure near the forward end of the cargo bay. The instrument is about 36 inches long, 30 inches wide, and 23 inches high. It weighs 203 pounds and consumes about 65 watts of electrical power.

The MAPS instrument is based on a technique called gas filter radiometry. The MAPS instrument determines the CO mixing ratio in the atmosphere by comparing the measured thermal energy from the atmosphere to the thermal energy of a known quantity of CO carried aboard the instrument. Heat, or thermal energy, is emitted by the Earth's surface and passes upward through the atmosphere. As the thermal energy passes through the atmosphere, it is absorbed by atmospheric carbon monoxide and retransmitted at a thermal energy frequency unique to CO.

The MAPS instrument is designed to be sensitive to the thermal energy at this unique CO frequency. This unique frequency can be thought of as an atmospheric CO "fingerprint." The thermal energy from the atmosphere enters the MAPS instrument and is split into three beams. One beam is passed through a gas cell containing CO and then falls upon an electronic detector which measures the amount of thermal energy in the filtered beam. The second beam falls directly onto a second electronic detector without passing through any gas filter. The difference in the amount of voltage between the first and second detectors is used to determine the amount of CO present in the atmosphere.

The third beam of thermal energy passes through a gas cell containing nitrous oxide then falls upon a third detector. This third beam is used to determine the amount of nitrous oxide in the lower atmosphere. Generally the amount of nitrous oxide in the lower atmosphere is relatively constant worldwide. Any changes in the levels of nitrous oxide measured by the MAPS instrument indicates that some portion of the atmosphere may have clouds present and the MAPS instrument cannot measure CO through clouds.

15.3.5 The MAPS Data

The MAPS measurements were recorded on a tape recorder aboard the instrument, and were transmitted to the ground in real-time through the Space Shuttle telemetry system. The real-time data transmissions were processed at the Payload Operations Control Center at the Johnson Space Center to produce "quick look" maps of the measured carbon monoxide distribution. Real-time data analysis by the MAPS operations team and observations by the astronaut crew helped scientists on the ground evaluate the MAPS data and determine those regions where more measurements that are detailed should be made by the MAPS instrument.

Chapter 16

Global Environmental Issues: Green House Effect, Ozone Layer Depletion, Acid Rain

16.1 RADIATION BALANCE OF THE EARTH

The earth continuously receives energy from the sun, a part of which is absorbed, while the remaining is emitted back into space. The earth maintains its heat balance within narrow limits, due to complex mechanism of energy transfer. The sun acts like a black body at 6000°K and radiates energy. Out of the solar radiation reaching the earth 92% consist of radiation in the range 315–1400 nm. 45% of this is in the visible region. (400-700nm). The earth absorbs radiations in the infra-red region (2–40μ with maximum at 10μ).

The heat equivalent of the solar radiation reaching the earth is estimated to be 2.68×10^{24} joules per year. Out of this energy 50% is reflected before it reaches the earth's surface, 15% is reflected by the earth's surface, 5.3% is absorbed by the soil .27.8% is utilized for heating and evaporation of water and the remaining 1.9% is absorbed by marine & land vegetation. The energy transport plays a vital role in maintaining the earths radiation balance and this proceeds through various mechanisms such as :

Conduction of energy through the interaction of atoms, molecules and other species.

Convection of energy via massive air circulation.

Radiation of energy from earth in the infrared region (2 to 40μ).

Re-absorption of most of the outgoing infra-red radiation (2 to 40μ) by water vapor (4–8μ), CO_2 (12 to 16.3μ) and other gases such as CH_4 and reemitting a part of this radiation to the earth's surface.

The particulate matter in the atmosphere which are released by natural forces (e.g. wind, sea sprays and volcanoes) or by anthropogenic activities (*e.g.*, agricultural & industrial activities which release dust, fumes, smoke) also exert cooling or heating effect, depending upon the nature of the particles which may reflect, scatter or absorb radiations.

16.2 GREEN HOUSE EFFECT

The earth is heated by sunlight and some of the heat that is absorbed by the earth is radiated back into space. However there are certain gases like CO_2, water vapors, CH_4 and man made chlorofluorocarbons (CFC) in the lower atmosphere which act like a glass in a green house *i.e.*, allows the solar radiations in the range 300 to 2500 nm to pass while filtering the dangerous u.v. radiations but do not allow the earth to reradiate the heat into space. A part of the heat so trapped in these atmospheric gases is reemitted to the earth's surface. The net result is the heating of the earth's surface by this phenomenon, called "**green house effect**".

The radiations in the range of 8000–12000 nm escape unabsorbed and are known as the region of atmospheric window. In fact, these green house gases particularly CO_2 & H_2O vapors are responsible for keeping our planet warm & thus sustaining life on earth. Nevertheless, if the concentration of these green house gases increases largely, then it may threaten the very existence of life on the earth. Every year the world-wide concentration of CO_2 is increasing at a rate of 0.75 ppm and the temperature is rising at a rate of 0.05 °C per year. If this continues, the world will go on warming up more & more. This could ultimately melt the glaciers, polar ice caps and result in flooding of many low lying areas.

The measures taken to reduce global warming or to reduce the effect of green house are:

Extensive afforestation

Conservation of forests

Encouraging community forestry

Reduction in the use of automobiles

Research in development of more efficient automobile engines.

Ban on CFC's and nuclear explosions

Development of environmentally compatible technologies with the help of intensive inter-disciplinary research effective check on the growth of population and imparting of non-formal and formal environmental education.

16.3 FORMATION AND DEPLETION OF OZONE LAYER

Ozone (O_3) s an allotrope of oxygen and is produced in the stratosphere. The ozone layer present in the stratosphere acts as a protective shield for the life on earth. It strongly absorbs ultra-violet radiations from the sun and protects the life on earth from severe radiation damages such as DNA mutation and skin cancer.

Ozone is formed in the stratosphere by photochemical reaction:

$O_2 + hv \rightarrow O + O$

$O + O_2 + M$ (third body, such as N_2 or O_2) $\rightarrow O_3 + M$

The third body absorbs the excess energy liberated stabilizing the ozone molecule. Thus, ozone is constantly formed in the stratosphere. At the same time it is also destroyed by chlorine, released due to volcanic activity and also by reaction with (a) nitric oxide (b) atomic oxygen and (c) reactive hydroxyl radical which are also present in the atmosphere,

(a) $O_3 + NO \rightarrow NO_2 + O_2$

(b) $O_3 + O \rightarrow O_2 + O_2$

(c) $O_3 + HO^o \rightarrow O_2 + HOO^o$ (hydro per oxyl)

(d) $HOO^o + O \rightarrow HO^o + O_2$

Ozone in the stratosphere, is also found to be destroyed by man made CFC's which are used as coolants in refrigerators, AC's, propellants in aerosol sprays and in plastic foams such as "theremocole" or Styrofoam.

The CFC molecules escaping into the atmosphere decompose to release chlorine in the ozone layer and each atom of chlorine, thus liberated is capable of attacking several ozone molecules:

$Cl^o + O_3 \rightarrow Cl\,O^o + O_2$

$ClO^o + O \rightarrow Cl^o + O_2$

Which regenerates Cl atom, so that a long chain process is involved which conserves Cl atoms.

16.4 CHEMICAL & PHOTOCHEMICAL REACTIONS OF VARIOUS SPECIES IN ATMOSPHERE

The various species present in the atmosphere are ions, radicals & particles.

Ions: The u.v. radiations from the sun are mostly responsible for the formation of the ionic species in the ionosphere. The various ions present in the atmosphere are O_2^{+}, O^+, NO^+ etc.

Radicals: The various free radicals (generated by photo-chemical reactions or electro magnetic radiations) present in the atmosphere are HO^o, CH^o_3, SO^o_2, ROO^o, NO^o_2 and HCO^o.

Particles: The various particles existing in nature include dust, smoke, fog, pollen grains, volcanic ash and bacteria.

Atmosphere is tremendously dynamic system with wide fluctuations of the parameter viz composition, temperature, humidity and intensity of sunlight, so different processes will be observed under varying atmospheric conditions. Some typical chemical and photochemical reactions are as follows:

Ozone & Ozone chemistry as described in formation & depletion of ozone layer.

Reactions involving SO_2.

SO_2 absorbs solar radiations in the region 300–400 nm particularly in the lower atmosphere to produce electronically excited states of SO_2.

$SO_2{}^o + h\nu \rightarrow SO^{\circ}_2$ (a)

$SO_2{}^o$ further oxidizes to SO_3 & finally to H_2SO_4 as follows:

$SO_2{}^o + O_2 \rightarrow SO^{\circ}_4$

$SO_4{}^o + O_2 \rightarrow SO_3 + O_3$ (b)

$SO_3 + H_2O \rightarrow H_2SO_4$

In natural sunlight at 5–30 ppm level of SO_2 and 30–90% relative humidity the over all reaction may be represented by

$SO_2 + \frac{1}{2}\ O_2 + H_20 \rightarrow H_2SO_4$

Solid particles such as soot provide heterogenous phases for catalyzing the oxidation of SO_2. Soot is formed during combustions of solid are liquid fuels in domestic and industrial operations and automobile emissions.

Sulphur dioxide is a pollutant responsible for smog formation, acid rains and corrosion of metals and alloys.

16.5 REACTION INVOLVING OXIDES OF NITROGEN

The oxides of nitrogen present in the atmosphere are N_2O. NO and NO_2

In the stratosphere, N_2O undergoes photochemical decomposition to NO, which in turn, depletes the protective ozone layer.

$N_2O + hv \rightarrow N_2 + O$

$N_2O + O \rightarrow NO + NO$

$NO + O_3 \rightarrow NO_2 + O_2$

The most important primary photochemical reaction is the dissociation of NO_2

$NO_2 + hv \rightarrow NO + O$

The NO so formed may be oxidized by O_3 or more slowly by O_2, thus leading to a cyclic chain reaction.

$2\,NO + O_2 \rightarrow 2\,NO_2$

$NO + O_3 \rightarrow NO_2 + O_2$

$2\,NO_2 + O_3 \rightarrow N_2O_5 + O_2$

$4\,NO_2 + O_2 + 2\,H_2O \rightarrow 4\,HNO_3$

$N_2O_5 + H_2O \rightarrow 2\,HNO_2$

HNO_2 & HNO_3 may also undergo photochemical dissociation as follows :

$HNO_2 + hv \rightarrow NO_2 + H^{o}$

$HNO_2 + hv \rightarrow NO + HO^{o}$

$HNO_3 + hv \rightarrow NO_2 + HO^{o}$

In the stratosphere NO_2 may react with the HO^{o} free radical, forming HNO_3

$NO_2 + HO^{o} \rightarrow HNO_3$

The HNO_3 so formed is removed as acid rain or is converted into particulate nitrate due to neutralization by NH_3 or particulate lime.

Oxidation of organic compounds

Organic compounds such as hydrocarbons, aldehydes and ketones absorb solar radiations. Due to this they undergo various photo chemical and chemical reactions involving free radicals.

$CH_4 + O_2 \rightarrow H_3C^{o} + HO$

$CH_4 + HO^{o} \rightarrow H_3C^{o} + H_2O$

$H_3C^{o} + O_2 + M$ (third body) $\rightarrow H_3COO^{o} + M$

$RCHO + hv \rightarrow R^{o} + HCO^{o}$

The alkyl on aryl radicals may react with oxygen to form a peroxyl radical which in turn may react with NO_2 to give PAN.

$$RCOO^{o} + NO_2 \rightarrow RC00NO_2$$

Peroxyacetyl nitrate (PAN)

Metal oxides and Charcoal in particulate matter catalyse the oxidation of hydrocarbons. Organic compounds in the atmosphere play an important role in Photochemical smog formation.

16.6 GREENHOUSE GASES

Greenhouse gases are gases in an atmosphere that absorb and emit radiation within the thermal infrared range. This process is the fundamental cause of the greenhouse effect. The main greenhouse gases in the Earth's atmosphere are water vapor, carbon dioxide, methane, nitrous oxide, and ozone. In our solar system, the atmospheres of Venus, Mars and Titan also contain gases that cause greenhouse effects. Greenhouse gases greatly affect the temperature of the Earth; without them, Earth's surface would be on average about 33°C (59°F) colder than at present. The burning of fossil fuels since the Industrial revolution has increased the levels of greenhouse gases in the atmosphere.

In order, Earth's most abundant greenhouse gases are:

Water vapor
Carbon dioxide
Methane
Nitrous oxide
Ozone
Chlorofluorocarbons

The contribution to the greenhouse effect by a gas is affected by both the characteristics of the gas and its abundance. For example, on a molecule-for-molecule basis, methane is about eight time's stronger greenhouse gas than carbon dioxide, but it is present in much smaller concentrations so that its total contribution is smaller. When these gases are ranked by their contribution to the greenhouse effect, the most important are:

Water vapor, which contributes 36–72%
Carbon dioxide, which contributes 9–26%
Methane, which contributes 4–9%

It is not possible to state that a certain gas causes an exact percentage of the greenhouse effect. This is because some of the gases absorb and emit radiation at the same frequencies as others, so that the total greenhouse effect is not simply the sum of the influence of each gas. The higher ends of the ranges quoted are for each gas alone; the lower ends account for overlaps with the other gases. The major non-gas contributor to the Earth's greenhouse effect, clouds, also absorb and emit infrared radiation and thus have an effect on radiative properties of the greenhouse gases.

In addition to the main greenhouse gases listed above, other greenhouse gases include sulfur hexafluoride, hydrofluorocarbons and perfluorocarbons. Some greenhouse gases are not often listed. For example, nitrogen trifluoride has a high global warming potential (GWP) but is only present in very small quantities.

Atmospheric absorption and scattering at different electromagnetic wavelengths. The largest absorption band of carbon dioxide is in the infrared. Scientists who have elaborated on Arrhenius's theory of global warming are concerned that increasing concentrations of greenhouse gases in the atmosphere are causing an unprecedented rise in global temperatures, with potentially harmful consequences for the environment and human health. Although contributing to many other physical and chemical reactions, the major atmospheric constituents, nitrogen (N_2), oxygen (O_2), and argon (Ar), are not greenhouse gases. This is because molecules containing two atoms of the same element such as N_2 and O_2 and monatomic molecules such as Ar have no net change in their dipole moment when they vibrate and hence are almost totally unaffected by infrared light. Although molecules containing two atoms of different elements such as carbon monoxide (CO) or hydrogen chloride (HCl) absorb IR, these molecules are short-lived in the atmosphere owing to their reactivity and solubility. Therefore they do not contribute significantly to the greenhouse effect and are not often included when discussing greenhouse gases.

16.6.1 Greenhouse Gas Emissions

List of countries by carbon dioxide emissions and List of countries by greenhouse gas emissions per capita Measurements from Antarctic ice cores show that before industrial emissions started atmospheric CO_2 levels were about 280 parts per million by volume (ppmv), and stayed between 260 and 280 during the preceding ten thousand years. Carbon dioxide concentrations in the atmosphere have gone up by approximately 35 percent since the 1900s, rising from 280 parts per million by volume to 387 parts per million in 2009. One study using evidence from stomata of fossilized leaves suggests greater variability, with carbon dioxide levels above 300 ppm during the period seven to ten thousand years ago[36], though others have argued that these findings more likely reflect calibration or contamination problems rather than actual CO_2 variability. Because of the way air is trapped in ice and the time period represented in each ice sample analyzed, The pores in the ice close off slowly to form bubbles deep within the firn. It figures represent averages of atmospheric concentrations of up to a few centuries rather than annual or decadal levels.

16.6.2 Recent year-to-year Increase of Atmospheric CO_2

Since the beginning of the Industrial Revolution, the concentrations of most of the greenhouse gases have increased. For example, the concentration of carbon dioxide has increased by about 36% to 380 ppmv, or 100 ppmv over modern pre-industrial levels. The first 50 ppmv increase took place in about 200 years, from the start of the Industrial Revolution to around 1973; however the next 50 ppmv increase took place in about 33 years, from 1973 to 2006. Recent data also shows the concentration is increasing at a higher rate. In the 1960s, the average annual increase was only 37% of what it was in 2000 through 2007. The other greenhouse gases produced from human activity show similar increases in both amount and rate of increase. Many observations are available online in a variety of Atmospheric Chemistry Observational Databases.

16.6.3 Human-Related Sources and Sinks of Carbon Dioxide

A variety of human activities lead to the emission (sources) and removal (sinks) of carbon dioxide (CO2). The largest source of CO_2 emissions globally is the combustion of fossil fuels such as coal, oil and gas in power plants, automobiles, industrial facilities and other sources.

A number of specialized industrial production processes and product uses such as mineral production, metal production and the use of petroleum-based products can also lead to CO_2 emissions.

Carbon sequestration is the process by which growing trees and plants absorb or remove CO_2 from the atmosphere and turn it into biomass *e.g.*, wood, leaves, etc. Deforestation, conversely, can lead to significant levels of CO_2 emissions in some countries. Carbon dioxide can be captured from power plants and industrial facilities before it is released into the atmosphere, and then injected deep underground.

16.6.4 Fossil Fuel Combustion

When fossil fuels are burned to produce energy the carbon stored in them is emitted almost entirely as CO^2. The main fossil fuels burned by humans are petroleum (oil), natural gas and coal. CO2 is emitted by the burning of fossil fuels for electricity generation, industrial uses, transportation, as well as in homes and commercial buildings. In 2006, petroleum supplied the largest share of domestic energy demands, accounting for an average of 47 percent of total fossil-fuel-based energy consumption in 2006. Coal and natural gas followed in order of importance, accounting for 27 and 26 percent of total fossil fuel consumption, respectively. The figure below displays emissions for each of these sectors, by fuel type in 2006.

16.6.5 Electricity Generation

The process of generating electricity is the single largest source of CO^2 emissions in the United States, representing 41 percent of all CO^2 emissions. The electric power industry includes all power producers - both regulated utilities and other entities (*e.g.*, independent power producers, cogenerators, etc.). Total national emissions in the U.S. depend upon the amount of electricity generated and the mix of fuels used to produce the electricity. For example, increases and decreases in the share of electricity generated by burning coal can affect total national emissions. Emissions from electricity generation can be reduced by:

Increasing the share of electricity generated from low carbon fuel or renewable sources. EPA's Clean Energy Programs are designed to help consumers improve their knowledge about their Clean Energy options by providing objective information, creating networks between the public and private sector and providing technical assistance. Lowering total electricity consumption by consumers through improvements in energy efficiency. For more information on how to improve energy efficiency. EPA's Acid Rain Program is designed to minimize emissions of sulfur dioxide and nitrogen oxides within parts of the U.S. The Acid Rain program tracks emissions of these gases and CO^2, and makes the data publicly available at its Data and Maps Web site.

EPA's Emissions and Generation Resource Integrated Database (EGRID) provides comprehensive information on the environmental characteristics of almost all electric power generated in the United States.

Industry: The industrial sector engages in activities such as manufacturing, construction and mining. Within manufacturing, six industries — petroleum refining, chemical production, primary metal production, paper, food, and mineral production — represent the majority of energy use. Industry consumes significant amounts of electricity, but in the national inventory, only direct onsite CO_2 emissions are allocated to this sector. Since 1990, industrial output in the United States has grown significantly, but CO_2 emissions experienced only a modest increase. A number of industrial companies have joined EPA's Climate Leaders program and taken on voluntary commitments to reduce their emissions of greenhouse gases.

Residential and Commercial: The residential and commercial sectors are heavily reliant on electricity for meeting their energy needs, particularly for lighting, heating, air conditioning and appliances. The main source of direct CO_2 emissions is the burning of natural gas and oil for heating and cooling of buildings. For more information on how to improve energy efficiency in the residential and commercial sectors.

Transportation: The transportation sector is the second largest source of CO_2 emissions in the U.S. Almost all of the energy consumed in the transportation sector is petroleum based, including gasoline, diesel and jet fuel. Automobiles and light-duty trucks account for almost two-thirds of emissions from the transportation sector and emissions have steadily grown since 1990. Other sources of transportation emissions are freight trucks, aircraft, trains and boats. Emissions from transportation depend on the number of trips or miles traveled by each type of vehicle each year, which are in turn influenced by larger economic trends and consumer behavior. Over the long term, changes in the fuel efficiency of vehicles (e.g., mileage), and in the type of fuel used can influence the level of emissions.

16.7 MAIN SOURCES OF CARBON DIOXIDE EMISSIONS

The three main sectors that use fossil fuels are:

a. Transportation
b. Utilities (power, gas, oil etc...)
c. Industrial production
d. Trans portation

16.7.1 Trans portation

The most important source of CO_2 emissions worldwide is caused by the transportation of goods and people. The emissions caused by people traveling by car, plane, train, etc. are examples of direct emissions since people can chose where they are going and by what method. The emissions caused by the transportation of goods are examples of indirect emissions since the consumer has no direct control of the distance between the factory and the store. Since the distance between the manufacturer and the consumer is constantly growing, more pressure is put on the transportation industry to bridge this gap and this ends up creating more indirect emissions. What's worse is that 99% of the energy used to transport people and goods all over the world comes from the combustion of fossil fuels.

Trends in today's modern economy. The impact that transporting people and good. This trend started in the 1990's and has continued ever since causing an increase in indirect emissions. The fact of the matter is that a person can only travel so much before they get exhausted but manufactured goods can travel limitless distances. U.S. automobiles, motorcycles, trucks, and buses drove over 2.8 trillion miles in 2002. That's almost 1/12th the distance to the nearest star beyond the solar system. It's like driving to the sun and back 13,440 times.

16.7.2 Utilities (power, gas, oil etc...)

Depending on the energy mix of your local power company you may find that the electricity that you use at home and at work has a considerable impact on greenhouse gas emissions. All industrialized nations (with the exception of Canada and France) get the majority (between 60–80%) of their electricity from the combustion of fossil fuels. Below is a chart for all G8 nations, for the complete list of all nations click here.

16.7.3 Production

Manufacturing and industrial processes all combine to produce large amounts of each type of greenhouse gas but specifically large amounts of CO_2 because of two reasons. First, many manufacturing facilities directly use fossil fuels to create heat and steam needed at various stages of production. Second, their energy intensive activities use more electricity than any other sector so unless they are using renewable sources the energy that they use is responsible for vast amounts of emissions. By industrial production, we are mainly talking about manufacturing, construction, mining, and agriculture. Manufacturing is the largest of the 4 and can be broken down into 5 main categories: paper, food, petroleum refineries, chemicals, and metal/mineral products. These categories account for the vast majority of the energy use and CO_2 emissions by the sector.

16.8 A NEW GLOBAL WARMING STRATEGY

How Environmentalists are Overlooking Vegetarianism as the Most Effective Tool against Climate Change in Our Lifetimes.

16.8.1 Global Warming and Carbon Dioxide

The environmental community rightly recognizes global warming as one of the gravest threats to the planet. Global temperatures are already higher than they've ever been in at least the past millennium, and the increase is accelerating even faster than scientists had predicted. The expected consequences include coastal flooding, increases in extreme weather, spreading disease, and mass extinctions. Unfortunately, the environmental community has focused its efforts almost exclusively on abating carbon dioxide (CO_2) emissions. Domestic legislative efforts concentrate on raising fuel economy standards, capping CO_2 emissions from power plants, and investing in alternative energy sources. Recommendations to consumers also focus on CO_2: buy fuel-efficient cars and appliances, and minimize their use.

This is a serious miscalculation. Data published by Dr. James Hansen and others show that CO_2 emissions are not the main cause of observed atmospheric warming. Though this may sound like the work of global warming skeptics, it isn't: Hansen is Director of NASA's Goddard Institute for Space Studies who has been called "a grandfather of the global warming theory." He is a longtime supporter of action against global warming, cited by Al Gore and often quoted by environmental organizations, who has argued against skeptics for subverting the scientific process. His results are generally accepted by global warming experts, including bigwigs like Dr. James McCarthy.

The focus solely on CO_2 is fueled in part by misconceptions. It's true that human activity produces vastly more CO_2 than all other greenhouse gases put together. However, this does not mean it is responsible for most of the earth's warming. Many other greenhouse gases trap heat far more powerfully than CO_2, some of them tens of thousands of times more powerfully. Wh en taking into account various gases' global warming potential—defined as the amount of actual warming a gas will produce over the next one hundred years—it turns out that gases other than CO_2 make up most of the global warming problem.

Even this overstates the effect of CO_2, because the primary sources of these emissions—cars and power plants—also produce aerosols. Aerosols actually have a cooling effect on global temperatures, and the magnitude of this cooling approximately cancels out the warming effect of CO_2. The surprising result is that sources of CO_2 emissions are having roughly zero effect on global temperatures in the near-term.

This result is not widely known in the environmental community, due to a fear that polluting industries will use it to excuse their greenhouse gas emissions. For example, the Union of Concerned Scientists had the data reviewed by other climate experts, who affirmed Hansen's conclusions. However, the organization also cited climate contrarians' misuse of the data to argue against curbs in CO_2. This contrarian spin cannot be justified.

While CO_2 may have little influence in the near-term, reductions remains critical for containing climate change in the long run. Aerosols are short-lived, settling out of the air after a few months, while CO_2 continues to heat the atmosphere for decades to centuries. Moreover, we cannot assume that aerosol emissions will keep pace with increases in CO_2 emissions. Nevertheless, the fact remains that sources of non-CO_2 greenhouse gases are responsible for virtually all the global warming we're seeing, and all the global warming we are going to see for the next fifty years. If we wish to curb global warming over the coming half century, we must look at strategies to address non-CO2 emissions. The strategy with the most impact is vegetarianism.

16.8.2 Methane and Vegetarianism

The most important non-CO_2 greenhouse gas is methane, and the number one source of methane worldwide is animal agriculture. Methane is responsible for nearly as much global warming as all other non-CO_2 greenhouse gases put together. Methane is 21 times more powerful a greenhouse gas than CO_2. While atmospheric concentrations of CO_2 have risen by about 31% since pre-industrial times, methane concentrations have more than doubled. Whereas human sources of CO_2 amount to just 3% of natural emissions, human sources produce one and a half times as much methane as all natural sources. In fact, the effect of our methane emissions may be compounded as methane-induced warming microbial decay of organic matter in wetlands the primary natural source of methane.

Methane emissions, causing nearly half of the planet's human-induced warming, methane reduction must be a priority. Methane is produced by a number of sources, including coal mining and landfills—but the number one source worldwide is animal agriculture. Animal agriculture produces more than 100 million tons of methane a year. Moreover, this source is on the rise: global meat consumption has increased fivefold in the past fifty years, and shows little sign of abating. About 85% of this methane is produced in the digestive processes of livestock, and while a single cow releases a relatively small amount of methane, the collective effect on the environment of the hundreds of millions of livestock animals worldwide is enormous. An additional 15% of animal agricultural methane emissions are released from the massive "lagoons" used to store untreated farm animal waste, and already a target of environmentalists for their role as the number one source of water pollution in the U.S.

The conclusion is simple: arguably, the best way to reduce global warming in our lifetimes is to reduce or eliminate our consumption of animal products. Simply by going vegetarian we can eliminate one of the major sources of emissions of methane, the greenhouse gas responsible for almost half of the global warming.

16.8.3 Advantages of Vegetarianism over CO_2 Reduction

In addition to having the advantage of immediately reducing global warming, a shift away from methane-emitting food sources is much easier than cutting carbon dioxide. First, there is no limit to reductions in this source of greenhouse gas that can be achieved through vegetarian diet. In principle, even 100% reduction could be achieved with little negative impact. In contrast, similar cuts in carbon dioxide are impossible without devastating effects on the economy. Even the most ambitious carbon dioxide reduction strategies fall short of cutting emissions by half.

Second, shifts in diet lower greenhouse gas emissions much more quickly than shifts away from the fossil fuel burning technologies that emit carbon dioxide. The turnover rate for most ruminant farm animals is one or two years, so that decreases in meat consumption would result in almost immediate drops in methane emissions. The turnover rate for cars and power plants, on the other hand, can be decades. Even if cheap, zero-emission fuel sources were available today, they would take many years to build and slowly replace the massive infrastructure our economy depends upon today.

Similarly, unlike carbon dioxide that can remain in the air for more than a century, methane cycles out of the atmosphere in just eight years, so that lower methane emissions quickly translate to cooling of the earth. Third, efforts to cut carbon dioxide involve fighting powerful and wealthy business interests like the auto and oil industries. Environmental groups have been lobbying for years to make fuel-efficient SUVs available or phase out power plants that don't meet modern environmental standards without success. At the same time, vegetarian foods are readily available, and cuts in agricultural methane emissions are achievable at every meal.

In addition, polls show that concern about global warming is widespread, and environmental activists often feel helpless to do anything about it. Unless they happen to be buying a car or major appliance, most people wanting to make a difference are given little to do aside from writing their legislators and turning off their lights. Reducing or eliminating meat consumption is something concerned citizens can do every day to help the planet. Finally, it is worth noting that reductions in this source of greenhouse gas have many beneficial side effects for the environment. Less methane results in less tropospheric ozone, a pollutant damaging to human health and agriculture. Moreover, the same factory farms responsible for these methane emissions also use up most of the country's water supply, and denude most of its wilderness for rangeland and growing feed. Creating rangeland to feed western nations' growing appetite for meat has been a major source of deforestation and desertification in third world countries. Factory farm waste lagoons are a leading source of water pollution in the U.S. Indeed, because of animal agriculture's high demand for fossil fuels, the average American diet is far more CO_2-polluting than a plant-based one.

16.9 CAUSES OF OZONE DEPLETION

Ozone depletion occurs when the natural balance between the production and destruction of stratospheric ozone is tipped in favour of destruction. Although natural phenomena can cause temporary ozone loss, chlorine and bromine released from man-made compounds such as CFCs are now accepted as the main cause of this depletion.

It was first suggested by Drs. M. Molina and S. Rowland in 1974 that a man-made group of compounds known as the chlorofluorocarbons (CFCs) were likely to be the main source of ozone depletion. However, this idea was not taken seriously until the discovery of the ozone hole over Antarctica in 1985 by the British Antarctic Survey.

Chlorofluorocarbons are not "washed" back to Earth by rain or destroyed in reactions with other chemicals. They simply do not break down in the lower atmosphere and they can remain in the atmosphere from 20 to 120 years or more. Because of their relative stability, CFCs are instead transported into the stratosphere where they are eventually broken down by ultraviolet (UV) rays from the Sun, releasing free chlorine. The chlorine becomes actively involved in the process of destruction of ozone. The net result is that two molecules of ozone are replaced by three of molecular oxygen, leaving the chlorine free to repeat the process:

$Cl + O_3\ ClO + O_2$

$ClO + O\ Cl + O_2$

Ozone is converted to oxygen, leaving the chlorine atom free to repeat the process up to 100,000 times, resulting in a reduced level of ozone. Bromine compounds, or halons, can also destroy stratospheric ozone. Compounds containing chlorine and bromine from man-made compounds are known as industrial halocarbons.

Emissions of CFCs have accounted for roughly 80% of total stratospheric ozone depletion. Thankfully, the developed world has phased out the use of CFCs in response to international agreements to protect the ozone layer. However, because CFCs remain in the atmosphere so long, the ozone layer will not fully repair itself until at least the middle of the 21st century. Naturally occurring chlorine has the same effect on the ozone layer, but has a shorter life span in the atmosphere

16.10 OZONE HOLE

The "Ozone hole" is a region of atmosphere over Antarctica from which "total ozone" has extremely decreased. Every year, the hole appears in August (austral spring) and develops during September early October; after that, it declines gradually, and finally vanishes during the end of November and December (austral summer). A stream of air that swirls around the South Pole, the so-called polar night or vortex. It develops in Antarctic winter stratosphere, which isolates the stratosphere above the Antarctic from the surrounding atmosphere. During the winter, the polar night zone receives almost no light from the sun inside polar vortex, air temperature become so low that nitric acid and water freezes to form ice crystal's clouds called polar stratospheric clouds. Through chemical reaction on the surfaces of ice crystals of these polar stratospheric clouds, chlorine gas is produced in the Ozone layer from inactive chlorides such as chlorine nitrate and hydrogen chloride.

The chlorine gas that accumulates during the winter releases chlorine atoms when spring comes and the sun shine on it, and this chlorine begins to reduce ozone. As such the Ozone hole is born, through absorption of solar radiation toward summer, the polar night vortex gradually warms up from its inside and therefore weakens, finally dissipating completely; exchange of air begins between inside of the vortex and outside, then the Ozone hole disappears. The Ozone poor air, on this occasion, flows away from Antarctica and reduces Ozone layer of the Southern Hemisphere surrounding the

16.11 ATMOSPHERIC OZONE

The chemical formula of Ozone is O_3. The molecule of Ozone consists of the atoms and is form of high energy of the element Oxygen O_2. It is an unstable pale bluish gas with a characteristic pungent penetrating Odour. It is liquefied at minus 112°C and solidified at minus 251°C. It is dense, soluble in water and is a more active oxidizing agent, acting directly on mercury and Silver to form oxides, affecting many organic compounds.

Ozone is rare in our atmosphere. It is mainly found in two regions of the Earth's atmosphere. About 90% of Ozone is found in layer surrounding the Earth's atmosphere between approximately 10 and 50 kilometers *i.e.*, about 6 to 30 miles above the Earth's surface. This region of Earth's atmosphere is known as stratosphere and the layer of Ozone found there is called Stratospheric Ozone Layer. The remaining Ozone is in the lower region of Earth's atmosphere, the troposphere, which extends from the Earth's surface up to 10 kilometers.

Chapter 17

Sound Pollution: Causes Controlling Measures

17.1 NOISE POLLUTION

The present generation and the coming generations have to solve three grave problems, namely, population poverty and pollution if they have to survive properly. Pollution being the most dangerous problem likes cancer in which death is sure but slow. Environment pollution is assuming dangerous proportions all through the globe and India is not free from this poisonous disease. This is the gift of modern living, industrialization and urbanization.

"Any undesirable and unwanted sound may be considered noise. However, its perception is subjective. One person's noise may be music to the ears of others." Regardless, the exposure to high levels of noise or music may have harmful physical or emotional effects. It may be manifested in minor psychological irritation, or severe, sometimes extreme pain to the ear.

The physical damage to the ear could be temporary hearing loss (temporary threshold shift or TTS) manifested in reduced perception of low level sound. If the patient is removed from the noisy environment, recovery could be expected within a couple of months. Permanent loss of hearing is possible (noise-induced permanent threshold shift or NIPTS). It means that the patient will not perceive low level sounds, and the condition may be corrected only with the use of electronic hearing aids.

Although some individuals may be more sensitive to noise than others, the exposure to loud (100 decibel) music — so fashionable today — may eventually lead to NIPTS, 10–15 decibel hearing loss at the lower end of the perception range.

The extent of the loss in ones hearing depends on the level and duration of the exposure. It is likely that one hour of exposure to 100 decibel noise may cause short term TTS, with a recovery period of one to five days. Continuous exposure to high levels of sound, in the vicinity of 90 decibel, for a period of more than 5 years, may eventually lead to 15–20 decibels of NIPTS. The emotional impact could be far more severe, but again the research data is woefully inadequate to draw "iron clad" conclusions. It is however undeniable that continuous exposure to elevated noise levels will cause irritability, anxiety, stress and in extreme cases depression.

In noisy factories, unless the workers are protected with earplugs or specially designed muffs, mental fatigue and loss of concentration is common, leading to lower levels of productivity, and in extreme cases accidents. Construction sites where hydraulic equipment (jackhammers) is used, the accident rate have been significantly reduced by the introduction of ear muffs to the operators of such machinery.

In a community the impact of high noise level is significant, since it interferes with sleep as well as conversation. The psychological effects could be far reaching. For example, if the rumors can be counted on, in an American University a research application is pending to examine the divorce rates in communities under the approaches to major airports. It may take many years of concentrated research and impact studies to connect these sociological problems to noise pollution, in such manner that it would stand up in the court of law.

One may therefore conclude that noise pollution is not just a minor annoyance, but serious and sometimes fatal environmental hazard. Public health officials should look into the physical and emotional impact of noise pollution especially in communities exposed to frequent low level overflight.

17.1.1 Measurement

A decibel is the standard for the measurement of noise. The zero on a decibel scale is at the threshold of hearing, the lowest sound pressure that can be heard, on the scale acc. To smith, 20 db is whisper, 40 db the noise in a quiet office. 60 db is normal conversation, 80 db is the level at which sound becomes physically painful. The Noise quantum of some of the cities in our country indicate their pitch in decibel in the nosiest areas of corresponding cities, *e.g.*, Delhi-80 db, Kolkata-87, Bombay-85, Chennai-89 db etc.

Sources of Noise Pollution: Noise pollution like other pollutants is also a by-product of industrialization, urbanizations and modern civilization. Broadly speaking, the noise pollution has two sources, *i.e.*, industrial and non-industrial. The industrial source includes the noise from various industries and big machines working at a very high speed and high noise intensity. Non- industrial source of noise includes the noise created by transport or vehicular traffic and the neighborhood noise generated by various noise pollution can be divided in the categories, namely, natural and manmade. Most leading noise sources will fall into the following categories: roads traffic, aircraft, railroads, construction, industry, noise in buildings.

17.1.2 Causes of Noise Pollution

1. **Road Traffic Noise:** In the city, the main sources of traffic noise are the motors and exhaust system of autos, smaller trucks, buses, and motorcycles. This type of noise can be augmented by narrow streets and tall buildings, which produce a canyon in which traffic noise reverberates.
2. **Air Craft Noise:** Now-a-days, the problem of low flying military aircraft has added a new dimension to community annoyance, as the nation seeks to improve its nap-of the earth aircraft operations over national parks, wilderness areas, and other areas previously unaffected by aircraft noise has claimed national attention over recent years.
3. **Noise from railroads:** The noise from locomotive engines, horns and whistles, and switching and shunting operation in rail yards can impact neighboring communities and railroad workers. For example, rail car retarders can produce a high frequency, high level screech that can reach

peak levels of 120 dB at a distance of 100 feet, which translates to levels as high as 138 or 40 dB at the railroad worker's ear.

4. **Construction Noise:** The noise from the construction of highways, city streets, and buildings is a major contributor to the urban scene. Construction noise sources include pneumatic hammers, air compressors, bulldozers, loaders, dump trucks (and their back-up signals), and pavement breakers.
5. **Noise in Industry:** Although industrial noise is one of the less prevalent community noise problems, neighbors of noisy manufacturing plants can be disturbed by sources such as fans, motors, and compressors mounted on the outside of buildings Interior noise can also be transmitted to the community through open windows and doors, and even through building walls. These interior noise sources have significant impacts on industrial workers, among whom noise- induced hearing loss is unfortunately common.
6. **Noise in building:** Apartment dwellers are often annoyed by noise in their homes, especially when the building is not well designed and constructed. In this case, internal building noise from plumbing, boilers, generators, air conditioners, and fans, can be audible and annoying. Improperly insulated walls and ceilings can reveal the soundof-amplified music, voices, footfalls and noisy activities from neighboring units. External noise from emergency vehicles, traffic, refuse collection, and other city noises can be a problem for urban residents, especially when windows are open or insufficiently glazed.
7. **Noise from Consumer products:** Certain household equipment, such as vacuum cleaners and some kitchen appliances have been and continue to be noisemakers, although their contribution to the daily noise dose is usually not very large.
8. **Harmful Effects on Human Being, Animal and Property:** Noise has always been with the human civilization but it was never so obvious, so intense, so varied and as pervasive as it is seen in the last of this century. Noise pollution makes men more irritable. The effect of noise pollution is multifaceted and interrelated. The effects of Noise Pollution on Human Being, Animal and property are as follows:

   (i) **It decreases the efficiency of a man:** Regarding the impact of noise on human efficiency there are number of experiments that print out the fact that human efficiency increases with noise reduction. A study by Sinha & Sinha in India suggested that reducing industrial booths could improve the quality of their work. Thus, human efficiency is related with noise.

   (ii) **Lack of concentration:** For better quality of work there should be concentration, Noise causes lack of concentration. In big cities, mostly all the offices are on main road. The noise of traffic or the loud speakers of different types of horns divert the attention of the people working in offices.

   (iii) **Fatigue:** Because of Noise Pollution, people cannot concentrate on their work. Thus, they have to give their more time for completing the work and they feel tiring.

   (iv) **Abortion:** There should be cool and calm atmosphere during the pregnancy. Unpleasant sounds make a woman of irriative nature. Sudden Noise causes abortion in females.

   (v) **It causes Blood Pressure:** Noise Pollution causes certain diseases in human. It attacks on the person's peace of mind. The noises are recognized as major contributing factors in accelerating the already existing tensions of modern living. These tensions result in certain disease like blood pressure or mental illness etc.

(vi) **Temporary of permanent Deafness:** The effect of nose on audition is well recognized. Mechanics, locomotive drivers, telephone operators etc. All have their hearing impairment because of noise at the place of work. Physictist, physicians and psychologists are of the view that continued exposure to noise level above 80 to 100 db is unsafe, loud noise causes temporary or permanent deafness.

(vii) **Effect on vegetation:** Poor quality of Crops—Now is well known to all that plants are similar to human being. They are also as sensitive as man is. There should be cool and peaceful environment for their better growth. Noise pollution causes poor quality of crops in a pleasant atmosphere.

(viii) **Effects on animal:** Noise pollution damages the nervous system of animal. Animal looses the control of its mind. They become dangerous.

(ix) **Effect on property:** Loud noise is very dangerous to buildings, bridges and monuments. It creates waves that struck the walls and put the building in danger condition. It weakens the edifice of buildings.

17.1.3 Noisy Oceans

Shipping, the mining and petroleum industries, military activities, acoustic thermometry, and fisheries all contribute to the relentless increase in sound levels in the oceans. With globalisation, the merchant fleet has doubled in size and quadrupled in tonnage. All of these ships (tankers, tug-boats, freighters, ice-breakers, etc.) fill every nook and cranny of the seas with a constant rumbling in the frequency band around 500 Hz. the danger for whales. In spite of what Jacques Cousteau has said, the oceans are a long way from being a "world of silence". The wind, tectonic plate movement, and whale song compose a complex web of sound. Nevertheless, for fifty years now, human activities have completely transformed this sound web. Biologists have coined the term "noise pollution" and are worried about what effects it may have on marine mammals. Why? One reason is that the oceans have become very noisy, and the level of noise is on the increase. Another reason is that marine mammals depend on sound in order to find their bearings as well as to feed, reproduce, and socialise. First, there was hunting, then habitat loss and chemical contamination. Does noise also represent a serious threat to whales?

17.2 NOISE POLLUTION CONTROL

Long term monitoring of the impact of noise pollution on life in the seas in general, and on marine mammals in particular, is essential. International co-operation should also be fostered to help find solutions to questions raised and to create practical ways of applying standards aimed at reducing noise pollution. These are huge challenges when we consider the vast range of activities that bring about noise pollution in the oceans. In fact, this type of pollution is but one aspect of a larger problem, one of the concerns of the United Nations' environmental programme: our growing use of the seas.

17.2.1 Occupational Human Health

Principal noise health effects are both health and behavioral in nature.. The following discussion refers to sound levels that are present within 30 to 150 meters from a moderately busy highway.

Hearing

The mechanism for chronic exposure to noise leading to hearing loss is well established. The elevated sound levels cause trauma to the cochlear structure in the inner ear, which gives rise to irreversible hearing loss. The pinna (visible portion of the human ear) combined with the middle ear amplifies sound levels by a factor of 20 when sound reaches the inner ear. In Rosen's seminal work on serious health effects regarding hearing loss and coronary artery disease, one of his findings derived from tracking Maaban tribesmen, who were insignificantly exposed to transportation or industrial noise. This population was systematically compared by cohort group to a typical U.S. population. The findings proved that aging is an almost insignificant cause of hearing loss, which instead is associated with chronic exposure to moderately high levels of environmental noise.

Cardiovascular Health

High noise levels can contribute to cardiovascular effects and exposure to moderately high (*e.g.*, above 70 dBA) levels during a single eight hour period causes a statistical rise in blood pressure of five to ten mm Hg; a clear and measurable increase in stress [1]; and vasoconstriction leading to the increased blood pressure noted above as well as to increased incidence of coronary artery disease.

Annoyance

Though it pales in comparison to the health effects noted above, noise pollution constitutes a significant factor of annoyance and distraction in modern artificial environments. The meaning listeners attribute to the sound influences annoyance, so that, if listeners dislike the noise content, they are annoyed. What is music to one is noise to another. If the sound causes activity interference, noise is more likely to annoy (for example, sleep disturbance)

If listeners feel they can control the noise source, the less likely the noise will be annoying. If listeners believe that the noise is subject to third party control, including police, but control has failed, they are more annoyed. The inherent unpleasantness of the sound causes annoyance.

Contextual sound. If the sound is appropriate for the activity it is in context. If one is at a race track the noise is in context and the psychological effects are absent. If one is at an outdoor picnic the race track noise will produce adverse psychological and physical effects. A 2005 study by Spanish researchers found that in urban areas households are willing to pay approximately four euros per decibel per year for noise reduction.

Environment

Noise pollution can also be harmful to animals. High noise levels may interfere with the natural cycles of animals, including feeding behavior, breeding rituals and migration paths. The most significant impact of noise to animal life is the systematic reduction of usable habitat, which in the case of endangered species may be an important part of the path to extinction. Perhaps the most sensational damage caused by noise pollution is the death of certain species of beaked whales, brought on by the extremely loud (up to 200 decibels) sound of military sonar.

Personal Protection

Disposable foam earplugs: out of the ear with coins for scale (top) and inserted into the wearer's ear (bottom).Two common forms of protection against noise are earplugs and earmuffs. These are available in a range of applications, effectiveness and quality.

Fig. 19.1

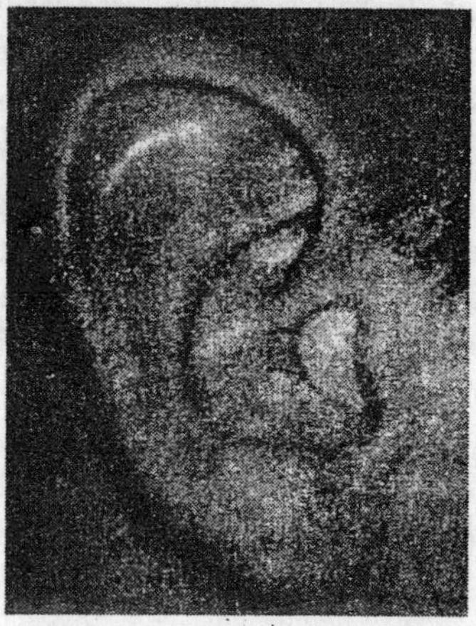

19.2

Mitigation and Control of Noise

There is also technology that has been applied with the aim of mitigating or containing noise as much as possible, if it has a sufficiently localized source. Roadway noise is the most widespread environmental component of noise pollution worldwide. There are a variety of effective strategies for mitigating adverse sound levels including: use of noise barriers, limitation of vehicle speeds, alteration of roadway surface texture, limitation of heavy duty vehicles, use of traffic controls that smooth vehicle flow to reduce braking and acceleration, innovative tire design and other methods. Thousands of case studies in the U.S. alone have been documented starting in 1970, indicating substantial improvement in roadway planning and design. The most important factor in applying these strategies is a computer model for roadway noise, that is capable of addressing local topography, meteorology, traffic operations and hypothetical mitigation.

Costs of building in mitigation are often quite modest, provided these solutions are sought in the planning stage of a roadway project. Aircraft noise can be reduced to some extent by design of quieter jet engines, which activity was pursued vigorously in the 1970s and 1980s. This strategy has had limited but noticeable improvement on urban sound levels. Operational controls, such as altering flight paths and time of day runway use, have demonstrated significant benefits for residential populations near airports. FAA sponsored residential retrofit (insulation) programs initiated in the 1970s has also enjoyed widespread success in reducing interior residential noise in thousands of affected residences across the United States.

Industrial noise for worker exposure has the longest history of scientific study, having been addressed since the 1930s. This practice has emphasized redesign of industrial equipment, shock mounting assemblies and physical barriers in the workplace. These pursuits have had considerable success; however, the costs of retrofitting existing systems are often rather high.

Legal Status

Governments up until the 1970s viewed noise as a "nuisance" rather than an environmental problem. In the United States, there are federal standards for highway and aircraft noise; states and local governments typically have very specific statutes on building codes, urban planning and roadway development. In Canada and the EU there are few national, provincial, or state laws that protect against noise. As a result, in Canada and the EU, most regulation has been left up to municipal authorities.

Noise laws and ordinances vary widely among municipalities and indeed do not even exist in some cities. An ordinance may contain a general prohibition against making noise that is a nuisance, or it may set out specific guidelines for the level of noise allowable at certain times of the day and for certain activities. Exceptions are generally made for activities considered essential public services such as refuse collection and emergency vehicles.

Most city ordinances prohibit sound above threshold intensity from trespassing over property line at night, typically between 10 p.m. and 6 a.m., and during the day restrict it to a higher decibel level; however, enforcement is uneven. Many municipalities do not follow up on complaints. Even where a municipality has an enforcement office, it may be unwilling to do more than issue warnings, since taking offenders to court is expensive. For persistent nuisances, individuals may have to seek damages through the civil courts. Many jurisdictions, such as New York City and Chicago, Illinois authorize police to impound cars with loud stereos and to hold the cars as evidence until the citation has been adjudicated.

Many conflicts over noise pollution are handled by negotiation between the emitter and the receiver. If this has no effect, the next step is typically a phone call to the non-emergency police number, and filing of a written report. Clear documentation, repetitive complaints, getting neighbors involved, and forming a Neighborhood Watch can be effective at obtaining enforcement, as can contacting one's police chief, city manager, mayor or local area representative. Noise pollution often persists because only five to ten percent of people affected by noise will lodge a formal complaint. Many citizens are not aware of their legal right to quiet and do not know how to register a complaint

17.3 NOISE CONTROL

Noise control can be effectively controlled by taking the following measures:

1. **Control at receiver's end:** For people working in noisy installations,ear protection aids like ear-plugs, ear–muffs,noise helmets,headphones etc must be provided to reduce occupational exposure.
2. **Acoustic zoning:** Increased distance between souce ant receiver by zoning of noisy industrial areas,bus terminals and railwy stations,aerodomes etcawy from the residential ares would go long way in minimizing noise pollution.
3. **Sound insulation at construction stages**: Sound insulation can be done by constructing windows with double or triple panes of glass and filling the gaps with sound absorbing materials.acoustical tiles, perforated plywood etc can be fixed on walls, ceilings, floors etc to

reduce noise.

4. **Planting of Trees:** Planting green trees and shrubs along roads, hospitals, educational institutions etc help in noise reduction to a considerable extent.
5. **Legislative Measures:** Strict legislative measures need to be enforced tio curb the mance of noise pollution.some of these measures could be:
   (a) Minimum use of loudspeakers and amplifiers especially near silence zones
   (b) Banning pressure horns in automobiles
   (c) Framing a separate noise pollution act

Regardless, the exposure to high levels of noise or music may have harmful physical or emotional effects. It may be manifested in minor psychological irritation, or severe, sometimes extreme pain to the ear. The physical damage to the ear could be temporary hearing loss (temporary threshold shift or TTS) manifested in reduced perception of low level sound. If the patient is removed from the noisy environment, recovery could be expected within a couple of months. Permanent loss of hearing is possible (noise-induced permanent threshold shift or NIPTS). It means that the patient will not perceive low level sounds, and the condition may be corrected only with the use of electronic hearing aids. Although some individuals may be more sensitive to noise than others, the exposure to loud (100 decibel) music — so fashionable today — may eventually lead to NIPTS, 10-15 decibel hearing loss at the lower end of the perception range.

Chapter 18

Measurement of Sound Pollution

18.1 UNIT OF MEASUREMENT FOR NOISE POLLUTION

Noise may be defined as, the undesirable sound that interferes significantly with the comfort, health or welfare of persons, or with the full use or enjoyment of property. Loudness is the most significant criteria which converts sound into noise. Noise pollution is the result of modern industrialized urban life and congestion due to over population.

Even though noise pollution is not fatal to human life, yet its importance cannot be overlooked because repeated exposure to noise reduces the sleeping hours and concentration or efficiency of human being.it affects the peace of mind and invades the privacy of a human being.

Decibel (db)is used in the environmental noise pollution as a measure of sound power level,sound intensity level,and sound pressure level. A decibel (one tenth of a bel) is a physical unit based on the weakest sound that can be detected by the human ear. Decibel (db) is not an absolute physical unit like metre, volt, etc.; but it is a ratio expressed on logarithmic scal this logarithmic scale takes care of wide range of sound power, intensity and pressure.

18.2 SOURCES OF NOISE POLLUTION

18.2.1 Major sources of noise pollution are

Industrial sources: Progress in the technology has resulted in creating noise pollution.textile mills, printing press, engineering establishments and metal works etc. contribute heavily towards noise pollution. In industrial cities due to the allotment of land in residential area to small scale industries causes' annoyance, comfort and irritation to the residents exposed to the noise that is inevitably produced.

Transport vehicles: Automobiles revolution in the urban cemters has proved to be big source of noise pollution.increasing traffic has given rise to the traffic jams in conjested areas where the repeated hoofing of horns by impatient drivers pierces the eras of all road users.

Household: The household is an industry in itself and is a source of many indoor noises such as the banging of doors, noise of playing children, crying of infants, moving of furniture's etc.besides these there are the entertainment equipment in the house, nmely radio, recorder, players and television sets.

Public address system: In India people need, only the slightest of an excuse for using loud speakers.the reason may be religious function, birth, marriage or it can be anything.public system therefore contributes in its own way towards noise pollution.

Agricultural machines: Tractors, thrashers, harvesters, tubewells, powered tillers etc have all made agriculture highly mechanical but at the same time highly noisy.noise level 90 db to 98 db due to running of farm machines have been recorded in the state of Punjab.

Defence equipment: A lot of noise pollution is added to the atmosphere by artillery, tanks, lunching of rockets, explosions, exercising of military airplanes practices.screams of jet enjines and sonic booms have a deafening impact on the ears and in extreme cases have been known to shatter the window panes and old dilapidated buildings.

Miscellaneous sources: The automobile repair shops, construction-works, blasting, bulldozing, stone crushing etc are other sources of noise pollution.

18.3 EFFECTS OF NOISE

Noise is generally harmfull and a serious health hazrd it has far reaching consequences and has many physical, physiologiocal and psychological effects on the human beings.

18.3.1 Physical Effects

The physical manifestation of noise pollution is the effect on hearing ability .repeated exposure to noise may result in temporary or permanent shifting of the threshold of a person depending upon the level and duration of exposure.the immediate and acute effect of noise pollution is impairment of hearing(*i.e.,* total deafness)

18.3.2 Physiological Effects

The physiological manifestation of noise pollution is:

(a) Headache by dilating blood vessels of the brain
(b) Increase in the rate of heart beat
(c) Narrowing of arteries
(d) Pain in the heart
(e) Decrease in heart output
(f) Impairment of night vision
(g) Lowering of concentration and affect on memory.
(h) Muscular strain and nervous breakdown.

18.3.3 Psychological Effects

The psychological manifestations of noise pollution are:

(a) Depression and fatigue which considerably readuces the efficiency of a person.
(b) Insomnia because of lack of undisturbed and refreshing sleep.
(c) Emotional imbalance

Therefore, noise is annoying and the annoyance depends on factors not merely the intensity of the sound but also repetition, because even a sound of small intensity (*e.g.,* dripping tap or clickimg of clock) may become annoying, simply by repetition.

Chapter 19

Industrial and Non-Industrial Sounds

19.1 NOISE POLLUTION

Noise pollution may be defined as 'a sound of unpleasant and annoying nature.' It is physical form of pollution that is different from the oil, water and soil pollutions. Noise pollution is the result of increased industrialization, urban and over populations.

Sources of Noise Pollution:

Industrial sources such as:

Steel rolling mills

Printing presses

Transportation sources such as:

Auto vehicles

Trains

Aeroplanes

Household sources such as:

Indoor noises

Domestic gadgets

Public address system sources such as:

Loud speaker at the occasion of festival, religious function, marriage function, demonstration etc.

Effects of Noise Pollution:

Physical effects such as:

Temporary impairment of hearing

Permanent deafness

Damage to tympanic membrane

Damage to ear drum

Physiological effects such as:

Head ache
Pain in heart
Reduced right vision
Nervous breakdown
Eye strain
Reduced concentration of memory

Psychological effects such as:

Depression
Disturbed sleep
Reduced efficiency
Irritation
Fatigue
Emotional disturbance
Frustration
Reduced recreation

REVIEW QUESTIONS

SHORT ANSWER

1. Define atmosphere.
2. Name the principal gases of atmosphere.
3. State the importance of mangrove forest.
4. Define biogeochemical cycle.
5. State the impact of land degradation on agriculture.
6. What is carrying capacity of environment?
7. What is Green Bench?
8. What is biodiversity?
9. What is a cyclone?
10. What is acid rain?
11. Give an outline of natural and man-made disasters.
12. State the importance of wetland.
13. What is Agenda 21?
14. Explain what is biomagnifications.
15. Explain what is composting.
16. What is wildlife sanctuary?
17. Describe two major air pollutants emitted by automobiles.

18. What is BOD?
19. What is biomass?

SHORT NOTES, WRITE NOTES ON THE FOLLOWING:

1. oil
2. Chipko movement
3. Silent Valley Movement
4. Ozone layer depletion
5. Human Rights
6. Rain water harvesting
7. Asbestosis
8. Silicosis
9. Byssinosis
10. Carrying capacity of the earth

DIFFERENTIATE BETWEEN THE

1. National park and sanctuary
2. In-situ and ex-situ conservation
3. Species and genetic biodiversity
4. Endangered and extinct species

LONG ANSWER

1. What is wetland? Name two important wetlands in India.
2. What are the measures to be taken to prevent water pollution-related diseases?
3. What is nitrogen cycle? State the role of bacteria in nitrogen cycle.
4. Name two Project Tiger Reserves in West Bengal. Define a producer (in ecology) giving an example.
5. What is the permissible noise level at night as prescribed by the Central Pollution Control Board in (i) residential areas and (ii) in silent zones?
6. Explain what is biodiversity and the necessity for its preservation.
7. Name two non-conventional energy sources and mention their possible applications in the Indian context.
8. What are the renewable and non-renewable energy sources? Give one example for each.
9. Give a brief account of the environmental policies of the government of India relating to (i) forests, and (ii) biosphere State the environmental laws relating to
10. Name three sources of odour pollution. Explain the importance of Environmental Impact Assessment (ETA) for development projects.
11. Elucidate: "India has rich heritage in environmental ethics but failed to lead the world in this area."

OBJECTIVE TYPE QUESTIONS

1. Population stabilisation is essential for
   (a) agriculture
   (b) economic growth
   (c) sustainable development
   (d) the atmosphere
2. Human Development Index (HDI) is based on the parameters
   (a) life span, literacy and standard of living
   (b) growth of population and industry
   (c) income and education of an adult
   (d) the atmosphere
3. In India, 50 per cent population
   (a) have good standard of living
   (b) live below the poverty line
   (c) have no access to safe drinking water
   (d) the atmosphere
4. India loses topsoil
   (a) 5 billion tonnes a year
   (b) 1 billion tonnes a year
   (c) 25 billion tonnes a year
   (d) the atmosphere
5. Soil erosion or loss of topsoil is caused by
   (a) agriculture
   (b) deforestation
   (c) drought and flood
   (d) agriculture
6. Freshwater available for our use is
   (a) less than 5 per cent of total water resources
   (b) more than 10 per cent of total water resources
   (c) less than 1 per cent of total water resources
   (d) the agriculture
7. Once water, vast water resources (97 per cent) is
   (a) good for agriculture
   (b) unfit for human consumption
   (c) useful for coastal vegetation
   (d) the agriculture

8. Compared to sea water and lake water, groundwater contains
   (a) same mineral salts, nitrate, "and bicarbonate
   (b) less mineral salts, nitrate and bicarbonate
   (c) more mineral salts, nitrate and bicarbonate
   (d) less mineral
9. The symptoms of polluted water are
   (a) no change in physical appearance
   (b) no external matter on the surface
   (c) foul smell, bad taste, oil and grease
   (d) the agriculture
10. Organic pollutants in water include
   (a) soap and detergents
   (b) mine drainage (acid)
   (c) domestic sewage, pesticides, paper mill tanneev wastes
   (d) the agriculture
11. Eutrophication results from
   (a) Agricultural run-off and domestic sewage input
   (b) industrial effluent
   (c) vehicular exhausts
   (d) The agriculture
12. Pesticide residues in crops enter the human bodies through
   (a) birds and insects
   (b) human food chain
   (c) animals only
   (d) The agriculture

Unit-IV

Chapter 20

Water Pollution, and Pollutants in Water, Adverse Effects of Water Pollution

20.1 WATER POLLUTION

When toxic substances enter lakes, streams, rivers, oceans, and other water bodies, they get dissolved or lie suspended in water or get deposited on the bed. This results in the pollution of water whereby the quality of the water deteriorates, affecting aquatic ecosystems. Pollutants can also seep down and affect the groundwater deposits. Water pollution has many sources. The most polluting of them are the city sewage and industrial waste discharged into the rivers. The facilities to treat waste water are not adequate in any city in India. Presently, only about 10% of the waste water generated is treated; the rest is discharged as it is into our water bodies. Due to this, pollutants enter groundwater, rivers, and other water bodies. Such water, which ultimately ends up in our households, is often highly contaminated and carries disease-causing microbes.

Agricultural run-off, or the water from the fields that drains into rivers, is another major water pollutant as it contains fertilizers and pesticides. It amounts to a very small fraction of the sewage by weight. Nevertheless, it is large by volume and contains impurities such as organic materials and plant nutrients that tend to rot. The main organic materials are food and vegetable waste, plant nutrient come from chemical soaps, washing powders, etc. Domestic sewage is also very likely to contain disease-causing microbes. Thus, disposal of domestic waste water is a significant technical problem. Sewage generated from the urban areas in India has multiplied manifold since 1947.

Today, many people dump their garbage into streams, lakes, rivers, and seas, thus making water bodies the final resting place of cans, bottles, plastics, and other household products. The various substances that we use for keeping our houses clean add to water pollution as they contain harmful chemicals. In the past, people mostly used soaps made from animal and vegetable fat for all types of washing. However, most of today's cleaning products are synthetic detergents and come from the petrochemical industry. Most detergents and washing powders contain phosphates, which are used to soften the water among other things. These and other chemicals contained in washing powders affect the health of all forms of life in the water.

20.2 AGRICULTURAL RUN OFF

The high nitrate content in groundwater is mainly from irrigation run-off from agricultural fields where chemical fertilizers have been used indiscriminately.

The use of land for agriculture and the practices followed in cultivation greatly affect the quality of groundwater. Intensive cultivation of crops causes chemicals from fertilizers (*e.g.*, nitrate) and pesticides to seep into the groundwater, a process commonly known as leaching. Routine applications of fertilizers and pesticides for agriculture and indiscriminate disposal of industrial and domestic wastes are increasingly being recognized as significant sources of water pollution.

20.3 INDUSTRIAL EFFLUENTS

Waste water from manufacturing or chemical processes in industries contributes to water pollution. Industrial waste water usually contains specific and readily identifiable chemical compounds. During the last fifty years, the number of industries in India has grown rapidly. However, water pollution is concentrated within a few subsectors, mainly in the form of toxic wastes and organic pollutants. Out of this, a large portion can be traced to the processing of industrial chemicals and to the food products industry. In fact, a number of large- and medium-sized industries in the region covered by the Ganga Action Plan do not have adequate effluent treatment facilities. Most of these defaulting industries are sugar mills, distilleries, leather processing industries, and thermal power stations. Most major industries have treatment facilities for industrial effluents. However, this is not the case with small-scale industries, which cannot afford enormous investments in pollution control equipment as their profit margin is very slender.

20.4 EFFECTS OF WATER POLLUTION

The effects of water pollution are not only devastating to people but also to animals, fish, and birds. Polluted water is unsuitable for drinking, recreation, agriculture, and industry. It diminishes the aesthetic quality of lakes and rivers. More seriously, contaminated water destroys aquatic life and reduces its reproductive ability. Eventually, it is a hazard to human health. Nobody can escape the effects of water pollution. The individual and the community can help minimize water pollution. By simple housekeeping and management practices, the amount of waste generated can be minimized.

20.5 CAUSES OF WATER POLLUTION

Industrial Effluents

Sewage

Agriculture discharges

Artificial fertilizers

Pesticides

Herbicides

Toxicants

20.5.5 Industrial Wastes

These come from chemical industries, petrochemical industries, tanneries, thermal power plant, nuclear power plants etc. Besides other things, these also include:

Mercury
Lead
Other metals

20.2 EFFECTS OF WATER POLLUTION

Its major effects are:
Industrial effluents
Phosphorus and nitrates
Domestic, commercial and industrial effluents
Water borne infectious diseases
Non-biodegradable pesticides
Thermal pollution
Oil pollutants
Radioactive pollutants
Fluoride
Water-logging floods and land undulations etc.
Disposal of medical waste
Wet lands due to always fuel irrigational canals.

Chapter 21

Soil Pollution and Soil Profiles

21.1 PROBLEM WITH THE SKIN OF EARTH

The United Nations has set aside one day in the year to devote attention to a problem that is going to be of immense importance to the world, especially India, in the coming years. The problem of desertification and drought affects the livelihood of around 1.2 billion people world-wide who depend on land for most of their needs. June 17th reminds the world every year of the consequences of desertification for the global village. Land degradation means migration of the dependent population to land areas that are not denuded. Hence, migration of the affected people and greater burden on the remaining land.

The theme reflects this concern. "Social Dimensions of Desertification: Migration and poverty." More than 135 million people equivalent to the population of Germany and France combined are at risk of being displaced because of desertification. By 2020, about sixty million people are likely to eventually move from the desertified areas in Sub-Saharan Africa towards northern Africa and Europe.

What is desertification? It is the slow process of land degradation that occurs due to climate and human-induced factors. It has been likened to a "skin disease" over the planet where in patches of degrades land, erupting separately, gradually join, creating desert-like conditions. Over-cultivation, overgrazing, deforestation, poor irrigation practices, all contribute towards desertification. The topsoil, which takes centuries to build up, can be lost in just a few through such practices.

Land that recovered quickly in the past after long droughts and dry periods now tends to lose its biological and economic productivity if not sustainable managed. Economic forces can encourage people to over-exploit their land for short-term gains. Ignorance, errors, natural disasters such as floods and droughts as well as man-made disasters, like war and national emergencies, can destroy land productivity by placing undue pressure on it.

The circle of desertification and poverty is a vicious one. One factor leads to the other. Degraded land means poverty for those living off it and poverty causes those dependent on the land to overexploit it for food, energy, housing and income.

India figures prominently in the United Nations Environment Programme, UNEP's World Atlas of Desertification. This shows the largest degraded area of agricultural land in the world. 1475 million ha to be in Asia. The annual loss of productivity due to soil erosion in the South Asia region is estimated at about US $5.4 billion. The reclassification of some towns in India as being not drought prone but desert prone is also significant in this regard. The Centre and the states have launched a number of programmes to combat the menace of desertification such as the Drought Prone Area Programme, The Integrated Watershed Management Programme and others. The need is for concerted action for sustainable development with a "bottom-up" approach.

21.2 SOIL POLLUTION

It may be defined as the contamination caused by chemicals and other substances resulting in loss of productivity of soil.

21.2.1 Sources of Soil Pollution

Human and animal excreta
Organic insecticides
Chemical pollutants such as from following industries
Soap
Drugs
Dyes
Detergents
Cement
Pesticides
Radioactive substances
Nuclear power plants
Nitrification
Urban wastes
Garbage
Rubbish
Useless goods
Industrial pollutants

21.2.2 Causes of Soil Pollution

Direct Causes:
Poor management of solids and liquids waste disposal such as
Sewage and sludge
Domestic waste
Industrial waste
Agriculture waste
Use of chemicals the crop yields
Improper sanitation method
Salivation
Soil erosion

21.2.3 Effects of Soil Pollution

1. Water mixed with human excretes; sewage and sludge kill the microorganism and reduces the fertility of soil.
2. Garbage, sludge and dead animals create bad odour that causes chronic disease.

   Urban solid wastes such as rubbish, broken articles etc.

   Pesticides affect the Normal metabolism and tissues.

Chapter 22

Pollutants in Soil, their Adverse Effects, Controlling Measures

22.1 PHYTOREMEDIATION FOR CONTAMINATED SOILS

Plant-based remediation techniques are showing increasing promise for use in soils contaminated with organic and inorganic pollutants. Two contrasting approaches to remediation are being pursued: pollutant-stabilization and containment, where soil conditions and vegetative cover are manipulated td reduce the environmental hazard; and decontamination, where plants and their associated micro flora are used to eliminate the contaminant from the soil.

Over the past century, mining, manufacturing and urban activities have all contributed to extensive soil contamination. Various physical, chemical and bio-logical processes are already being used to remediate contaminated soil. These processes either 'decontami-nate' the soil, or 'stabilize' the pollutant within it. Decontamination reduces the amount of pollutants within the soil by removing them; stabilization does not reduce the quantity of pollutant at a site, but makes use of soil amendments to alter the soil chemistry and sequester or absorb the pollutant into the matrix so as to reduce or eliminate environmental risks.

The choice of remediation strategy depends on the nature of the contaminant(s). Metal contaminants are notoriously hard to remediate. Soils that are contami-nated with metals are usually excavated and land filled, although some sites are now treated by acid leaching, physical separation of the contaminant, 6r electro-chemical processes. Soils contaminated with organics are treated by vapor stripping or thermal desorption (for volatiles and semi-volatiles), soil washing (for leach able materials), incineration (for all organics not otherwise treatable) and some land filling. Certain organic contaminants, primarily petroleum hydro-carbons, are amenable to microbiological treatment, although the volume of material currently treated in this manner is relatively small. Biological soil-treatment systems include 'land farming' of some petroleum hydrocarbons, and ex situ techniques such as composting, 'bio-piles' and slurry reactors.

The costs associated with soil remediation are highly variable and depend on the contaminant, soil properties, site conditions and the volume of material to be remediated. Techniques that remediate a soil in situ are generally less expensive than those that require ex-cavation. On average, remediation costs are US$10-100 per m^3 of soil for volatile or water-soluble pollutants remediate in situ, US$60-300 per m^3 for compounds handled by land filling or low-temperature thermal treatment, and US$200-70 per m^3 for materials requiring special landfill arrangements or high temperature thermal treatments. The incineration of contaminated soil can cost up to US$100 per m_3. Certain materials (e.g. radionuclide) require even more intensive management techniques that can cost well beyond US$1000–3000 per m^3 of soil.

22.1.1 Phytoremediation of Contaminated Soils

Phyto- (or green-plant based-) remediation is not a new concept. Constructed wetlands, reed beds and floating-plant systems have been common for the treatment of some types of wastewater for many years. Current research efforts now focus on expanding phytoremediation to address contaminated soils and atmospheric pollutants. As far as soils are concerned, phytoremediation includes 'phytodecontamination' and 'phytostabilization' techniques.

22.1.2 General limitations of phytoremediation

Plants are alive; their roots require oxygen, water and nutrients. Soil texture, pH, salinity, pollutant concen-trations and the presence of other toxins must be within the limits of plant tolerance. Contaminants that are highly water soluble may leach outside the root zone and require containment. Phytoremediation is also and quaintly slower than physico-chemical processes, and may be considered as a long-term re-mediation process. Despite these limitations, in cases where large surface areas of relatively immobile contaminants exist in the surface soils, phytoremediation may be appropriate.

22.1.3 General Advantages of Phytoremediation

To facilitate comparison with physical remediation systems, we have redefined plants as 'solar-driven pumping and filtering systems that have measurable loading, degrading, and fouling capacities'. Roots may similarly be described as exploratory, liquid-phase extractors that can find, alter and or translocate elements and compounds against large chemical gradients. Plants can also be a cost-effective alternative to physical remediation systems. Cost ranges of between US$200 and 10000 hectare-1 for cropping sys-tems represent a treatment cost of US$0.02-1.00 m^3 per year (with roots down to one meter), which is many orders of magnitude less than costs associated with physico-chemical remediation technologies.

22.1.4 Phytodecontamination strategies involve

Phytoextraction, where plants accumulate the con-taminants and are harvested for processing. Postharvest processing of contaminants includes thermal, microbial and chemical treatments. Phytodegradation, where plants, or plant-associated microflora, convert pollutants into nontoxic materials.

Phytostabilization is where pollutants precipitate trom solution or are absorbed or entrapped in either plant tissue or the soil matrix. Sequestration can be enhanced either by amendments to the soil or through the action of the plant and its microflora.

22.2 PHYTOEXTRACTION OF CONTAMINANTS

The concept of soil remediation through plant extraction was first proposed for cadmium (Cd) more than a decade ago. However, little progress had been made until relatively recently. Engineering calcu-lations suggested that the successful decontamination of even moderately contaminated soils would require metal-removal rates of as much as 200—1000 kg metal per hectare per year over a 20-year period. Dividing these removal rates by the biomass of even a high-biomass crop, such as maize, suggested tissue concentration requirements in excess of 1—2%. To most researchers at the time, such levels of heavy metals (*e.g.*, zinc, cop-per, nickel and lead) seemed biocidal. However, it now seems that such concentrations may be tolerable.

Most plants growing on contaminated soils effec-tively exclude heavy metals from their tissues. Although plants take up and accumulate certain essential nutrients from soils to concentrations as high as 1–3%, levels of heavy metals only accumulate to 0.1—100mgkg-1 (Ref. 3) in most plants. Some non-essential elements that are not particularly harm-ful (*e.g.*, silicon and sodium) may accumulate in large amounts, but plants that hyper accumulate normally toxic metals are rare4. Such hyper accumulators are taxonomically widespread throughout the plant kingdoms. One such plant, which grows on outcroppings of metalliferous soils, is Sebertia accuminata, a small tree with sap that is 25% nickel by dry weight.

A member of the Brassica family, Thlaspi caerulescens, can accumulate up to 4% zinc in its tissue without apparent damage. However, the potential for application of hyper accumulators in bioremediation is limited by several factors: hyper accumulators often accumulate only a specific element and have not been found for all elements of interest; most hyper accumulators grow slowly and have small biomass; little is known about their agronomic characteristics, pest management, breeding potential and physiology. The plants are often rare and grow in remote regions; in certain cases, their habitat is threatened by mining, development and other activities. Using wild plants as a seed source is, therefore, also unreliable.

Given these limitations, efforts are being made to develop traditional crop plants with 'hyper accumulator tendencies'. One proposed strategy, as yet unsuccessful, is to cross hyper accumulators with high biomass relatives. Over the past four years, many crop and related weed species have been screened for metal uptake, translocation and tolerance. Much effort has centered on the Brassica family to which many hyper accumulator species belongs. To date, the results of these screening efforts indicate that, although many heavy-metal cations are easily taken up and accumu-lated in plant roots8, translocation of these cations to the shoots, as well as tolerance to these metal levels, is often limited.

Screening for mutants might yield useful hyper accumulators. For example, a mutant of Pisum sativum, mutated in a single gene, accumulates 10–1 OO-fold more iron than the wild type[9,10]. Similarly, a manganese accumulating mutant of Arabidopsis accumulates ten fold more manganese than does the wild type.

Effective genetic engineering of metal transport and tolerance in plants requires a better understanding of the mechanisms involved. However, increased metal tolerance has already been obtained, both by the introduction of metallothioneins, and by the introduc-tion of a semi-synthetic gene encoding MerA (bacterial mercuric ion reductase. The transgenic Arabidopsis tolerates levels of mercuric ion up to 100? M by reducing the toxic cation to Hg(O), which is then volatilized. Other possible tolerance mecha-nisms under investigation include alterations in phytochelatins andmetal-binding peptides. Ways of increas-ing the translocation of metals from root to shoot are also needed. Augmenting the uptake of relatively immobile contaminants is being attempted by alter-ing root morphology through Agrobacterium rhizogenes transformation14.

Phytoextraction should have economic advantages over traditional engineering techniques, especially in cases where the extracted metals are 'biomining' targets and have economic value (*e.g.*, nickel and copper). Phytoextraction of some inorganic as volatile forms (*e.g.*, selenium as dimethyl selenide16) may also be possible; this would further improve the economics by omitting harvesting and processing steps.

22.3 PHYTODEGRADATION OF ORGANIC CONTAMINANTS

Successful phytodegradation requires organic contaminants to be biologically available for absorption to, or uptake and metabolism by, plant or plant-associated microbial systems. Bioavailability depends on the relative lipophilicity of the compound17, the soil type (organic matter content, pH, and clay content and type18) and the age of the contaminant. Traditional analytical protocols cannot determine the bioavailability of a contaminant. Soils may contain biodegrad-able contaminants yet, due to the nature of the soil or the age of the contaminant, the material can prove to be recalcitrant.

A rough idea of bioavailability can be obtained using a laboratory microbial bioassay for biodegradability, to help indicate the potential for phytodegradability contaminants that, are tightly ad-sorbed to soil particles and resist uptake by microbes or plants make poor targets for phytodegradation. However, if these contaminants are similarly no interactive with other organisms (soil arthropods, herbivores), are not readily mobile (shown by leaching assays), or are not readily absorbed in the human gastro-intestinal tract, phytostabilization should be considered.

Once inside the plant, compounds are either stored unchanged, are bound to plant structural constituents, are metabolized, or are passed through the plant and volatilized. Plants have evolved in an environment where they are continually assaulted with a wide array of microbial, plant and, more recently, manmade toxins. In addition, they have significant metabolic activities in the root and the shoot that may be exploited for phytoremediation. Increasing the inherent degradative capacity of plants has been the aim of a number of molecular biology programs. One widely reported strategy is the creation of herbicide-resistant plants by the incorporation of bacterial degradative genes. Other (no microbial) resources for metabolic genes for plant transformation include mammalian livers[23] and pesticide-resistant insects.

Not all plant-associated degradative capacities need to be internal to the plant. Plant oxidoreductases have been proposed for the decontamination of phenolics and anilines in water-treatment systems. When fresh water sediments were screened for five specific enzy-matic capacities (dehalogenase, nitroreductase, per-oxidase, laccase and nitrilase), the enzymatic activity in all cases was found to have been of plant origin. This "Suggests that plant enzymes released into the environment following plant death might have sig-nificant catalytic effects and be useful for phyto-remediation.

The metabolic capacity of plant-associated mi-crobial systems is also tinder investigation. Bioremedi-ation through exploitation of the plant rhizosphere has received much of this attention26; however, plant-leaf microtlora and endophytic organisms are also being explored. In the rhizosphere, accelerated rates of degradation for many pesticides, as well as trichloro-ethylene and petroleum hydrocarbons, have been observed. To date, however, the rate and quantity of degradation have been slow. Managing the plant microbe interface to accelerate this degradation is an active area of research in many laboratories. Investigating the mechanisms and parameters of phytoremediation of organic contaminants under field conditions poses significant analytic challenges. Mass-balance studies for a contaminant are often incomplete, as is an understanding of the fate and metabolic impact of the contaminant. Heterogeneously contaminated matrixes are particularly difficult to study. Processes such as plant and microbial metabolism, as well as incorporation into plant lignin or soil humus, are difficult to follow analytically, even with the use of radio labeled compounds.

With few exceptions (*e.g.*, nitrate contamination), phytodecontamination techniques are still in the early stages of research and development. No soil has been successfully decontaminated by either phytoextraction or phytodegradation. Pilot projects that target organic contaminants in the water phase [*e.g.*, trinitrotoluene (TNT), trichloroethylene (TCE)] look promising; however, more research on iess-mobile contaminants [*e.g.*, polychlorinated biphenyls (PCB), polyaromatic hydrocarbons (PAHs)] is needed before they undergo large-scale field testing. Results nom field trials involving metal phytoextraction show that metal-removal rates currently remain too low to be commercially useful. New plant- and soil-management practices will need to be developed before large-scale pilot trials can be planted.

22.4 PHYTOSTABILIZATION OF SOIL CONTAMINANTS

Phytostabilization techniques exploit these processes to decrease bioavailability further, with the aim of greatly reducing, or even eliminating, further environmental harm or human health risk posed by the contaminants at the site. The practice is well advanced for contaminating metals at mining sites; however, such processes are also applicable to organic contaminants.

In biologically active soils, organic and inorganic contamihants[29] form chemical and biological associations of varying intensities. Although many of these associations effectively decrease contaminant availability for bioremediation, they also reduce the likelihood of leaching. Such sequestration processes include incorporation of organics into lignin or soil humus, and precipitation or sequestration of metals into iron hydroxide/ oxide coatings that form on soil particles and are trapped within small pores within the soil structure. In some cases, the reduction in bioavailability may preclude biological decontamination strategies.

Phyt-ostabilization of metal-contaminated soils exploits experience in reclaiming and revegetating soils associated with mine spoils, dredged materials and smelter emissions[31], as well as in the fate of metals in sewage sludges. Soil amendments can be used to alter soil chemistry and sequester the metal contaminant, thus having a dramatic effect on the presumed environ-mental hazard33. Amendments that have been used include composts and sludges, inorganic anions {*e.g.*, phosphates) and metallic oxides and hydroxides. The role of plants is to increase the sequestration of the contaminant by altering water flux through the soil, incorporating residual see contaminant into roots, and preventing wind and rain erosion. Plants can be chosen that alter or further sequester pollutants by mechanisms, such as: redox reactions [*e.g.*, chromium (VI) to chromium (III)]; precipitating the contaminant into an insoluble form (lead into lead phosphate); or incorporat-ing organics into the plant lignin (subsequently unextractable in chemical solvents and animal feeding tests).

Phytostabilization techniques are most appropriate for relatively immobile materials and large surface areas, and may work better with heavier textured soils and soil with a high organic matter content. The technique is currently acceptable for remediation at mining sites, but relatively few urban or industrially contaminated sites. Field tests and discussions are ongoing in a number of countries. Additional technical development should expand the acceptability of the technique to other sites and more contaminants.

22.5 FUTURE EFFORTS

Phytoremediation is a nascent technology that seeks to exploit the metabolic capabilities and growth habits of plants. However, delivering a 'remediation' system that is applicable to specific contaminated soils is a relatively recent focus. There is a significant need to pursue both fundamental and applied research: at a basic level, we do not understand the limiting factors in increasing uptake, translocation and tolerance of soil contaminants by plants. The mechanisms of seques-tration and the fate of many contaminants within the plant are also only vaguely understood. Without this basic understanding, it will be difficult to exploit many of the recent advances in plant molecular biology. The phytoremediation community looks towards the biotechnology community:

Provide research tools (*e.g.*, paired plants that differ in only a single trait, such as root morphology or a specific metabolic pathway). Much current testing involves plant species with numerous phenotYPic differences, such that results of these experiments are hard to interpret and 'causative' relationships are difficult to ascertain; produce products (*e.g.*, poplar trees with higher translocation rates; larger-biomass hyperaccumulators; or higher lignin or oil contents in the roots); and

Interact with the agronomic, engineering and chemical-remediation experts to produce integrated 'hybrid' technologies (*e.g.*, design a plant that absorbs and degradessurfactants and pollutants following sur-factant flushing of an aquifer, hence eliminating the need for recovery wells and post-recovery processing. Exploring the synergy between traditional disciplines may eventually provide low-cost, low-impact, visually benign and environmentally sound remediation strategies.

However, the use of plants to remove toxic metals ('phytoextraction') affords a low-cost alternative, which is ecologically preferable because it reclaims the original soil permanently. Phytoextraction requires plants that accumulate and tolerate high metal concentrations in their aboveground biomass, which can be harvested and disposed of or processed for industry or commerce. In practice, metal accumulation by plants is restricted by metal bioavailability in the soil. As accumulator plants have access only to metal in the soil solution, which might represent only a small fraction of the metal in the soil, this limits the amount that can be extracted.

The use of chemical chelates, which remove metals from their binding sites in the soil, was once proposed as a solution to this problem. However, although the accumulation of metals by plants can be enhanced by the addition of chemical chelates, these compounds can purge the soil of metals too efficiently, resulting in pollution of the water table. An analogous approach, proposed by Steven Whiting and his colleagues at the University of California at Berkeley (Whiting et al., 2001), is to employ natural soil microorganisms (bacteria and fungi) to increase the bioavailability of metals in contaminated soils. This has two advantages. First, microbial chelates are likely to occur predominantly in the vicinity of the roots (rhizosphere). Second, their persistence in the soil is likely to be shorter than that of chemical chelates. It is possible that natural chelates might be produced industrially and added to contaminated soils to aid phytoremediation, or one might consider constructing a 'designer rhizosphere' with microbial activities matched to both the plants' requirements and the soil conditions – but perhaps this has already arisen in nature and is just waiting to be discovered. The hypothesis that Ca^{2+} ?spiking plays a role in nodule formation, and directly suggests a mechanism whereby ethylene might constitute part of an auto-regulatory feedback loop controlling nodule number in response to the nitrogen status of the plant.

Stimulants, unable to respond to ethylene signals, are unable to downregulate their responses to Nod factor, resulting in the super-nodulated phenotype. Because ethylene also inhibited early nodulin gene expression and other 'downstream' responses, it has yet to be determined whether this downregulation operates at a single point, at or upstream of Ca^2 spiking, or whether multiple steps are affected independently. Further elucidation of Nod factor signal transduction and the molecular components involved is necessary before many of the questions raised can be answered. In the meantime, it is intriguing to consider possible mechanisms whereby ethylene modulation of the Ca^{2+} signal might influence nodulation.

If, for example, as in ligand-induced Ca^{2+} spiking in animal systems, spike characteristics encode information influencing downstream cellular responses, then it is conceivable that ethylene modulation of spiking frequency or amplitude also influences early nodulin gene expression and other cellular responses associated with nodule morphogenesis. Land contaminated by toxic metals threatens both the environment and human health. Generally, the contamination has arisen through human activities, such as the mining and smelting of metalliferous ores, the burning of fossil fuels, the disposal of sewage and municipal wastes, or the use of fertilizers and pesticides in agriculture. To return this land to agricultural or amenity use, the toxic metals must be removed or rendered inaccessible. Conventional approaches to the reclamation of contaminated land are expensive, and based on either the removal ('dig and dump') or fixation ('immobilize and cover') of toxic metals.

Indeed, enhanced phytoextraction was only observed when bacteria (or filtered solutions in which bacteria had been cultured) raised the concentration of watersoluble zinc. It is currently believed that plants take up zinc as the cation. The bacteria could produce zinc-chelating metallophores, which might also be taken up by the plant. It will be interesting to analyse the zinc complexes in the soil solution and determine which, if any, are taken up by plants. It will also be worth investigating how microorganisms release metals from their binding sites in the soil, and identifying useful microbial chelates, their biostability, specificity for binding metals, and whether plants produce similar compounds.

REVIEW QUESTIONS

Short notes, Write notes on the following:

1. oil
2. Chipko movement
3. Flyash
4. Carrying capacity
5. aquifer
6. aerosol
7. EIA
8. geothermal energy
9. Silent Valley Movement

10. biogas
11. sustainable development
12. ozone layer
13. Green Bench

DIFFERENTIATE BETWEEN THE

1. National park and sanctuary
2. In-situ and ex-situ conservation
3. Species and genetic biodiversity
4. Endangered and extinct species

LONG ANSWER

1. Briefly mention the role of biotic components of an ecosystem.
2. State the function of decomposers in an ecosystem.
3. State the ecological and economical importance of biodiversity.
4. Briefly explain hydrological cycle.
5. State how population growth and natural resources are related.
6. Explain (Jaia hypothesis.
7. Give an outline of environmental ethics.

SHORT ANSWER

1. What is El-Nino?
2. What is plate tectonics?
3. What is quarantine?
4. What is biodiversity?
5. What is a cyclone?
6. What is acid rain?
7. What is meant by environmental studies?
8. What is succession?
9. Define wetland.
10. What is biomagnification?
11. What is ecosystem?
12. Mention the major causes of air pollution in the urban areas.
13. What is biogas?
14. Define sustainable development.
15. State the importance of ozone layer
16. What is Green Bench?
17. State the role of bacteria in nitrogen cycle.

18. What is meant by non-conventional energy?
19. What is exponential growth of population?
20. What is flyash?
21. Define carrying capacity.
22. What is aquifer?
23. Define aerosol.
24. What is EIA
25. What is geothermal energy?

OBJECTIVE TYPE QUESTIONS

1. Thermal pollution originates from discharge of waste water from
   (a) steel plant
   (b) nuclear power plant
   (c) thermal power plant
   (d) the atmosphere
2. Arsenic contamination of groundwater arises from
   (a) excessive pumping of groundwater by shallow tube wells for irrigation
   (b) seepage of surface water
   (c) leaching of arsenopyrite mineral into groundwater
   (d) the atmosphere
3. Arsenic poisoning from drinking water leads to
   (a) loss of hair, brittle nails, gangrene and cancer
   (b) diarrhoea, dysentery, etc.
   (c) pneumonia, typhoid, etc
   (d) the atmosphere
4. The Ganga river is heavily polluted at
   (a) Rishikesh and Haridwar
   (b) Kanpur, Varanasi and Kolkata
   (c) Patna and Allahabad
   (d) the atmosphere
5. The Ganga pollution is due to dumping of
   (a) domestic and industrial sewage
   (b) waste from forests
   (c) food wastes
   (d) Roorkee
6. The Ganga Action Plan is based on
   (a) mixing with rainwater

(b) preventing input of domestic and industrial wastes
(c) recycling of water after waste treatment
(d) hydrosphere

7. Primary and secondary wastes water treat ment are based on
(a) screening of solid matter only
(b) injecting air stream only
(c) screening, sedimentation, aerobic digestion and sedimentation
(d) the agriculture

8. The important water quality parameters are
(a) calcium, magnesium, iron
(b) lead, zinc mercury
(c) dissolved oxygen, chemical oxygen demand, chloride and arsenic
(d) the agriculture

9. Desalination of sea water means
(a) removal of salts from sea water
(b) dumping of oil into sea water
(c) removal of suspended solids from sea water
(d) the arsenic

10. Water treatment for drinking water supply requires
(a) filtration through sand bed
(b) Disinfection by chlorination to kill viruses, bacteria, etc
(c) sedimentation
(d) TDS

11. The major components of the atmosphere are
(a) rare gases
(b) carbon dioxide and argon
(c) nitrogen, oxygen and water vapour
(d) the ammonia

12. The important chemical species in the tropoc sphere are
(a) oxygen, nitric oxide
(b) nitrogen, oxygen, carbon dioxide and water vapour
(c) sulphur dioxide, carbon monoxide
(d) clouds

Unit-V

Chapter 23

Society and Ethics

23.1 VALUE EDUCATION

The socio-economic and culture progress of a country depends upon education. Education does not simply mean acquiring knowledge and information but also its right use within the framework of ethical values. Values are closely related with aims of education. Values are ideas, beliefs or norms that a society holds. Although the scientific and technological advancement has brought a revolutionary change in our day to day life but at the same time, we are losing the values of life. Therefore, value based education has a very significant role in children's education. It teaches them to be compassionate, helpful, peace loving, generous and tolerant, so that they can make their future more harmonies, peaceful, enjoyable and sustainable.

Value Based Environmental Education: The environment belongs to each one of us and our actions affect the environment. When the environment gets degraded, it affects our health, well being and our future. Therefore, we should inculcate following values in our attitude and behavior about environment.

We must recognize 'men in nature' rather then 'nature for man'.

We must have love compassion tolerance and justice towards nature.

We should not exploit nature without nurturing her. Our culture customs and rituals in many ways teach us to nurture and respect nature. For example, treating many plants, Animals Rivers, mountains and forest as sacred.

We should learn that the human civilization is a part of the Earth and various natural phenomenons are interconnected and interlinked with special bonds of hormony. If we disturb this harmony anywhere, there will be an ecological imbalance leading to catastrophic results. We should develop the principles of self restrain, self discipline, reduction of wants, freedom from greed and severity in our attitude. Such values will help us in attaining the goal of sustainable development and environmental conservation.

23.2 ENVIRONMENTAL AESTHETIC AND ETHICAL RESPONSIBILITY OF A CITIZEN TOWARDS PROTECTING THE ENVIRONMENT

Other wildlife values are less tangible than maintaining stable ecosystems or providing recreation. If wildlife had no other value it would still be worth preserving for its sheer beauty and appeal to the human spirit. Aldo Leopold, an Iowan, author, and great conservationist, wrote of a "land ethic" in which plants and animals should have "at least in spots, their continued existence in a natural state." According to Leopold, humans must change from "conqueror of the land community to a plain member and citizen of it." His sentiments give definition to the aesthetic and ethical values of wildlife.

Values related to wildlife are expressed in many different cultures through legends, myths. religious teachings and writings, symbols, protocols, and ceremonies. To a citizen of the United States, the bald eagle is much more than a large bird of prey. It symbolizes many things %u2013 freedom, power, courage. It has values beyond that of its place in the natural world. These values vary from person to person and culture to culture.

23.3 IMPORTANCE OF WILDLIFE

People have utilized wildlife throughout the ages. Prehistoric people, Native Americans, and Euro-American settlers depended on wildlife for food, clothing, and even shelter. Wildlife is often a part of many Native American religious ceremonies.

23.4 BIODIVERSITY

Biodiversity describes a variety of natural systems (ecosystem diversity), the number of different species in a given area (species diversity), or variety within individual living things (genetic diversity). Biodiversity has declined over the past century due to intensive agriculture and urban development. Iowa has the unfortunate distinction as being perhaps the most ecologically altered state in the nation. We have lost over 99 percent of our native prairies, 95 percent of our wetlands, and 70 percent of our forests. Native ecosystems were reduced in size and diversity. Many species of wildlife declined in numbers or disappeared from the state.

Each plant and animal species may represent solutions to biological problems. Plants and animals provide medicines, food, and fibers. Most advances in biological and medical research have come through the studies of wild, or formerly wild, animals and plants. Individual animals and plants also contribute to the well-being of the ecosystems they inhabit. If even one, seemingly unimportant, species is removed this delicate balance may be disturbed. People have only begun to understand the intricate relationships among species. A species becoming extinct creates situations that cannot be reversed.

Maintaining biodiversity is an important goal of wildlife management. For example, the IDNR prairie seed harvest team grows their own plants to augment prairie plantings on both public and private lands. Adding established plants (especially Forbes) to new prairie seedings increases their diversity. IDNR also is reintroducing species into suitable habitats to increase biodiversity.

23.5 RECREATION

People have always been dependent on wildlife. They used wildlife for food, clothing, shelter, utensils, medicines, and religious objects throughout history. In the United States, wildlife now is more important for recreation. Food and fur are still important products of hunting and trapping, but many values being outdoors and/or hunting with friends as much as or more than, gathering food.

Non-consumptive uses of wildlife include bird watching, wildlife photography, feeding birds, landscaping for wildlife, hiking, bicycling, backpacking, camping, canoeing, etc. Recent state park visitor profiles show these forms of recreation are increasing. Eighty-one percent of Iowans say they participate in viewing wildlife. Nearly half travel away from their homes to view or photograph wildlife.

23.6 AESTHETIC AND ETHICAL VALUE

Other wildlife values are less tangible than maintaining stable ecosystems or providing recreation. If wildlife had no other value it would still be worth preserving for its sheer beauty and appeal to the human spirit. Aldo Leopold, an Iowan, author, and great conservationist, wrote of a "land ethic" in which plants and animals should have "at least in spots, their continued existence in a natural state." According to Leopold, humans must change from "conqueror of the land community to a plain member and citizen of it." His sentiments give definition to the aesthetic and ethical values of wildlife.

Values related to wildlife are expressed in many different cultures through legends, myths, religious teachings and writings, symbols, protocols, and ceremonies. To a citizen of the United States, the bald eagle is much more than a large bird of prey. It symbolizes many things%u2013freedom, power, courage. It has values beyond that of its place in the natural world. These values vary from person to person and culture to culture.

In this crucial period of transition, it is necessary for Ukraine to search for ways of overcoming current difficulties and securing a brighter future. Decision-makers and government representatives must, therefore, focus their attention on ensuring economic and societal development that respect the environment and improve quality of life, on a long-term basis. For this endeavour to be successful priorities should be clearly defined and, to avoid mistakes of the past, a new vision and new models are seriously needed.

Since its inception in 1985, the Biopolitics International Organisation (B.I.O.) has been raising awareness of the urgent need to shift from an anthropocentric to a biocentric system of values in society, in order to curb environmental deterioration and place respect for the gift of bios- life- at the core of every action and thought. Within this framework, the B.I.O. has been promoting the implementation of environmental principles in every human endeavour, since concern for the environment is perhaps the most potent unifying agent in modern society. Long-term, multilateral initiatives for environmental conservation are the only option for guaranteeing the rights of future generations, currently jeopardised by irresponsibility and oversight. A millennium approach to decision-making can provide the necessary objectives for the essential duty of developing policy with a view to the future.

At a time when global priorities are rapidly changing, accommodating environmental protection, as the most important parameter in management and administration procedures, becomes a critical task. The potential shutdown of the Chernobyl Nuclear Power Plant should be viewed as an excellent opportunity for the dynamic implementation of this new policy in Ukraine. Slavutich can serve as a model for the development of employment opportunities, which will guarantee economic growth in the region and will take advantage of the available infrastructure, in an effective manner. The evolution of Slavutich into a "biopolis" model, where every endeavour would be geared towards environmental appreciation, can help restore confidence in the population, and promote constructive and productive enterprise.

Chernobyl, a place of destruction, can serve as a powerful model to help society acknowledge the importance of embracing biocentric values and preserving bios on our planet. A biocentric vision can help create a balanced society, with the appropriate legal framework to support both technological progress and environmental protection.

23.7 HUMAN INFLUENCES ON THE ECOSYSTEM

23.7.7 Changes in Human Population

Early humans lived in family groups and acted as hunter/gatherers. They needed very little raw materials and moved around as supplies of food varied. About 10,000 years ago the agricultural revolution began; people settled, began farming land and affected their environment in a more permanent way. At the end of the 20th century, the human population was increasing exponentially.

Because of human activities [anthropogenic] the needs for food, raw materials, energy & land have increased, as have the production of waste materials and pollution. All of these factors have a big influence on the natural ecosystems around us.

Fig. 24.1

23.7.2 Changes In Land Use

Deforestation

Indigenous **tribes normally clear small areas, farm/harvest for a few seasons then move on.** With low density populations, the forest regenerates & recovers. In addition, the forest can be managed sustainable for its productivity and controlled reafforestation replenishes its stock.

Causes: Large scale deforestation is due to Hardwood timbers used for furniture & building.

Area converted to agriculture for food–growing crops and grazing animals.

Wood cut down as source of fuel.

Land used for homes, factories, also infrastructure eg road, rail, airports, and seaports. Often areas cleared by **'SLASH & BURN'** creating more air pollution.

. Rivers used for hydroelectric power stations.

Areas cleared for mining of minerals [manganese, tin and iron].

Forestry products used for extraction of medicines

EFFECTS OF DEFORESTATION

Trees normally retain water and release it slowly into soil, streams and water vapour to the air. Surface runoff increases, washing soil into streams and rivers. Nutrients are mainly retained within the trees but natural recycling is rapid. Without the trees, nutrients are lost and soil fertility decreases rapidly.

Soil is exposed to the sun, desiccates & erosion increases.

Sediment blocks rivers and leads to flooding.

Usually **less CO_2 is used** by the replacement crop plant, so increasing Greenhouse effect.

Solutions

Governments to encourage sustainable use of forest resources, including **Reforestation** = planting of trees in areas that were previously forested. & **Afforestation** = planting trees in areas which were not previously forest. This can only be done through **managed systems, control of logging, financial support** of indigenous populations to **encourage use of renewable resources** eg nuts, publicising use of sustainable wood for furniture etc around the world.

Managed systems in Britain include **Coppice woodlands** [*eg.,* hazel, alder, and maple Willow poplar]. At intervals, different areas of trees are cut close to ground to form stumps, new side shoots or stools are allowed to grow for 10–15 years, these are then harvested as poles for broom handles, fencing and furniture legs, etc. Some trees, standards, are allowed to grow to full size and felled areas regenerate naturally from seedlings. Species diversity is supported as neighbouring areas have different aged stands of trees.

Desertification = 'land degradation in arid, semi-arid and dry sub-humid areas arising mainly from adverse human impact'

Causes: Natural deserts are caused by low and intermittent rainfall [<250 mm per yr].

Pressures on Arid land are due to need for grazing animals and for gathering fuel. A dry season or increasing human population can tip the balance so that herds exceed the carrying capacity and the little vegetation is destroyed.

Effects: Lack of vegetation exposes soil to sunlight causing desiccation and erosion.

Salination occurs as the water evaporates and salts from ground water are left behind. Soil is then unsuitable for plant growth. Salination also results from poorly designed irrigation systems. Fertilisers and pesticides make the situation worse. Lack of vegetation affects humidity, rainfall and climate patterns.

Solutions

Terrace the land to prevent run-off.

Plant trees to provide shade and wind shelter. Leguminous trees increase soil fertility.

Use stones at base of trees to retain moisture.

Intensive Farming Methods: Use of Monocultures increases yield but disease and pest spread faster.

Selective breeding and genetic engineering decreases species diversity and decreases gene pools.

Use of Fertilisers and Pesticides increases water pollution and disrupt food chains.

Irrigation increases salinity of soils.

Mechanisation destroys hedgerows, habitats and decreases species diversity.

Atmospheric Pollution: Increased atmospheric pollution is linked directly to increasing human population and growth of urban and industrial societies. Damage affects people, their crops, buildings, wildlife & global climate.

Acid Rain - Causes: Rain is naturally mildly acidic [~pH 5.6] due to CO2 dissolving in air moisture to form carbonic acid. **Acid rain is pH 5.5 or lower due to burning of fossil fuels releasing SO_2 and NOx.** Study of glaciers and diatoms in lake sediments has confirmed the increase in acidity of precipitation. Pollutants travel with prevailing air currents and are high in Scandinavia and mountain regions where rainfall is higher.

Effects: Lakes with pH < 4.5 have no fish because trout do not produce the enzyme needed to break out of egg coating so larvae get trapped inside. Aluminium ions increase causing excess of sticky mucus on gills, so gas exchange is reduced and less salt is absorbed affecting osmoregulation. Neutralising by adding lime gives short-term benefits. Phytoplankton decrease affecting food chains. Coniferous forests show poorer growth, lower productivity, and discolouration of needles, shallow roots and die-back of crowns. Heavy metal ions [cadmium, lead, mercury] are released into soils and may contaminate drinking water. Mercury poisoning may occur in unborn foetuses. Copper causes diarrhoea in young children, Aluminium is linked with Alzheimer's disease.

23.3 GREENHOUSE EFFECT

A natural phenomenon maintains life on Earth. Radiation from the Sun reaches the Earth, most of the short wavelengths [*eg.,* 400–700nm visible spectrum] pass through the atmosphere easily and warms the surface. Longer wavelengths [4000–100,00 nm] radiate away from the Earth, but more is absorbed by the troposphere and radiates back as heat. This effect has **increased** due to more greenhouse gases from human activities.

Causes of Increase

CO_2 from increased combustion of fossil fuels and respiration including increase of domesticated animals. Deforestation means more 'slash & burn' and less CO_2 removed by photosynthesis.

Chlorofluorocarbons [CFCs] from aerosols & fridges, last for >60 yrs, absorb 7000 times the infrared radiation that CO_2 does and are entirely anthropogenic.

Methane from ruminant animals [*eg.,* cattle] and anaerobic bacteria in rice fields and landfill rubbish tips.

Nitrous Oxide from combustion of fossil fuels, activity of denitrifying bacteria on nitrate fertilisers & decomposition of animal and human waste.

Ozone [O3] from car exhausts.

Water Vapour from burning fossil fuels and increasing evaporation with increasing global temperatures.

23.4 WATER POLLUTION

Water or Hydrological Cycle **controlled through evaporation, transpiration, condensation & precipitation may be affected by human activities.**

Factors which affect water systems & are altered by pollution;

Water movement—stagnant in ponds & lakes, slow to fast in rivers & streams.

Nutrient Status—depends on bedrock, soil & vegetation. **Oligotrophic** = poor nutrients, **Mesotrophic** = intermediate nutrient level, **Eutrophic** = rich in nutrients.

Oxygen – decreases with increasing temp. but increases with turbulence. Diurnal fluctuation – increased by photosynthesis during day. Also seasonal fluctuations due to changes in temp and light. Biochemical Oxygen Demand [BOD] = amount of O_2 used by living organisms (measured at 20°C over 5 days) will increase as microbes decompose polluting organic material, so BOD used as a measure of pollution.

CO_2 - forms carbonic acid which dissociates into H^+ and $HCO3^-$ causing fluctuations in pH, which is also affected by photosynthesis.

Temperature – affects density of water and may cause barriers between layers in large lakes. Water temp is relatively stable.

Light Intensity – decreases with depth and suspended solids

Plant life – microscopic phytoplankton are important in primary productivity and number vary hugely with seasons and nutrient level.

Animal life – is greatly affected by O_2 levels so some species act as indicators of this.

23.5 OIL POLLUTION

Oil pollution affects mainly marine ecosystems and usually occurs as oil spills from tankers or oil installations and emptying of ballast water in tankers. As some lighter oil fractions evaporate the denser oil reacts to produce tar. Oil on water surface reduces exchange of O_2, killing those species that breathe on the surface. Toxins from oil kill plankton, shellfish, fish and birds and reduce reproduction rates in birds. Oil coats birds' feathers, which then die from toxins as they clean them. In addition, the birds can't fly, hunt for food and loose the normal insulation of the feathers.

Biodegradation: Oil slicks will breakdown naturally, as wave, action disperses oil into smaller droplets and micro-organisms digest it. Then chemical reactions occur in the presence of light to complete the breakdown into CO_2 & H_2O. This process takes weeks to many years.

Bioremediation: A polluted area is deliberately seeded with micro-organisms to speed up recovery.

Mechanical aids can be used to trap the oil with booms then skim it off the surface. It can be shovelled off beaches. Chemical dispersants and detergents can be used to break up the oil but may be more toxic to organisms than the oil.

23.6 THERMAL POLLUTION

Thermal pollution is where human activities raise the water temperature above normal [usually 5-10°C], due to effluent from industries & hot water from power stations. Effects vary, sometimes beneficial as well as harmful. As temperature increases, O_2 solubility decreases. Different species have different temperature tolerances and it affects development, growth rate, migration, spawning and the time taken for eggs to hatch [called day-degrees]. Trout are killed above 25°C and their eggs need 300 day-degrees to hatch, *i.e.,* 30 days at 10°C, but only 20 days at 15°C. The communities in an ecosystem will change with thermal pollution, some species will die out, others will multiply e.g. algal blooms may form.

23.6.1 Measures to Control Pollution

Modern society relies heavily on fossil fuels and a 'throw away' economy. To control pollution we need to reduce carbon and sulphur emissions, use of pesticides and artificial fertilisers and use of new raw materials. However, a balance needs to be found between practical measures to control pollution and the economic needs of society, locally and globally. Both local, national & global agreements and laws are made e.g.;

Clean Air Act [1956 &1968] – smoke cont: ol on domestic and industrial fuels..

EU Directives [1970s & 1990s] – limit smoke and sulphur dioxide emissions, set up pollution monitoring stations, phased out leaded petrol to protect health.

EU Directives on water quality for fish and shellfish, drinking water and 'Blue Flag' awards for bathing beaches with low microbe counts.

23.7 SOCIAL ISSUE AND ENVIRONMENT

23.7.1 Biodiversity

The variety of life on Earth, its biological diversity, is commonly referred to as biodiversity. The number of species of plants, animals, and microorganisms, the enormous diversity of genes in these species, the different ecosystems on the planet, such as deserts, rainforests and coral reefs are all part of a biologically diverse Earth. Appropriate conservation and sustainable development strategies attempt to recognize this as being integral to any approach. In some way or form, almost all cultures have recognized the importance of nature and its biological diversity for their societies and have therefore understood the need to maintain it. Yet, power, greed and politics have affected the precarious balance.

Biodiversity boosts ecosystem productivity where each species, no matter how small, all have an important role to play. For example, a larger number of plant species means a greater variety of crops; greater species diversity ensures natural sustainability for all life forms; and healthy ecosystems can better withstand and recover from a variety of disasters. Therefore, while we dominate this planet, we still need to preserve the diversity in wildlife.

23.7.2 Loss of Biodiversity and Extinctions

It is feared that human activity is causing massive extinctions. From various animal species, forests and the ecosystems that forests support, marine life. The costs associated with deteriorating or vanishing ecosystems will be high. However, sustainable development and consumption would help avert ecological problems.

23.7.3 Nature and Animal Conservation

Preserving species and their habitats is important for ecosystems to self-sustain themselves.

Yet, the pressures to destroy habitat for logging, illegal hunting, and other challenges are making conservation a struggle

23.8 CLIMATE CHANGE AFFECTS BIODIVERSITY

The World Resources Institute reports that there is a link between biodiversity and climate change. Rapid global warming can affect an ecosystems chances to adapt naturally. What have governments around the world been trying to do about it?

23.8.1 Coral Reefs

One type of ecosystem that perhaps is neglected more than any other is perhaps also the richest in biodiversity—the coral reefs.

Coral reefs are useful to the environment and to people in a number of ways. However, all around the world, much of the world's marine biodiversity face threats from human and activities as well as natural. It is feared that very soon, many reefs could die off.

The February 1999 Biodiversity Protocol meeting in Colombia broke down because USA, not even a signatory to the Convention on Biological Diversity, to which the protocol is meant to be part of, and five other countries of the "Miami Group" felt that their business interests were threatened. The safety concerns were unfortunately overridden by trade concerns. Some technological advances, especially in genetically engineered food, have been very fast paced and products are being pushed into the market place without having been proven safe. All over the world, concerned citizens and governments have been trying to take precautionary measures. However, 1999 was not a successful year in that respect.

A Biosafety Protocol meeting was hosted in Montreal, Canada January 24 to January 28. Compared to the fiasco of the previous year, this time, there had been a somewhat successful treaty to regulate the international transport and release of genetically modified organisms to protect natural biological diversity. However, there were a number of important and serious weaknesses too.

23.9 CLIMATE CHANGE AND GLOBAL WARMING

The climate is changing. The earth is warming up, and there is now overwhelming scientific consensus that it is happening, and human-induced. With global warming on the increase and species and their habitats on the decrease, chances for ecosystems to adapt naturally are diminishing. Many are agreed that climate change may be one of the greatest threats facing the planet. Recent years show increasing temperatures in various regions, and/or increasing extremities in weather patterns.

This section explores some of the effects of climate change. It also attempts to provide insights into what governments, companies, international institutions, and other organizations are attempting to do about this issue, as well as the challenges they face. Some of the major conferences in recent years are also discussed.

The climate is changing. The earth is warming up, and there is now overwhelming scientific consensus that it is happening, and human-induced. With global warming on the increase and species and their habitats on the decrease, chances for ecosystems to adapt naturally are diminishing.

Many are agreed that climate change may be one of the greatest threats facing the planet. Recent years show increasing temperatures in various regions, and/or increasing extremities in weather patterns.

23.10 GLOBAL DIMMING

Research has shown that air pollutants from fossil fuel use make clouds reflect more of the sun's rays back into space. This leads to an effect known as global dimming whereby less heat and energy reaches the earth. At first, it sounds like an ironic savior to climate change problems. However, it is believed that global dimming caused the droughts in Ethiopia in the 1970s and 80s where millions died, because the northern hemisphere oceans were not warm enough to allow rain formation. Global dimming is also hiding the true power of global warming. By cleaning up global dimming-causing pollutants without tackling greenhouse gas emissions, rapid warming has been observed, and various human health and ecological disasters have resulted, as witnessed during the European heat wave in 2003, which saw thousands of people die.

23.11 UN FRAMEWORK CONVENTION ON CLIMATE CHANGE

The world mostly agrees that something needs to be done about global warming and climate change. The first stumbling block, however, has been trying to get an agreement on a framework. In 1988, the Intergovernmental Panel on Climate Change (IPCC) was created by the United Nations Environment Programme (UNEP) and the World Meterological Organization (WMO) to assess the scientific knowledge on global warming. The IPCC concluded in 1990 that there was broad international consensus that climate change was human-induced. That report led way to an international convention for climate change, the United Nations Framework Convention on Climate Change (UNFCCC), signed by over 150 countries at the Rio Earth Summit in 1992. This section looks at this Convention and some of the main principles in it.

23.12 REACTIONS TO CLIMATE CHANGE NEGOTIATIONS AND ACTION

The United States plus a few other countries, and many large corporations, have been against climate change treaties due to the fear of the threat to their economy and profits if they have to make substantial changes. However, as more climate change science has emerged over the years, many businesses are accepting this and even asking their governments for more action so that there is quick clarification on the new rules of the game so they can get on with their businesses.

For many years, large, influential businesses and governments have been against the idea of global warming. Many have poured a lot of resources into discrediting what has generally been accepted for a long time as real. Now, the mainstream is generally worried about climate change impacts and the discourse seems to have shifted accordingly. Even some businesses that once engaged in disinformation campaigns have changed their opinions, some even requesting governments for regulation and direction on this issue. However, a few influential companies and organizations are still attempting to undermine climate change action and concerns. All this mean a different type of spin and propaganda with attempts at green washing and misleading information becoming the norm, or will there now be major shift in attitudes to see concrete solutions being proposed and implemented.

23.13 CLIMATE JUSTICE AND EQUITY

For a number of years, there have been concerns that climate change negotiations will essentially ignore a key principle of climate change negotiation frameworks: the common but differentiated responsibilities.

This recognizes that historically:

Industrialized nations have emitted far more greenhouse gas emissions (even if some developing nations are only now increasing theirs); Rich countries therefore face the biggest responsibility and burden for action to address climate change; and Rich countries therefore must support developing nations adapt—through financing and technology transfer, for example. This notion of climate justice is typically ignored by many rich nations and their mainstream media, making it easy to blame China, India and other developing countries for failures in climate change mitigation negotiations. Development expert, Martin Khor, calculated that taking historical emissions into account, the rich countries owe a carbon debt because they have already used more than their fair quota of emissions. Yet, by 2050 when certain emission reductions are needed by, their reduced emissions will still add up to be go over their fair share:

However, rather than continue down the path of unequal development, industrialized nations can help pay off their carbon debt by truly helping emerging countries develop along a cleaner path, such as through the promised-but-barely-delivered technology transfer, finance, and capacity building. So far, however, rich nations have done very little within the Kyoto protocol to reduce emissions by any meaningful amount, while they are all for negotiating a follow on treaty that brings more pressure to developing countries to agree to emissions targets. In effect, the more there will be delay the more the poor nations will have to save the Earth with their sacrifices (and if it works, as history shows, the rich and powerful will find a way to rewrite history to claim they were the ones that saved the planet.

23.14 CLIMATE CHANGE FLEXIBILITY MECHANISMS

Flexibility mechanisms were defined in the Kyoto Protocol as different ways to achieve emissions reduction as part of the effort to address climate change issues. These falls into the following categories: Emissions Trading, Joint Implementation and Clean Development Mechanism.

However, these have been highly controversial as they were mainly included on strong US insistence and to keep the US in the treaty (even though the US eventually pulled out). Some of the mechanisms face criticism for not actually leading to a reduction in emissions, for example.

23.15 CARBON SINKS, FORESTS AND CLIMATE CHANGE

A mechanism suggested for tackling climate change and warming has been the idea of using Carbon Sinks to soak up carbon dioxide. To aid in this, reforestation, or planting of new forests, have been suggested. This is a popular strategy for the logging industry and nations with large forests interests. While there may be some potential in this solution, it cannot be effective on its own. This is because it legitimizes continued destruction of old-growth and pristine forests which are rich ecosystems and have an established biodiversity base (albeit shrinking now) that naturally maintain the environment (at no cost!). Creating new forest areas would require the creation of entire ecosystems. It is also criticized for being a quick fix that does not tackle the root causes effectively and does not lead to, or promote actual emissions reduction.

23.16 GLOBAL WARMING AND POPULATION

It seems there has been a recent interest in associating climate change/global warming with "over population" and that countries such as China and India have to do more to help contain global warming.

Yet rich countries have a lot to do themselves. There were agreed reasons why developing countries were exempt from initial greenhouse gas emission targets: it was the emissions from rich countries that accumulated in the atmosphere for so long to trigger climate change.

23.17 DECLINING AMPHIBIAN POPULATIONS

Amphibians are particularly sensitive to changes the environment. Amphibians have been described as a marker species or the equivalent of "canaries of the coal mines" meaning they provide an important signal to the health of biodiversity; when they are stressed and struggling, biodiversity may be under pressure. When they are doing well, biodiversity is probably healthy. Unfortunately, as has been feared for many years now, amphibian species are declining at an alarming rate.

Bio-ethics: Bio-ethics is an essential part of modern Biopolitics. It can be considered both a conceptual science with a philosophical dimension, and, at the same time, a direction of practical activities. Since 1985, the B.I.O. has been promoting a shift from anthropocentric to biocentric values in society. This shift requires the participation not only of governments and large business corporations, but also of all individuals. This basic thinking, that all life has equal value, must be present in every human endeavour. As each person takes a small step and applies biocentric thinking to his or her actions, a huge step is taken by society.

The bios theory promotes bio-ethics as one of its major components. Bio-ethics provides the ethical and philosophical foundations for peaceful and harmonious co-evolution of humanity and the bio-environment. Bio-ethics is an essential part of modern biopolitics. Biopolitics in general is aimed at maintaining and promoting life, bios. Bio-ethics is primarily concerned with the ethical issues pertaining to all forms of life. In this way, bio-ethics supplements bio-legislation, the field of biopolitics dealing with the legal problems associated with bios. In many instances, bio-ethics and bio-legislation should be used in concert. For example, genetic engineering has raised issues with both legal and ethical dimensions. Bio-ethics can be considered both a conceptual science with a philosophical dimension and, at the same time, a direction of practical activities. From a philosophical perspective, bio-ethics is closely related to the principle of reverence for life. Of paramount importance for bio-ethics is the philosophical idea that any individual, any form of bios is of unique, absolute value. The underlying philosophical idea of intrinsic unity of human and non-human life entails increased responsibilities.

The pressing problem of our time concerns the fate of the bio-environment, currently endangered by human activities. This problem includes an ethical dimension. A human being is closely related to, and dependent on, all the life on Earth. How, then, can we reconcile our existence with the rapid deterioration of bios? In order to achieve the attitudinal changes desired, a number of practical steps including pollution taxes waste reduction policy and using representative polluting substances as indicators of pollution, have been designed. Important initiatives pertaining to environmental ethics have been recently launched.

Chapter 24

Solid Waste Managemet (Nuclear, Thermal, Plastic, Medical Waste)

24.1 SOLID WASTE

The sight of a dustbin overflowing and the stench rising from it, the all too familiar sights and smells of a crowded city. You look away from it and hold your nose as you cross it. Have you ever thought that you also have a role to play in the creation of this stench. That you can also play a role in the lessening of this smell and making this waste bin look a little more attractive if you follow proper methods of disposal of the waste generated in the house. Since the beginning, humankind has been generating waste, be it the bones and other parts of animals they slaughter for their food or the wood they cut to make their carts. With the progress of civilization, the waste generated became of a more complex nature. At the end of the 19th century, the industrial revolution saw the rise of the world of consumers. Not only did the air get more and more polluted but also the earth itself became more polluted with the generation of nonbiodegradable solid waste. The increase in population and urbanization was also largely responsible for the increase in solid waste.

Each household generates garbage or waste day in and day out. Items that we no longer need or do not have any further use for fall in the category of waste, and we tend to throw them away. There are different types of solid waste depending on their source. In today's polluted world, learning the correct methods of handling the waste generated has become essential. Segregation is an important method of handling municipal solid waste. Segregation at source can be understood clearly by schematic representation.One of the important methods of managing and treating wastes is composting.

As the cities are growing in size and in problems such as the generation of plastic waste, various municipal waste treatment and disposal methods are now being used to try and resolve these problems. One common sight in all cities is the rag picker who plays an important role in the segregation of this waste. Garbage generated in households can be recycled and reused to prevent creation of waste at source and reducing amount of waste thrown into the community dustbins.

24.2 MUNICIPAL SOLID WASTE

Municipal solid waste (MSW), also called urban solid waste, is a waste type that includes predominantly household waste (domestic waste) with sometimes the addition of commercial wastes collected by a municipality within a given area. They are in either solid or semisolid form and generally exclude industrial hazardous wastes. The term residual waste relates to waste left from household sources containing materials that have not been separated out or sent for reprocessing.

- Biodegradable waste: food and kitchen waste, green waste, paper can also be recycled
- Recyclable material: paper, glass, bottles, cans, metals, certain plastics, etc.
- Inert waste: construction and demolition waste, dirt, rocks, debris.
- Composite wastes: waste clothing, Tetra Packs, waste plastics such as toys.
- Domestic hazardous waste (also called "household hazardous waste") toxic waste: medication, E-waste, paints, chemicals, light bulbs, fluorescent tubes, spray cans, fertilizer and pesticide containers, batteries, shoe polish.

24.3 THE FUNCTIONAL ELEMENTS OF SOLID WASTE

- Waste generation
- Waste handling and separation, storage and processing at the source
- Collection
- Separation and processing and transformation of solid wastes
- Transfer and transport
- Disposal
- Energy Generation

24.4 THE FUNCTIONAL ELEMENTS OF SOLID WASTE

24.4.1 Waste Generation

Waste generation encompasses activities in which materials are identified as no longer being of value and are either thrown away or gathered together for disposal.

Waste handling and separation, storage and processing at the source

Waste handling and separation involves the activities associated with management of waste until they are placed in storage container for collection. Handling also encompasses the movement of loaded containers to the point of collection. Separation of waste components is an important step in the handling and storage of solid waste at the source.

24.4.2 Collection

The functional element of collection includes not only the gathering of solid waste and recyclable materials, but also the transport of these materials, after collection, to the location where the collection vehicle is emptied. This location may be materials processing facility, a transfer station or a landfill disposal site.

24.4.3 Separation, Processing and Transformation of Solid Wastes

The types of means and facilities that are now used for the recovery of waste materials that have been separated at the source include curbside collection, drop off and buy back centers. The separation and processing of wastes that have been separated at the source and the separation of commingled wastes usually occur at a materials recovery facility, transfer stations, combustion facilities and disposal sites.

24.4.4 Transfer and Transport

This element involves two steps:

(i) The transfer of wastes from the smaller collection vehicle to the larger transport equipment

(ii) The subsequent transport of the wastes, usually over long distances, to a processing or disposal site

24.4.5 Disposal

Today the disposal of wastes by land filling or land spreading is the ultimate fate of all solid wastes, whether they are residential wastes collected and transported directly to a landfill site, residual materials from Materials Recovery facilities (MRFs), residue from the combustion of solid waste, compost or other substances from various solid waste processing facilities. A modern sanitary landfill is not a dump; it is an engineered facility used for disposing of solid wastes on land without creating nuisances or hazards to public health or safety, such as the breeding of fatties and insects and the contamination of ground water.

24.4.6 Energy Generation

Municipal solid waste can be used to generate energy. Several technologies have been developed that make the processing of MSW for energy generation cleaner and more economical than ever before, including landfill gas capture, combustion, paralysis, gasification, and plasma arc gasification. While older waste incineration plants emitted high levels of pollutants, recent regulatory changes and new technologies have significantly reduced this concern. EPA regulations in 1995 and 2000 under the Clean Air Act have succeeded in reducing emissions of dioxins from waste-to-energy facilities by more than 99 percent below 1990 levels, while mercury emissions have been reduced by over 90 percent. The EPA noted these improvements in 2003, citing waste-to-energy as a power source "with less environmental impact than almost any other source of electricity.

24.4.7 Plasma arc Waste Disposal

Plasma is a highly ionized or electrically charged gas. An example in nature is lightning, capable of producing temperatures exceeding 12,600°F (6,980 °C). A gasifier vessel utilizes proprietary plasma torches operating at +10,000°F (5,540°C) (the surface temperature of the Sun) in order to create a gasification zone of up to 3,000°F (1,650°C) to convert solid or liquid wastes into a singes. When municipal solid waste is subjected to this intense heat within the vessel, the waste's molecular bonds break down into elemental components. The process results in elemental destruction of waste and hazardous materials.

According to the U.S. Environmental Protection Agency, the U.S. generated 250 million tons of waste in 2008 alone, and this number continues to rise. About 54% of this trash (135,000,000 short tons (122,000,000 t)) ends up in landfills and is consuming land at a rate of nearly 3,500 acres (1,400 ha) per year. In fact, land filling is currently the number one method of waste disposal in the US. Some states no longer have capacity at permitted landfills and export their waste to other states. Plasma gasification offers states new opportunities for waste disposal, and more importantly for renewable power generation in an environmentally sustainable manner.

24.5 LANDFILL

Landfill Operation in Hawaii

Disposing of waste in a landfill involves burying the waste, and this remains a common practice in most countries. Landfills were often established in abandoned or unused quarries, mining voids or borrow pits. A properly-designed and well-managed landfill can be a hygienic and relatively inexpensive method of disposing of waste materials. Older, poorly-designed or poorly-managed landfills can create a number of adverse environmental impacts such as wind-blown litter, attraction of vermin, and generation of liquid leach ate. Another common byproduct of landfills is gas (mostly composed of methane and carbon dioxide), which is produced as organic waste breaks down an aerobically. This gas can create odor problems, kill surface vegetation, and is a greenhouse gas.

24.6 A LANDFILL COMPACTION VEHICLE IN ACTION

Design characteristics of a modern landfill include methods to contain leach ate such as clay or plastic lining material. Deposited waste is normally compacted to increase its density and stability, and covered to prevent attracting vermin (such as mice or rats). Many landfills also have landfill gas extraction systems installed to extract the landfill gas. Gas is pumped out of the landfill using perforated pipes and flared off or burnt in a gas engine to generate electricity.

24.7 BIOMEDICAL WASTE

Biomedical waste consists of solids, liquids, sharps, and laboratory waste that are potentially infectious or dangerous. It must be properly managed to protect the public, specifically healthcare and sanitation workers who are regularly exposed to biomedical waste as an occupational hazard. Biomedical waste differs from other types of hazardous waste, such as industrial waste, in that it comes from biological sources or is used in the diagnosis, prevention, or treatment of diseases. Common producers of biomedical waste include hospitals, health clinics, nursing homes, medical research laboratories, offices of physicians, dentists, and veterinarians, home health care, and funeral homes.

Components: The following is a list of materials that are generally considered biomedical waste:

Solids:

Catheters and tubes
Disposable gowns, masks, and scrubs
Disposable tools, such as some scalpels and surgical staplers
Medical gloves
Surgical sutures and staples
Wound dressings

Liquids:

Blood

Body fluids and tissues

Cell, organ, and tissue cultures

Sharps

Blades, such as razor or scalpel blades

Lancets

Materials made of glass, such as corvettes and slides

Metal stylist

Needles

Plastic pipettes and tips

Syringes

Laboratory waste

Animal carcasses

Hazardous chemicals with biological components

Media

Medicinal plants

Radioactive material with biological components

Supernatants

Exceptions:

Cadavers, urine, faces, and cytotoxic drugs are not considered biomedical waste.

Management

24.8 Sorting of Medical Wastes in Hospital

At the site where it is generated, biomedical waste is placed in specially-labeled bags and containers for removal by biomedical waste transporters. Other forms of waste should not be mixed with biomedical waste as different rules apply to the treatment of different types of waste. Biomedical waste is treated by any or a combination of the following methods: incineration; discharge through a sewer or septic system; and steam, chemical, or microwave sterilization. Any tools or equipment that encountered potentially infectious material and is not disposable or designed for single-use is sterilized in an autoclave.

Household biomedical waste usually consists of needles and syringes from drugs administered at home (such as insulin), soiled wound dressings, disposable gloves, and bed sheets or other cloths that have come into contact with bodily fluids. Disposing of these materials with regular household garbage puts waste collectors at risk for injury and infection, especially from sharps as they can easily puncture a standard household garbage bag. Many communities have programs in place for the disposal of household biomedical waste. Some waste treatment facilities also have mail-in disposal programs. Biomedical waste treatment facilities are licensed by the local governing body that maintains laws regarding the operation of these facilities. The laws ensure that the public is protected from contamination of air, soil, groundwater, or municipal water supply.

Chapter 25

Agricultural, Domestic and E-waste

25.1 HOSPITAL WASTE

Hospital waste is generated during the diagnosis, treatment, or immunization of human being or animals or in research activities in these fields or in the production or testing of biological. It may include wastes like sharps, soiled waste, disposables, anatomical waste, cultures, discarded medicines, chemical waste, etc. These are in the form of disposable syringes, swabs, bandages, body fluid, human excreta, etc. The moisture content is 85% and there are 5% non-combustible solids. The heating value is around 2.510^6 J/kg. This waste is highly infectious and can be a serious threat to human health if not managed in a scientific and discriminate manner.

25.2 INDUSTRIAL WASTE

They include chemicals, paints, sand, metal ore processing, fly ash, sewage treatment sludge etc. Manufacturing industries produce wastes that are solid or semisolid. This waste can be self-igniting, explosive, toxic or radioactive. Chemical process industries generate a variety of waste, both organic and inorganic, which are mixtures with wide range of component concentration.

25.3 AGRICULTURAL WASTE

These include farm animal manure and crop residue etc. animal and vegetable waste contain valuable minerals and nutrients. Humus from agricultural wastes contains nitrong phosphorus potash and trace elements which are vital to the fertility of the soil and optimum plant growth burning of wastes as fuel in the conventional manner makes poor use of the lea India agricultural wastes contains around 2 Kg/Person/day.

25.4 CAUSES OF SOLID WASTE

The main causes for the repaid growth in the quantity of solid waste are:

(i) Overpopulation: Due to increasing industrialization and population, large quantities of wastes are being generated in different forms such as-solid, liquid sludge and gases. Each city produces tones of solid wastes daily from house holds, hospitals, industry offices, market centers etc. come of these are biodegradable come are non biodegradable and hazardous waste. Wastes are directly thrown away on the street roads, city garbage collecting places etc out of which most of it still remain there, which later pile up and chocks cities drainage lines.

(*ii*) Urbanization: due to pressure of urbanization most of the cities are growing fast and something they beyond the planned limits generally the unplanned areas of the city contain a quarter of the total population, where the spatial information is missing because of non-availability of up to date maps. Earlier waste disposal did not pose problem due to less population and lack of public awareness but due to repaid urbanization, proportionate increase in domestic and industrial solid waste generation was observed in large cities.

(*iii*) *Affluence:* With the affluence, there is a tendency to declare items as being in or out of fashion and the item; those are out of fashion results solid waste pollution.

Technology: as the country achieves the economical goals the country invest more over technology. With the development in technology, there is a shift form natural goods to the artificial ones theses are generally no- biodagrable by nature such a plastic, polythen etc. These non-biodegradable products are largely responsible for causing solid waste pollution because they persist unchanged in disposal operations such as landfills.

25.5 EFFECTS OF SOLID WASTE

Hazardous solid wastes are injurious to human healthy; some have acute effects while others pose a health hazard others pose a health hazard after prolonged period of exposure. Improper disposal of such wastes has resulted in the death of human and animals through contamination of crops and water supplies.

Solid waste disposal increases the rate of breeding of disease vectors primarily files and rats.

There is danger of water pollution when the leachate from a solid waste dump enters surface water or ground water resource.

In addition uncontrolled burning of open dumps can cause objectionable odour and air pollution.

Improper handling of solid waste causes damage to the environment the environment damage caused by solid waste is mostly destroys the beauty of the country-site.

25.6 MANAGEMENT OF SOLID WASTE

Some of the can be recovered and reprocesses a procedure commonly known as recycling. However, before the waste can be disposed of effectively they must the collected efficiently. These activities *i.e.,* collection disposal and/or recovery are known as solid waste management four R's (refuse reuse, recycle and reduce.) to be followed for waste management.

(*a*) *Refuse:* Instead of buying new containers from the market use the ones that are in the house. Refuse to buy new item though you may think they are prettier than the ones you already have.

(*b*) *Reuse:* Do not throw away the soft drink cans or the bottles; cover them with homemade paper or paints or them and use them as pencil stants or small vases.

(*c*) *Recycle:* Use shopping bags made of cloth or jute, so that they can be used repeatedly will this come under recyle or reduce. Segregate your waste to make sure that it is collected and use them as pencil stands or small vases.

(*d*) **Reduce** reduce the generation of unnecessary waste, eg carry your own shopping bag when you go the market and put all your purchases directly into it.

25.7 CONTROL MEASURES

Solid waste management is a manifold task involving many activities like-

Collecting of solid waste: The essential parts of the overall solid waste management programme are effective collection and transportation the basic mode of collection of from communal storage point. The waste is delivered to fixed storage bins usually built from concrete block to the location from where the collection vehicle will ultimately transport it to the site of disposal. Daily collection is essentially because the organic matter in the waste tends to decompose rapidly in the hot climate.

Disposal of solid waste: As cities are growing in size with a rise in the population, the amount of waste generated is increasing becoming unmanageable the local corporations have adapted different methods for the disposal of waste-open dumps landfills, sanitary landfills composting and incineration plants.

25.8 OPEN DUMPS

Open dumping of solid waste is done in low lying areas and outskirts of the towns and cities. Being comparatively cheaper and required no planning this method of disposal is used extensively in India. Open dumps refer to uncovered areas tat are used to dump solid waste of all kinds. The waste is untreated uncovered, and not segregated it is the breeding ground for flies, rats and others insects that spread disease the rainwater run-off from these dumps contaminates nearby land water thereby spreading disease. They also become a source of objectionable odours and causes air pollution when the wastes are burned I order of reduce their volume and conserve space.

25.8.1 Landfills

Landfills are generally located ion urban areas where a large amount of waste is generated and has to be dumped in a common place. Unlike an open dump, a pit is dug in the ground. The garbage is dumped and the pit is covered thus preventing the breeding of flies and rats. At the end of each day, a layer of soil is scattered on top of it and some mechanism usually earth-moving equipment is used to compress the garbage, which now forms a cell thus every day garbage is dumped and becomes a cell. After the landfill is full, the final layer is covered by final cover of about one meter of earth to prevent rodents from buffing into the refuse and scattering and the site can thereafter be developed as a parking lot or a park. Landfills have many problems as all type of waste are dumped in landfills and when water seeps thought them it gets contaminated and in turns pollutes the surrounding area. This contamination of groundwater and soil through landfills is known as leaching.

25.8.2 Sanitary landfills

Sanitary land filling involves the disposal of municipal wastes on or in the upper layers of the earth's mantel especially in degraded area in the need the upper layers of the earth's mantle especially in degreded area in the need of restoration. An alternative to landfills, which will solve the problem of leaching to some extent, is a sanitary landfill that is more hygienic and built in a methodical manner. Theses are lined with materials that are impermeable such as plastic and clay and are also build over impermeable soil. The advantages of sanitary landfills as apposed to an open dump are.

The public health problems are minimized because fillies, rates and other pests are unable to breed in the covered refuse.

There is no air pollution from burning.

Fire hazards are minimal.

Constructing sanitary landfills is very costly and they are having their own problems, some atonalities claim that often the plastic liner develops cracks as it reacts with various chemical solvents present in the waste. The rate of decomposition on sanitary landfills is also extremely variable this can be due to the fact that less oxygen is available as the garbage is compressed very tightly. It has also been observed that some biodegradable materials do not decompose in a landfill. Another major problem is the development of methane gas, which occurs when little oxygen is present i.e during anaerobic decomposition in some countries the methance being produced from sanitary landfills is tapped and sold as fuel.

25.9 INCINERATION PLANTS

This process of burning waste in large furnaces is known as incineration is these plants the recyclable material is segregated and the highly combustible wastes like plastics, cardboard, paper, rubber and combustible wastes like cartons, wood scrap, floor sweepings food wastes etc are subjected to incineration i.e. burning at very high temperatures. At the end of the process all that is lef behind is ash during the process some of the ash floats out with the hot air. This is called fly ash. Both the fly ash and the ash that is left in the furnace after burning have high concentrations of dangerous toxins such as dioxins and heavy metals. Disposing of this ash is a problem. The ash that is buried at the landfills leaches the area and causes severe contamination.

Burning garbage is not a clean process as it produces tones of toxic ash and pollutes the air and water. A large amount of the waste that is burnt here can be recovered and recycled. In fact at precent incineration is kept as the last resort and is used mainly for treating the infectious waste. The advantages in incineration included wide range ability for handling varying load and small space requirement for ultimate disposal. However the method requires fairly high level of maintenance and the operation of sanitary landfill.

25.10 COMPOSTING

Organic matter constitutes 35 % – 40% of the municipal solid waste generated in India. This waste can be recycled by the method of compositing one of the oldest forms of disposal. It is the natural process of decomposition of organic waste that yields manure of compost, which is very rich in nutrients. Composting is a biological process in which microorganism mainly fungi and bacteria convert degradable organic waste into humus like substance. This finished product, which looks like soil is high in carbon and nitrogen and is an excellent medium for growing plants it recycles the nutrients and returns them to the soil as nutrients.

Apart form being clean, cheap and safe composting can significantly reduces the amount of disposable garbage. The organic fertilizer can be used instead of chemical fertilizers and is better specially when used for vegetables it increases the soil's ability to hold water and makes the soil easier to cultivate it helped the soil retain more of the plant nutrients.

25.10.1 Composting: Some benefits

Compost allows the soil retain more pant nutrients over a longer period.

- It supplies part of the 16 essential elements needed by the plants
- It helps reduce the adverse effects of excessive alkalinity acidity or the excessive use of chemical fertilizer.
- It makes soil easier to cultivate
- It helps keep the soil cool in summer and warm in winter.
- It aids in preventing soil erosion by keeping the soil covered
- It helps in controlling the growth of weeds in the garden.

25.11 PYROLSIS OR DESTRUCTIVE DISTILLATION

In this disposal method, the solid wastes are heated under anaerobic conditions i.e. burning without oxygen. The organic components of the solid wastes split up into gaseous liquid and gaseous fractions (CO, CO_2 , CO_4 tar charred carbon) unlike the highly exothermic process of combustion paralysis is a highly endothermic processes and that is why it is also called destructive distillation.

(i) Land Farming: The organic wastes are either applied on top of the land or injected below the soil surface with suitable equipment, where they undergo bacterial and chemical decomposition. At frequent intervals, the land farming sites can be reused without any adverse effects proded the land-farming site is properly managed.

(ii) Waste Utilization: A developing country can not afford wastage. By proper utilization of solid waste a developing counter like India can avail of many advantages many solid wastes generated by industries can be utilized directly fly ash and bottom ash from power plants can be used commercially largely as cement substitute, new uses are developed for fly ash *e.g.*, to make bricks to dewater industrial wastewater sludge, as a land cover etc recycling involves the collection of used and discarded materials processing these material and taking them into new products it reduces the amount of waste that is thrown the community dustbins thereby making the environment cleaner and the air fresher to breathe.

25.12 BIO-PEACE-GLOBAL HARMONY IN THE NEXT MILLENNIUM

Regional conflicts, constantly erupting all over the world, are severely jeopardising global security. Without a new and revised approach to the issue of international co-operation, it is doubtful whether we will ever be successful in attaining harmony and peace, and progress toward a world made up of responsible and affected citizens. Our society is governed by a system of Darwinian ethics, where survival of the fittest is regarded as the optimal strategy.

The fate of the world cannot keep resting in the hands of the few and "powerful." Global peace cannot become a reality if we allow these trends to continue, and it is the responsibility of every citizen in the world to ensure that a new set of values and ethics prevails. Within the framework of this new set of ethics, the global community has to learn the joy of sharing. It is not to anyone's advantage to separate the world into developed and under-developed regions. Poverty and the unequal distribution of resources not only affect the countries that suffer most by it, but threaten the stability of the entire planet.

It is up to us to render the concept of a "Third World" obsolete and work together to reconcile environmental harmony with the need for economic prosperity and growth. As the present century is ending, technological achievements seem almost unreal, as though this rapid progress images intangible concepts. Our future development and survival will depend on our ability to assimilate the explosive progress of technology towards a new bio-culture, webbed with unifying values and based on a better assimilation and appreciation of the gift of bios. Within this framework, culture and technology can co-evolve and enrich each other with positive new dimensions. Waves of light, waves of music and communication can provide hope and encouragement to help us face the challenges of the new millennium.

The solution is staring us in the face. We all share the gift of bios, the most precious possession on our planet. Political systems have come and gone, financial regimes have succeeded and failed, but bios, in unlimited varieties and forms, have existed for millions of years. Bios and the bio-environment are the most powerful agents for the attainment of world peace and stability. The pursuit of bio-peace, through the development of concrete action plans for world-wide co-operation on bio-environmental conservation, can alleviate conflict and division and contribute to a new era of international understanding, and global security and order. The unifying aspects of bios and the bio-environment hold the key to our future. If we all adopt this principle as our guide, then perhaps global peace will become a reality in the 21st century.

Chpater 26

Studies Regarding Environmental Protection Acts

26.1 MAN AND HIS ENVIRONMENT

Evolution of life, plants and animals, heredity and environment-Genetics, cells, chromosomes, genes. Knowledge of the human body-nutrition, balanced diet, substitutes foods. Public health and sanitation including control of epidemics and common diseases. Environmental pollution and its control food adulteration, proper storage and preservation of food grains and finished products, population explosion, population control. Production of food and raw materials breeding of animals and plants, artificial insemination, manures and fertilizers, crop protection measures, high yielding varieties and green revolution, main cereal and cash crops of India.

The Air (Prevention and Control of Pollution) Act, 1981: The Air (Prevention and Control of Pollution) Act was enacted by the Parliament in 1981 with an objective to prevent, control and abatement of air pollution. Under Section 19 of this act, the whole of National Capital Territory of Delhi has been declared as air pollution control area by the Central Government. Under this section, the government approved fuels to be used in the air pollution control area.

The following are the important provisions of the Air (Prevention and Control of Pollution) Act:

Under Section 21(1): Person cannot establish or operate any industrial unit in National Capital Territory of Delhi without obtaining prior consent of the DPCC. The consent application will be disposed off within 4 months of receipt of the consent application. However, DPCC may either grant consent or reject the application within 4 months for reasons to be recorded in writing. It may also revoke previous, consent to the industry before expiry of the same after giving a reasonable opportunity of being heard.

Any consent requires the compliance with the following conditions:

Control equipment of such specification as the State Board may approve.

I Control equipment referred above shall be kept at all times in good running condition.

Any other such conditions as the state board may specify.

State Board can also approach the court to stop any person from doing air pollution.

No person operating any industrial plant, in any air pollution control area shall discharge or cause or permit to be discharged the emission of any air pollution in excess of the standards laid down by the state board.

Under Section 22: No person operating any industrial plant, in any air pollution control area shall discharge or cause or permit to be discharged the emission of any air pollution in excess of the standards laid down by the state board.

Under Section 22(A): State Board can also approach the court to stop any person from doing air pollution

Under Section 24(i), 26(i): DPCC office have powers to inspect any premises in performance of their duties, take samples, examine records, documents etc. or performing any other duty entrusted to him by the board. Every person operating any equipment is bound to provide all assistance to the person who is inspecting. When samples taken, officials can collect the samples after informing the person of the industry. Any analysis of the samples done in the air lab can be produced as evidence in a court.

Under Section 31: Any person aggrieved by an order made by the state board under this act may, within 30 days from the date on which order is communication to him, prefer an appeal to the authorized authority who in the case of Delhi is the Joint Secretary, Ministry of Environment & Forest.

Under Section 31(A): The state board can give directions to any person or office or authority in writing and such person or officer or authority is bound to comply with such directions that include:

(i) The closure, prohibition or regulation of any industry, operation or process or

(ii) Stoppage or regulation of electricity, water or any other services

Under Section 37: Any person failing to comply with the provisions of Section 21 or Section 22 or directions issued under Section 31(A) can be imprisoned from 1-1/2 years to 6 years, with fine or with a fine upto ₹.5000/- per day.

If violation continues beyond one year, imprisonment can be increased up to 7 years with fine

Under Section 39: Whoever contravenes any of the provisions of this Act or any order or directions issued there under, for which no penalty has been elsewhere provided in this act, shall be punishable with imprisonment for a term which may extend to three months or with fine which may extend to ten thousand rupees or with both, and in case of continuing contravention with an additional fine which may extend to ₹.5000/- for every day during which such contravention continues after conviction for the first such contravention

26.2 POWERS AND FUNCTIONS OF BOARDS

1. Functions of Central Board

(1) Subject to the provisions of this Act, and without prejudice to the performance, of its functions under the Water (Prevention and Control of Pollution) Act, IL974 (6 of 1974), the main functions of the Central Board shall be to improve the quality of air and to prevent, control or abate air pollution in the country.

(2) In particular and without prejudice to the generality of the foregoing functions, the Central Board may:

(a) Advise the Central Government on any matter concerning the improvement of the quality of air and the prevention, control or abatement of air pollution;

(b) Plan and cause to be executed a nation-wide programmed for the prevention, control or abatement of air pollution;

(c) Co-ordinate the activities of the State and resolve dispute among them;

(d) Provide technical assistance In addition, guidance to the State Boards, carry out and sponsor investigations and research relating to problems of air pollution and prevention, control or abatement of air pollution;

(e) Plan and organize the training of persons engaged or to be engaged in programs for the prevention, control or abatement of air pollution on such terms and conditions as the Central Board may specify;

(f) Organize through mass media a comprehensive program regarding the prevention, control or abatement of air pollution;

(g) collect, compile and publish technical and statistical data relating to air pollution and the measures devised for its effective prevention, control or abatement and prepare manuals, codes or guides relating to prevention, control or abatement of air pollution;

(h) Lay down standards for the quality of air.

(i) Collect and disseminate information in respect of matters relating to air pollution;

(j) Perform such other functions as may be prescribed.

(3) The Central Board may establish or recognize a laboratory or laboratories to enable the Central Board to perform its functions under this section efficiently.

(4) The Central Board may:

(a) Delegate any of its functions under this Act generally or specially to any of the committees appointed by it;

(b) Do such other things and perform such other acts as it may think necessary for the proper discharge of its functions and generally for carrying into effect the purposes of this Act.

2. Functions of State Boards

(1) Subject to the provisions of this Act, and without prejudice to the performance of its functions, if any, under the Water (Prevention and Control of Pollution) Act, 1974 (Act 6 of 1974), the functions of a State Board shall be:

(a) To plan a comprehensive program for the prevention, control or abatement of air pollution and to secure the execution thereof;

(b) To advise the State Government on any matter concerning the prevention, control or abatement of air pollution;

(c) To collect and disseminate information relating to air pollution;

(d) To collaborate with the Central Board in organizing the training of persons engaged or to be engaged in programs relating to prevention, control or abatement of air pollution and to organize mass-education program relating thereto;

(e) To inspect, at all reasonable times, any control equipment, industrial plant or manufacturing process and to give, by order, such directions to such persons as it may consider necessary to take steps for the prevention, control or abatement of air pollution;

(f) To inspect air pollution control areas at such intervals as it may think necessary, assess the quality of air therein and take steps for the prevention, control or abatement of air pollution in such areas;

(g) To lay down, in consultation with the Central Board and having regard to the standards for the quality of air laid down by the Central Board, standards for emission of air pollutants into the atmosphere from industrial plants and automobiles or for the discharge of any air pollutant into the atmosphere from any other source whatsoever not being a ship or an aircraft:

Provided that different standards for emission may be laid down under this clause for different industrial plants having regard to the quantity and composition of emission of air pollutants into the atmosphere from such industrial plants;

(h) To advise the State Government with respect to the suitability of any premises or location for carrying on any industry which is likely to cause air pollution?

(i) To perform such other functions as may be prescribed or as may, from time to time, be entrusted to it by the Central Board or the State Government;

(j) To do such other things and to perform such other acts as it may think necessary for the proper discharge of its functions and generally for carrying into effect the purposes of this Act.

(2) A State Board may establish or recognize a laboratory or laboratories to enable the State Board to perform its functions under this section efficiently.

26.3 PREVENTION AND CONTROL OF AIR POLLUTION

1. Power to declare air pollution control areas:

(i) The State Government may, after consultation with the State Board, by notification in the Official Gazette declare in such manner as may be prescribed, any area or areas within the State as air pollution control Area or areas for the purposes of this Act.

(ii) If the State Government, after consultation with the State Board, is of opinion that the use of any fuel, other than an approved fuel, in any air pollution control area or part thereof, may cause or is likely to cause air pollution, it may, by notification in the Official Gazette, prohibit the use of such fuel in such area or part thereof with effect from such date (being not less than three months from the date of publication of the notification) as may be specified in the notification.

(iii) The State Government may, after consultation with the Sate Board, by notification in the Official Gazette, direct that with effect fr6m such date as may be specified therein, no appliance, other than an approved appliance, shall be used in the premises situated in an air pollution control area:

Provided that different dates may be specified for different parts of an air pollution control area or for the use of different appliances.

(iv) If the State Government, after consultation with the State Board, is of opinion that the burning of any material (not being fuel) in any air pollution control area or part thereof may cause or is likely to cause air pollution, it may, by notification in the Official Gazette, prohibit the burning of such material in such area or part thereof.

2. Power to give instructions for ensuring standards for emission from automobiles: With a view to ensuring that the standards for emission of air pollutants from automobiles laid down by the State Board tinder clause (g) of sub-section (1) of section 17 are complied with, the State Government shall, in consultation with the State Board, give such instructions as may be deemed necessary to the concerned authority in charge of registration of motor vehicles under the Motor Vehicles Act, 1939 (Act 4 of 1939), and such authority shall, notwithstanding anything contained in that Act or the rules made there under be bound to comply with such instructions.

3. Persons carrying on industry, etc., and to allow emission of air pollutants in excess of the standard lay down by State Board: No person operating any industrial plant, in any air pollution control area shall discharge or cause or permit to be discharged the emission of any air pollutant in excess of the standards laid down by the State Board under clause (g) of sub-section (1) of section 17.

4. Power of Board to make application to court for restraining person from causing air pollution:

(i) Where it is apprehended by a Board that emission of any air pollutant, in excess of the standards laid down by the State Board under clause (g) of sub-section (1) of section 17, is likely to occur by reason of any person operating an industrial plant or otherwise in any air pollution control area, the Board may make an application to a court, not inferior to that of a Metropolitan Magistrate or a Judicial Magistrate of the first class for restraining such person from emitting such air pollutant.

(ii) On receipt of the application under sub-section (1), the court may make such order as it deems fit.

(iii) Where under sub-section (2), the court makes an order restraining any person from discharging or causing or permitting to be discharged the emission of any air pollutant, it may, in that order:

(a) Direct such person to desist from taking such action as is likely to cause emission;

(b) Authorize the Board, if the direction under clause (a) is not compiling with by the person to whom such direction is issued, to implement the direction in such manner as may be specified by the court.

(iv) All expenses incurred by the Board in implementing the & actions of the court under clause (b) of sub-section (3) shall be recoverable from the person concerned as an-ears of land revenue or of public demand.

5. Power to take samples of air or emission and procedure to be followed in connection therewith:

(i) A State Board or any officer empowered by it in this behalf shall have power to take, for the purpose of analysis, samples of air or emission from any chimney, flue or duct or any other outlet in such manner as may be prescribed.

(ii) The result of any analysis of a sample of emission taken under subsection (1) shall not be admissible in evidence in any legal proceeding unless the provisions of sub-sections (3) and (4) are complied with.

(iii) Subject to the provisions of sub-section (4), when a sample of emission is taken for analysis under sub-section (1), the person taking the sample shall-

(a) Serve on the occupier or his agent, a notice, then and there, in such form as may be prescribed, of his intention to have it so analyzed;

(b) In the presence of the occupier or his agent, collect a sample of emission for analysis;

(c) Cause the sample to be placed in a container or containers which shall be marked and sealed and shall also be signed both by the person taking the sample and the occupier or his agent;

(d) Send, immediately, the container to the laboratory established or recognized by the State Board under section 17 or, if a request in that behalf is made by the occupier or his agent when the notice is served on him under clause (a), to the laboratory established or specified under sub-section (1) of section 28.

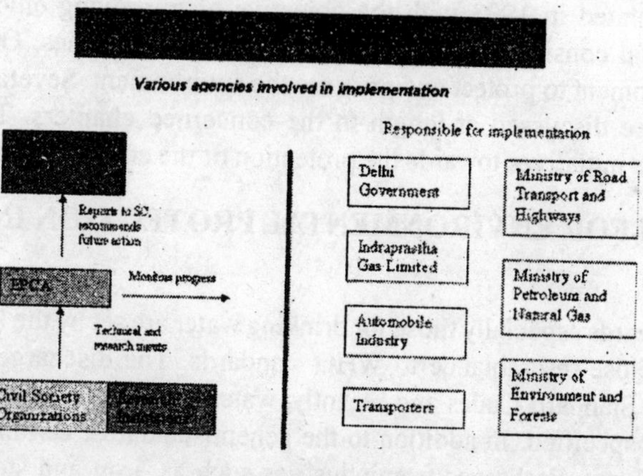

Fig. 33.1

26.4 LAW RELATED TO ENVIRONMENTAL PROTECTION

26.4.1 Introduction

Over the years, together with a spreading of environmental consciousness, there has been a Change in the traditionally-held perception that there is a trade-off between environmental Quality and economic growth as people have come to believe that the two are necessarily complementary. The current focus on environment is not new—environmental considerations have been an integral part of the Indian culture. The need for conservation and sustainable use of natural resources has been expressed in Indian scriptures, more than three thousand years old and is reflected in the constitutional, legislative and policy framework as in the international commitments of the country.

Even before India's independence in 1947, several environmental legislation existed but thereal impetus for bringing about a well-developed framework came only after the UNConference on the Human Environment. Under the influence of thisdeclaration, the National Council for Environmental Policy and Planning within the Department of Science and Technology was set up in 1972. This Council later evolved into a full-fledged Ministry of Environment and Forests (MoEF) in 1985 which today is the apexadministrative body in the country for regulating and ensuring environmental protection.

After the Stockholm Conference, in 1976, constitutional sanction was given to environmentalconcerns through the 42nd Amendment, which incorporated them into the Directive Principlesof State Policy and Fundamental Rights and Duties.

Since the 1970s an extensive network of environmental legislation has grown in the country.The MoEF and the pollution control boards (CPCB i.e. Central Pollution Control Board and SPCBs *i.e.*, State Pollution Control Boards) together form the regulatory and administrativecore of the sector.

A policy framework has also been developed to complement the legislative provisions. ThePolicy Statement for Abatement of Pollution and the National Conservation Strategy andPolicy Statement on Environment and Development were brought out by the MoEF in 1992,2 to develop and promote initiatives for the protection and improvement of the environment.The EAP (Environmental Action Programme) was formulated in 1993 with the objective of improving environmental services and integrating environmental considerations in to development programmes. Other measures have also been taken by the government to protect and preserve the environment. Several sector-specific policies have evolved, which are discussed at length in the concerned chapters. This chapter attempts to highlight only legislative initiatives towards the protection of the environment.

26.5 LEGISLATION FOR ENVIRONMENTAL PROTECTION IN INDIA

26.5.1 Water

Water quality standards especially those for drinking water are set by the Indian Council ofMedical Research. These bear close resemblance to WHO standards. The discharge ofindustrial effluents is regulated by the Indian Standard Codes and recently, water qualitystandards for coastal water marine outfalls have also been specified. In addition to the generalstandards, certain specific standards have been developed for effluent discharges fromindustries such as, iron and steel, aluminium, pulp and paper, oil refineries, petrochemicalsand thermal power plants. Legislation to control water pollution are listed below.

Water (Prevention and Control of Pollution) Act, 1974

This Act represented India's first attempts to comprehensively deal with environmentalissues. The Act prohibits the discharge of pollutants into water bodies beyond a givenstandard, and lays down penalties for non-compliance. The Act was amended in 1988 toconform closely to the provisions of the EPA, 1986. It set up the CPCB (Central Pollution Control Board) which lays down standards for the prevention and control of water pollution. At the State level, the SPCBs (State Pollution Control Board) function under the direction ofthe CPCB and the state government.

Water (Prevention and Control of Pollution) Cess Act, 1977

This Act provides for a levy and collection of a cess on water consumed by industries andlocal authorities. It aims at augmenting the resources of the central and state boards forprevention and control of water pollution. Following this Act, *The Water (Prevention and Control of Pollution) Cess Rules* were formulated in 1978 for defining standards andindications for the kind of and location of meters that every consumer of water is required to install.

26.5.2 AIR

Air (Prevention and Control of Pollution) Act, 1981

To counter the problems associated with air pollution, ambient air quality standards wereestablished, under the 1981 Act. The Act provides means for the control and abatement of air pollution. The Act seeks to combat air pollution by prohibiting the use of polluting fuels andsubstances, as well as by regulating appliances that give rise to air pollution. Under the Actestablishing or operating of any industrial plant in the pollution control area requires consent from state boards. The boards are also expected to test the air in air pollution control areas, inspect pollution control equipment, and manufacturing processes.

National Ambient Air Quality Standards (NAAQS) for major pollutants were notified by the CPCB in April 1994. These are deemed to be levels of air quality necessary with an adequatemargin of safety, to protect public health, vegetation and property. The NAAQS prescribe specific standards for industrial, residential, rural andother sensitive areas. Industry-specific emission standards have also been developed for ironand steel plants, cement plants, fertilizer plants, oil refineries and the aluminium industry. The ambient quality standards prescribed in India are similar to those prevailing in many developed and developing countries.

To empower the central and state pollution boards to meet grave emergencies, the *Air (Prevention and Control of Pollution) Amendment Act*, 1987, was enacted. The boards wereauthorized to take immediate measures to tackle such emergencies and recover the expensesincurred from the offenders. The power to cancel consent for non-fulfilment of the conditions prescribed has also been emphasized in the Air Act Amendment.

The Air (Prevention and Control of Pollution) Rules formulated in 1982, defined the procedures for conducting meetings of the boards, the powers of the presiding officers, decision-making, the quorum; manner in which the records of the meeting were to be set etc.They also prescribed the manner and the purpose of seeking assistance from specialists andthe fee to be paid to them.

Complementing the above Acts is the *Atomic Energy Act* of 1982, which was introduced todeal with radioactive waste. In 1988, the *Motor Vehicles Act,* was enacted to regulatevehicular traffic, besides ensuring proper packaging, labelling and transportation of the hazardous wastes. Various aspects of vehicular pollution have also been notified under the EPA of 1986. Mass emission standards were notified in 1990, which were made more stringent in 1996. In 2000 these standards were revised yet again and for the first time separate obligations for vehicle owners, manufacturers and enforcing agencies werestipulated. In addition, fairly stringent Euro I and II emission norms were notified by the

Supreme Court on April 29, 1999 for the city of Delhi. The notification made it mandatory for car manufacturers to conform to the Euro I and Euro II norms by May 1999 and April 2000, respectively, for new non-commercial vehicle sold in Delhi.

26.5.3 Forests and wildlife

The Wildlife (Protection) Act, 1972, Amendment 1991

The WPA (Wildlife Protection Act), 1972, provides for protection to listed species of floraand fauna and establishes a network of ecologically-important protected areas. The WPA empowers the central and state governments to declare any area a wildlife sanctuary, national park or closed area. There is a blanket ban on carrying out any industrial activity inside the seprotected areas. It provides for authorities to administer and implement the Act; regulate the 5 hunting of wild animals; protect specified plants, sanctuaries, national parks and closed areas; restrict trade or commerce in wild animals or animal articles; and miscellaneous matters. TheAct prohibits hunting of animals except with permission of authorized officer when an animalhas become dangerous to human life or property or so disabled or diseased as to be beyond recovery (WWF-India, 1999). The near-total prohibition on hunting was made more effectiveby the Amendment Act of 1991.

The Forest (Conservation) Act, 1980

This Act was adopted to protect and conserve forests. The Act restricts the powers of the statein respect of de-reservation of forests and use of forestland for non-forest purposes (the term 'non-forest purpose' includes clearing any forestland for cultivation of cash crops, plantationcrops, horticulture or any purpose other than re-afforestation).

26.6 General

Environment (Protection) Act, 1986 (EPA): This Act is an umbrella legislation designed to provide a framework for the co-ordination ofcentral and state authorities established under the Water (Prevention and Control) Act, 1974 and Air (Prevention and Control) Act, 1981. Under this Act, the central government isempowered to take measures necessary to protect and improve the quality of the environmentby setting standards for emissions and discharges; regulating the location of industries; management of hazardous wastes, and protection of public health and welfare. From time to time the central government issues notifications under the EPA for the protection of ecologically-sensitive areas or issues guidelines for matters under the EPA.

Some notifications issued under this Act are:

- *Doon Valley Notification* (1989), which prohibits the setting up of an industry inwhich the daily consumption of coal/fuel is more than 24 MT (million tonnes) per dayin the Doon Valley.
- *Coastal Regulation Zone Notification* (1991), which regulates activities along coastalstretches. As per this notification, dumping ash or any other waste in the CRZ isprohibited. The thermal power plants (only foreshore facilities for transport of rawmaterials, facilities for intake of cooling water and outfall for discharge of treated waste water/cooling water) require clearance from the MoEF.

- *Dhanu Taluka Notification* (1991), under which the district of Dhanu Taluka has been declared an ecologically fragile region and setting up power plants in its vicinity is prohibited.
- *Revdanda Creek Notification (1989)*, which prohibits setting up industries in the beltaround the Revdanda Creek as per the rules laid down in the notification.
- *The Environmental Impact Assessment of Development Projects Notification*, (1994 and as amended in 1997). As per this notification:
  - All projects listed under Schedule I require environmental clearance from the MoEF.
  - Projects under the delicenced category of the New Industrial Policy also require clearance from the MoEF.
  - All developmental projects whether or not under the Schedule I, if located in fragile regions must obtain MoEF clearance.
  - Industrial projects with investments above ₹.500 million must obtain MoEF clearance and are further required to obtain a LOI (Letter of Intent) from the Ministry of Industry, and an NOC (No Objection Certificate) from the SPCB and the State Forest Department if the location involves forestland. Once the NOC is obtained, the LOI is converted into an industrial licence by the state authority.
  - The notification also stipulated procedural requirements for the establishment and operation of new power plants. As per this notification, two-stage clearance for sites pecificprojects such as pithead thermal power plants and valley projects is required. Site clearance is given in the first stage and final environmental clearance in the second. A public hearing has been made mandatory for projects covered by this notification. This is an important step in providing transparency and a greater role to local communities.
- *Ash Content Notification* (1997), required the use of beneficiated coal with ashcontent not exceeding 34% with effect from June 2001, (the date later was extended to June 2002). This applies to all thermal plants located beyond one thousand kilometres from the pithead and any thermal plant located in an urban area or,sensitive area irrespective of the distance from the pithead except any pithead powerplant.
- *Taj Trapezium Notification* (1998), provided that no power plant could be set up within the geographical limit of the Taj Trapezium assigned by the Taj Trapezium Zone Pollution (Prevention and Control) Authority.
- *Disposal of Fly Ash Notification* (1999) the main objective of which is to conserve the top soil, protect the environment and prevent the dumping and disposal of fly ashdischarged from lignite-based power plants. The salient feature of this notification is that no person within a radius of 50 km from a coal-or lignite-based power plant shallmanufacture clay bricks or tiles without mixing at least 25% of ash with soil on aweight-to-weight basis. For the thermal power plants the utilisation of the fly ash would be as follows:
  - Every coal- or lignite-based power plant shall make available ash for at least ten years from the date of publication of the above notification without any payment or any other consideration, for the purpose of manufacturing ash-based products such ascement, concrete blocks, bricks, panels or any other material or for construction of roads, embankments, dams, dykes or for any other construction activity.

- Every coal or lignite based thermal power plant commissioned subject to environmental clearance conditions stipulating the submission of an action plan forfull utilisation of fly ash shall, within a period of nine years from the publication of this notification, phase out the dumping and disposal of fly ash on land in accordancewith the plan.

Rules for the Manufacture, Use, Import, Export and Storage of Hazardous Microorganisms/ Genetically Engineered Organisms or Cell were introduced in 1989 with the viewto protect the environment, nature and health in connection with gene technology and microorganisms,under the Environmental Protection Act, 1986. The government in 1991, furtherdecided to institute a national label scheme for environmentally-friendly products called the'ECOMARK'. The scheme attempts to provide incentives to manufactures and importers toreduce adverse environmental impacts, reward genuine initiatives by companies, and improvethe quality of the environment and sustainability of available resources. Besides the aboveattempts, notifications pertaining *to Recycled Plastics Manufacture and Usage Rules, 1999* were also incorporated under the Environment (Protection) Act of 1986.

The Environment (Protection) Rules, 1986: These rules lay down the procedures for setting standards of emission or discharge ofenvironmental pollutants. The Rules prescribe the parameters for the Central Government,under which it can issue orders of prohibition and restrictions on the location and operation ofindustries in different areas. The Rules lay down the procedure for taking samples, servingnotice, submitting samples for analysis and laboratory reports. The functions of thelaboratories are also described under the Rules along with the qualifications of the concernedanalysts.

The National Environment Appellate Authority Act, 1997: This Act provided for the establishment of a National Environment Appellate Authority tohear appeals with respect to restriction of areas in which any industry operation or process orclass of industries, operations or processes could not carry out or would be allowed to carryout subject to certain safeguards under the Environment (Protection) Act, 1986.

In addition to these, various Acts specific to the coal sector have been enacted. The firstattempts in this direction can be traced back to the *Mines Act, 1952*, which promoted healthand safety standards in coal mines. Later the *Coal Mines (Conservation and Development) Act* (1974) came up for conservation of coal during mining operations. For conservation anddevelopment of oil and natural gas resources a similar legislation was enacted in 1959.

Overexploitation of the country's resources be it land or water and the industrialization process has resulted in considerable environmental degradation of resources along with the pollution of these and the other environmental parameters. The demographics and socio-economic factors have also influenced the environment, though indirectly.

Hence, with an aim to provide a comprehensive picture of India's environment pollution and protection scenario, the State section deals with the analysis of extent of environmental degradation in the country over the years; Pressure section analyses the factors responsible for such changes and the Response section deals with the interventions made by the government by way of policy reforms, institutional, legislative and regulatory mechanisms as well as the non-governmental initiatives, if any. Broadly divided into three chapters — Air, Water and Land, these would almost completely cover the entire spectrum of environment pollution. Land degradation is observed to be largely a rural phenomenon whereas water and air pollution are more pervasive in urban areas. Municipal solid waste too has lately become a major environmental issue of concern especially in the urban areas

26.7 POLLUTION IN INDIA

Ambient air quality has a significant localized impact and the percentage of population exposed is much higher in urban areas and in particular metropolitan cities. Therefore since these areas have emerged as greatly stressed, the emphasis is on studying the causes for air pollution and interventions to ameliorate the condition in urban areas. Four reasons being — emissions from vehicles, thermal power plants, industries and refineries. The problem of indoor air pollution though an issue of concern in rural areas and urban slums has assumed significant attention lately. Water has been divided into two sections - groundwater and surface water. Groundwater exploitation is a serious matter of concern today and legislations and policy measures taken till date, by the state governments (water is a state subject) have not had the desired effect on the situation. Agriculture, forestry and mining being the three most important activities effecting land use and degradation, a sectoral impact of each of these can been discussed separately.

Municipal solid waste is limited to the solid waste generated by households, commercial establishments and offices and does not include the industrial or agricultural waste. Municipal solid waste management is more of an administrative and institutional mechanism failure problem rather than a technological one, hence the number of non-governmental initiatives in solving the same have been many. Environmental movements arise largely due to the clash between economic development and exploitation of natural resources in the process of doing so. People in different parts of India have participated in such movements in the past and these are raged even today when the supposedly development projects, taken up in the name of prosperity and better living conditions, affect the local people adversely. Movements were/are meant as means to safeguard the interests of people (generally poorest and marginalised sections of society) over and above the endless aspirations of decision makers to promote extensive industrial activity and expansion of energy and resource in the context of limited resource availability.

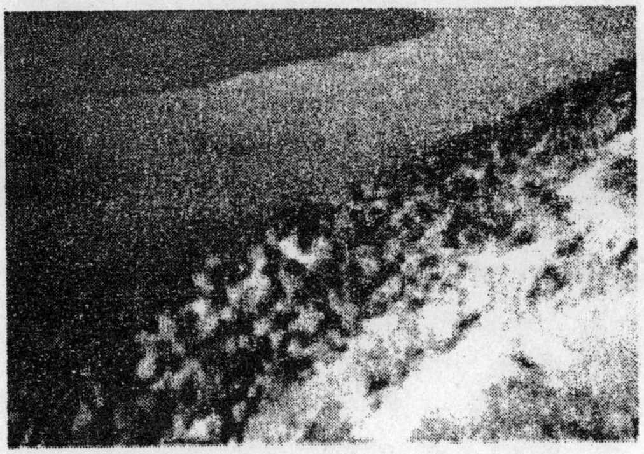

Fig. 26.2

Such as against ms, mineral resources, exploitation of forest resources, natural disasters and major chemical accidents/incidents.

26.8 TRENDS IN POPULATION GROWTH AND ENVIRONMENTAL DEGRADATION

The issues of population, environment and development should be treated not as separate sets of issues, but as three interactive factors. Considerable debate has taken place in recent years on the complex issue of the environmental implications of population change. The rapid population growth, which affects patterns of production and consumption, is a principal source of pressure on the environment especially in a developing country like India. The environment has to sustain not only the basic human needs for survival, but also the conversion of raw materials into products and services. India is the second largest populous country of the world, with its current population figures standing at one billion. Of this, 276 million people reside in urban areas implying urbanization level of 28.9%.

The urbanization levels of the country have been increasing consistently since 1971. Almost 20 % of the country's population lived in the urban areas in 1971, while in 1991 the figure had risen to approximately 26%. Most of this urban population is concentrated in the Class I cities (cities with a population of 100,000 and above). The total population in the metros accounts for nearly one-third of total urban population. Over 50% of the population of these metros lives in the five giant conglomerates - Mumbai, Kolkata, Delhi, Chennai, and Bangalore.

Fig. 26.3: From stacks showing Air pollution

Fig. 26.4: Air pollution from World War II production

26.9 SMOG OVER SANTIAGO

Air pollution is the introduction of chemicals, particulate matter, or biological materials that cause harm or discomfort to humans or other living organisms, or damages the natural environment, into the atmosphere. The atmosphere is a complex, dynamic natural gaseous system that is essential to support life on planet Earth. Stratospheric ozone depletion due to air pollution has long been recognized as a threat to human health as well as to the Earth's ecosystems.

26.10 POLLUTANTS

Before flue gas desulfurization was installed, the emissions from this power plant in New Mexico contained excessive amounts of sulfur dioxide.

Fig. 26.5

Schematic drawing, causes and effects of air pollution: (1) greenhouse effect, (2) particulate contamination, (3) increased UV radiation, (4) acid rain, (5) increased ozone concentration, (6) increased levels of nitrogen oxides

An air pollutant is known as a substance in the air that can cause harm to humans and the environment. Pollutants can be in the form of solid particles, liquid droplets, or gases. In addition, they may be natural or man-made. Pollutants can be classified as either primary or secondary. Usually, primary pollutants are substances directly emitted from a process, such as ash from a volcanic eruption, the carbon monoxide gas from a motor vehicle exhaust or sulfur dioxide released from factories.

Secondary pollutants are not emitted directly. Rather, they form in the air when primary pollutants react or interact. An important example of a secondary pollutant is ground level ozone—one of the many secondary pollutants that make up photochemical smog. Note that some pollutants may be both primary and secondary: that is, they are both emitted directly and formed from other primary pollutants. About 4 percent of deaths in the United States can be attributed to air pollution, according to the Environmental Science Engineering Program at the Harvard School of Public Health.

Major primary pollutants produced by human activity include: Sulfur oxides (SO_x)- especially sulfur dioxide, a chemical compound with the formula SO_2. SO_2 is produced by volcanoes and in various industrial processes. Since coal and petroleum often contain sulfur compounds, their combustion generates sulfur dioxide. Further oxidation of SO_2, usually in the presence of a catalyst such as NO_2, forms H_2SO_4, and thus acid rain.[2] This is one of the causes for concern over the environmental impact of the use of these fuels as power sources.

Nitrogen oxides (NO_x) - especially nitrogen dioxide are emitted from high temperature combustion. Can be seen as the brown haze dome above or plume downwind of cities. Nitrogen dioxide is the chemical compound with the formula NO_2. It is one of the several nitrogen oxides. This reddish-brown toxic gas has a characteristic sharp, biting odor. NO_2 is one of the most prominent air pollutants.

Carbon monoxide - is a colourless, odourless, non-irritating but very poisonous gas. It is a product by incomplete combustion of fuel such as natural gas, coal or wood. Vehicular exhaust is a major source of carbon monoxide.

Carbon dioxide (CO_2) - a greenhouse gas emitted from combustion but is also a gas vital to living organisms. It is a natural gas in the atmosphere.

Volatile organic compounds - VOCs are an important outdoor air pollutant. In this field they are often divided into the separate categories of methane (CH_4) and non-methane (NMVOCs). Methane is an extremely efficient greenhouse gas which contributes to enhanced global warming. Other hydrocarbon VOCs are also significant greenhouse gases via their role in creating ozone and in prolonging the life of methane in the atmosphere, although the effect varies depending on local air quality. Within the NMVOCs, the aromatic compounds benzene, toluene and xylene are suspected carcinogens and may lead to leukemia through prolonged exposure. 1,3-butadiene is another dangerous compound which is often associated with industrial uses.

Particulate matter - Particulates, alternatively referred to as particulate matter (PM) or fine particles, are tiny particles of solid or liquid suspended in a gas. In contrast, aerosol refers to particles and the gas together. Sources of particulate matter can be man made or natural. Some particulates occur naturally, originating from volcanoes, dust storms, forest and grassland fires, living vegetation, and sea spray. Human activities, such as the burning of fossil fuels in vehicles, power plants and various industrial processes also generate significant amounts of aerosols. Averaged over the globe, anthropogenic aerosols—those made by human activities—currently account for about 10 percent of the total amount of aerosols in our atmosphere. Increased levels of fine particles in the air are linked to health hazards such as heart disease, altered lung function and lung cancer.

Persistent free radicals connected to airborne fine particles could cause cardiopulmonary disease.[2][3]

26.11 TOXIC METALS, SUCH AS LEAD, CADMIUM AND COPPER

Chlorofluorocarbons (CFCs) — harmful to the ozone layer emitted from products currently banned from use.

Ammonia (NH_3) — emitted from agricultural processes. Ammonia is a compound with the formula NH_3. It is normally encountered as a gas with a characteristic pungent odor. Ammonia contributes significantly to the nutritional needs of terrestrial organisms by serving as a precursor to foodstuffs and fertilizers. Ammonia, either directly or indirectly, is also a building block for the synthesis of many pharmaceuticals. Although in wide use, ammonia is both caustic and hazardous.

Odors — such as from garbage, sewage, and industrial processes

Radioactive pollutants — produced by nuclear explosions, war explosives, and natural processes such as the radioactive decay of radon.

Secondary Pollutants Include

Particulate matter formed from gaseous primary pollutants and compounds in photochemical smog. Smog is a kind of air pollution; the word "smog" is a portmanteau of smoke and fog. Classic smog results from large amounts of coal burning in an area caused by a mixture of smoke and sulfur dioxide. Modern smog does not usually come from coal but from vehicular and industrial emissions that are acted on in the atmosphere by sunlight to form secondary pollutants that also combine with the primary emissions to form photochemical smog.

· Ground level ozone (O_3) formed from NO_x and VOCs. Ozone (O_3) is a key constituent of the troposphere (it is also an important constituent of certain regions of the stratosphere commonly known as the Ozone layer). Photochemical and chemical reactions involving it drive many of the chemical processes that occur in the atmosphere by day and by night. At abnormally high concentrations brought about by human activities (largely the combustion of fossil fuel), it is a pollutant, and a constituent of smog.

Peroxyacetyl nitrate (PAN) — similarly formed from NO_x and VOCs.

Minor air pollutants include: A large number of minor hazardous air pollutants. Some of these are regulated in USA under the Clean Air Act and in Europe under the Air Framework Directive.

A variety of persistent organic pollutants, which can attach to particulate matter. Persistent organic pollutants (POPs) are organic compounds that are resistant to environmental degradation through chemical, biological, and photolytic processes. Because of this, they have been observed to persist in the environment, to be capable of long-range transport, bioaccumulate in human and animal tissue, biomagnify in food chains, and to have potential significant impacts on human health and the environment.

26.12 WATER POLLUTION

26.12.1 Oil, Gasoline and Additive

Oil spills like the Exxon Valdez spill off the coast of Alaska or the more recent Prestige spill off the coast of Spain get lots of news coverage, and indeed, they do cause major water pollution and problems for local wildlife, fishermen, and coastal businesses. However, the problem of oil polluting water goes far beyond catastrophic oil spills. Land-based petroleum pollution is carried into waterways by rainwater runoff. This includes drips of oil, fuel, and fluid from cars and trucks; dribbles of gasoline spilled onto the ground at the filling station; and drips from industrial machinery. These sources and more combine to provide a continual feed of petroleum pollution to all of the world's waters, imparting an amount of oil to the oceans *every year* that is more than 5 times greater than the Valdez spill.

Shipping is one of these non-spill sources of oil pollution in water: Discharge of oily wastes and oil-contaminated ballast water and wash water are all significant sources of marine pollution, and drips from ship and boat motors add their share. Drilling and extraction operations for oil and gas can also contaminate coastal waters and groundwater. As for gasoline and gas additives, leaking storage tanks are a big problem. The US Environmental Protection Agency (EPA) estimates that about 100,000 gasoline storage tanks are leaking chemicals into groundwater. In Santa Monica, California, wells supplying half the city's water have been closed because of dangerously high levels of the gasoline additive MTBE.

26.12.2 Noise Pollution

Noise pollution (or environmental noise) is displeasing human-, animal- or machine-created sound that disrupts the activity or balance of human or animal life. The word *noise* comes from the Latin word *nausea* meaning seasickness. The source of most outdoor noise worldwide is transportation systems, including motor vehicle noise, aircraft noise and rail noise.[1][2] Poor urban planning may give rise to noise pollution, since side-by-side industrial and residential buildings can result in noise pollution in the residential area.

Other sources of indoor and outdoor noise pollution are car alarms, emergency service sirens, office equipment, factory machinery, construction work, groundskeeping equipment, barking dogs, appliances, power tools, lighting hum, audio entertainment systems, loudspeakers, and noisy people.

26.12.3 Noise Health Effects

Noise health effects are both health and behavioural in nature. The unwanted sound is called noise. This unwanted sound can damage physiological and psychological health. Noise pollution can cause annoyance and aggression, hypertension, high stress levels, tinnitus, hearing loss, sleep disturbances, and other harmful effects.[3][4][5][6] Furthermore, stress and hypertension are the leading causes to health problems, whereas tinnitus can lead to forgetfulness, severe depression and at times panic attacks. Chronic exposure to noise may cause noise-induced hearing loss. Older males exposed to significant occupational noise demonstrate significantly reduced hearing sensitivity than their non-exposed peers, though differences in hearing sensitivity decrease with time and the two groups are indistinguishable by age 79. A comparison of Maaban tribesmen, who were insignificantly exposed to transportation or industrial noise, to a typical U.S. population showed that chronic exposure to moderately high levels of environmental noise contributes to hearing loss.

High noise levels can contribute to cardiovascular effects and exposure to moderately high levels during a single eight hour period causes a statistical rise in blood pressure of five to ten points and an increase in stress and vasoconstriction leading to the increased blood pressure noted above as well as to increased incidence of coronary artery disease. Noise pollution is also a cause of annoyance. A 2005 study by Spanish researchers found that in urban areas households are willing to pay approximately four Euros per decibel per year for noise reduction.

26.13 ENVIRONMENTAL EFFECTS

Noise can have a detrimental effect on animals by causing stress, increasing risk of death by changing the delicate balance in predator or prey detection and avoidance, and by interfering with their use of sounds in communication especially in relation to reproduction and in navigation. Acoustic overexposure can lead to temporary or permanent loss of hearing.

An impact of noise on animal life is the reduction of usable habitat that noisy areas may cause, which in the case of endangered species may be part of the path to extinction. Noise pollution has caused the death of certain species of whales that beached themselves after being exposed to the loud sound of military sonar.

Noise also makes species communicate louder, which is called Lombard vocal response. Scientists and researchers have conducted experiments that show whales' song length is longer when submarine-detectors are on. If creatures don't "speak" loud enough, their voice will be masked by anthropogenic sounds. These unheard voices might be warnings, finding of prey, or preparations of net-bubbling. When one species begins speaking louder, it will mask other species' voice, causing the whole ecosystem to eventually speak louder.

European Robins living in urban environments are more likely to sing at night in places with high levels of noise pollution during the day, suggesting that they sing at night because it is quieter, and their message can propagate through the environment more clearly. Interestingly, the same study showed that daytime noise was a stronger predictor of nocturnal singing than night-time Light pollution, to which the phenomenon is often attributed.

Zebra finches become less faithful to their partners when exposed to traffic noise. This could alter a population's evolutionary trajectory by selecting traits, sapping resources normally devoted to other activities and thus lead to profound genetic and evolutionary consequences.

Figures compiled by Rockwool, the mineral wool insulation manufacturer, based on responses from local authorities to a Freedom of Information Act (FOI) request reveal in the period April 2008 - 2009 UK councils received 315,838 complaints about noise pollution from private residences. This resulted in environmental health officers across the UK serving 8,069 noise abatement notices, or citations under the terms of the Anti-Social Behaviour (Scotland) Act. In the last 12 months, 524 confiscations of equipment have been authorised involving the removal of powerful speakers, stereos and televisions. Westminster City Council has received more complaints per head of population than any other district in the UK with 9,814 grievances about noise, which equates to 42.32 complaints per thousand residents. Eight of the top 10 councils ranked by complaints per 1,000 residents are located in London.

26.14 MITIGATION AND CONTROL OF NOISE

Fig. 26.6: Noise mitigation

The *sound tube* in Melbourne, Australia, designed to reduce roadway noise without detracting from the area's aesthetics. Technology to mitigate or remove noise can be applied as follows: There are a variety of strategies for mitigating roadway noise including: use of noise barriers, limitation of vehicle speeds, alteration of roadway surface texture, limitation of heavy vehicles, use of traffic controls that smooth vehicle flow to reduce braking and acceleration, and tire design. An important factor in applying these strategies is a computer model for roadway noise, that is capable of addressing local topography, meteorology, traffic operations and hypothetical mitigation. Costs of building-in mitigation can be modest, provided these solutions are sought in the planning stage of a roadway project.

Aircraft noise can be reduced to some extent by design of quieter jet engines, which was pursued vigorously in the 1970s and 1980s. This strategy has brought limited but noticeable reduction of urban sound levels. Reconsideration of operations, such as altering flight paths and time of day runway use, has demonstrated benefits for residential populations near airports. FAA sponsored residential retrofit (insulation) programs initiated in the 1970s has also enjoyed success in reducing interior residential noise in thousands of residences across the United States. Exposure of workers to Industrial noise has been addressed since the 1930s. Changes include redesign of industrial equipment, shock mounting assemblies and physical barriers in the workplace. Noise Free America, a national anti-noise pollution organization, regularly lobbies for the enforcement of noise ordinances at all levels of government.

26.15 ENVIRONMENT PROTECTION

The need for the protection of environment is increasing the world over day by day. Various steps have been taken both at national and international level. However, these steps and measures adopted are not sufficient to meet the menace of pollution. The rapid increase in pollution, accelerated exploitation of natural resources and industrialization, unchecked use of chemicals etc. lead to more pollution. The gulf war threw new challenges to the champions of environmental pro tection movement. The dangerous impact it had on the environment and the pollution it caused would need years for even restoring the status quo. Even natural calamities like typhoon, earthquake etc. also affect environment. Destruction of environment will result in depletion of life on this Earth. The task is Himalayan, the resources are scarce. We must pool all our resources, knowledge and means to check pollution of water, air, destruction of forests and other natural resources to ensure health and life for us and for our future generations. Scientists, jurists, administrators must join their heads and hearts in this task.

Chapter 27

Environmental Impact Assessment

27.1 ENVIRONMENTAL IMPACT ASSESSMENT

The purpose of EIA is to help design the projects for the maintenance of the quality of the environment by examining alternatives and mitigating measures throughout the ventire course of planning and development.

27.1.1 Goals of EIA

The goals of environment impact assessment are:

1. Resource conservation
2. Wastes minimizations
3. Recovery of by-product
4. Efficient equipment

To ensure environmental quality measures must be taken before the damage.

27.2 METHODOLOGY OF ENVIRONMENTAL IMPACT ASSESSMENT

Earlier it was perceived that environmental conservation is a necessary need in development and productivity. It has been realized that man activities have many undesirable environmental effects. Environmental impact assessment is a procedure that ensures that developmental activities cause minimum environmental side effects without disturbing natural systems. EIA can identify major areas of environmental damage due to developmental activities in a systematic and comprehensive manner if carried out properly. Environmental impact assessment consists of four phases,:

1. Organizing the task
2. Performing the assessment
3. Writing the Environmental impact statement (EIS)
4. Review of the EIS

27.3 Organizing the Task

In this step, the action or project is identified and an interdisciplinary (ID) team is constituted to conduct the analysis for the success of the analysis. It is important to include appropriate specialists in the formation of the interdisciplinary team. as specialists are bound to be a variety of problems necessitating the inclusion of geologists, agronomists, hydrologists, meteorologists, biologists and cultural scientists etc.

A time frame for the conduct of the analysis and knowledge of the relevant rules regulations and limitations on the part government are necessary. Finally, a frame is prepared to document particulars concerning the project. its sponsors the participants of the ID team the activities that need to be accomplished and specify responsibilities time frame cost estimate etc. this from is distributed to each member of the ID team.

27.4 Performing the Assessment

This phase of EIA consists of the following steps:

1. Visit of site by the interdisciplinary team to determine the possible environmental impact of the proposed project and recording the description of the environmental impact.
2. Identification and evaluation of the likely beneficial or adverse environmental effects of the proposed project.
3. Discussion of the alternatives, *i.e.,*
   (a) What are the alternate uses of the site where the project or activity proposed to take place?
   (b) Are there any alternate means of obtaining the objectives of the proposed project?
4. Preparation of a check list for EIA to ensure complete coverage of all the possible consequences of the proposed activity so that it can be determined as to what administrative action be taken because of this activity.

27.5 Measurement of Environmental Impact

For identifying, the impact of a project on an environmental attribute the impact is required to be measured which is difficult to do quantitatively however using the check list method a comprehensive list is made of the environmental attributes related to the particular action A change in the environmental attributes reflects impacts on environmental resulting from a particular action.

Environmental Parameter	Environmental Attributes
(1) Air	- Odour Diffusion factor - Carbon monoxide
- Nitrogen oxide	- Hydrogen oxide
- Sulfur oxide	- Photocmical oxidants
- Hazardous toxicants	
(2) - Dissolved oxygen- BOD	
	- Dissolved Solids
	- Nutrients
	- Acid and Alkali

- Thermal Pollution
- Oil pollution
- Radioactivity
- Toxic Compound
- Flow variations
- Aquatic safe yield
- Auqtic life

(3) Land

Land-use patterns
- Natural calamities
- Soil stability

(4) Ecology
- Natural land vegetation
- Auatic plants
- Auatic animals
- large animals (wild as well as Domestic)
- Field crops
- Predatory birds

(5) Sound
- **Psychological effects**
- Communication effects
- Performance effects
- Social behavior effects

(6) Resources(fuel resource, non-fuel resource)

(7) Anthropogenic aspects
- Lifestyles
- Physiolgical
- Psycholgical
- Community needs
- Aesthetics

(8) Economics (regional economic stability, public economic precipitate consumption

27.6 Criteria for Choosing an EIA Methodology

In view of the large number of models and methodology being used in EIA studies, one must choose between the two extremes: complete uniformity or complete uniqueness. As both these approaches, have their limitations. Many specialists on EIA have may be their own methodologies for each one of the projects.

27.7 Preparation of Environmental Impact Statement (EIS)

EIS is the conclusion of the EIA, as the results of the assessment are reported through it. EIS is prepared by the concerted effort of an interdisciplinary team it includes the following:

(*i*) Description of the site where the proposed project is to take place.

(*ii*) Description of the proposed project. Purpose of the action-its goals and objectives, magnitude of the action, area, extent equipments, manpower and material requirement

The environmental impact of the proposed projects (*i.e.*, on air water, land, and ecology sound socio-economics). The environmental adverse edicts resulting from the activity. Alternatives of then activity Relations of the proposed activity to the existing land use plans, i.e. conformity or conflict with other land-use plans and policies when in conflict–extents of recommendations and reasons for proceeding with action. Relationship between the local short-term uses and long -term productivity of affects. Identifying the modifications that can be taken in order to minis to the adverse effects incompetent the modifications in the proposed project. Finally, the EIS written in a clear and comprehensive manner is presented to the public, competent authorities and independent experts. It is reviewed cruelly before any decision is talked in favor or against passing the proposed project.

27.8 REVIEW OF THE EIS

After written the EIS is presented to the public to make the role of public participation more effective in developmental planning process. Concerned and responsible public participation is important in order to maintain a safe and healthy environment and to upgrade the standard of living by taking advantage of new technological developments without exploiting the environment. The proposed project is made available for public inspection by advertising though the press. This coupled with discussion sessions of the government agency the proponent and the public, further information and comment from the public and competent authorities are useful for the maintenance of good environment.

A period of at least one month is given for public inspection and submission of comments of the EIS for final decisive comments of the competent authority. After the final review of least one month is given to public for submission of comments of the EIS for Final Decisive Comments of the Competent Authority. After the final review beneficial and adverse environmental impact and cost benefit analysis etc., a decision is ultimately taken to either approve or reject the project or approve the most acceptable alternative in actual or modified form.

Cost effectiveness of EIA can be improved by:

(*i*) Reducing unnecessary assessment and monitoring by better screening

(*ii*) Making use of available data and experience

(*iii*) Assigning responsibilities to the members of the analysis team thereby avoiding duplication or overlapping of duties and activities.

(*iv*) Simplifying administrative producers

27.9 LIMITATION OF THE ENVIRONMENTAL IMPACT ASSESSMENT

EIA is the major instrument for the assessment of developmental activities indicating the quality of the before, during and after the proposed developmental activity although it suffers form the following limitation.

(*i*) EIA in undertaken at the project level whereas it should be done at the policy and planning level because most environmental impacts in the development process arise at decision related to plans and policies.

(*ii*) Range of possible alternative in project often small if EIA is implemented at the level of district plan in than a reasonable number of implemented at the level of district planning then a reasonable number of alternative are available to the developer in the light of the proceeding development and available carrying capacity of the local environment.

(*iii*) There are no criteria to decide that what type and scale of projects are to undergo, EIA if there was screening a lot of unnecessary expense and delays in project clearance could be avoided as there are many project that do not require an EIA in depth.

(*iv*) Lack of a comprehensive environmental information base, limitation of time manpower financial resources etc make EIA very cumbersome and time consuming if EIA includes studying only a limited number of relevant significant issues rather than elaborately studying all environmental parameters then this limitation could be overcome.

(*v*) More research and development of improved methodologies is required to overcome limitations relating to the uncertainties in data (sampling and measurement error)

(*vi*) EIA reports are too academic, bureaucratic and lengthy containing numerous tables of collected data (relevant as well as irrelevant) without any data analysis interpretation and environmental implications.

This makes the EIA reports difficult for a common man to Understand.

Environmental policy: Environmental policy is any action deliberately taken [or not taken] to manage human activities with a view to prevent, reduce, or mitigate harmful effects on nature and natural resources, and ensuring that man-made changes to the environment do not have harmful effects on humans.

Definition: It is usefull to consider that environmental policy comprises two major terms: environment and policy. Environment primarily refers to the ecological dimension (ecosystems), but can also take account of social dimension (quality of life) and an economic dimension (resource management). Policy can be defined as a "course of action or principle adopted or proposed by a government, party, business or individual". Thus, environmental policy focuses on problems arising from human impact on the environment, which retroacts onto human society by having a (negative) impact on human values such as good health or the 'clean and green' environment.

Environmental issues generally addressed by environmental policy include (but are not limited to) air and water pollution, waste management, ecosystem management, biodiversity protection, and the protection of natural resources, wildlife and endangered species. Relatively recently, environmental policy has also attended to the communication of environmental issues.

Rationale: The rationale for governmental involvement in the environment is market failure in the form of externalities, including the free rider problem and the tragedy of the commons. An example of an externality is a factory that engages in water pollution in a river. The cost of such action is paid by society-at-large, when they must clean the water before drinking it and is external to the costs of the factory. The free rider problem is when the private marginal cost of taking action to protect the environment is greater than the private marginal benefit, but the social marginal cost is less than the social marginal benefit. The tragedy of the commons is the problem that, because no one person owns the commons, each individual has an incentive to utilize common resources as much as possible. Without governmental involvement, the commons is overused. Examples of tragedies of the common are overfishing and overgrazing.

27.10 ENVIRONMENTAL POLICY INSTRUMENTS

Environmental policy instruments are tools used by governments to implement their environmental policies. Governments may use a number of different types of instruments. For example, economic incentives and market-based instruments such as taxes and tax exemptions, tradable permits, and fees can be very effective to encourage compliance with environmental policy.

Voluntary measures, such as bilateral agreements negotiated between the government and private firms and commitments made by firms independent of government pressure, are other instruments used in environmental policy. Another instrument is the implementation of greener public purchasing programs.

Often, several instruments are combined in an instrument mix formulated to address a certain environmental problem. Since environmental issues often have many different aspects, several policy instruments may be needed to adequately address each one.

Furthermore, instrument mixes may allow firms greater flexibility in finding ways to comply with government policy while reducing the uncertainty in the cost of doing so. However, instrument mixes must be carefully formulated so that the individual measures within them do not undermine each other or create a rigid and cost-ineffective compliance framework. Also, overlapping instruments lead to unnecessary administrative costs, making implementation of environmental policies more costly than necessary. In order to help governments realize their environmental policy goals, the OECD Environment Directorate studies and collects data on the efficiency of the environmental instruments governments use to achieve their goals as well as their consequences for other policies. The site serves as a complementary database detailing countries' experience with the application of instruments for environmental policy.

The current reliance on a market based framework is controversial; however, with many prominent environmentalists arguing that a more radical, overarching, approach is needed than a set of specific initiatives, to deal coherently with the scale of the climate change challenge. For an example of the problems, energy efficiency measures may actually increase energy consumption in the absence of a cap on fossil fuel use, as people might drive more efficient cars further and they might sell better. Thus, for example, Aubrey Meyer calls for a 'framework based market' of contraction and convergence examples of which is ideas such as the recent Cap and Share and 'Sky Trust' proposals.

In the study of environment, it is essential to identify each possible environmental aspect and impact of it on our surroundings. The various environmental aspects each have a number of different impacts on the environment. Potential impacts must also be identified.

27.11 COMMONLY USED DEFINITIONS IN THE STUDY OF ENVIRONMENTAL ASPECT AND IMPACT

1.1. *Environmental Impact:* Any change to the environment whether adverse or beneficial (wholly or partially) resulting from an organization's activities products or services.

1.2. *Significant Impact:* The activity that results in substantial breach of statutory regulations under abnormal conditions.

Knowledge of environmental aspect and impact is necessary in order to have a thorough awareness of the world we live in.

2. Identification of Environmental Aspect and Impact *Inputs and Outputs of a manufacturing process*
3. Cause and Effect **Activity** Spray Painting

   Aspect Emissions of Solvent to air

   Impact Global Warming plus Ozone Depletion

   Activity At start up of spray painting

   Aspect Emissions of Solvent to water

   Impact Water Pollution

   Activity Spray on to the ground for 5 seconds **Aspect** Contamination of land **Impact** Land Pollution
4. Potential Environmental Impacts Let us now list out a number of environmental aspects. We shall discuss each environmental aspect and impact that each has on the environment

4.1 Natural Resources Possible Aspect: Over consumption

Impact: Depletion of minerals, raw materials, and energy sources

Possible Aspect: Habitat destruction **Impact** Depletion of living resources

4.2 Air Possible Aspect: CO_2, CH_4 fossil fuel combustion

Impact: Global warming

Possible Aspect: CFCs, halons, other chlorinated compounds

Impact: Ozone layer depletion

Possible Aspect: SO_2 Nox NH_3

Impact: Acid precipitation

Possible Aspect: Automobile, bus, truck emissions

Impact: Rising ground level ozone

Possible Aspect: Industrial emissions: evaporation

Impact: Exposure to hazardous gases

Possible Aspect: Energy installations

Impact: Exposure to smoke

Possible Aspect: Nuclear installation, wastes, natural sources

Impact: Exposure to radioactivity

4.3 Land Possible Aspect: Hazardous or radioactive waste, air deposition

Impact: Contamination

Possible Aspect: Mining, construction, drainage

Impact: Disturbance and soil erosion, loss of soil cover, water logging, disturbs groundwater, loss of habitats

4.4 Visual, Noise, Nuisance **Possible Aspect** Construction **Impact** Visual

Possible Aspect Production, processes, waters

Impact Dust

Possible Aspect Machinery, traffic

Impact Odor, noise, vibration

27.12 POLLUTION

Pollution is the introduction of contaminants into an environment that causes instability, disorder, harm or discomfort to the ecosystem i.e. physical systems or living organisms. Pollution can take the form of chemical substances or energy, such as noise, heat, or light. Pollutants, the elements of pollution, can be foreign substances or energies, or naturally occurring; when naturally occurring, they are considered contaminants when they exceed natural levels.

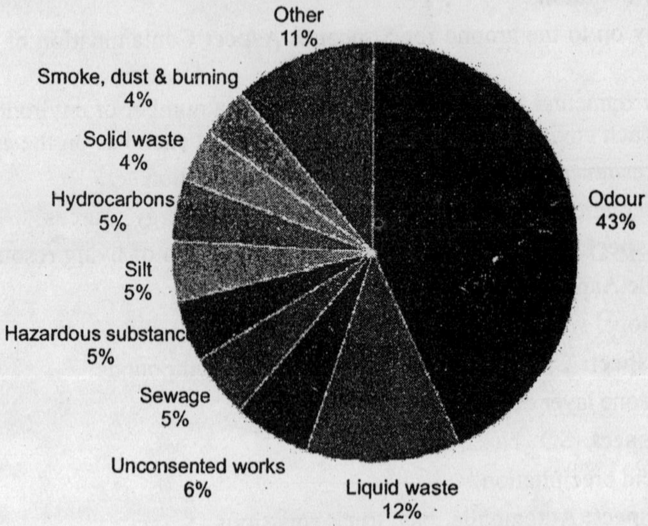

Fig. 27.1

27.12.1 Forms of Pollution

The major forms of pollution are listed below along with the particular pollutants relevant to each of them:

Air pollution, the release of chemicals and particulates into the atmosphere. Common gaseous air pollutants include carbon monoxide, sulfur dioxide, chlorofluorocarbons (CFCs) and nitrogen oxides produced by industry and motor vehicles. Photochemical ozone and smog are created as nitrogen oxides and hydrocarbons react to sunlight.

Water pollution, by the release of waste products and contaminants into surface runoff into river drainage systems, leaching into groundwater, liquid spills, wastewater discharges, eutrophication and littering.

Soil contamination occurs when chemicals are released by spill or underground leakage. Among the most significant soil contaminants are hydrocarbons, heavy metals, MTBE, herbicides, pesticides and chlorinated hydrocarbons.

Radioactive contamination, resulting from 20th century activities in atomic physics, such as nuclear power generation and nuclear weapons research, manufacture and deployment.

Noise pollution, which encompasses roadway noise, aircraft noise, industrial noise as well as high-intensity sonar.

Light pollution, includes light trespass, over-illumination and astronomical interference.

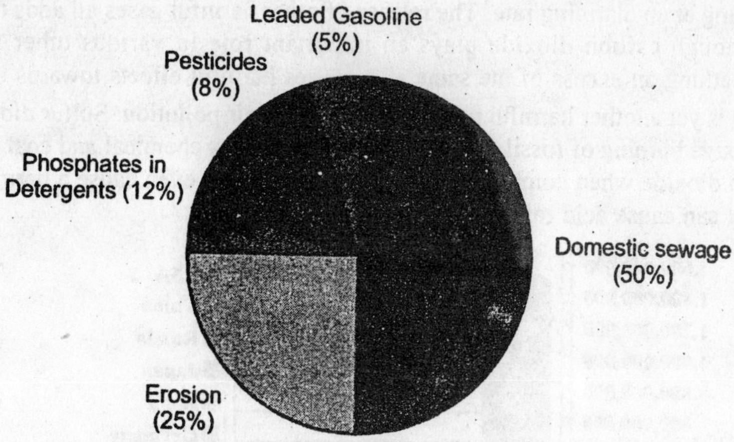

Fig. 27.2

27.12.2 Cause of Pollution

Cause of Water Pollution: Discharge of contaminated or heated water that has been used for industrial purposes. The surface runoff that contains spilled petroleum products. The surface runoff from farms, construction sites or other impervious surfaces. The improper disposal of solid wastes like littering on a localized scale. Addition of excessive nutrients by runoff containing detergents or fertilizers called as eutrophication. The geology of aquifers where groundwater is abstracted. Maltreated sewage discharged in a wrong manner. Slash and burn farming practice is a component in shifting cultivation agricultural systems.

Radioactive substances from nuclear power plants and industrial, medical and scientific use are also contributive. Uranium and thorium mining and refining are some of the examples. Heat is a leading cause as it results in the death of several aquatic organisms. A discharge of cooling water by factories and power plants lowers the temperature of the water bodies. Oil pollution is very harmful for coastal wildlife. Oil spreads on huge areas to form oil slicks. If there are trials to sink the oil or chemically treat it, the marine and beach ecosystems may be further disrupted.

Cause of Air Pollution: Carbon dioxide is one the main pollutants that causes air pollution. This is because, although living beings do exhale carbon dioxide, this gas is harmful when emitted from other sources, which are caused due to human activity. An additional release of carbon dioxide happens due to various such activities. Carbon dioxide gas is used in various industries such as the oil industry and the chemical industry. The manufacturing process of most products would require the use of this gas. Various human activities add to the increased proportions of carbon dioxide in the atmosphere. The combustion of fossil fuels and the harmful effects of deforestation have all contributed towards the same. Show that amongst the various gasses emitted during a volcanic eruption, carbon dioxide remains to be at least 40% of the emission. Scientists have now therefore identified carbon dioxide as one of those elements that have contributed to global warming.

Causes of air pollution are not limited to this, the combustion of fuels in automobiles, jet planes etc all cause the release of several primary pollutants into the air. The burning of fossil fuels in big cities which is seen at most factories, offices and even a large number of homes, it is no wonder that air pollution is increasing at an alarming rate. The release of other harmful gases all adds to the state that we see today. Although carbon dioxide plays an important role in various other processes like photosynthesis, breathing an excess of the same also causes harmful effects towards one's health.

Sulfur dioxide is yet another harmful pollutant that causes air pollution. Sulfur dioxide is emitted largely to the excessive burning of fossil fuels, petroleum refineries, chemical and coal burning power plants etc. Nitrogen dioxide when combined with sulfur dioxide can even cause a harmful reaction in the atmosphere that can cause acid rain.

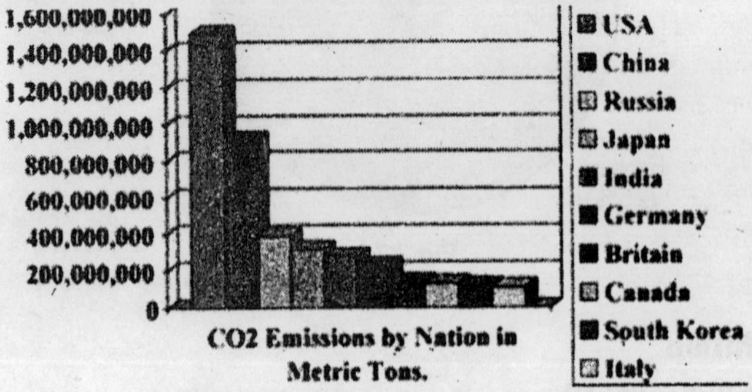

Fig. 27.3

27.12.3 Cause of Noise Pollution

Traffic noise is the main source of noise pollution caused in urban areas. With the ever-increasing number of vehicles on road, the sound caused by the cars and exhaust system of autos, trucks, buses and motorcycles is the chief reason for noise pollution. With the low flying military aircrafts soaring over the national parks. wasteland and other vacant areas, the level of noise pollution has drastically increased in these previously unaffected zones.

People living beside railway stations put up with a lot of noise from locomotive engines, horns and whistles and switching and shunting operation in rail yards. This is one of the major sources of noise pollution. To meet the demands of the necessity of living, the construction of buildings, highways and city streets causes a lot of noise. Pneumatic hammers, air compressors, bulldozers, loaders, dump trucks and pavement breakers are the major sources of noise pollution in construction sites. However, not a prime reason, industrial noise adds to the noise pollution. Machinery, motors and compressors used in the industries Create a lot of noise that adds to the already detrimental state of noise pollution.

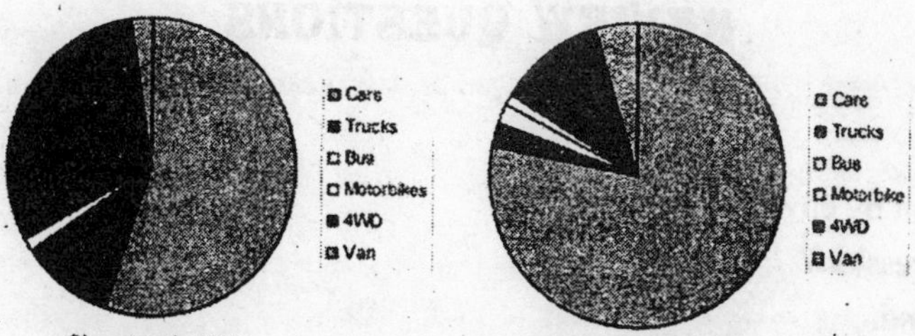

Fig. 27.4

27.12.4 Cause of Soil Pollution

Increase in urbanization: Construction uses up forestland. More constructions means increase in demand for raw materials like timber. This leads to the exploitation and destruction of forests. There is more demand for water. Reservoirs are built leading to the loss of land.

Increase in agricultural land: As the human population grew, there was a greater demand for food. This caused more land allocated to agriculture. Forests were cut down for this purpose.

Domestic waste: Every single day, tons and tons of domestic waste are dumped ranging from huge pieces of rubbish such as unused refrigerator to fish bones. If all these wastes are not disposed of properly, the damage they can do to the environment and humankind can be devastating. While waste collected from homes, offices and industries may be recycled or burnt in incinerators, a large amount of rubbish is neither burnt nor recycled but is left in certain areas marked as dumping grounds. We throw away more things today and there is an increase in the quantity of solid waste. This has given rise to problems as new dumping grounds have to be found.

Agricultural activities: Besides domestic waste, pesticides and herbicides used by farmers to increase crop yields also pollute the land when they are washed into the soil.

Industrial activities: Industrial activities also are a contributing factor to land pollution. For example, in open cast mining, huge holes are dug in the ground and these form dangerously deep mining pools. Heaps of mining waste is left behind and these wastes often contain several poisonous substances that will contaminate the soil.

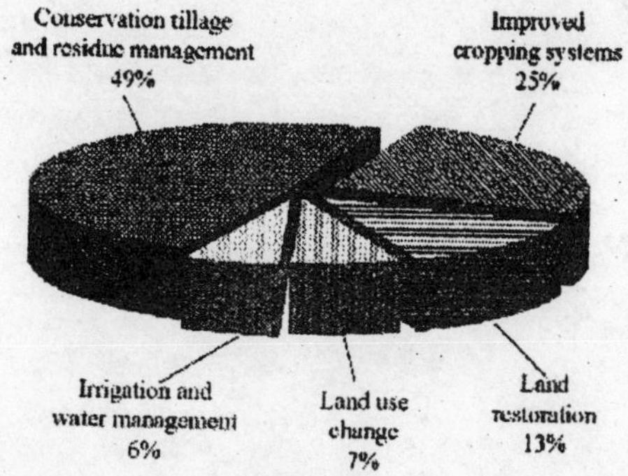

Fig. 27.5

REVIEW QUESTIONS

Short answer

1. What is meant by environmental studies?
2. What is succession?
3. Define wetland.
4. State the function of decomposers in an ecosystem.
5. What is biomagnification?
6. What is ecosystem?
7. Mention the major causes of air pollution in the urban areas.
8. What is biogas?
9. Answer any ten questions (with 2-3 lines):
10. State two causes of landslide
11. Name two nitrogen-fixing bacteria.
12. What is an inverted pyramid?
13. What is wasteland?
14. What is social forestry?
15. What is carrying capacity?
16. What is photochemical smog?
17. What is ozone hole?
18. What is urbanization?
19. What is Chipko Movement?
20. What is bioremediation?
21. What is environmental ethics?
22. What is bio-diesel?
23. What is El-Nino?
24. What is plate tectonics?
25. What is quarantine?

Short notes

Write notes on the following:

1. oil
2. Ozone layer depletion
3. Human Rights
4. Rain water harvesting
5. Chipko movement
6. Silent Valley Movement

Differentiate between the

1. National park and sanctuary
2. In-situ and ex-situ conservation
3. Species and genetic biodiversity
4. Endangered and extinct species

Long answer

1. Briefly mention the role of biotic components of an ecosystem.
2. State the ecological and economical importance of biodiversity.
3. Briefly state the air-pollution status of Kolkata city.
4. Describe the importance of land-use planning.
5. Briefly state your view about the river linking proposals in Indian context.
6. State the reasons of wildlife extinction.
7. State the function of decomposers in an ecosystem.
8. What is biomagnification?
9. What is ecosystem?
10. What is a Biome?
11. What is Green belt?
12. What is Minamata disease?
13. What is Sanctuary?
14. What is Biofertilizer?
15. What is Biological warfare?
16. Sources and effects of radioactive pollution.
17. State the impact of economic development on environment in India.
18. Discuss your view about the importance of water conservation in our country.

Objective Type Question

1. The life-saving gas in the atmosphere is
   (a) ozone in the stratosphere
   (b) water vapour in the troposphere
   (c) oxygen (charged) in the mesosphere
   (d) the atmosphere
2. Global warming is
   (a) a cean phenomenon
   (b) an tmospheric phenomenon and hydrosphere
   (c) asoil phenomenon
   (d) the atmosphere

3. The Greenhouse Effect is due to
   (a) carbon dioxide, water vapour, methane and chlorofluorocarbons
   (b) nitrogen oxides
   (c) sulphur oxides
   (d) the atmosphere
4. The Greenhouse Effect cause global disasters
   (a) by favouring forest fires
   (b) by increasing the frequencies of cyclones
   (c) by affecting agricultural production, sea food production and raising the sea levels due to melting of polar ice caps
   (d) the atmosphere
5. The protective shield for life on earth is
   (a) carbon dioxide
   (b) oxygen
   (c) ozone
   (d) the atmosphere
6. Ozone hole is formed by interaction of ozone with
   (a) hydrocarbons
   (b) chlorofluorocarbons and nitric oxide
   (c) carbon dioxide
   (d) the atmosphere
7. El Nino starts from
   (a) Mediterranean coast
   (b) Chinese coast
   (c) South American coast
   (d) the atmosphere
8. Automobile exhausts consist of
   (a) hydrocarbons, carbon monoxide and nitric oxide
   (b) carbon, zinc and lead vapour
   (c) sulphur dioxide
   (d) the atmosphere
9. Auto emissions are controlled by
   (a) using oxygen stream in the exhaust pipes of automobiles
   (b) using catalytic converters in the engines
   (c) replacing petrol/diesel by alcohol
   (d) the atmosphere

10. Photochemical smog arises from
    (a) ozone and methane in the presence of sunlight
    (b) carbon monoxide and sulphur dioxide
    (c) plotochemical reactions of hydrocarbons, ozone, carbon monoxide and nitrogen oxides
    (d) the atmosphere
11. Primary air pollutants are
    (a) oxygen, nitrogen and water vapour
    (b) carbon monoxide, nitrogen oxides, sulphur oxides, hydrocarbons and particulates
    (c) carbon dioxide, sulphur dioxide and ozone
    (d) the atmosphere
12. Acid rain consists of
    (a) acetic acid and phosphoric acid
    (b) acetic and sulphuric acids
    (c) hydrogen chloride, nitric and sulphuric acids

REVISION QUESTION WITH ANSWERS

Q.1. What is Ecosystem? With the help of suitable models, explain the energy flow in Ecosystem?

Ans. The term ecosystem was given by A.G. Tensely in 1935 defined the ecosystem as the system resulting after the integration of all biotic and abiotic parts of this environment.

Energy flow in ecosystem: Energy is defined as the ability to do work.energy flow is the moment of energy through an ecosystem,organism and back to enciornment there are two models given to explain the energy flow.

1. Single channel energy model
2. Y-shaped energy flow model

In single channel energy flow the flow of energy is unidirectional.there is a successive reduction of energy flow at successive tropic levels so shorter the food chain greater the food energy available.

Q.2. Write short note on:

a. autotrophs and hetrotrophs,

b. food chain and food web

Ans: autotrophs: It includes the organism which are self nourishing. The component take radient energy from the sun during photosynthesis process use of simple organic substance like CO_2 and H_2O.

Hetrotrophs: It include all living organisms which are depends up on autotrophs. These are two types macro type and micro type.

b. food chain and food web

Food chain: Transfer of food energy from the producers through series of organisms with repeated eating. This is called food chain. It is of two type:

1. **Grazing food chain**
2. **Detritus food chain**

Food web:- web means network. The network of interconnected food chain is called food web. The individual food chain in ecosystem is connected through different type of organisms. This interconnection is called food web.

c: Productivity of ecosystem: The productivity of an ecosystem is refer to the rate of production i.e., amount of organic matter produced in any unit time. It is of three types.

1. Primary productivity
2. Secondry productivity
3. Net productivity

Primary productivity:- the rate at which radient energy is stored by photosynthesis of products.

Gross primary productivity:- the total productivity as a result of photosynthesis is called gross primary productivity.

Net primary productivity:- this is the rate of production when loss due to respiration deducted out of the gross production rate.

Secondary productivity:-this is the rate of energy storage at consumer level.

Net productivity:-organic matter not used by consumer.

Q.3. What is biodiversity? Explain genetic and ecosystem diversity?

Ans. Biodiversity comes from the phrase biological diversity and simply means the variety of life.

Genetic diversity: It refer to the variation of the jeans within species.this cause distinct production of same species or genetic variation within production.

Ecosystem diversity: Depending upon the availability of abiotic resources. Ecosystem can dovelope its own community of living organisms.eg. lake ecosystem is always differ in compare to ocean ecosystem because each ecosystem has different kind of climate conditions. According of these conditions they are doveloping there species.

Q.4. Write a short note on habitat destruction?

Ans. Destruction of natural habitat is main reason for biodiversity. Following are the main cause for habitat destruction.

1: expending population

2: human settlement

3: industrialization

4: human activities

5: agriculture

6: mining, etc.

Deforestation is the biggest and main cause of biodiversity. This decrease the population of many species. Reduction in animals strength is also due to reduction in area for their movement.

Major problems associated with reduction of area are:-

1. **Poaching :-** killing of prohibited wild animals for illegal trading of wildlife products. Wildlife items like fur, horns, bones and other products worth millions of rupees.
2. **Need of more space:-** the way in which our population is growing up it also a major factor. More population needs more space for their every purpose.

Q.5. Define natural resources? Give its classification? Point out the major reasons for resource depletion.

Ans:- Environment is derived from the French word "environ" which means the surrounds.

All the biological and nonbiological things are surrounding an organism are thus includes in environment. Environment is the total sum of water, air and land. Interrelation among themselves and also with the human beings, other living organisms and property.

Q.6. Explain:

a: Extinct species: according to IUCN red list a taxon is extinct when there is no reasonable doubt that last individual has died.

b: Endangered: a species is said to be endangered when it is facing an extremely high risk of extinctsium in the wild in the immediate future. These are the species standing on the edge of extinctsium.

c: Threatened species: these are the species which are comes next to the endangered species. There is a thread of there extinction in near future. If not protected they might come in the category of extinct.

d: Vulnerable species: these are the species which are not in so much danger of extinct but can come in future if not protected *eg.*, Elephant.

Q.7. What are the hot spots of Biodiversity. Explain with the help of eastern himalaya and western ghat hot spot?

Ans: Hot spot are the area that are rich in endangered species. This term is introduced by Myer in 1988. Hot spots are the areas that are extremely rich in species. Have high endemism and are under constant threat.

Area which have high species richness as well as high species endemism are termed as the hot spot of biodervisity.

There are total 25 recognized hot spot of biodiversity

North and central America (3)

South America (5)

Europe and Central Asia (2)

Africa (5)

Mainland Asia (3)

Asia Pacific (7)

Eastern Himalaya

They display a ultra varied topography that forest species diversity and endemism. There are

numerous deep and semi–isolated valleys sikkim which are extremely rich in endemic plant species. In an area of 7298 km^2 of sikkim about 4250 plant species are found of which 60% are endemic. The forest cover of eastern Himalaya has changed to about 1/3rd of its original cover. Certain species like sapria Himalayan was sighted only in this region in the last 70 years.

Appendices

APPENDIX—1. THE TIME SCALE OF EVOLUTION

Time	Event
6.5—7.00-billion years ago	The big bang
4.50-billion years ago	The earth was born
3.50-billion years ago	The blue green algae (Plant) was formed
3.00-billion years ago	The Animal appeared
0.0025—0.0030-billion (25–30 lakh) years ago	The man appeared

APPENDIX—2. DRINKING WATER QUALITY

Standards

In this table, the permissible limits for water quality parameters, as laid down by the United States Public Health (USPH) Standard for drinking water and Indian Standards Institution (151), are listed for comparison. The 15 values, available for only a few parameters, are found to be much higher than those for USH for no valid reasons. All the units, except for pH and E. coli, are in ppm or mg/ml.

Parameters	USPH Standard	ISI Standard
pH 6.0—8.5 6.0—9.0Dissolved Oxygen (D.O.)	4.0—6.0	3.0
Chemical Oxygen 4.0—Dsemand (COD)		
Total dissolved solids	500	—
Suspended solid 5.0		
Chloride	250	600
Sulphate	250	1000
Cyanide	0.05	—
Nitrate + Nitrite	<10	—
Fluoride	1.5	3.0
Phosphate	0.1	—
Ammonia	0.5	—
Total hardness (as CaCO 500)	—	
Calcium	100	—
Magnesium	30	—
Arsenic	0.05	0.2
Cadmium	0.01	—

Chromium (VI)	0.05	0.05
Iron (filterable)	< 0.3	—
Lead	0.05	0.01
Mercury	0.001	—
Zinc	5.5	
—		
Phenols	0.001	0.005
E Coli (coliform cells)/1000 nil		
— (Bacteriological parameter)	100	—

APPENDIX—3. Toxic CHEMICALS IN THE ENVIRONMENT

There are a number of chemicals in the environment. Some of them are toxic while the rest are non-toxic. The toxic chemicals are discharged by the industries into air, water and soil. They enter our biological system through food chain and disturb the metabolic processes, leading in some cases to fatal results.

At present, there are four million known chemicals in the world and we are adding to the list 30,000 new com pounds every year among these 60,000–70,000 chemicals are commonly used. Apart from their benefit to increasing production, living standards and health, many of them are potentially toxic.

Toxic Chemicals in Air

- Acrylonitrile, Arseni; Asbestos
- Banzenc, Beryllium
- Cadmium, Chromium, Chlorinated solvents, Coke oven emissions, Chlorofluorocarbons
- Ethylene dibromide, Ethylene oxide
- Lead, Mercury
- Owne
- Polycyclic aromatic hydrocarbons
- Sulphur dioxide

Toxic Chemicals in Water

Trace Elements

- Arsenic
- Beryllium,
- Cadmium,
- Fluoride
- Lead
- Manganese, Mercury, Molybdenum
- Selenium

• Zinc
• Pesticides (from agricultural run-off)

APPENDIX—4. THE HAVES AND HAVE-NOTS (Developed And Developing Countries)

80:20 Ratio Twenty per cent of the world's population (developed countries) consume 80 per cent of the world's resources (natural), generate 75 per cent of total solid wastes and are responsible for 70 percent of global environmental damage.

USA. with about half of India's population and double of India's area, discharges 5000 million tonnes of carbon dioxide every year—five times more than India. Al Gore, Ex-Vice President of USA—IJNEP magazine vol. 6, No. 2, 1994—The North (developed countries) accounts for over consumption of resources while the South (developing countries) for population explosion and poverty.

APPENDIX—5. ONE EARTH, ONE FAMILY (Global Village)

The UNEP (United Nations Environment Programme) theme for 1994 was One Earth, One Family:

The Earth is not merely a "hotel"—it is our "home".

It is a place, where we should not use the resources and then move to another spot for further exploration.

— It is a place that we should cherish and need to protect.

It is not merely a "resource" or "retreat", which we use, enjoy and then leave.

— It is our Mother.

APPENDIX—6. INDIA'S RANK IN THE WORLD

Parameter	Rank
Population	2 (next to China)
Area	7
Value added in agriculture	5
Electricity generation	8
Value added in manufacturing	14
Gross Domestic Product	15
Export of goods and services	30
Human Development Index	128

Suggested Readings

S. Deshwal & A. Deshwal , Dhanpat Rai & Co. (P) Ltd, Delhi

A.K. De—Environmental Chemistry, 6th edition, New Age International (P) Ltd. New, Delhi (2006).

A.K. De—Environmental Studies, Rural Technology Centre. University of Burdwan (1999), chapters 14.

A.K. Mitra—Urban Environment in Crisis, New Age International (P) Ltd., New Delhi (2000).

A.K: Agarwal (Editor)—The State India Environment, (1984–85); Centre for Science and Environment, New Delhi (1985).

Agarwal D., Pushpendra and Gupta A. K. (2009). Eco-introspection of Hazardous Waste Management in India - Disaster Manager's Perspective, Second India disaster management congress new Delhi, 4–6 Nov, 2009 Pp 31-31.

Agarwal, SK. and Dubey, RS., Environmental Controversies. APH Publishing Corporation, New Delhi, 2002.

Agarwal, Y. K., Pushpendra, Srisvatava, P. C., Sharma B. and Kaushik, S. D., (2008) "Accumulation of cadmium in the roots of different plant species grown in cadmium spiked sandy loam soil". Proceeding of seminar on Sanitation the Challenges Ahead, Organized by Institute of Engineering & Technology and Indian Water Works Association, with U.P Pollution Control Board Lucknow pp. 23–28.

Agarwal.R.K & Sangal.V.K (2007). *Environmental Studies* Krishna Prashan Media Pvt Ltd., Meerut

Ahmed, R., A. van de Klundert, and Lardinois. Rubber Waste, Urban Solid Waste Series, Vol. 3. Amsterdam and Gouda: Tool, Transfer of Technology for Development and WASTE Consultants, 1996.

Air Pollution: M. N. Rao & H. V. N. Rao, Tata McGraw-Hill Publishing Company Ltd., New Delhi

Alam Aftab (Ed.), Human Rights in India: Issues and Challenges, Raj Publications. De 2000.

Anuj K Gautam, Pushpendra and Rakesh K (2010) Bioremediation of anaerobically treated distillery spent wash using axenic culture of Proteces microbilis, Bacillus spp, Kleibsiella planticola, Enterobactor sokazaki; MSc theses deptt of biotechnology, Adhunic institute of education and research Delhi Meerut road Duhai, Ghaziabad.

Atchia, M., and Tropp, S. (Eds.), Environmental Management: Issues and solu tions, John Wiley & Sons, 1995.

Bagad. A (2007) *Environmental Studies* Technical Publications., Pune.

Beede, David N., and David E. Bloom, "The Economics of Municipal Solid Waste." The World Bank Research Observer, Vol. 10, No. 2, August, 1995, pp. 113–150.

Bishnoi N R, Goyal S, Pushpendra and Malik. S. 2010. Effect of Cadmium on the Seed Yield of Different Plant Species (National Seminar on Medicinal Plants: conservation, cultivation and utilization, (National Symposium on impacts of trends in climate change on biodiversity and faunistic system Deptt. of Zoology and Env. Sc., GKV, Haridwar-249404, Feb. 19–20th, 2010) p. 65–65.

Chadha, S.K., (ed.), 1988, *Himalayas: ecology and environment*. Delhi: Mittal Publications.

Chary, SN. and Vyasulu, V. (Eds) Environmental Management, An Indian Per spective, MacMillan India Ltd., 2001.

Chaube, S.K., (ed.), 1985, *The Himalayas: profiles of modernisation and adaptation*. New Delhi: Sterling Publishers.

Chaudhary, R., Pushpendra and Firdos, S (2010). Environmental Pollution and Alteration of Brain Chemistry by Exposure of Toxic Metals, National seminar on Aggression and violence: challenges for social well-being March 17-18, 2010, department of psychology Jamia Millia Islamia New Delhi p. 54.

Chaudhary, R., Pushpendra and Singh, R. P. (2007). Psychological effects of medicinal plant extracts, (National Seminar on Medicinal Plants: conservation, cultivation and utilization II, Deptt. of Zoology and Env. Sc., GKV, Haridwar-249404, March 9-11, 2007) p. 55–55.

Chaudhary, R., Singh, R. P., Mishra, S. N., Pushpendra and Sharma A. K. (2009). Protection of Mental Health from Hazardous Radiation, National Seminar on Mental Health and Current Scenario 20-21 March 2009, Deptt. of Psychology Gurukul Kangri University, Haridwar- 249404, p. 45-46.

Cunningham, W. and Cunningham, MA., Princtivles of Environmental Science:

D AK., Environmental Chemistry, New Age International (p) Ltd. Publishers, New Delhi, 3rd edition, 1996.

D.D. Monte—Temples or Tombs? Centre Science and Environment, New Delhi (1985).

Das. R.R. (2006) *Environmental Studies* Paragon International Publishers., New Delhi

Deswal.S & Deswal.A (2005). *Environmental Studies* Dhanpat Rai &Company Ltd. Delhi

Dewan, M.L., 1990, *People's participation in Himalayan eco-system development*. New Delhi: Concept Publishing Company.and B.D. Joshi, (eds.), 1993, *Vedic philosophy for Himalayan eco-system development*. New Delhi: Concept Publishing Company.

Dhama, C. P. S. (1998) "Swasthya Rksha Ke Saral Upay" Veenapani (1998-99), DAV College Muzaffar Nagar, U.P.-251001. pp. 64-67.

Dhama, P S., (1998) "The Company of Books" Veenapani, English Section (1998–99) DAV College Muzaffar Nagar, U.P. – 251001, p.13–14.

Dhama, P., Sharma, A D and Sharma, K. (2005) "A Comparative study of some physico-chemical properties of effluent treatment plant–A case. study of I.T.C. Ltd., Saharanpur". Indian Science Congress held at Ahmedabad.

Dhameja.S.K. (2008) *Environmental Science* S.K. Kataria & Sons., Delhi

Dhar, B.B., Mining and environment, APE. Publishing Corporation, New Delhi, 2000.

Dhar, T.N. and Sharma P.N., (eds.), 1987, *Himalayan energy systems*. Nainital: Gyanodaya Prakashan.

Down to Earth, Centre for Science and Environment, New Delhi.

Ecology and Environment: P. D. Sharma' Rastogi Publishers Meerut.

Elements of Environmental Science and Engineering: P. Meenakshi, Prentice Hall of India Pvt. Ltd, New Delhi.

Enquiry and Applications, Tata McGraw Hill Publication, New Delhi, 2nd edition, 2003.

Environmental Chemistry: A. K. De' New Age International (P) Ltd.

Environmental Chemistry: B.K. Sharma & H. Kaur, Goel Publishing House, Meerut.

Environmental Engineering: P. Aarne Vesilind/ Susan M. Morgan, Tomson Asia Pvt Ltd., Singapore

Environmental Pollution Control Engineering: C.S. Rao, New Age International (P) Ltd.

Environmental Studies: Benny Joseph, Tata McGraw-Hill Publishing Company Ltd., New Delhi

Environmental Studies: Dr. Suresh K. Dhameja, S. K. Kataria & Sons Publishers, Nai sarak, Delhi.

Environmental Studies: K.M. Gupta, Umesh Publications, Nai Sarak, Delhi.

Environmental Studies: R.K. Agarwal & V. K. Sangal, Krishna Prakashan Media (P) Ltd. Meerut.

Firdos, S., Pushpendra and Singh, R P 2010. Phytoextraction: A green technology to control soil pollution and recovery of metals (National conference on eco-friendly manufacturing for sustainable development. Institute of engineering & technology GLA university , Mathura (UP) India 19–21 November. 2010) p.31.

Foundation of Environmental Studies: Prof. Dr. Devendra S. Bhargava, A Publication of the U.P. Technical University Lucknow.

G.D. Friedman—Primer of Epidemiology, 3rd McGraw New York (1988).

Glasbergen, P. and Blowers, A. (Eds). Perspectives on Environmental Problems. Arnold, 1997.

Goel, P.K., Water Pollution; Causes, Effects and Control, New Age International (P) Ltd., Publishers, 1997.

Gupta S. and Pushpendra (2010) importance of the implementation of the environmental science subject to graduation level in India. Quest the search AKGEC, Ghaziabad-201009 India, p31-32.

Gupta, Krishna Murti, (ed.), 1990. *Himalaya: man and nature*. New Delhi: Lancers Books.

Gupta.K.K (2006). *Environmental Studies 2nd Edition* Umesh Publications Delhi

INFORM Inc., and Recourse Systems, Inc. Business Recycling Manual. 1991.

Introduction Text of Environmental Policies & Laws: V. K. Garg, M.S. Bishnoi & C.P. Malik, Kalyani Publishers, New Delhi.

Introduction to Environmental Engineering & Science: Gilbert M. Masters, Prentice Hall India Pvt. Ltd., New Delhi.

Introduction to Environmental Science and Technology: Dr. S. Amal Raj, Laxmi Publications (P) Ltd., Ne New Delhi.

Ison, S., Peake, S. and Wall, S., Environmental Issues and Policies, Prentice Hall, 2002.

Jackson, A.R.W. and Jackson IM., Environmental Science, Longrnan Group Ltd., 1998.

Jayal, N.D. and Motwari Mohan, (eds.), 1986, *Conservation, tourism and mountaineering in the Himalayas*. Dehradun: Natraj Publishers.

Kaur. H (2007) *Environment And Ecology* Pragati Prakashan. Meerut

Kaur. H (2008) *Environmental Studies* Pragati Prakashan. Meerut

Kaushik. A, Kaushik C.P (2007) *Environmental Studies* New Age International Pvt Ltd, Publishers., New Delhi

Khanna, S., Pushpendra, Chauhan, B. S., Goyal, S., and Giri, P. P. (2009). Protection of Children from Hazardous Environmental Pollutants, National Seminar on Mental Health and Current Scenario 20-21 March 2009, Deptt. of Psychology Gurukul Kangri University, Haridwar- 249404, p. 8.

Khoshoo, T.N., 1988, *Environmental concerns and strategies*. New Delhi: Ashish Publishing House., 1995, *Mahatma Gandhi: apostle of applied human ecology*. New Delhi: Tata Applied Research Institute.

Kreith, Frank, ed. Handbook of Solid Waste Management. New York: McGraw-Hill, 1994.

Kumar, H.P., Forest Resources; Conservation and Management. Affiliated East West Press Pvt. Ltd., 2001.

Kumar, K., Kumar, T. and Pushpendra (2005) "Role of Ca^{+2} and Ethylene in the Microbes assisted phytoremediation" (National Conference on Recent Trends in surface Chemistry, Deptt. of Chemistry, G.J.U., Hisar, March 13–14, 2005) p. 53–54.

Kumar, K., Rishi, Singh, J., Somvir and Pushpendra (2005) "Biochemical and Physiological aspects of Cadmium toxicity" (National Conference on Recent Trends in surface Chemistry, Deptt. of Chemistry, G.J.U., Hisar, March 13-14, 2005) p 51–52.

Kumar, K., Pushpendra, Gangal, V. and Khanna, D. R. (2003) Performance Study of Distillery Effluent Treatment Plant (National Seminar on Emerging Environmental Issues and Technological Challenges, Deptt. of Env. Sc. and Engg. G.J.U., Hisar, Sept. 1-2, 2003) p. 86–87.

Kumar, K., Singh R. P. and Pushpendra (2005) "Cadmium tolerant plant growth promoting Rhizobacteria in *Brassica juncea*". (National symposium on plant disease diagnosis, Epidemiology and Management. Annual meeting Indian Society of Plant Pathologists and Indian Phytopathological Society. Deptt. of Plant Pathology CCS HAU, Hisar-125004, Dec., 21-22, 2005) p. 71.

Kumar, V., Pushpendra and Singh R P 2010. Phytoextraction: A Green Technology to control soil pollution and recovery of metal, (National conference on recent trends in the exotic materials, school of Engg. and technology , Sharda university plot no 32-34, knowledge park-III Greater Noida UP India, 26-28 Aug. 2010) p. 25.

Lardinois, 1. and A. van de Klundert. Organic Waste, Urban Solid Waste Series, Vol. 1. Amsterdam and Gouda: Tool, Transfer of Technology for Development and WASTE Consultants, 1994.

Malik A., Bishnoi, N R and Pushpendra (2010). Environmental pollution, brain biochemistry, neurotoxicity and criminal violence, National seminar on Aggression and violence: challenges for social well-being March 17-18, 2010, department of psychology Jamia Millia Islamia New Delhi pp. 50-51.

Malik S, Anil, Bishnoi N R., and Pushpendra 2010. Effect of Cadmium Concentration on the Growth and Biomass Yield of Various Plant Species dj college

Malik S., Kumar, V and Pushpendra 2010. Phytoextraction: A recent technology for the decontamination of agricultural lands using different plant species, (National Seminar on agriculture poverty and environment: issues and challenges, Feb. 20-21, 2010 Deptt. of Geography, Digamber Jain PG College, Baraut Baghpat-UP) p 38-38.

Malik, S, Anil, Bishnoi N R., and Pushpendra 2010. Effect of Cadmium Concentration on the Growth and Biomass Yield of Various Plant Species (National Seminar on Medicinal Plants, conservation, cultivation and utilization II, Deptt. of Zoology and Env. Sc., GKV, Haridwar-249404, March 9-11, 2007) pp. 66-66.

Miller, G. Tyler, Environmental Science, Brooks/Cole, Thomas Learning, Inc., USA. 8th edition, 2001.

Miller, G. Tyler, Living in the Environment, Brooks/Cole, Thomas Learning, Inc. 12th edition, USA, 2002.

Mishra, S. N., Pushpendra and Singh A. (2009). Effect of different Cadmium concentrations on the Yield of Different Plant Species, Journal of Management & Technology, Agra Vol. 1 No. 1, 2009 Jan. Pp 35-47.

Mishra, S. N., Singh R.P. and Pushpendra 2010. Cadmium Concentration affects the Root Biomass Yield of Different Plant Species (National Seminar on Medicinal Plants: conservation, cultivation and utilization, (National Symposium on impacts of trends in climate change on biodiversity and faunistic system Deptt. of Zoology and Env. Sc., GKV, Haridwar-249404, Feb 19-20th, 2010). 66

Monga, G.S., Environment and Development, Deep & Deep Publications Put. Ltd., New Delhi, 2001.

N R Bishnoi[1], Sanjeev Goyal[2], Pushpendra[3] and Subhash Malik[4] Effect of Cadmium on the Seed Yield of Different Plant Species communicated

N.C.E.R,T., Journal of Value Education: Special Issue on Environmental Values, Vol. 3(2), 2003.

Negi, S.S., 1990, *Himalayan forest and forestry*. New Delhi: Indus Publishing Company.

Nitya Nand and Kamlesh Kumar, 1989, *The holy Himalaya: a geographical interpretation of Garhwal*. New Delhi: Daya Publishing House.

Odum, ER, Fundamentals of Ecology, WB. Saunders Company, Japan, 3rd ed., 1971.

Pani.B (2007) *Environmental Sciences & Engineering* Galgotia Publication Pvt.Ltd. New Delhi

Pathak, A., Kumari, P. and Pushpendra (2007). Heavy Metals Evaluation of Fly Ash and Potentials Hazards Associated with River Ecology due to its Disposal, Tall 2007, Ministry of Environment and Forest 12th World Lake Conference, pp. 146-146.

Pathak, A., Singh, R. P., Kumar, A. and Pushpendra (2005). "Role of micorrhiza in heavy metals contaminated soil". (National symposium on plant disease diagnosis, Epidemiology and Management and Annual meeting Indian Society of Plant Pathologists and Indian Phytopathological Society. Deptt. of Plant Pathology CCS HAU, Hisar-125004, Dec., 21-22, 2005) p. 71.

Pokhriyal, H.C., 1994, *Human environment and socio-economic development in the Himalayas*. Delhi: B.R. Publishing Corporation.

Polesthya, A., Sharma, S., Pushpendra and Khanna. D. R. (2008) Study of physico- chemical characteristics of treated effluent of sugar Industry. 11th Punjab congress, Feb. 7, 9, (2008) The sciences technology: opportunities & challenge organized by Thaper University, Patiala, 109.

Prakriti, 1993, Information brochure on an exhibition on man in harmony wi h the elements. New Delhi: Indira Gandhi National Centre for the Arts.

Pushpendra (2008) Is 'small' really the big thing and impacts may be ignored? Udgar An Expression Raj Kumar Goel Institute of Technology, Delhi Meerut Road, opp. Jain Tube Co., Ghaziabad.

Pushpendra (2010) Review Article, Bio removal of hazardous heavy metals from contaminated soils: Environmental concerns and opportunities, Quest the search AKGEC, Ghaziabad-201009 India, p.38-42.

Pushpendra (2010). Impact of EDTA application on the translocation of cadmium from root to shoot in Chenopodium murrale grown in cadmium spiked sandy loam soil, (National seminar on recent trends in chemical research 4-6 September 2010, dept of chemistry Meerut College Meerut-250001, India p.29.

Pushpendra 2009 Text book of Environment & Ecology, Vayu Education of India, 2/25, Ansari road, Darya Ganj, New Delhi-110002, ISBN No.-81-8283-077-X.

Pushpendra 2009 Text book of Environmental Science & Ethics, Vayu Education of India, 2/25, Ansari road, Darya Ganj, New Delhi-110002, ISBN No.-81-8283-077-X.

Pushpendra 2009 Text book of Environmental Studies, Vayu Education of India, 2/25, Ansari road. Darya Ganj, New Delhi-110002, ISBN No.-81-8283-077-X.

Pushpendra 2009 Text book of NCER, Vayu Education of India, 2/25, Ansari road, Darya Ganj, New Delhi-110002, ISBN No.-81-8283-077-X.

Pushpendra 2009 Text book of psychology, Vayu Education of India, 2/25, Ansari road, Darya Ganj, New Delhi-110002, ISBN No.-81-8283-077-X.

Pushpendra 2009 Text book of psychology, Vayu Education of India, 2/25, Ansari road, Darya Ganj, New Delhi-110002. ISBN No.-81-8283-077-X.

Pushpendra 2010. Instruments to control air pollution and need of engineering to improve efficiency (National conference on eco-friendly manufacturing for sustainable development, Institute of engineering & technology GLA university , Mathura (UP) India 19-21 November, 2010) p.30.

Pushpendra 2010. Effect of Cadmium Contamination on the Root Biomass Yield of Different Hyperaccumulator Plant Species (National Seminar on Medicinal Plants: conservation, cultivation and utilization, (National Seminar on Medicinal Plants, conservation, cultivation and utilization II, Deptt. of Zoology and Env. Sc., GKV, Haridwar-249404, March 9-11, 2007) pp. 87-88.

Pushpendra and Bishnoi N. R. (2010). Phytoremediation: A Technology for Control of Pollution and Recovery of Metal, National Conference on, Recent Advances in Materials and Methods of Chemistry RAMMC-2010, SRM University, Kattankulathur Tamilnadu-603203 pp 222-225.

Pushpendra and Bishnoi N. R. (2010). Phytoremediation: A Technology for Control of Pollution and Recovery of Metal, National Conference on, Recent Advances in Materials and Methods of Chemistry RAMMC-2010, SRM University, Kattankulathur Tamilnadu-603203 pp 222-225.

Pushpendra and Malik, S. 2010. Impact of heavy metal pollution on various Plant Species (National conference on recent trends in the exotic materials, school of Engg. and technology , Sharda university plot no 32-

34, knowledge park-III Greater Noida UP India, 26-28 Aug 2010) p. 71.

Pushpendra and Singh R. P. (2007). Role of conventional breeding methods and molecular markers for improvements of medicinal traits, (National Seminar on Medicinal Plants: conservation, cultivation and utilization II Deptt. of Zoology and Env. Sc., GKV, Haridwar-249404, March 9-11, 2007) p. 54-55.

Pushpendra and Singh R. P. (2010). Detection of Heavy Metal Concentration in Fly Ash for Its Management, Journal of Management & Technology, Agra Vol. 2 No. 1, 2010 Jan. pp 33-38.

Pushpendra and Singh R. P. (2010). Detection of Heavy Metal Concentration In Fly Ash For Its Management, Journal of Management & Technology, Agra Vol. 1 No. 1, 2009 Jan. pp 35-47.

Pushpendra, (2010). Psychological Impacts of War on the Environment and Human Health National seminar on Aggression and violence: challenges for social well-being March 17-18, 2010, department of psychology Jamia Millia Islamia New Delhi pp 51-52.

Pushpendra, Agarwal, Y. K., Gupta, K. K., Polestya A., and .Singh, R. P., (2008). "Enhanced Organic Loading Rate in Hybrid Anaerobic Reactor for Treatment of Distillery Effluents". Proceeding of seminar on Sanitation- The Challenges Ahead, Organized by Institute of Engineering & Technology and Indian Water Works Association, with U.P Pollution Control Board Lucknow, pp17-22.

Pushpendra, Agarwal, Y. K., Tomar, R. K., and Singh, R. P., (2007), Proceeding of National conference on Strategies and Innovation in teaching at Higher Education level, Dept. of Education, Vidyavati Mukund Lal (PG) Girls College, and Ghaziabad. pp. 83-84.

Pushpendra, Anil and Bishnoi, NR (2010). Environmental Pollution and Its Contribution to a Life of Crime through Violence, National seminar on Aggression and violence: challenges for social well-being March 17-18, 2010, department of psychology Jamia Millia Islamia New Delhi pp 50-51.

Pushpendra, Anil, Agarwal D. and Mishra S. N. (2010). Effect of Cadmium Concentration on the Root Biomass Yield of Various Plant Species, International Conference on Green Technologies For Greener Environment 27-30 January 2010 Department of Chemistry Ch. Charan Singh University, Meerut- 250005, India pp 90.

Pushpendra, Anil, Agarwal D. and Mishra S. N. (2010). Effect of Cadmium Concentration on the Root Biomass Yield of Various Plant Species, International Conference on Green Technologies For Greener Environment 27-30 January 2010 Department of Chemistry Ch. Charan Singh University, Meerut- 250005, India Pp 90.

Pushpendra, Anil, Bishnoi N R and Malik S 2010. Effect of Cadmium Concentration on the Growth and Biomass Yield of Various Plant Species (dj college

Pushpendra, Chaudhary, R., and Giri, P.P. (2007). Over exploitation of medicinal plants: A global issue, (National Seminar on Medicinal Plants: conservation, cultivation and utilization, (National Seminar on Medicinal Plants, conservation, cultivation and utilization II, Deptt. of Zoology and Env. Sc., GKV, Haridwar-249404, March 9-11, 2007) p. 87-88.

Pushpendra, Chaudhary, R., Mailk, A., and Polestya, A., (2007). "Graduate Science Education", Proceeding of National conference on Strategies and Innovation in teaching at Higher Education level, Dept. of Education, Vidyavati Mukund Lal (PG) Girls College, Ghaziabad, pp. 81-82.

Pushpendra, Gautam A K, Kumar V and Malik S 2010. Variation in the Root Biomass Yield of Different Plant Species Due To Cadmium Contamination in Agricultural Lands (dj college

Pushpendra, Kumar V., Bishnoi N. R. and Malik S. (2010). Metal Recovery Using Phytoremediation Technology, International Conference on Green Technologies For Greener Environment 27-30 January 2010 Department of Chemistry Ch. Charan Singh University, Meerut- 250005, India pp. 113.

Pushpendra, Kumar V., Bishnoi N. R. and Malik S. (2010). Metal Recovery Using Phytoremediation Technology, International Conference on Green Technologies For Greener Environment 27-30 January 2010 Department of Chemistry Ch. Charan Singh University, Meerut- 250005, India pp. 113.

Pushpendra, Kumar, K. and Chopra, A. K. (2003) Physico-Chemical Characterization of Different Sites of ETP of India Tobacco Company Ltd., Saharanpur, (National Seminar on Emerging Environmental Issues and Technological Challenges, Deptt. of Env. Sc. and Engg. G.J.U., Hisar, Sept. 1-2, 2003) pp. 36-37.

Pushpendra, Kumar, K. and Polestya, A. (2006). "Extraction of drugs from Medicinal Plants, (National Seminar on Medicinal Plants: conservation, cultivation and utilization, Deptt. of Zoology and Env. Sc., GKV, Haridwar- 249404, March 9-11, 2006) pp. 116.

Pushpendra, Kumar, M. and Mishra, S. N. (2009). Production of biomass for the production of energy and metal recovery using phytoremidiation technology, National Seminar on Energy & Environment Problems and Solutions in 21st Century, 30-31 March 2009, Sir Chhotu Ram Institute of Engineering & Technology, C C S University, Meerut- 250004, pp. 40

Pushpendra, Kumar, R., Sunil and Bishnoi, N R. (2005) "Effect of mixed cadmium and zinc upon Alfa alfa growth" (National Conference on Recent Trends in surface Chemistry, Deptt. of Chemistry, G.J.U., Hisar, March 13-14, 2005) pp. 65-66.

Pushpendra, Kumar, V. and Sharma, A K 2010. Phytoextraction of cadmium to control soil and water pollution in contaminated agricultural soil (National conference on eco-friendly manufacturing for sustainable development, Institute of engineering & technology GLA university , Mathura (UP) India 19-21 November, 2010) pp. 31.

Pushpendra, Panwar, D., Chaudhary, R. 2010 Text book of Human Values & Professional Ethics, ISBN No. 81-8283-099-0 Krishna Prakashan Media (P) Ltd., Meerut.

Pushpendra, Pathak, A., Gautam P. and Singh, R. P. (2006). Harvesting of Medicinal Plants: A Global Issue (National Seminar on Medicinal Plants: conservation, cultivation and utilization, Deptt. of Zoology and Env. Sc., GKV, Haridwar- 249404, March 9-11, 2006) p. 117.

Pushpendra[1] Vinod Kumar[2], Subhash Malik[2] and N R Bishnoi[4] Phytoremediation: A Technology for Control of soil Pollution in contaminated agricultural soil communicated

Pushpendra[1], Anil[2] , N R Bishnoi[3] and Subhash Malik[4] Effect of Cadmium Concentration on the Growth and Biomass Yield of Various Plant Species communicated

Pushpendra[1], Sanjeev Goyal[2] Munish Kumar[3], and Amarjeet Singh Effect of Cadmium on the Seed Yield of Different Plant Species communicated

Qasim, S.Z., 1993, *National policy for integrated development in the Himalayas*. New Delhi: Planning Commission.

Raha, M.K., (ed), 1987, *The Himalayan heritage*. Delhi: Gian Publishing House.

Rajan, Madhu, 1993, ' Man against nature? *The Tribune*, New Delhi, 20 June.

Rajni Ranjan Mani, Pushpendra and Tyagi Ambika (2010) Optimization of bioremediation of PMDE (post methylated distillery effluents) by analyzing the environmental factors and inoculums ratio, MSc theses deptt of biotechnology, Adhunic institute of education and research Delhi Meerut road Duhai, Ghaziabad.

Rustomji, N.K. and C. Ramble, (eds.), 1990, *Himalayas: Environment and Culture*. Shimla: Indian Institute of Advanced Study; New Delhi: Indus Publishing Company.

Sawyer.C.N, McCarty.P.L & Parkin. G.F (2002) *Chemistry For Environmental Engineering.* Tata McGrawHill Publishing Company Limited.New Delhi

Shah, S.D. Bhatt and R.K. Pande, R.K., (eds.), 1990, *Himalaya: environmeent, resources and development*. Almora: Shree Almora Book Depot.

Shah, S.D. Bhatt and R.K. Pande, R.K., (eds.), 1990, *Himalaya: environmeent, resources and development*. Almora: Shree Almora Book Depot. Source:

Sharma A. K., Pushpendra, Srivastava, D., Sharma, A. and Mishra, S. N. (2009). Removal of cadmium from the contaminated sandy loam soil with the production of biomass for metal recovery and energy production using different plant species, National Seminar on Energy & Environment Problems and Solutions in 21st Century, 30-31 March 2009, Sir Chhotu Ram Institute of Engineering & Technology, C C S University, Meerut- 250004, pp. 25

Sharma, A.K, Pushpendra, Mishra S N 2010 Cadmium Removal from the Contaminated Soil Using Different Hyper Accumulator Plant Species for the Production of Energy and Recovery of Metal (National Symposium on impacts of trends in climate change on biodiversity and faunistic system Deptt. of Zoology and Env. Sc., GKV, Haridwar-249404, Feb 19-20th, 2010) p. 65-65.

Sharma, ES. and Khan TI. (Editors), Environmental Conservation Depleting Resources and Sustainable Development, Aavishkar Publishers, Distribu tors, Jaipur, 2003.

Sharma. J.P (2006) *Environmental Studies* Laxmi Publication , New Delhi.

Singh PV., Pushpendra and Yadav A K (2010) Effect of cadmium concentration on the root biomass yield of different plant species, Chem Enviro- Interdisciplinary annual publication 2010, BBD Group of educational institutions Lucknow campus, Lucknow-227105, pp. 9-15.

Singh R P., Pushpendra, Kumar, V. and Malik, S. 2010. Variation in the Root Biomass Yield of Different Plant Species Due to heavy metal Contamination in Agricultural Lands (National conference on recent trends in the exotic materials, school of Engg. and technology, Sharda university plot no 32-34, knowledge park-III Greater Noida UP India, 26-28 Aug 2010) p 70.

Singh R P., Sharma AK ., Pushpendra , Kumar, V., Malik, S (2010) REMOVAL OF CADMIUM from the contaminated sandy loam soil using different Brassica Species, (National seminar on recent trends in chemical research 4-6 September 2010, dept of chemistry Meerut College Meerut- 250001, India pp. 93.

Singh R.P., Verma B B., Pushpendra and Mishra S. N. (2010). Phytoextraction a green technology for control of pollution and recovery of metals, International Conference on Green Technologies For Greener Environment 27-30 January 2010 Department of Chemistry Ch. Charan Singh University, Meerut- 250005, India pp. 110.

Singh, R P., Gautam, P and Pushpendra (2006). Role of Tribal ethnomedical knowledge of plants (National Seminar on Medicinal Plants: conservation, cultivation and utilization, Deptt. of Zoology and Env. Sc., GKV, Haridwar-249404, March 9-11, 2006) pp. 117-118.

Singh, R P., Verma, B B., Pushpendra, and Mishra S N., (2010) Effect of Cadmium Concentration on the root biomass yield of various plant species, (2nd National seminar on recent trends in the advancement of mathematical and physical sciences 30-31 Jan, 2010, D N College Meerut- UP, India) pp. 110.

Singh, R P., Verma, B B., Pushpendra, and Mishra S N., (2010) Effect of Cadmium Concentration on the root biomass yield of various plant species, (2nd National seminar on recent trends in the advancement of mathematical and physical sciences 30-31 Jan, 2010, D N College Meerut- UP, India) pp. 110.

Singh, S., Pushpendra, Chauhan, B. S., Goyal, S., and Batra, A. (2009). Pollutants Responsible for Children's Brain Damage Risk, National Seminar on Mental Health and Current Scenario 20-21 March 2009, Deptt. of Psychology Gurukul Kangri University, Haridwar- 249404, pp. 8-9.

Singh.S (1998) *Environmental Geography* Prayag Pustak Bhawan, Allahabad

Singhal.S, Singhal.N (2007) *Environmental Studies* Pragati Prakashan . Meerut

Sodhi, 0.5., Fundamental Concepts of Environmental Chemistry, Narosa Pub lishing House, New Delhi, 2000.

Subba Rao, S., Ethics of Ecology and Environment, Rajat Publications, New Delhi, 2001.

Subhash Malik[1], Anil[2], N R Bishnoi[3] and Pushpendra[1] Effect of Cadmium Concentration on the Growth and

Biomass Yield of Various Plant Species............communicated

T.M. Das—Ls the Earth for Man Only? Jonaki Publishers, Kolkata, 4th edition, (1995).

T.M. Das—Man, an Endangered Species, Shaibya Prakashan, Kolkata (1995).

T.M. Khosoo—Environmental Prioritie in India and Sustainable Development, Indian Sciflce Congress Association, New Delhi (1986).

Tchobanoglous George, Hilary Theisen, and Samuel Vigil. Integrated Solid Waste Management. Engi-neering Principles and Management Issues. New York: McGraw-Hill, 1993.

Tiwari.M, Khulbe.K & Tiwari.A(2007) *Environmental Studies* I.K.International Publishing House Pvt. Ltd.,NewDelhi

UNEP-IETC, International Source Book on Environmentally Sound Technologies for Municipal Solid Waste Management. Technical Publication Series no. 6. Osaka/Shiga: UNEP International Environmental Technology Centre, 1996 (pp. 421-427)

United States, Government of, Environmental Protection Agency. Decision Makers Guide to Solid Waste Management. Washington: US Environmental Protection Agency, 1989.

United States, Government of, Office of Technology Assessment (OTA). Facing America's Trash: What Next for Municipal Solid Waste? Washington: OTA, 1989.

Varshney, C,1C. and Sardesai, P.R. (Eds.), Environmental Challenges, Wiley East em Ltd., 1993.

Waste Water Engineering; Treatment, Disposal, Refuse: Metcalf & Eddy, Tata McGraw-Hill Publishing Company Ltd., New Delhi.

Wilson, E.O. 1988 (Ed.) Biodiversity, NationalAcademic Press, Washington, D.C.

Glossary of Important Terms

Abandoned Well: A well whose use has been permanently discontinued or which is in a state of such disrepair that it can not be used for its intended purpose.

Abatement Debris: Waste from remediation activities.

Abatement: Reducing the degree or intensity of, or eliminating, pollution.

Absorbed Dose: In exposure assessment, the amount of a substance that penetrates an exposed organism's absorption barriers (*e.g.*, skin, lung tissue, gastrointestinal tract) through physical or biological processes.

Absorption Barrier: Any of the exchange sites of the body that permit uptake of various substances at different rates (*e.g.*, skin, lung tissue, and gastrointestinal-tract wall)

Absorption: The uptake of water, other fluids, or dissolved chemicals by a cell or an organism (as tree roots absorb dissolved nutrients in soil).

Accident Site: The location of an unexpected occurrence, failure or loss, either at a plant or along a transportation route, resulting in a release of hazardous materials

Acid rain (Acid Precipitation). Precipitation of acids like sulphuric acid and nitric acid formed from the gases such as SO_2 and NO_2 in the atmosphere as pollutants. Rain water containing mixtures of acids (nitric, hydrochloric and sulfuric acid) from polluted air is known as acid rain. It damages lakes, forests and marble sculptures.

Afforestation. Plantation of trees to grow new forests.

Age-structure: Percentage of men and women in the young, adult and old age group in the population.

Agricultural Pollution: Farming wastes, including runoff and leaching of pesticides and fertilizers; erosion and dust from plowing; improper disposal of animal manure and carcasses; crop residues, and debris.

Agricultural Waste: Poultry and livestock manure, and residual materials in liquid or solid form generated from the production and marketing of poultry, livestock or fur-bearing animals; also include grain, vegetable, and fruit harvest residue.

Agroecosystem: and used for crops, pasture, and livestock; the adjacent uncultivated land that supports other vegetation and wildlife; and the associated atmosphere, the underlying soils, groundwater, and drainage networks.

AHERA Designated Person (ADP): A person designated by a Local Education Agency to ensure that the AHERA requirements for asbestos management and abatement are properly implemented.

Air Binding: Situation where air enters the filter media and harms both the filtration and backwash processes.

Air Pollutants: Gases and particles which cause air pollution are called air pollutants. Various gaseous pollutants from natural and man-made source enter the atmosphere and have adverse effects on the normal properties of air. This leads to air pollution, which is harmful for man and environment.

Air Quality: Each pollutant in air has a limiting concentration, which if exceeded. causes public health hazards.

Algaecide: Substance or chemical used specifically to kill or control algae.

Alkaline: the condition of water or soil, which contains a sufficient amount of alkali substance to raise the ph above 7.0.

Alpha Radiation: alpha rays consist of nuclei of the element helium and carry a positive charge. Penetrates the least, but does great damage in a small area, (see radiation).

Alternative Fuels: substitutes for traditional liquid, oil–derived motor vehicle fuel like gasoline and diesel. Includes mixture of alcohol based fuels with gasoline, methanol, ethanol compressed natural gas and other.

Ambient Air: any unconfined portion of the atmosphere: open air, surrounding air. Ambient temperature: temperature of the surrounding air or other medium. Anaerobic: a life or process that occurs in, or is not destroyed by the absence of oxygen.

Anaerobic Decomposition: reduction of the net energy level and change in chemical composition of organic matter caused by microorganisms in oxygen–free environment.

Antarctic-ozone Hole: refers to the seasonal depletion of ozone in the upper atom-sphere above a large are of Antarctica (see ozone hole).

Anthropogenic: Caused by man or man-made things.

Aquifer: a geological formation on group of formation in the ground which is usually composed of rock gravel sand or other porouse material and which yields water to wells or springs can be polluted by introduction of pollutants through poorly capped wells injection waste disposal and other entries below ground. A highly permeable layer of sediment or rock containing water.

Area source: Any source of air polluztion that is released over a relatively small are but which cannot be classified as a point source such sources may include vehicles and other small engines small business and household activities or biogenic sources such as a forest that releases hydrocarbons.

Ash: the mineral content of product remaining after complete combustion.

Assimilation: The ability of a body of water to purify itself if pollutants.

Assimilative capacity: The capacity of a natural body of water to receive the burnt gases from the engine of automobile have the potential to cause pollution which is know is automobile pollution.

B. O.D.: Biological oxygen demand—amount of dissolved oxygen required by micro-organisms to breakdown organic matter present in water.

Back Pressure: A pressure that can cause water to backflow into the water supply when a user's waste water system is at a higher pressure than the public system.

Backflow/Back Siphonage: A reverse flow condition created by a difference in water pressures that causes water to flow back into the distribution pipes of a drinking water supply from any source other than the intended one.

Background Level: 1. The concentration of a substance in an environmental media (air, The concentration of a substance in an environmental media (air water or soil) that occurs naturally or is not he results of human activities 2 in exposure assessment the concentration of a substance in a defined control area during a fixed period of time before during or after a date- gathering operation.

Background radiation: Radiation that occurs naturally in the environment from cosmic rays and radon or from atomic tests carried out by man.

Bacteria: (singular bacterium) Microscopic living organisms that can aid in pollution control by metabolizing organic meter in sewage oil spills or other pollutants however bacteria in soil water or air can also cause human animal and plant health problems.

Bactericide: A pesticide used to control or destroy bacteria typically in the home, schools or hospitals.

Baffle chamber: in incinerator design, a chamber designed to promote the settling of fly ash and coase particulate matter by changing the direction or reducing the velocity of the gases produced by the combustion of the refuse or sludge.

Baffle: A flat board or plate deflector guide or similar device constructed or placed in flowing water or slurry systems to cause more uniform flow velocities to observe energy and to divert guide or agitate liquids.

Baghouse filter: large fabric bag, usually made of glas fibers used to eliminate intermediate and large (greater than 20 pm in diameter) particles. This device operates like the bag of an electric vacuum cleaner, passing the air and smaller particles while entrapping the large ones.

Balanced Ecosystem: balanced ecosystem is an ecosystem where optimum amount of nutrient gases and species are present and there is equilibrium between them.

Bar screen: in wastewater treatment ad device used to remove large solides.

Bioaccumulants: Substances that increase in concentration in living organisms as they take in contaminated air water or food because the substances are very slowly metabolized or exerted (See: biological magnification).

Bioaccumulation: Accumulation of non-biodegradable substances in the body (e.g., lead, mercury, DDT etc.) through food chain.

Biodiversity: Genetic variety among individual species and between species of plants, micro-organism and animals. There are about 10 million species of plants, micro-organisms and animal on earth. These living natural resources are essential for the welfare of mankind.

Biogeochemical Cycle: is a circular pathway by which a chemical element or molecule moves through biotic and a biotic compartments of an ecosystem. Circulation of nutrients in cycles among air, soil, water and micro-organisms.

Biological Contaminants: living organisms or derivatives (*e.g.*, viruses, bacteria, fungi, and mammal and bird antigens) that can cause harmful effects when inhaled, swallowed, or otherwise taken into the body.

Biological Magnification: Refers to the process where by certain substances such as pesticides or heavy metals move up the food chain, work their way into rivers or lakes, and are eaten by large birds, animals or humans. The substance becomes concentrated in tissues or internal organs as they move up the chain. Refers to the process whereby certain substances such as pesticides or heavy metals move up the food chain, work their way into rivers or lakes, and are eaten by aquatic organisms such as fish, which in turn are eaten by large birds, animals or humans. The substances become concentrated in tissues or internal organs as they move up the chain. the contaminants.

Biological Oxidation: Decomposition of complex organic materials by microorganisms. Occurs in self purification of water bodies and in activated sludge wastewater treatment.

Biological Oxygen Demand (BOD): an indirect measure of the concentration of biologically degraded material present in organic wastes. It usually reflects the amount of oxygen consumed in five days by biological process breaking down organic waste.

Biological pesticides: Certain microorganism, including bacteria, fungi, viruses, and protozoa that are effective in controlling paste. These agents usually do not have toxic effects on animals and people and do not leave toxic effects or persistent chemical residue in the environment.

Biological Treatment: A treatment technology that uses bacteria to consume organic waste.

Biomagnification: The process of increases in the concentration of a pollutant with increasing trophic level in a food chain. Increase in concentration of nondegradable substance (*e.g.*, lead, mercury, DDTetc.) at successive trophic levels in a food chain (same as bioaccumulation above).

Biomass: all of the living material in a given area; often refers to vegetation.

Biomass: Organise matter produced by living organisms.

Biome: Entire community of living organisms in a single major ecology area.

Bionie: A broad region-based ecosystem with distinct climate, soil, flora and funna

Bioremediation: use of living organisms to clean up oil spills or remove other pollutants from soil, water or wastewater use of organisms such as non harmful insects to remove agricultural pests or counteract diseases of trees, plants, and garden soil.

Biosphere Reserve: World heritage sites, identified by ICECN, due to their high biodiversity and unique ecosystem *e.g.*, Silent Valley Kerala.

Biosphere: Composite environment consisting of land, air, water, micro-organism, plants, animals and man. Biosphere and environment have close interaction with each other. The portion of earth and its atmosphere that can support life.

Biota: The animal and plant life of a given region.

Biotic Community: A naturally occurring assemblage of plants and animals that live in the same environment and are mutually sustaining and interdependent. Removed mechanically; a concentration of non combustible material, which may include toxics.

BOD (Biochemical Oxygen Demand): The amount of dissolved oxygen needed by microorganism in decomposing the organic waste present in water.

By-Product: Material, other than the principal product, generated because of an industrial process or as a breakdown product in a living system.

Cadmium (Cd): A heavy metal that accumulates in the environment.

Capillary Action: Movement of water through very small space due to molecular forces called capillary forces.

Carbon Adsorption: A treatment system that removes contaminants from ground water or surface water by forcing it through tanks containing activated carbon treated to attract impurities and charged matter

Carbon and Hydrogen: The molecular structure of hydrogen compounds varies from the simplest, methane (CH_4) , top heavier and more complex molecules such as octane, (C_gH_{lg}), a constituent of crude oil. Crude oil and natural gas are often referred to as hydrocarbons or hydrocarbon Fuels.

Carbon Monoxide (CO): A colorless, odorless, poisonous gas produced by incomplete combustion of carbon

Carboxyhemoglobin: Hemoglobin in which the iron is bound to carbon monoxide (co)instead of oxygen.

Carcinogen: any substance that can cause or aggravate cancer. Chemicals promoting cancer *e.g.*, benzo-a pyrene, arsenic, DDT etc.

Carrying Capacity: 1.In recreation management, the amount of use a recreation area can sustain without loss of quality.2. In wildlife management, the maximum number of animal an area can support during a give period.

Carrying Capacity: Maximum population size that a given system can support over a given period of time.

Case Study: A brief fact sheet providing risk, cost and performance information on alternative, voluntary efforts, etc.

Catalyst: A substance that change the speed or yield of a chemical reaction.

Catalytic Converter : an air pollution abatement device that removes pollutants from motor vehicle exhaust , either by oxidizing them into carbon dioxide and water or reducing them to nitrogen.

Cavitations: The formation and collapse of gas pockets or bubbles on the blade of an impeller or the gate of a valve; collapse of these pockets or bubbles drive water with such force that it can cause pitting of the gate or valve surface.

Chemical Oxygen Demand (COD): A measure of the oxygen required to oxidize all compounds, both organic and inorganic, in water.

Chemical Treatment: any one of a variety of technologies that use chemicals or a variety of chemical processes to treat Waste.

Chiorofluorocarbons (CFC): Used as solvent, refrigerant, fire retardant etc. Responsible for ozone hole and greenhouse effect. A family of inert, nontoxic, and easily liquefied chemicals used in refrigeration, air conditioning, packaging, insulation, or as solvent and aerosol propellants.

Chronic Effect: An adverse effect on a human or animals in witch symptoms recur frequently or develop slowly over a long period.

Chronic Exposure: Multiple exposures occurring over an extended prided of time organism lifetime, Usually seven years to a lifetime.

Clean Flues: Blends or substitutes for gasoline fuels including compressed natural gas methanol ethanol and liquefied petroleum gas.

Climate Change: Also referred to as global climate change. The them climate change is sometimes used to refer to all forms of climatic inconsistency but because the earth climate is never static the term is more properly used to imply a significant change from one climatic condition to another In some cases clement change has been used synonymously whit the term global warming scientists however tend to use the term in the wider sense to also include antacid changes in climte see global warming.

Coagulation: Clumping of partial in wastewater to settle out impurities often induced by chemicals such as lime alum and iron salts.

Combustion: 1. Burning or rapid oxidation accompanied by energy in the form of heat and light. 2 Refers to controlled burning of waste in which heat chemically alters organic compounds converting into stable inorganic such as carbon dioxide band water.

Commercial waste: The actual compartment where is burned in an incinerator combustion product substance produced during the brining or oxidation of a material.

Community: In ecology an assemblage of populations of different species within a specified such in space and time. Sometimes a particular sub grouping may be specified such as the fish community is a lake or the soil arthropod community in a forest. Population of various species living and interacting in a given area.

Compaction: Reduction of the bulk of solid waste by rolling and tamping. The relatively stable humus material that is produced from a composting process in which bacteria in soil mixed with garbage and degradable trash break down the mixture into organic fertilizer. The controlled biological decomposition of organic material in the presence of air to form a humus-like material controlled methods of vapors are relatively non-ozone producing however vehicles fueled with CNG do emit a significant quantity of nitrogen oxides .

Compaction: All solid waste emanating from business establishments such as stores markets office buildings shopping centers and theaters.

Compost: A nutrient rich soil produced by decomposition of organic matter under aerobic conditions.

Concentration: The relative amount of a substance mixed with another substance. An example is five ppm of carbon monoxide in air or 1 mg/1 of iron in water.

Condensate: 1. liquid formed when warm landfill gas cools as it travels through a collection system. 2. Water created by cooling steam or water vapor.

Conductivity: A measure of the ability of a solution to carry an electrical current.

Cone of Depression: A depression in the water table that develops around a pumped well.

Confined Aquifer: An aquifer is in which ground water confined under pressure that is significantly greater than atmospheric pressure.

Conservation: Preserving and renewing, when possible, human and natural resources. The use protection, and improvement of natural resources according to principles that will ensure their highest economic or social benefits.

Construction and Demolition Waste: Waste building materials, dredging materials, tree stumps, and rubble resulting from construction, remodeling, repair, and demolition of homes, commercial building and other structures and pavements May contain lead, asbestos or other hazardous substances.

Contaminant: Any physical, chemical, biological, or radiological substance or matter that has an adverse effect on air, water, or soil.

Contamination: Introduction into water, air, soil of microorganisms, chemical, toxic substance, wastes, or wastewater in a concentration that makes the medium unfit for its next intended use. Also applies to surfaces of objects, buildings, and various household and agricultural use products.

Contour Strip Farming: A kind of contour farming in which row crops are planted in scripts, between alternating strips of close-growing, erosion- resistant forage crops.

Conventional Systems: Systems that have been traditionally used to collect municipal wastewater in gravity sewers and convey it to a central primary or secondary treatment plant prior to discharge to surface waters.

Corrosion: the dissolution and wearing away of metal caused by a chemical reaction such as between water and the pipes, chemicals touching a metal surface, or contact between two metals.

DDT: Pesticide useful in agriculture eradication of malaria.

Dead End: The end of a water main, which is not connected to other parts of the distribution system.

Deadmen: Anchors drilled or cemented into the ground to provide additional reactive mass for DP sampling rigs.

Deforestation: The loss of tropical forests due to collection of fuel wood, commercial logging, shifting, cultivation, grazing, road construction, ranching, mining and fire. Leads to soil erosion and flooding and endangers wildlife though habitat destruction.

Dependency Ratio: Ratio of people 65 + (above 65) and 15 (under 15) to the rest of the population.

Desertification: 1. A process whereby the productivity of the land is reduced through deforestation. Water logging and salinization, chemical degradation by nutrient leaching, range mismanagement such as overgrazing, soil erosion and aridity and semi-aridity.

Detergent: Synthetic washing agent that helps to remove dirt and oil. Some contain compounds, which kill useful bacteria and encourage algae growth when they are in wastewater that reaches receiving waters.

Diffusion: The movement of suspended or dissolved particles (or molecules) from a more concentrated to a less concentrated area. The process tends to distribute the particles or molecules more uniformly.

Digestion: The biochemical decomposition of organic matter, resulting in partial gasification, liquefaction, and mineralization of pollutants.

Discharge: Flow of surface water in a steam or canal or the outflow of groundwater from a flowing artesian well, ditch, or spring can also apply to discharge of liquid effluent from a facility or to chemical emissions into the air through designated venting mechanisms.

Disinfectant: A chemical or physical process that kills pathogenic organisms in water, air, or on surface. Chlorine is often used to disinfect sewage treatment effluent, water supplies, wells, and swimming pools.

Disposables: Consumer products, other items, and packaging used once or a few times and discarded.

Disposal: Final placement or destruction of toxic, radioactive, or other wastes, surplus or banned pesticides or other chemicals, polluted soil, and drums containing hazardous materials from removal actions or accidental releases. Disposal may be accomplished through use of approved secure landfills, surface impoundments, land farming deep-well injection, ocean dumping, or incineration.

Dissolved Oxygen (DO): The oxygen freely available in water, vital to fish and other aquatic life and for the prevention of odors do levels are considered a most important indicator of water body's ability to support desirable aquatic life. Secondary and advanced waste treatment are generally designed

Dissolved Solids: Disintegrated organic and inorganic material in water excessive amounts make water unfit drink or use in industrial processes.

Distillation: The act of purifying liquids through boiling, so that the steam or gaseous vapors condense to a pure liquid. Pollutants and contaminants may remain in a concentrated residue.

Dobson Unit (DU): Units of ozone level measurement. If, for example, 100 DU of ozone were brought to the earth's surface they would from a layer one millimeter thick. Ozone levels very geographically, even in the absence of ozone depletion.

Doubting Time: Period during which population doubles itself. It is about 100 years in developed countries and 40 years in India.

Dry deposition. Refers to wind blown acidic gases and particles which settle down on the ground.

Dump: A site used to dispose solid waste without environmental controls.

Earthquake. A short term vibration of the ground surface capable of shaking buildings apart and causing gaping fissures to open in the ground.

Ecological Exposure: Exposure of a non-human organism to a stressor.

Ecological Impact: The effect that a man-caused or natural activity has on living organisms and their non-living (abiotic) environment.

Ecological/Environmental Sustainability: Maintenance of ecosystem components and functions for future generations.

Ecology: Study of interactions of living organisms with their biotic and a biotic environments. The relationship of living things to one another and their environment the study of such relationships.

Ecosphere: The "bio-bubble" that contains life on earth, in surface waters, and in the air. (See: biosphere)

Ecosystem Structure: Attributes related to the instantaneous physical state of an ecosystem, example includes species population density, species richness or evenness, and standing crop biomass.

Ecosystem: 1.The interacting system of a biological community and its nonliving environmental surroundings. A biological community and its physical environment exchanging matter and energy.

Effluent: Wastewater – treated or untreated – that flows out of a treatment plant, sewer, or industrial outfall. Generally refer to wastes discharged into surface waters.

Electromagnetic Radiation: Are the electromagnetic waves which are produced by the motion of electrically charges particles.

Electrostatic Precipitator (ESP): A devise that removes particles from a gas stream (smoke) after combustion occurs. The ESP imparts as electrical charge to the particles, causing them to adhere to metal plates inside the precipitator. Rapping on the plates causes the particles to fall into a hopper for disposal.

Emission: Pollution discharged into the atmosphere from smokestacks, other vents, and from surface areas of commercial or industrial facilities, from residential chimneys, and from motor vehicle, locomotive, or aircraft exhausts.

Energy Recovery: Obtaining energy from waste through a variety of processes (e.g. combustion).

Environment: Something that environs i.e., encircles all our surroundings—the natural world in which we live — the living and non-living objects around us in our day-to day living.

Environmental Audit: An independent assessment of the current status of a party's compliance with applicable environmental requirements or of a party's environmental compliance policies, practices, and controls.

Environmental Impact Assessment (EIA): A systematic analysis of the effects of a major development project on environment.

Environmental Studies: The studies of the quality of environment and all aspects of human environment, their degradation etc. comprise environmental studies.

Environmental Sustainability: long-term maintenance of ecosystem components and functions for future generations.

Episode (Pollution): An air pollution incident in a given area caused by a concentration of atmospheric pollutants under meteorological conditions that may result in a significant increase in illnesses or deaths May also describe water pollution events or hazardous material spills.

Erosion: The wearing away of land surface by wind or water, intensified by land-clearing practices related to farming, residential or industrial development, road building, or logging.

Estuary: Region of interaction between rivers and near-short Ocean waters where tidal action and river flow mix fresh and salt water. Such areas include bays, mouths of rivers, salt marshes, and lagoons. These brackish water ecosystems shelter and feed marine life, birds, and wildlife. (see wetlands)

Eutrophication. The process of nutrient enrichment of water, and consequent loss of species diversity. Overnourishment of waterbodies due to excessive nitrates and phosphate through run off—it is harmful for the water. The slow aging process during which a lake, estuary or bay evolves into a bog or marsh and eventually disappears. During the later stages of eutrophication, the water body is choked by abundant plant life due to higher levels of nutritive compounds such as nitrogen and phosphorus. Human activities can accelerate the process.

Evaporation Ponds: Areas where sewage sludge is dumped and dried.

Evapo transpiration: The loss of water from the soil both by evaporation and by transpiration from the plants growing in the soil.

Exposure: The amount of radiation or pollutant present in a given environmental that represents a potential health threat to living organisms.

Extinction: Los pecies on earth as natural or man made process.

Fabric Filter: A cloth device that catches dust particles from industrial emissions.

Financial Assurance for Closure: Documentation or proof that an owner or operator of a facility such as a landfill or other waste repository is capable of paying the projected costs of closing the facility and monitoring it afterwards as provided in RCRA regulations.

Fluorides: Gaseous, solid or dissolved compounds containing fluorine that result from industrial processes. Excessive amounts in food can lead to fluorosis.

Fluorocarbons (FCs): Any of a number of organic compounds analogous to hydrocarbon in which one or more hydrogen atoms are replaced by fluorine. Once used in the United States as a propellant for domestic aerosols they are now found mainly in coolants and some industrial processes. FRS containing chlorine is called chlorofluorocarbons (CFCs). They are believed to be modifying the ozone layer in the stratosphere thereby allowing more harmful solar radiation to reach the Earth surface.

Fly Ash: Non-combustible residual particles expelled by flue gas. The air borne combustion residue from burning of coal or other fuels Consists mainly of various oxides and silicates. Major sources are pulverized coal-burning boilers.

Food Chatin: Series in an ecosystem *e.g.*, plant animals than

Fossil Fuel: Fuel derived from ancient organic remains e.g. peat coal crude oil and natural gas. Fuels produced by fossilization of plants! animals such as petroleum, coal, natural gas.

Fungicide: Pesticides, which are used to control deter or destroy fungi.

Fungus (Fungi): Molds mildews yeasts mushrooms and puffballs a group of organisms lacking in chlorophyl (*i.e.*, are not photosynthetic) and which are usually non-mobile filamentous and multicellular. Some grow in soil others attach themselves to decaying trees and other plants whence they obtain nutrients. Some are pathogens others stabilize sewage and digest composted waste.

Funna: All the annim cies present in a given region.

Game Fish: Species like trout, salmon, or bass, caught for sport. Many of them show more sensitivity to environmental change than "rough" fish.

Gamma rays: Electromagnetic rays similar to X-rays emitted in an unstable atom nucleus, which travel in straight paths at the speed of light, penetrate matter readily, but do not make the material radioactive. They penetrate a greater area then alpha or beta rays but do less damage they are weaker from of radiation.

Garbage: Animal and vegetable waste resulting from the handling storage sale preparation, cooking and serving of foods.

Garbage: Animal and vegetable waste resulting from the handling, storage, and sale, preparation, cooking, and serving of foods.

Gas Chromatograph/Mass Spectrometer: Instrument that identifies the molecular composition and concentrations of various chemicals in water and soil samples.

Gasahol: Mixture of gasoline and ethanol derived from fermented agricultural products containing at least nine percent ethanol. Gasohol emissions contain less carbon monoxide than those from gasoline.

Gasification: conversation of solid material such as coal into a gas for use as a fuel.

Gasification: Conversion of solid material such as coal into a gas for use as a fuel. \par Habitat: The place where a population (*e.g.*, human, animal, plant, microorganism) lives and its surroundings, both living and non-living.

Gasohol: Mixture of gasoline and alcohol is known as gasohol, used as a fuel in Brazil for running cars and buses.

Geographic Information System (GIS): A computer System designed for storing, manipulating, analyzing, and displaying data in a geographic context.

GNP (Gross National Product): An index of a country's economic status based on consumerism i.e., commodities purchased per year, consumer durables and financial status of consumer.

Gray Water: Domestic wastewater composed of wash water from kitchen, bathroom, and laundry sinks, tubs, and washers.

Greenhouse Effect (Global Warming): Rise in temperature of the earth's surface due to indrease in the levels of greenhouse gases viz., carbon dioxide, methane etc. The latter trap heat from the earth'

surface arid returns it thereby raising the earth's surface temperature. This phenomenon is similar to trapping of heat in glass-covered green house (used for growth of vegetables and flowers during winter) and hence called greenhouse effect.

Greenhouse Effect: The warning of the Earth's atmosphere attributed to a buildup of carbon dioxide or other Gases.

Greenhouse Gas: A gas, such as carbon dioxide or methane, which contributes to potential climate change.

Greenhouse Gases: Gases such as carbon dioxide; methane water vapour etc. which absorb earth's infra-red radiation, return it to the earth's surface thereby raising the temperature (global warming).

Ground Cover: Plants grown to keep soil from eroding.

Ground water Discharge: Groundwater entering near coastal waters which has been contaminated by landfill leachate, deep well injection of hazardous waste, septic tanks, etc.

Groundwater: The supply of fresh water found beneath the Earth's surface, usually in aquifers, which supply wells and springs. Because groundwater is a major source of drinking water, there is growing concern over contamination from leaching agriculture or industrial pollutant or leaking underground storage tanks. Water held in aquifers 50% below the earth's surface. This is the major source (0.66%) for freshwater.

Gully Erosion: Severe erosion in which trenches are cut to a depth greater than 30 centimeter (A foot). Generally, ditches deep enough to cross with farm equipment are considered gullies.

Habitat Indicator: A physical attribute of the environment measured to characterize conditions necessary to support an organism, population, or community in the absence of pollutants; *e.g.*, salinity of estuarine waters or substrate type in streams or lakes.

Habitat: The place where population (*e.g.*, human, animal, plant, microorganism) lives and its surrounding, both living and non-living.

Half-Life: The time required for a pollutant to lose one-half of its original concentration examples, the biochemical half-life of DDT in the environment is 15 years.

Halon: Bromine-containing compounds with long atmosphere life-times.

Hazard: Potential for radiation, a chemical or other pollutant to cause human illness or injury.

Hazardous Air Pollutants: Air pollutants which are not covered by ambient air quality standards but which, as defined in the Clean Air Act, may present a threat of adverse human health effects or adverse environmental effects. Such pollutants include asbestos, beryllium, mercury, benzene, coke, oven emissions, radio nuclides, and vinyl chloride.

Hazardous Substance: By-products of society that can pose a substantial or potential hazard to human health or the environment when improperly managed. Possesses at least one of four characteristics (ignitability, corrosivety, reactivity, or toxicity), or appears on special EPA lists. Any material that poses a treat to human health and/or the environment. Typical hazardous substances are toxic, corrosive, ignitable, explosive, or chemically reactive.

Hazardous Waste Landfill: An excavated or engineered site where hazardous waste is deposited and covered.

Heavy Metals: Metallic elements with high atomic weight, (e.g. mercury, chromium, cadmium, arsenic, and lead), can damage living things at low concentration and tend to accumulate in the food chain. (See toxic metal).

Herbivore: An animal that feeds on plants.

Heterotroph: Organism that can't synthesize its own food and derives its nourishment by feeding on other.

Household Hazardous Waste: Hazardous products used and disposed of by residential as opposed to industrial consumers. Includes paints, stains, varnishes, solvent, pesticides, and other material or products containing volatile chemical that can catch fire, react or explode, or that are corrosive or toxic.

Household Waste (Domestic Waste): Solid waste composed of garbage and rubbish, which normally originates in private home or apartment house. Domestic Waste may contain a significant amount of toxic or hazardous waste.

Humus: A dark amorphous substance that is partially degraded and serves as a major source of nutrients to plants.

Hurricanes. Cyclonic storms with heavy rains and wind with speed exceeding 119 km/h.

Hydro Geological Cycle: Movement or exchange of water between the atmosphere and Earth.

Hydrogen Sulphide (H_2S): Gas emitted during organic decomposition also a by-product of oil refining and burning. Smells like rotten eggs and, in heavy concentration, can kill or cause illness.

Hydrogeology: The geology of ground water, with particular emphasis on the chemistry and movement of water.

Hydrology: The science dealing with the properties, distribution, and circulation of water.

Identification Code or EPA I.D. Number: The unique code assigned to each generator, transporter, and treatment, storage, or disposal facility by regulating agencies to facilitate identification and tracking of chemicals or hazardous waste.

Ignitable: Capable of burning or causing a fire.

IM240: A high-tech, transient dynamometer automobile emissions test that takes up to 240 seconds.

Imhoff Cone: A clear, cone-shaped container used to measure the volume of settleable solids in a specific volume of water.

Infant Mortality: Number of Infants born per 1000 who die before their first birthday.

Ion: An **ion** is an atom or molecular which has lost or gained one or more valence electron giving it a positive or negative electrical charge.

Jar Test: A laboratory procedure that simulates a water treatment plant's coagulation/flocculation units with differing chemical doses, mix speeds, and settling times to estimate the minimum or ideal coagulant dose required to achieve certain water quality goals.

Karst: A geologic formation of irregular limestone deposits with sinks, underground streams, and caverns.

Lagoon: A shallow pond where sunlight, bacterial action, and oxygen work to purity wastewater, also used for storage of wastewater or spent nuclear fuel rods.

Land Application: Discharge of wastewater onto the ground for treatment or reuse.

Land Ban: Phasing out of land disposal of most untreated hazardous wastes, as mandated by the 1984 RCRA amendments.

Land Disposal Restrictions: Rules that require hazardous wastes to be treated before disposal on land to destroy or immo-bilize hazardous constituents that might migrate into soil and ground water.

Land Farming (of Waste): A disposal process in which hazardous waste deposited on or in the soil is degraded naturally by microbes.

Landfills: Sanitary landfills are disposal sites for non-hazardous solid waste spread in layers, compacted to the smallest practical volume, and covered by material applied at the end of each operating day.

Landscape: The traits, patteıns, and structure of a specific geographic area, including, its biological composition, its physical environment, and it's anthropogenic and repeated in similar form.

Landslides. Mass movement of rock or soil down hill.

Leaching: The process by which soluble constituents are dissolved and through the soil by a percolating fluid. (See: leachate)

Lead (Pb): A heavy metal that is hazardous to health if breathed or swallowed its use in gasoline, paints, and plumbing compounds has been sharply restricted or eliminated by federal laws and regulations. (See: heavy metal)

Leads to sedimentation and siltation of water-ways, which destroy aquatic and marine habitats, make water undrinkable, clog water-dependent industrial machinery, and other intake equipment.

Life Expectancy: Average number of years a new-born baby is expected to survive.

Lithosphere: Outer shell of the earth's crust made of the mantle of rocks. It includes the soil which covers the rock's crust in many places.

Magma: Molten rock below the earth's surface.

Management Plan: Under the Asbestos Hazard Emergency Response Act (AHERA), a document that each Local Education Agency is required to prepare, describing all activities planned and undertaken by a school to comply with AHERA regulations, including building inspections to identify asbestos-containing materials, response actions, and operations and maintenance programs to minimize the risk of exposure.

Managerial Controls: Methods of non point source pollution control based on decisions about managing agricultural wastes or application times or rates for agrochemicals.

Mandatory Recycling: Programs which by law require consumers to separate trash so that some or all recyclable materials are recovered for recycling rather than going to landfills.

Manifest: A one-page form used by haulers transporting waste that lists EPA identification numbers, type and quantity of waste, the generator it originated from, the transporter that shipped it, and the storage or disposal facility to which it is being shipped. It includes copies for all participants in the shipping process

Mercury (Hg): Heavy metal that can accumulate in the environment and is highly toxic if breathed or swallowed. (See heavy metals)

Microbial Growth: The amplification or multiplication of microorganisms such as bacteria, algae, diatoms, plankton, and fungi.

Mining Waste: Residues resulting from the extraction of raw materials from the earth.

Mist: Liquid particles measuring 40 to 500 micrometers (pm), are formed by condensation of vapor. By comparison, fog particles are smaller than 40 micrometers (pm).

Mitigation: Measures taken to reduce adverse impacts on the environment.

Monoculture: Cultivation of a single crop of tree.

Mortality: Death rate.

Municipal Solid Waste: Common garbage or trash generated by industries, businesses, institutions, and homes.s

National Emissions Standards for Hazardous Air Pollutants (NESHAPS): Emissions standards set by EPA for an air poll-utant not covered by NAAQS that may cause an increase in fatalities or in serious, irreversible, or incapacitating illness. Primary standards are designed to protect human health, secondary standards to protect public welfare (*e.g.*, building f-a-c-ades, visibility, crops, and domestic animals).

National Environmental Performance Partnership Agreements: System that allows states to assume greater responsibility for environmental programs based on their relative ability to execute them.

National Estuary Program: A program established under the Clean Water Act Amendments of 1987 to develop and implement conservation and management plans for protecting estuaries and restoring and maintaining their chemical, physical, and biological integrity, as well as controlling point and non point pollution sources.

Natural Gas: Underground deposits of gases containing mainly methane and small amounts of propane and butane. It is a cleaner fuel than fossil fuel as it produces less carbon dioxide on burning.

Natural Hazards: Hazards from natural sources (earthquake, volcanic eruption etc.) which destroy or damage human lives, houses etc.

Necrosis: Death of plant or animal cells or tissues. In plants, necrosis can discolor stems or leaves or kill a plant entirely.

Neutralization: Decreasing the acidity or alkalinity of a substance by adding alkaline or acidic materials, respectively.

Neutron: Nuclear particle with zero charge and mass, (relative to it).

Nitrate: compounding containing nitrogen that can exist in the atmosphere or as a dissolved gas in water and which can have harmful effects on humans and animals. Nitrates in water can cause severe illness infants and domestic animals. A plant nutrient and inorganic fertilizer, nitrate is found in septic systems, animal feed lots, agricultural fertilizers, manure, industrial waste waters, sanitary landfills, and garbage dumps.

Nitric Oxide (NO): A gas formed by combustion under high temperature and high pressure in n internal combustion engine, it is converted by sunlight and photochemical processes in ambient air nitrogen oxide. NO is a precursor of ground-level ozone pollution or smog.

Nitrogen Cycle: Continuous exchange of nitrogen within the ecosystem: air soil

Nitrogen Dioxide (NO_2): The result of nitric oxide combining with oxygen in the atmosphere, major component of photochemical.

Nitrogen Fixation: Conversion of atmospheric nitrogen gas into ammonia by nitrogen fixing bacteria/cyanobacteria

Oxides of Nitrogen (NO_x): The result of photochemical reactions of nitric oxide in ambient air, major component of photochemical smog. Product of combustion from transportation and stationary sources and a major contributor to the formation of ozone in the troposphere and to acid deposition.

Noise: Product-level or product volume changes occurring during a test that are not related to a leak but may be mistaken for one.

Non-point source Pollution: A type of pollution if pollutants emitting from an unconfined or unchanelled source, including agricultural runoff, drainage or seepage and air contamination from landfills or surface impoundments.

Non-Point Sources: Diffuse pollution source (*i.e.,* without a single point of origin or not introduced into a receiving stream from a specific outlet). Common non point sources are agricultural, forestry, urban, mining, construction, dams, channels, land disposal, saltwater intrusion, and city streets.

Nuclear Fission: Splitting of nucleus (uranium! plutonium) into two or more fragments with release of tremendous amount of energy. This is the source of nuclear power (electricity generation).

Nutrient Cycle: (See biogeochemical cycle)

Nutrient Pollution: contamination of water resources by excessive inputs of nutrients. In surface waters, excess algal production is a major concern.

Nutrient: any substance assimilated by living things that promotes growth. The term is generally applied to nitrogen and phosphorus in waste water, but is also applied to other essential and trace element.

Ocean Discharge Waiver: A variance from Clean Water Act requirements for discharges into marine waters.

Odor Threshold: The minimum odor of a water or air sample that can just be detected after successive dilutions with odor-less water. Also called threshold odor.

OECD Guidelines: Testing guidelines prepared by the Organization of Economic and Cooperative Development of the United Nations. They assist in preparation of protocols for studies of toxicology, environmental fate, etc.

Office Paper: High grade papers such as copier paper, computer printout, and stationary almost entirely made of uncoated chemical pulp, although some ground wood is used. Such waste is also generated in homes, schools, and elsewhere.

Off-Site Facility: A hazardous waste treatment, storage or disposal area that is located away from the generating site.

Oil Spill: An accidental or intentional discharge of oil which reaches bodies of water. Spills from ...nks and pipelines can occur away from water bodies, contaminating the soil, getting into sewer ... and threatening underground water sources. Can be controlled by chemical dispersion, ...echanical containment, and adsorption. Accidental discharge of petroleum in oceans or ...kers, offshore oil mining and oil exploration.

Open Dump: An uncovered site used for disposal of waste without environment controls. (see: dump)

Organic farming. Farming involving organic fertilizers and natural pest control, no use of inorganic fertilizers and pesticides.

Organism: Any form of animal or plants life.

Overburden: Rock and soil cleared away before mining.

Overgrazing: The practice of grazing too many ruminants on land unable to recover its vegetation or of grazing ruminants on land not suitable for grazing

Oxidation Pond: A man-made (anthropogenic) body of water in which waste is consumed by bacteria, used most frequently with other waste treatment processes; a sewage lagoon.

Oxidation: The chemical addition of oxygen to breakdown pollutants or organic waste; e.g. destructive of chemical such as cyanides, phenols, and organic sulphur compounds in sewage by bacterial and chemical means.

Ozone (O3): Found in two layers of the atmosphere, the stratosphere and the troposphere. In the stratosphere (the atmospheric layer 7 to 10 miles or more above the earth's surface) ozone is the natural form of oxygen that provides a protective layer shielding the earth from ultra violet radiation? In the troposphere (the layer extending up 7 to 10 miles from the earth's surface), ozone is a chemical oxidant and major component of photochemical smog. It can seriously impair the respiratory system. Ozone in the troposphere is produced through complex chemical reactions of nitrogen oxides, which are among the primary pollutants emitted by combustion, handling and processing of petroleum products, and sunlight.

Ozone Depletion: Destruction of the stratospheric ozone layer, which shields the earth from ultraviolet radiation harmful to life. This destruction of ozone is caused by the breakdown of certain chlorine and/or bromine containing compounds (chlorofluorocarbons or halons), which breakdown when they reach the stratosphere and then catalytically destroy ozone molecules. A potential effect of the loss of this protective layer could be a sharp rise in the incidence of skin cancer.

Ozone Hole: Thinking break in the stratospheric ozone layer. Designation of amount of such depletion as an "ozone hole" is made when the detected amount of depletion exceeds fifty percent. Seasonal ozone holes have been observed over both the Antarctic and Arctic regions, part of Canada, and the extreme northeastern United States.

Ozone Layer: The protective layer in the atmosphere, about 15 miles above the ground that absorbs some of the sun's ultraviolet rays thereby reducing the amount of potentially harmful radiation that reaches the earth's surface.

Packaging: The assembly of one or more containers and any other components necessary to ensure minimum compliance with a program's storage and shipment packaging requirements. Also, the containers, etc. involved.

Packed Bed Scrubber: An air pollution control device in which emissions pass through alkaline water to neutralize hydrogen chloride gas.

Packed Tower: A pollution control device that forces dirty air through a tower packed with crushed rock or wood chips while liquid is sprayed over the packing material. The pollutants in the air stream either dissolve or chemically react with the liquid.

PAN (Peroxy Acetyl Nitrate): A toxic product of photo-chemical smog reactions.

Particulate Matter: Solid particles or ligand droplets suspended in air. Examples are particles from combustion of fossil fuels.

Pest: and insect rodent nematode fungus weed or other from terrestrial or aquatic plant or animal life that is injurious to health or the environment

Pesticide: substances or mixture there of interded for precenting destroying repelling or mitigating any pest also any substance or mixture intended for use as a plant regulator defoliant or desiccant.

pH; a numerical designation of relative acidity and alkalinity of chemical solution may range form 0 to 14. The term pH tells how many hydrogen atoms (H+) are in a liquid. While a pH of 7.0 is natural, higher values indicate increasing alkalinity and lower values indicate increasing acidity. Natural waters usually have a pH between 6.5 and 8.5 some pH values of common Liquids are: bleach 12.7, ammonia 11.3, blood 7.3, milk 6.8, vinegar 2.8, battery acid 0.2.

Phosphorus: An essential chemical food element that can contribute to the eutrophication of lakes and other water bodies. Increased phosphorus levels result from discharge of phosphorus-containing materials into surface waters.

Photo Chemical Oxidants: Air pollutants formed by the action of sunlight on oxides of nitrogen and hydrocarbons.

Photo-chemical smog. A fogy smoke formed because of photo chemical reaction between the products of incomplete combustion of petrol and diesel and oxides of nitrogen. It is composed of O_3, PAN and N_2 Air pollution caused by chemical reactions of various pollutants emitted from different sources. (See: Photochemical Oxidants)

Photosgnthesis: Synthesis of food (carbohydrates) by green plants in the presence of sunlight using carbon dioxide from air and water from soil. The manufacture by plants of carbohydrates and oxygen from carbon dioxide mediated by chlorophyll in the presence of sunlight.

Photovoltaic Cell: Solar cell that converts solar energy into electricity.

Physical and Chemical Treatment: Processes generally used in large-scale wastewater treatment facilities. Physical processes may include air-stripping or filtration. Chemical treatment includes coagulation, chlorination, or ozonation. The term can also refer to treatment of toxic materials in surface and groundwater's, oil spills, and some methods of dealing with hazardous materials on or in the ground.

Phytoplankton: Small plants like algae, bacteria found floating on the surface of water. That portion of the plankton community comprised of tiny plants able to prepare their own food in presence of sunlight, *e.g.*, algae, diatoms.

Plankton: Tiny plants and animals that live in water.

Point Source: A stationary location or fixed facility from which pollutants are discharged, any single identifiable source of pollution, *e.g.*, pipe, ditch, ship, ore pit factory smokestack.

Pollutant: Generally, any substance introduced into the environment that adversely affects the usefulness of a resource of the health of humans, animals, or ecosystems.

Pollutants. The substances, responsible for environmental pollution.

Pollution: Generally, the presence of a substance in the environment that because of its chemical composition or quantity prevents the functioning of natural processes and produces undesirable environmental and health effects.

Population explosion: Excessive growth of population as in developing countries, to a size that exceeds the carrying capacity.

Population: A group of interbreeding organisms occupying a particular space, the number of humans or other living creatures in a designated area.

Porosity: Degree to which soil, gravel, sediment, or rock is permeated with pores or cavities through which water or air can move.

ppb: parts per billon.

ppm: Parts per million: a scientific unit commonly used to represent the level of pollutant concentration where concentrations are small. An example of 1 ppm would be 1 grain of brown rice in 1 million white grains.

Precipitation: removal of hazardous solids from liquid waste to permit safe disposal; removal of particles from airborne emission as in rain (*e.g.*, acid precipitation).

Precipitator: pollution control device that collects particles from an air stream.

Primary pollutants. The pollutants, which enter the atmosphere directly from various sources. Gaseous and particulate pollutants emissions. The gases thus discharged are carbon monoxide, nitrogen oxides, sulphur dioxide, and hydrocarbons.

Primary treatment: first stage of wastewater treatment in which solids are removed by screening and setting; screens and sedimentation tanks are used to remove most materials that float or will settle. Primary treatment removes about 30 per cent of carbonaceous biochemical oxygen demand from domestic sewage.

Producers: plants that perform photosynthesis and provide food to consumers.

Pyrolysis: decomposition of a chemical by extreme heat.

Qualitative Use Assessment: Report summarizing the major uses of a pesticide including percentage of crop treated, and amount of pesticide used on a site.

Radioactive decay: Spontaneous change in an atom by emission of changed particular and/ or gamma rays; also known as radioactive disintegration and radioactivity.

Radioactive Decay: Spontaneous change in an atom by emission of charged particles or gamma rays; also known as radioactive disintegration and radioactivity.

Radioactive substances: substances that emit ionizing radiation.

Radioactive Substances: Substances that emit ionizing radiation.

Radioactive waste: Any waste that emits energy as rays, waves, streams or energetic particles. Radioactive materials are often mixed with hazardous waste, from nuclear reactors research institutions or hospitals.

Radioactive Waste: Any waste that emits energy as rays, waves, streams or energetic particles. Radioactive materials are often mixed with hazardous waste, from nuclear reactors, research institutions, or hospitals.

Radioisotopes: Chemical variants of radioactive elements with potentially oncogenic, teratogenic, and mutagenic effects on the human body.

Recharge: The process by witch water is added to a zone of saturation, usually by percolation from the soil surface; e.g. the recharge of an aquifer.

Reclamation: (In recycling) restoration of materials found in the waste stream to a beneficial use which may be for purpose other then the original use.

Recycle/Reuse: minimizing waste generation by recovering and repressing usable products that might otherwise become waste the object *eg.,* satellite imaging, aerial photography and open path measurements.

Reservoir: any natural of artificial holding are used to store regulate or control water.

Residence Time: Length of time for which a chemical or molecule stays in the environment. For example, the residence time of CFC (chlorofluorocarbon) molecule in the stratosphere is 100 years.

Reuse: Using a product or component of municipal solid waster in its original from more than once; e.g. refilling a glass bottle that has been returned or using a coffee can to hold nuts and bots.

Rill: a small channel eroded into the soil by surface runoff; can be easily smoothed out or obliterated by normal tillage.

Rubbish: solid waste excluding food waste and ashes from homes institution and workplaces.

Run off: 1. That part of precipitation, snow melt or irrigation water that runs off the land into stream streams or there surface –water it can carry pollutants from the air and land into receiving waters.

Sacrifical Anode: An easily corroded material deliberately installed in a pipe or intake to give it up (sacrifice it) to corrosion while the rest of the water supply facility remains relatively corrosion-free.

Safe Water: Water that does not contain harmful bacteria, toxic materials, or chemicals, and is considered safe for drinking even if it may have taste, odor, color, and certain mineral problems.

Safe Yield: The annual amount of water that can be taken from a source of supply over a period of years without depleting that source beyond its ability to be replenished naturally in "wet years."

Safe: Condition of exposure under which there is a practical certainty that no harm will result to exposed individuals.

Safener: A chemical added to a pesticide to keep it from injuring plants.

Salinity: The percentage of salt in water.

Sanitary Landfill: Waste disposal site on land in which solid waste is spread with fresh layer of clay.

Screening: use of screen s to remove coarse floating and suspended solids from sewage.

Scrubber: An air pollution device that use a spray of water or reactant or a dry process to trap pollutants in emission.

Secondary pollutants. The pollutants that are formed by chemical reactions between primary air pollutants and other atmospheric constituents.Harmful pollutants generated from primary pollutants air, for example, sulphonic acid is a, secondary pollutant, produced by the primary pollutant sulphur dioxide by reaction with water vapour in air.

Secondary treatment: the second step in most publicly owned waste treatment systems in which bacteria consume the organic part of the waste in is accomplished by bringing together waster bacteria and oxygen in trickling filters or in the activated sludge process. This treatment removes floating and settable solids and about 90 per cent of the oxygen-demanding substance and suspended solids. Disinfection is the final stage of secondary treatment. (See primary, tertiary treatment)

Sedimentation Tanks: Wastewater tanks in which floating wastes skimmed is off and settled solids are removed for disposal.

Sedimentation: letting solids settle out of wastewater by gravity during treatment.

Sediments: Soil sand and mineral washed from land into water usually after rain. They pile up in Reservoirs River and harbors destroying fist and wildlife habitat and clouding the water so that sunlight cannot reach aquatic plants careless farming minning and building activities will expose sediment materials allowing them to wash off the land after rainfall.

Septic tank: an underground storage tank for wastes from home snot connected to a sewer line. Waster goes directly from the home to the tank.

Settling chamber: A series of screens placed in the way of lue gases to show the steam of air, thus helping gravity to pull particles into a collection device.

Settling tank: A holding area for wastewater, where heavier particles sink to the bottom for removal and disposal.

Sewage: the waste and wastewater produced by residential and commercial sources and discharged into swears.

Siltation: The same as sedimentation.

Sludge: Settled solids removed from waste waters or 1. a semi solid residue from any of a number of air or water treatment processes; can be a hazardous. 2. Solid, semi solid or liquid waste from municipal, commercial or industrial waste treatment facilities, waste-water treatment plants and air pollution control facilities.

Smog. A product of smog and fog air pollution typically associated with oxidants.

Smoke: Particles suspended in air after incomplete combustion.

Soil erosion: Movement of soil due to wind, rain and related natural forces that carries surface soil down slope toward streams and on into rivers and eventually bays and the oceans.

Solid Waste Disposal: The final placements of refuse that is not salvaged or recycled.

Solid waste Management: Supervised handling of waste materials their source through recovery processes to disposal.

Solid waste: 1. non liquid, non soluble materials ranging from municipal garbage to industrial wastes that contain complex and sometimes hazardous substance. Solid waste also includes sewage sludge, agricultural refuse, demolition wastes, and mining residues. Technically, solid waste also refers to liquids and gases container. 2. waste including, but not limited to, municipal, residual or hazardous waste, including solid, liquid, semi solid or contained gaseous materials. Some scientists theorized that in time this could create a hothouse effect, raising the temperature of the earth, causing glaciers to melt and the sea level to rise.

Soot. Black coloured particulate pollutants produced due to incomplete combustion of hydro carbons.

Species Extinction: Elimination of any species of living things because of habitat destruction, hunting for sport, trophies, and collection and hunting for food, pleasure, research and trade. "Incidental take" of mammals and other marine life during fishing threatens certain species.

Species: 1. A reproductively isolated aggregate of interbreeding organisms having common attributes usually designated by a common name. 2. An organism belonging to such a category.

Stack: A chimney, smokestack, or vertical pipe that discharges used air.

Stratosphere: The portion of the atmosphere 10–25 miles above the earth's surface. This region is above the troposphere at an altitude of li-SO km above the earth's surface. Here ozone acts as a protective shield against ultraviolet radiation from space and thus protects life on earth.

Sulfur Dioxide (SO_2): A pungent, colorless, gas formed primarily by the combustion of fossil fuels, becomes a pollutant when present in large amounts.

Surface Runoff: Precipitation, snow melt, or irrigation water in excess of what can infiltrate the soil surface and be stored in small surface depressions:

Sustainable Development: Improvement in quality of life over a long-term without degrading the environment or compromising the needs of future generations. Tectonic Plates: Huge blocks of earth's crust which slide along slowly. The concept of using resources in an ecologically sound manner so that they will be sustainable over the long term. Put another way, by the Executive Secretary of the U.N. Economic and Social Commission for Asia and the Pacific, it is "an approach to progress that meets the needs of the present without compromising the ability of future generations to meet their needs.

Tailings: Residue of raw material or waste separated out during the processing of crops or mineral ores.

Tectonic plates Huge blocks of earths crust that slide along slowly.

Terracing: Dikes built along the contour of sloping farm land that hold runoff and sediment to reduce erosion.

Tertiary Treatment: Advanced cleaning of waste water that goes beyond the secondary or biological stage, removing nutrients such as phosphorus, nitrogen, and most BOD and suspended solids. Advanced cleaning of wastewater that goes beyond the secondary or biological stage, removing nutrients such as phosphorus, nitrogen, and most BOD and suspended solids.

Theoretical Maximum Residue Contribution: The theoretical maximum amount of a pesticide in the daily diet of an average person. It assumes that the diet is composed of all food items for which there are tolerance-level residues of the pesticide. The TMRC is expressed as milligrams of pesticide/kilograms of body weight/day.

Therapeutic Index: The ratio of the dose required to produce toxic or lethal effects to the dose required to produce non adverse or therapeutic response.

Threshold Level: Time-weighted average pollutant concentration values, exposure beyond which is likely to adversely affect human health.

Threshold: 1. The lowest dose of a chemical a at which a specified measurable effect is observed and below which it is not observed. 2. The dose or exposure level below which a significant adverse effect is not expected.

Topography: The physical features of a surface area including relative elevation and the position of natural and man-made (anthropogenic) features.

Total Dissolved Solids (TDS): All material that passed the standard glass river filter, now called total filterable residue team is used to reflect salinity.

Total suspended solids (TSS): A measure of the suspended solids in wastewater, effluent or water bodies, determined by tests for "total suspended non filterable solids." (See suspended solids)

Toxic metals: often called heavy metals because most are dhigh density metallic elements such as mercury, chromium cadmium arsenic and lead, which are generally toxic to plant, are animal life in low concentrations.

Toxic substances: poisonous substances known or believed to be harfull to people's health ofter producing chronic irreversible physical problems and possibly harming subsequent generations examples are acrlonitrile arsenic asbestos benzene beryllium cadmium. chloroform chromates EDB ethylene oxide mercury PCB and many others.

Toxic waste: a waste that poses a substantial precent or potential hazard to

Toxicity: The degree to which a substance or mixture of substances can harm humans or animals. Acute toxicity involves harmful effect in an organism through a single or short – term exposure. Chronic toxicity is the ability of a substance or mixture of substances to cause harmful effects over an extended period usually upon repeated or continuous exposure sometimes lasting for the entire life of the exposed organism. Subchronic toxicity is the ability of the substance to cause effect for more than one year but less than the lifetime of exposed organism0.

Transpiration: Loss of water from plant surfaces. 'the bottom region of the atmosphere at an altitude of 0–11 km. It contains 70 per cent of air masses which are always in motion. Here temperature decreases with increasing altitude.

Transpiration: The process by which water vapor is lost to the atmosphere from living plants. The term can also be applied to the quantity of water thus dissipated.

Treatment: Any method technique or process designed to remove solids and/ or pollutants from solid waste waste-streams and air emissions Methods used to change the biological or composition of any regulated medical waste so as to substantially reduce or eliminate its potential for causing disease.

Troposphere: The layer of the atmosphere closest to the earth s surface

Tsunamis: Seismic waves caused by earthquakes traveling through sea water, generating high sea waves.

Tundra: A type of treeless ecosystem dominated by lichens mosses grasses and woody plants tundra is found at high latitudes (arctic tundra) and high altitudes (alpine tundra). Arctic tundra is underlain by permafrost and is usually water saturated (see: wetlands).

Turbidity: Haziness in air caused by the presences of particles and pollutants. A cloudy condition in water due to suspended silt or organic matter.

Ultra Clean Coal (UCC): Coal that is washed, ground into fine particles, and then chemically treated to remove sulfur, ash, silicone, and other substances; usually briquetted and coated with a sealant made from coal.

Ultraviolet Rays: Radiation from the sun that can be useful or potentially harmful. UV rays from one part of the spectrum (UV-A) enhance plant life. UV rays from other parts of the spectrum (UV-B) can cause skin cancer or other tissue damage. The ozone layer in the atmosphere partly shields us from ultraviolet rays reaching the earth's surface.

Unconfined Aquifer: An aquifer containing water that is not under pressure; the water level in a well is the same as the water table outside the well.

Under the Clean Water Act, for example, the term has been defined as the man-made or man-induced alteration of the physical, biological, chemical, and radiological integrity of water and other media.

Urbanization: Increasing population in cities by migration from villages and other states. India has a huge uroan population (about 300 million). Urbanization refers to a process in which an increasing proportion of entire population lives in cities and suburbs of cities.

Ventura scrubbers: Air pollution control devices that use water to remove particulate matter form emissions.

Venturi Scrubbers: Air pollution control devices that use water to remove particulate matter from emissions.

Vinyl Chloride: A chemical compound, used in producing some plastics, that is believed to be oncogenic.

Virgin Materials: Resources extracted from nature in their raw form, such as timber or metal ore.

Viscosity: The molecular friction within a fluid that produces flow resistance.

Volatile Organic Compound (VOC): Any organic compound that participates in atmospheric photochemical reactions except those designated by EPA as having negligible photochemical reactivity.

Volatile: Any substance that evaporates readily

Waste Characterization: Identification of chemical and microbiological constituents of a waste material.

Waste Exchange: Arrangement in which companies exchange their wastes for the benefit of both parties.

Waste Feed: The continuous or intermittent flow of wastes into an incinerator.

Waste Treatment plant: A facility containing a series of tanks screens filters and other processes by which pollutants are removed from water.

Waste: Unwanted materials left over from a manufacturing process. 2. Refuse from places of human or animal habitation.

Wastewater: The spent or used water from a home community farm or industry that contains dissolved or suspended matter.

Water logging: Soaking of agricultural land caused by rising water table or excessive irrigation. Compacts soil, deprives roots of oxygen and contributes to Stalinizations.

Water pollution: 1. The presence in water of enough harmful or objectionable material to damage the water quality. 2. the introduction of substances that make water impure compared with undisturbed water. Usually this comes from soil erosion, introduction of poisonous chemicals from industries and spills and introduction of domestic sewage or industrial and agricultural wastes.

Water Table: 1. the level of groundwater. 2. The top of the zone of saturation in the ground. See groundwater.

Water logging: Saturation of soil with irrigation water or excessive rain whereby water table rises close to surface.

Watershed Area: A topographic area within a line drew connecting the highest points uphill of a drinking water intake into which overland flow drains.

Watershed: Land area for which water drains under gravity to a common drainage channel. The land area that drains into a stream; the watershed for a major river may encompass a number of smaller watersheds that ultimately combine at a common point.

Wet deposition Refer to acidic water received through rain fog and snow.

Wetlands: An area that saturated by surface or ground water with vegetation adapted for life under those soil conditions, as swamps, bogs, fens, marshes and estuaries. Ecosystems with stagnant water pool and having rooted vegetation.

Xenobiota: Any biotum displaced from its normal habitat; a chemical foreign to a biological system

X-Rays: X- Ray is a form of electromagnetic radiation with a wavelength in the range 0.010 to 10 manometer, corresponding to frequency 30×10^{15} to 30×10^{18} hertz and energies in the range of 120 ev to 120 kev.

Yard Waste: The part of solid waste composed of grass clippings, leaves, twigs, branches, and other garden refuse.

Yeast: Yeast is unicellular fungi.

Yellow-Boy: Iron oxide flocculant (clumps of solids in waste or water); usually observed as orange-yellow deposits in surface streams with excess iron content

Zero Air: Atmospheric air purified to contain less than 0.1 ppm total hydrocarbons.

Zooplankton: Small (often microscopic) free-floating aquatic plants or animals